Political Affairs of the Heart

I0867334

TRANSITS:
LITERATURE, THOUGHT & CULTURE, 1650–1850

Series Editors
Miriam Wallace, New College of Florida
Mona Narain, Texas Christian University

A landmark series in long-eighteenth-century studies, *Transits* publishes monographs and edited volumes that are timely, transformative in their approach, and global in their engagement with arts, literature, culture, and history. Books in the series have engaged with visual arts, environment, politics, material culture, travel, theater and performance, embodiment, connections between the natural sciences and medical humanities, writing and book history, sexuality, gender, disability, race, and colonialism from Britain and Europe to the Americas, the Far East, the Middle/Near East, Africa, and Oceania. Works that make provocative connections across time, space, geography, or intellectual history, or that develop new modes of critical imagining are particularly welcome.

Recent titles in the series:

Families of the Heart: Surrogate Relations in the Eighteenth-Century British Novel
Ann Campbell

Eighteenth-Century Environmental Humanities
Jeremy Chow, ed.

Political Affairs of *the Heart: Female Travel Writers, the Sentimental Travelogue, and Revolution, 1775–1800*
Linda Van Netten Blimke

The Limits of Familiarity: Authorship and Romantic Readers
Lindsey Eckert

"Robinson Crusoe" after 300 Years
Andreas K. E. Mueller and Glynis Ridley, eds.

Transatlantic Women Travelers, 1688–1843
Misty Krueger, ed.

Laurence Sterne's "A Sentimental Journey": A Legacy to the World
W. B. Gerard and M-C. Newbould, eds.

Hemispheres and Stratospheres: The Idea and Experience of Distance in the International Enlightenment
Kevin L. Cope, ed.

For more information about the series, please visit www.bucknelluniversitypress.org.

Political Affairs of the Heart

FEMALE TRAVEL WRITERS, THE SENTIMENTAL TRAVELOGUE, AND REVOLUTION, 1775–1800

LINDA VAN NETTEN BLIMKE

Bucknell University | UNIVERSITY PRESS
LEWISBURG, PENNSYLVANIA

Library of Congress Cataloging-in-Publication Data

Names: Van Netten Blimke, Linda, author.
Title: Political affairs of the heart : female travel writers, the sentimental travelogue, and revolution, 1775-1800 / Linda Van Netten Blimke.
Description: Lewisburg, Pennsylvania : Bucknell University Press, [2022] | Series: Transits: literature, thought & culture 1650-1850 | Includes bibliographical references and index.
Identifiers: LCCN 2021044569 | ISBN 9781684484058 (paperback) | ISBN 9781684484065 (hardback) | ISBN 9781684484072 (epub) | ISBN 9781684484089 (mobi) | ISBN 9781684484096 (pdf)
Subjects: LCSH: Women—Political activity—Great Britain—History—18th century. | Travel writing—Great Britain—History—18th century. | Travel writers—Great Britain—History—18th century.
Classification: LCC HQ1236.5.G7 V36 2022 | DDC 305.420941/09033—dc23/eng/20211115
LC record available at https://lccn.loc.gov/2021044569

A British Cataloging-in-Publication record for this book is available from the British Library.

Copyright © 2022 by Linda Van Netten Blimke

All rights reserved

No part of this book may be reproduced or utilized in any form or by any means, electronic or mechanical, or by any information storage and retrieval system, without written permission from the publisher. Please contact Bucknell University Press, Hildreth-Mirza Hall, Bucknell University, Lewisburg, PA 17837-2005. The only exception to this prohibition is "fair use" as defined by U.S. copyright law.

References to internet websites (URLs) were accurate at the time of writing. Neither the author nor Bucknell University Press is responsible for URLs that may have expired or changed since the manuscript was prepared.

♾ The paper used in this publication meets the requirements of the American National Standard for Information Sciences—Permanence of Paper for Printed Library Materials, ANSI Z39.48-1992.

www.bucknelluniversitypress.org

Distributed worldwide by Rutgers University Press

Manufactured in the United States of America

For Matthew

The title of a work no longer announces its intention: books of travels are converted into vehicles of politics and systems of legislation. Female letter-writers teach us the arcana of government, and obliquely vindicate . . . manners and actions at which female delicacy should blush.

—Jane West, *A Tale of the Times*

CONTENTS

Political Affairs of the Heart

INTRODUCTION

Critical Contexts: Eighteenth-Century Women's Travel Writing

IN 1797, ANDREW AND MARY DOUGLAS privately published a joint travelogue of their harrowing experience of traveling back to Britain through France to escape the spread of war across Europe. *Notes of a Journey from Berne to England, through France* is remarkable for the unusual nature of its form: rather than integrate their voices, the Douglases' observations are printed as two separate documents, allowing readers to examine directly how gender factored into the production of the travelogue genre. That gender expectations were indeed formative can be traced through the different preoccupations and subject positions of each writer. Andrew's main motivation is to memorialize their journey; Mary writes to satisfy her husband's request that she record her observations in order to "awaken [her] attention and find [her] occupation," presumably to act as a distraction and to settle her nerves.[1] Andrew—although not immune to sentimental reflections—often relies on his wife to fill in the emotional blanks of their journey. Upon encountering an old, venerable beggar, he allocates the sentimental heavy lifting to his wife: "As I am sure my dear Mrs. Douglas will never forget the touching manner of the man, I hope she will allow herself to mention him with all that energy and delicacy of feeling, with which she can describe scenes of distress and tenderness."[2] Mary reciprocates by leaving the more meticulous political details to her husband: official correspondences, their visit to the Council of the Five Hundred, and sketches of military encampments. Read on the surface, this gendered back-and-forth seems to reinforce eighteenth-century gender categories on a textual level: woman = emotional/personal, man = objective/political. Yet a careful comparative reading of the Douglases' paired travelogues reveals not so much a division as a partnership. Andrew may provide more political facts, but Mary provides the emotional content that enlivens their joint politics. Her responsive body—feverish, melancholy, and anxious in turns—registers the past horrors of the French Revolution and the uncertainty of the new Directory, physically manifesting the impact of her political environment. Her emotional responsiveness becomes the means through which she both enters the travelogue genre (she writes to "find occupation" for her melancholic mind) and intervenes in political discourse.

Mary Douglas's relatively unknown travelogue provides an apt introduction to this book, which revolves around the dynamic intersections of gender, sensibility, mobility, and politics within eighteenth-century women's sentimental travel writing. *Political Affairs of the Heart* addresses the discursive constructions of nation and gender in British women's sentimental travel writing during the last quarter of the eighteenth century, and specifically during the American and French Revolutions. This study is predicated upon two major and intertwined contentions. First, that the convergence of sentimental discourse and the travelogue genre introduced in Laurence Sterne's *A Sentimental Journey* (1768) assisted women's gradual inclusion into the male-dominated genre of the travelogue. As Andrew Douglas's deferral to his wife's "delicacy of feeling" demonstrates, eighteenth-century theory, culture, and even science invested women with acute sensibility; their socially constructed expertise within the realm of feeling consequently allowed them particular authority within sentimental discourse. Sterne's emphasis on untutored response over erudite reflection and on sociability over critical detachment created a mode of travel writing tailored to women's putative natural abilities, ultimately contributing to the development of the female travel writer post-1768. Second, that Sterne's technique of grafting sensibility into the travelogue genre's heady array of political, economic, social, and cultural discourses provided female travel writers with a unique means of directing the sociopolitical transformation of the British nation during a period when its national identity was being challenged and consolidated through a series of political revolutions.[3] The sentimental travelogue licensed women to discuss a variety of broadly political topics, and to do so with the emotional intensity of a sentimental subject and with the eyewitness authority of a traveler.

The four travelogues at the center of this book manifest the repercussions of political revolution: Janet Schaw's *Journal of a Lady of Quality* (1774–1776) and Helen Maria Williams's *A Tour in Switzerland* (1798) provide firsthand accounts of the emergent or fully emerged revolutions in America, France, and Switzerland, while the anonymous author of *A Journey to the Highlands of Scotland* (1777) and Mary Morgan in *A Tour to Milford Haven* (1795) deal with the domestic effects of these political crises.[4] Their refraction of political, economic, social, and cultural discourses through the lens of sensibility is calculated to influence the collective political mood and to shape the contours of British national identity by manipulating the circulation of feeling both within and outside of the nation. Although the women included here pull from different ends of the political spectrum, the shared dislocations of travel and revolution help them to reimagine women's political subjectivity. The experiences, reflections, and self-representations they offer actively resist conventional definitions of femininity and envision a place for women within the British polity.

Only recently have the political dimensions of eighteenth-century women's travelogues been rediscovered by scholars. Current scholarship has moved away from the purely celebratory and/or biographical approaches to female travelers common among earlier explorations of the genre and has begun to chart the myriad of politics at work within these documents.[5] Early assessments of eighteenth-century women's travel writing are largely concerned with imperial contexts and situate their analyses within postcolonial frameworks, with particular attention to the question of whether or not women's contributions to colonial discourse diverge from the male imperialist perspective. Although the timeframe addressed in Sara Mills's *Discourses of Differences* (1993) is slightly outside of the period with which this book is concerned, her groundbreaking research on nineteenth- and twentieth-century women's travel writing must be mentioned as one of the first studies to analyze at length the serious political content of early women's travelogues. Mills draws attention to the imperial politics at work within women's travel texts, analyzing their contributions to colonialism and its various discourses to refute the notion of female travel writing as "simply the accounts of the lives of individual women."[6] The first full-length study of specifically eighteenth-century female travel writers is Elizabeth Bohls's *Women Travel Writers and the Language of Aesthetics, 1716–1818* (1995). Bohls—similar to Mills—interprets women's entrance into the travel writing genre as a strategic attempt to engage in the normatively masculine discourses from which they were conventionally excluded. She illuminates how women's appropriation of aesthetic conventions in their travel narratives exposed, challenged, and adopted the matrix of racist, classist, and gendered assumptions embedded in the foundations of eighteenth-century aesthetic discourse. More recently, scholars have turned their attention to negotiations of British nationhood and citizenship within the domestic and Continental tours of eighteenth-century female travel writers. In *British Travel Writers in Europe, 1750–1800* (2001) and *Women Writing the Home Tour* (2008), Katherine Turner and Zoë Kinsley respectively study the ways in which the texts of female travelers on the Grand Tour (Turner) or on the home tour (Kinsley) were invested in defining or redefining British national identity through their politically inflected representations of both home and away.

There is a general consensus across all of these studies that travel and travel writing served an emancipatory function for those privileged eighteenth-century women who traveled by choice; even where women continued to be more constrained than men (in terms of where they could travel and what they could say), the act and reportage of travel more often opened rather than shut doors. This strain of thought is explicitly developed in Yaël Schlick's fresh contribution to the field with *Feminism and the Politics of Travel after the Enlightenment* (2012). Schlick chronicles the ways in which the possibilities and ruptures opened by travel have often fostered women's feminist political agendas from the eighteenth century onward. Her work stresses the liberatory potential of travel for women and asks us to be continuously alert to the intersections among space, gender, and ideology.

These readings provide insightful and necessary strategies for thinking about women's travelogues as political documents and their journeys as political acts. Gone is the stereotype of the eccentric woman whose exploits solely serve as fodder for colorful anecdotes; in its place is the figure of the intellectually incisive, ambitious, and politicized female traveler whose texts represent significant socio-political interventions. This book seeks to contribute to the renewed acknowledgment of eighteenth-century women's travel texts as what Jane West referred to as "vehicles of politics and systems of legislation" by drawing attention to a still understudied aspect of their travelogues: the politics of sensibility within the female sentimental travelogue.[7] Very few works that address eighteenth-century women's travel narratives analyze the prevalence of sentimental discourse within these texts. The matter of feeling—presented in rich and complex detail across the spectrum of these travelogues—is often treated as a marginal or aberrant aspect of the text, but not evaluated as a unified strategy or as a deliberate mode of representation. Katherine Turner suggests that "few women mobilize sensibility to any great degree, doubtless because of its associations . . . with particular formulations of manliness—including sexual impulses—as well as its tendency towards social critique."[8] The impulse to underestimate or overlook the sentimental nature of women's travelogues is perhaps rooted in a desire to steer the discussion of their texts away from eighteenth-century stereotypes of frivolous female tourists and contemporary readings of early female travelers as curiosities, both of which suggest that the journeys and texts of female travelers lack intellectual rigor.[9] The handful of exceptional book chapters and articles that investigate the convergence of sentimental discourse and travel in eighteenth-century women's travelogues consistently affirm that female travel writers *did* mobilize sensibility to a significant degree, but much of this scholarship occurs within studies of sensibility rather than within studies of the travelogue.[10] Katrina O'Loughlin's *Women, Writing, and Travel in the Eighteenth Century* (2018) provides a welcome exception to this gap within the scholarship of women's travel writing. Her recent contribution to the field maps the ways in which eighteenth-century female travel writers deployed multiple modalities of sociality (including sensibility) to stage and endorse evolving forms of British subjectivity. In her discussion of Jane Vigor's sentimental travelogue, *Letters from a Lady, who Resided Some Years in Russia* (1775), she challenges the suggestion that female travel writers deliberately avoided sensibility; rather, O'Loughlin contends, female travel writers like Vigor "explicitly advocate feeling as a form of self-expression and authority for women, [and] they utilize sentiment as a tool of social comparison and critique."[11]

Political Affairs of the Heart builds on this emerging interest in the politics of emotion in eighteenth-century women's travel literature, participating in bridging the gap between studies of sensibility and studies of the travelogue. Where my approach differs from O'Loughlin's is both in my attention to the sentimental mode as a discrete form within the genre of eighteenth-century travel writing with its origins in Sterne's *A Sentimental Journey*, and in my focus on the productive interaction among the discourses of sensibility, gender, politics (and particularly the politics of revolution), and mobility in late eighteenth-century women's travel writing. Lynn Festa's definition of sentimentality as a "rhetorical structure that contains the potentially indiscriminate circulation of feeling" can be usefully applied to the sentimental mode within eighteenth-century travel writing.[12] By adopting a sentimental persona and its associated discourse, those female travel writers working within Sterne's legacy drew on a recognizable set of tropes, idioms, and gestures to manage their audience's identifications with the nations, communities, and events being described. Identifying the sentimental mode as a discernable "rhetorical structure" within eighteenth-century travel writing allows for a more nuanced, historically specific understanding of how feeling is operating within these texts and—crucially—for a way to discern how female travel writers working within this mode challenged and changed the very parameters in which they were operating. By focusing on the pervasiveness of revolutionary discourse in women's sentimental travelogues in the late eighteenth century, this book aims to demonstrate how the convergence of sensibility and mobility in Sterne's innovative form jointly sanctioned women writers to address explicitly political (and often controversial) issues—or how, to use West's words, they coalesced to convert "books of travel" into "vehicles of politics and systems of legislation."[13]

SOCIAL CONTEXTS: GENDER AND JOURNEYING

In Thomas Gisborne's popular conduct book *An Enquiry into the Duties of the Female Sex* (1797), he suggests that women's stasis is vital to the stability of the British nation. Women (particularly those who belong to the middle and upper classes) provide the glue that binds local communities together: their philanthropy secures the affection of the laboring class and their presence within the home keeps their husbands from wandering abroad and neglecting their domestic responsibilities. Gisborne argues that women's participation in Britain's traveling culture compromises the local ties that they are responsible for maintaining. "When the rage of rambling has seized a woman," he warns, "the ties of connection between them and the vicinity are broken. With the upper ranks, their intercourse is that of form and hurry; to the lower, they become distant, cold, and estranged."[14] Their absence inevitably displaces their husbands as well, disrupting the "friendly intercourse" between tenant and landowner and destabilizing the relationships of power that underpin Britain's governing structures.[15] "The absence of a common patron," he continues, "who used to conciliate differences, to encourage the meritorious, to overawe the refractory is severely felt in the neighbouring villages and hamlets."[16] He concludes by exhorting women to dutifully obey the biblical injunction to be a "keeper 'at home.'"[17] The sense of domestic and national disorder that Gisborne evokes in his depiction of the transient woman was part of an emerging discourse that firmly situated women's value and influence within the home; women were cast, to use John Donne's metaphor, as the "fixt foot" around which men moved—their domestic presence ensuring the stability of the "center" and the return of the adventuring male.[18] "The plot of the male journey," Karen Lawrence succinctly explains, "depends on keeping woman in her place. Not only is her place at home, but she in effect is home itself, for the female body is traditionally associated with earth, shelter, and enclosure."[19] However, although Gisborne naturalizes the private, domestic character of women and denies them a directly political role within society—establishing politics, law, philosophy, navigation, commerce, and warfare as strictly masculine affairs—it is important to note that his emphasis on their unique capacity for sociability inadvertently provides them with a distinctly public *and* political role.[20] Eighteenth-century women were quick to treat this quality as a loophole, using their socially sanctioned roles as mediators and as stewards as a means through which to claim active participation within British political culture, reifying their sociability into political property.

Amanda Gilroy observes that, in response to a culture that increasingly valorized their stasis, "an important consideration for many women was how they could operate in the public sphere of travel and writing and yet still preserve their association with the private sphere."[21] Those women who wanted to join the ranks of male travel writers were faced with the question of how to represent their travels in such a way that avoided suspicions of moral laxity, allegations of domestic negligence, or accusations of being a "petticoat pedant."[22] The immense cultural challenges faced by female travel writers can be seen in the very fact that in the first six decades of the eighteenth century—decades which witnessed the rapid rise of the female novelist—only two British women published accounts of their journeys, and one of those publications was released posthumously.[23] Those female travelers who did publish saw fit to vindicate their acts of travel and publication in the preface to their works, a convention that Turner describes as a "framework within which women writers fashion an apologetic . . . for the act of travelling itself."[24] Despite these challenges and displays of hesitation, female travelers increasingly sought to publish their travels in the last three decades of the eighteenth century.[25] Socioeconomic factors such as rising literacy rates, the gradual development of mass tourism, the increasing presence of women in the literary marketplace, and the popularity of Mary Wortley Montagu's *The Turkish Embassy Letters* (1763) certainly contributed to the development of women's travel writing at the end of the eighteenth century. Along with these broad socioeconomic changes, formal changes in the travelogue genre further propelled the rise of the female travel writer.

The contribution of *A Sentimental Journey*'s genric innovations to the development of women's travel writing should not be overlooked in the history of women's participation in this genre. Sterne's narrative crafted a textual persona and a literary form that allowed women to negotiate strategically the masculine domain of travel writing with their feminine roles and responsibilities. Organized around moments of sympathetic exchange rather than around topics "commercial, political, œconomical, and philosophical,"[26] the sentimental travelogue obscures its political commitments in the guise of sensibility; spectacles of sociability supplant political controversy, seemingly dissociating the sentimental travelogue from the realm of politics. It is this outward emphasis on the personal rather than the political, or on social rather than political spaces, that makes the sentimental travelogue a congenial form for women within which to represent their travels. Chloe Chard affirms that this shift within the genre to "an authority derived from an ability to respond emotionally to the objects of commentary" had significant implications for aspiring female travel writers, inadvertently admitting them "as capable of pronouncing on the foreign in a responsive manner."[27] Sterne's creation of the sentimental traveler—sympathetic, sociable, and emotionally responsive—and his protagonist's performance of travel as a "quiet journey of the heart" offered women an opportunity to extend their natural sociability and sensibility beyond the domestic sphere,[28] fostering on a national and international scale the "ties of connection" for which Gisborne claimed they were uniquely responsible.[29]

THEORETICAL CONTEXTS: THE POLITICS OF SENSIBILITY

Pointing to the ways in which travel writers—and specifically female travel writers—sublimated their political motivations and messages into alternate discourses, Ulrike Brisson calls for a diversity of approaches to "the politics of travel" in order to "tease out the complex ideological and sociopolitical transactions that attend the act of journeying."[30] *Political Affairs of the Heart* offers one such approach by remapping the sentimental discourse in eighteenth-century women's travel texts as political terrain, building on the vibrant bodies of work both in contemporary affect theory and eighteenth-century studies that have progressively recovered and theorized the political dimensions of emotion. Theorists within the field of affect studies have convincingly established the relevance of the history of emotions to political history—or, to put it more bluntly, have established that political history *is* a history of emotions. William Reddy, Barbara Rosenwein, and Jonathan Flatley all explore the ways in which political institutions, collectives, and movements are fundamentally grounded in (and vulnerable to) the manipulation of human emotions. Reddy's concept of "emotional regimes" and Rosenwein's concept of "emotional communities"[31]—although different in terms of their imagined scale and diversity—both schematize the socialized nature of emotions, suggesting that individual and communal emotional expressions are shaped by the emotional norms established within a given community. As a result, our overarching emotional environments ("regimes" or "communities") determine our deepest political values. "Emotional control," Reddy states, "is the real site of the exercise of power: politics is just a process of determining who must repress as illegitimate, who must foreground as valuable, the feelings that come up for them in given contexts and relationships."[32] Flatley's theory of "revolutionary counter-moods" interprets political revolutions as grand shifts in feeling.[33] He traces the ways in which normative emotional regimes (or what Flatley refers to as "moods") are challenged and even toppled by the emergence of new emotional collectives, formed through the public expression of oppositional feeling.[34] By alerting us both to the social constructedness of human emotions (shaped by existing emotional "regimes," "communities," or "moods") and to the emotional dimensions of sociopolitical organizations and movements (shaped by the emotional coalition of its members), these theorists illuminate the integral relationship between politics and emotion.

The field of eighteenth-century studies has been particularly receptive to the imbrication of political history and what is now being called "emotions history,"[35] as it has helped to make sense of the eighteenth century's complex and often bewildering (some critics have even suggested *embarrassing*) culture of sensibility.[36] For the past three decades, scholars have begun to rehabilitate the culture of sensibility and to rediscover its texts—with particular attention to the sentimental novel—as sites of political contest that intervened in all major sociopolitical issues. Markman Ellis (1996) and Brycchan Carey (2005) explore the convergence of sentimental and abolitionist discourses in the latter half of the eighteenth century, revealing how the culture of sensibility alternately challenged and defended Britain's involvement in the slave trade. Sarah Knott (2009), Nicole Eustace (2008), and Chris Jones (1993) expose the revolutionary potential of sensibility in their considerations of its function within the American and French Revolutions, while Evan Gottlieb (2007) and Juliet Shields (2010) turn their attention to the constitutive power of sympathy within the British nation following the Act of Union in 1707. In the area of gender politics, both G. J. Barker-Benfield (1992) and Gary Kelly (1993) recover the ways in which the culture of sensibility provided women with a powerful sociopolitical niche that enabled their participation in everything from humanitarian movements to revolutionary debate. Claudia Johnson (1995), meanwhile, complicates this symmetry between sensibility and female empowerment by arguing that the male appropriation of sentimentality effectively limited women's already restricted options for political participation, and reads moments of emotional excess within women's novels as politically inflected reactions to their deteriorating sociopolitical status. Julie Ellison (1999) further conceptualizes the specifically political relationship between masculinity and sensibility, arguing that the emergence of the eighteenth-century "man of feeling" is intimately connected to shifts in parliamentary culture. The remarkably broad scope of these studies—and this representative list is by no means complete—overwhelmingly confirms sensibility's political embeddedness in the eighteenth century. Far from operating as a purely personal, sequestered quality, sensibility was clearly understood and practiced as a social, political quality. "Rather than worrying about degenerating into sentimentality," Carey explains, "many aspired to it, recognizing an opportunity to tap directly into the heart of the human condition. If sentimental literature could put people in touch with their emotions, as many in the eighteenth century believed, it was clearly a powerful tool."[37] This book is situated within this ever-expanding field in eighteenth-century studies that explores the political nature and interventions of sensibility, with particular attention to the complicated position of women within this cultural movement. Both theoretically and historically grounded approaches to the political history of emotions provide my exploration of women's sentimental travelogues with a helpful framework for interpreting the performances of feeling within sentimental travel texts as emotives—affective gestures that, as Reddy explains, "do things to the world."[38]

Yet in order to understand how sensibility was deployed as a political tool, it is necessary to turn to the ways in which it was defined and theorized *within* eighteenth-century culture. In her study of the political valence of emotion within colonial America, Nicole Eustace reminds us that "we cannot simply assume that eighteenth-century emotional expression can now be understood transparently and without translation."[39] As various studies on the history of emotions have shown, emotions—as they are defined and even experienced—are historically contingent rather than transcendent.[40] As such, a historically accurate analysis of the eighteenth-century culture of sensibility must take into account the particular vocabulary and understanding of emotions available to eighteenth-century individuals.

Defining eighteenth-century sensibility for the purposes of this book is an essential, albeit daunting, imperative. Scholars who study the culture of sensibility often either gloss over the matter of definition or admit to the difficulty of distinguishing among the various terms. "The terms 'sensibility' and 'sentimental,'" Markman Ellis asserts, "denote a complex field of meanings and connotations in the late eighteenth century, overlapping and coinciding to such an extent as to offer no obvious distinction."[41] Chris Jones agrees with Ellis's statement that "it is not possible to legislate between the closely allied terms of 'sensibility' and 'sentimental' in the mid-eighteenth century," himself arguing that "sensibility was clearly not a uniform or unitary concept."[42] As the decisions of Ellis and Jones suggest, current confusion and contention over the precise definitions of sensibility and its attendant vocabulary of sympathy and sentimentalism are indicative of the lack of precision surrounding these terms in the eighteenth century. Messy as it is, however, there are also enough basic similarities in the eighteenth-century use of the various expressions associated with the culture of sensibility to justify provisional definitions in order to clarify the central terms of this study: sensibility, sympathy, and sentimentalism. *Sensibility* is here defined as acute emotional sensitivity. Samuel Johnson's eighteenth-century definition of the concept as "quickness of sensation and perception" is developed in Lynn Festa's and Stephen Ahern's more nuanced descriptions of sensibility as an "individual's susceptibility to particular kinds and degrees of feeling" (Festa) and as a "capacity for living intensely that is demonstrated in a heightened sensitivity to one's environment" (Ahern).[43] While sensibility denotes the capacity to feel, *sympathy* allows for the communication of that feeling between two or more people. According to Johnson, sympathy can be understood as "mutual sensibility; the quality of being affected by the affection of another."[44] His description finds current support in Juliet Shields's articulation of the eighteenth-century concept as "the mobility of emotion between different individuals."[45] I understand *sentimentalism* as a particular form within the culture of sensibility that draws on a recognizable set of tropes, themes, stereotypes, and rhetorical expressions. For this interpretation I am indebted to Ahern's explanation of eighteenth-century sentimentality as "a representational mode that operates according to various media and literary genres and includes two elements: a focus on the workings of heightened emotion . . . and an always implicit and often explicit goal to stimulate an affective response in the observer."[46]

All of these definitions—both the eighteenth-century descriptions and their contemporary interpretations—point to the powerful potential of feeling insofar as it was understood as a potent catalyst and an effective conduit. Enlightenment moral philosophy provided a theory of the emotions that developed the sociopolitical possibilities of sensibility by investing it with both moral and political agency. Particularly germane to this book are the theories of sympathy developed by David Hume and Adam Smith; both philosophers labored to invest the emotions with a formative role within society that rivaled the influence of formal politics or, in fact, was constitutive of political structures. By positioning sympathy at the core of individual and collective identity, they clearly demonstrate how sympathy could be understood as having political dimensions. Moreover, through their precise delineations of the mechanism of sympathy, Hume and Smith offer tools for the identification and explanation of the emotional orientations found within both individuals and communities. Their schematics provide the foundation for this investigation of the emotional networks embedded within sentimental travelogues.

Hume and Smith were reacting against environmental explanations of human behavior and social organization, against theories that posited the creative and unifying power of biology and geography.[47] Faced with a nation spilling out of its traditional borders and increasingly composed of varied racial groups, they realized that the method by which national character is formed had to be reconceived in order to accommodate the new reality represented by the British Empire. Both philosophers argue that individuals and nations are fundamentally shaped by psychosocial factors rather than by the interplay between the body and its physical environment, positing that the human impulse to "enter into the sentiments of others" constitutes both individual and collective identity.[48] Individuals both unconsciously (Hume) and consciously (Smith) change to fit the emotional contours of their immediate environment, and this emotional synchronicity forms the foundations of both personal and national identity. The formulation of individuals and societies as malleable constructs vulnerable to emotional energies exposes the political dimensions of feeling: as contemporary affect theorists have rediscovered, feeling was not understood simply as a personal attribute—limited in its scope—but as a catalyst of action and as a means of social transformation. Both philosophers imbue it with the power to create and to reform societies, arguing that social and political organizations are not only *made possible* but *made through* humankind's propensity for sympathy.

Hume's *A Treatise of Human Nature* (1738–1740) provides the theoretical foundation for his later and more direct consideration of the role of sympathy in the development of national identity in "Of National Characters" (1748). Hume's explanation of the operation of sympathy within society in *A Treatise* invests it with tremendous creative power; its seemingly uncontainable nature and formative and transformative capacity furnish it with a quasi-mystical quality. "Sympathy," he repeatedly asserts, "is a very powerful principle in human nature" (628). Hume suggests that the impulse to sympathize is so deeply rooted within the human psyche that the transmission of sympathy is an unconscious and uncontrollable process; we appear to spontaneously "enter into the sentiments of others" (367). He observes with a tone of wonder that "no quality of human nature is more remarkable . . . than that propensity we have to sympathize with others, and to receive by communication their inclinations and sentiments, however different from, or even contrary to our own" (367). Hume's comparisons of the operation of sympathy both to the inexorable movement of a virus (655) and to the rapid reverberation of sound waves across the taut strings of an instrument suggest the unstoppable nature of sympathy (626–627). "So close and intimate is the correspondence of human souls," he confidently asserts, "that no sooner any person approaches me, than he diffuses on me all his opinions, and draws along my judgment in a greater or lesser degree" (642–643). Through this psychic transfer of sentiments, we are interpolated by others' emotional states and these invasive sentiments are internalized to the extent that they "operat[e] as if originally our own" (437).

Humean sympathy largely blurs the boundaries between self and other; indeed, it can be said that self *is* other in Hume's theory, insofar as the self is shaped by and negotiated through our social interactions. Sympathy not only enables the *communication* of sentiments, it also allows for the *transformation* of sentiments from other into ours. By establishing sympathy as that which transmits and synthesizes sentiments, Hume institutes sympathy as the condition of possibility for society and as the source of collective identity. As Janet Todd asserts, he "makes community a spontaneous formation, a combination of self and other through sympathy and tenderness that elide individual differences."[49] This elision of "individual differences" facilitates the emergence of a shared identity that Hume describes in more detail in his essay "Of National Characters." Explaining the decisive role of sympathy in the development of national identity, he states:

> The propensity to company and society is strong in all rational creatures; and the same disposition, which gives us this propensity, makes us enter deeply into each other's sentiments, and causes like passions and inclinations to run, as it were, by contagion, through the whole club or knot of companions. Where a number of men are united into one political body, the occasions of their intercourse must be so frequent for defence, commerce, and government, that, together with the same speech or language, they must acquire a resemblance in their manners, and have a common or national character, as well as a personal one, peculiar to each individual.[50]

According to Hume, our inability to resist internalizing and reproducing the sentiments of those with whom we interact ultimately generates a cohesive national identity. He follows this assertion with a series of examples that verify his theory. Close contact between neighboring nations fosters "a similitude of manners, proportioned to the communication" (118); displaced groups of people can preserve their national identity if they "maintain a close society or communication together" (117); and nations spread across vast tracks of land can attain cohesion if the government consistently "communicates to every part a similarity of manners" (116). In short, sympathy has the power to actively constitute the nation.

Written two decades after Hume's *A Treatise* and receiving far more popular attention than his forerunner's text, Adam Smith's *The Theory of Moral Sentiments* reaffirms—and continues to affirm over the course of six revised editions and three decades—Hume's basic premise that sympathy is situated at the core of human nature and society. However, Smith attempts to stabilize sympathy by developing a more regulated version that divests it of the spontaneity that Hume perceives in its operation. He understands the sympathetic exchange as a deliberate process in which individuals consciously alter their behavior to achieve emotional correspondence. Although Smith concurs that humans possess a natural inclination toward sympathy, he does not believe that our identities are constructed of permeable membranes. "Though our brother is upon the rack," he contends, "as long as we ourselves are at ease, our senses will never inform us of what he suffers. They never did, and never can, carry us beyond our own person."[51] It is only through the rigorous work of the imagination that these bodily limits can be breached and "some correspondence of sentiments" (27) achieved. "The spectator," Smith explains, "must, first of all, endeavor, as much as he can, to put himself in the situation of the other, and to bring home to himself every little circumstance of distress which can possibly occur to the sufferer" (28). The activity of putting oneself in the "situation of the other" and internalizing "every little circumstance of distress" suggests an emotional and psychological exercise that contrasts with the more passive reception of emotions outlined in Hume's theory. Smith's revised description of the process of emotional identification portrays sympathy as a choice rather than as a contagion; as such, he appears to be arguing that individuals and collectives *can* monitor whom or what they become.

Yet it would be wrong to assume that Smith divests sympathy of its powerfully transformative capacity by regulating its process; rather, he reinforces the argument that sympathy has powerful personal and political implications. According to Smith, sympathy transforms both parties involved; the achievement of perfect sympathy depends upon a *correspondence* of sentiments between spectator and subject. While the spectator strives to "put himself in the situation of the other," the subject must reciprocate by modifying their emotions to reach that "pitch . . . in which the spectators are capable of going along with him" (28). The repeated action of assuming the circumstances of another shapes human behavior as it determines our emotional responses; we instinctively "accommodate and assimilate, as much as we can, our own sentiments, principles, and feelings, to those which we see fixed and rooted in the persons whom we are obliged to live and converse a great deal with" (264–265). Smith goes as far as to contend that all socialized individuals develop an internal censor that he calls the "impartial spectator," the function of which is to reproduce "sentiments and motives" (133) synchronous with our social environments. His emphasis on the role of self-regulation in the operation of sympathy ultimately enlarges the potential field for sympathetic energies. Our established patterns of sympathy train us to overcome our selfish preoccupations and put us in mind of the needs, desires, and conditions of the anonymous individuals that constitute the nation: "Not only we ourselves, but all the objects of our kindest affections, our children, our parents, our relations, our friends, our benefactors, all those whom we naturally love and revere the most, are commonly comprehended within [the state or sovereignty]; and their prosperity and safety depend in some measure upon its prosperity and safety. It is by nature, therefore, endeared to us, not only by all our selfish, but by all our private benevolent affections" (269).

Rather than generating insularity, networks of sympathy create the demand for the extension of sympathy to the nation as a whole. Comparing Smith's version of sympathy to Hume's earlier formulation, Evan Gottlieb concludes that Smith "rearticulates sympathy as a voluntary, 'achieved' state of emotional harmony capable of actively uniting disparate peoples."[52] By requiring its participants to exchange their personal desires for those of another (or others), sympathy not only enables actions that benefit the collective, but also enables the formation of the collective.

Aspects of Hume's and Smith's moral philosophies can be found woven throughout the travelogues of the female sentimental travel writers included in this book, who apply Enlightenment theories of sympathy in real-life contexts both to navigate and to represent their foreign environments. Although contemporary affect theory helps to confirm the political dimensions of emotions, understanding Hume's and Smith's theories of sympathy ultimately provides a way to grasp the sociopolitical implications of eighteenth-century female travel writers' sentimental performances and rhetoric. The philosophers' contention that we naturally absorb (Hume) or accommodate (Smith) other's emotions—thus fundamentally changing our own emotional composition—provides a way for these politically minded women to imagine and shape a viable form of political participation for themselves. By revealing their own emotional attachments and preferences through their sentimental representations of people, objects, and ideologies, they attempt to align their readers' sympathies with their own, either through the operation of emotional contagion or accommodation. At the same time, female sentimental travel writers police the flow of sympathetic traffic between different individuals or groups by engaging the caveats elaborated in Hume's and Smith's texts. Despite (or due to) the ambiguity of his definitions, Hume's emphasis on the importance of contiguity or resemblance in the circulation of feelings provides a useful way for female travel writers to rhetorically prevent the extension of sympathy to those that compromise their political vision. Similarly, Smith's insistence on the importance of reciprocity within the sympathetic exchange indirectly provides these shrewd authors with the means to interrupt objectionable emotional connections. If one party refuses to or is incapable of sympathizing with the other's "misfortunes," "grief," "injuries," or "resentments," Smith cautions that the sympathetic exchange is compromised: "We become intolerable to one another" (27).

The travel writers examined in this book carefully designate who deserves to be included in the sentimental community by representing the ability of particular individuals and groups to engage in the circulation of feelings. Although their feelings are often presented as organic, artless outpourings, their calculated application of Enlightenment theories of sympathy reveals the instrumental function of the feelings flooding their texts. Discussing philosophies of sympathy and their manifestations in sentimental literature, John Mullan argues that "neither type of text simply reflects social conditions or relations: both *produce* society; both seek to make society on the page."[53] Female sentimental travel writers' representations both of their society and the foreign societies they encounter accomplish a similar intervention; their portrayals are not static copies but dynamic impressions that attempt to remake the British nation according to their own ideals.

GENRIC CONTEXTS: THE CULTURAL AUTHORITY OF THE SENTIMENTAL TRAVELOGUE

Although a tremendous amount of ink has been spilled on the political investments of the sentimental novel, there are no comparable full-length studies on the sentimental travelogue. *Political Affairs of the Heart* departs from previous work on the political nature of sentimental literature by focusing on eighteenth-century travel writing, and particularly on the sentimental travelogue—a mode that is often (and understandably, given its genesis as a fictional narrative) read as an extension of the sentimental novel. Although the sentimental travelogue shares with the sentimental novel several defining characteristics—namely, an "interest in feeling and emotional states,"[54] a tendency toward "emotional and rhetorical excess," and "an always implicit and often explicit goal to stimulate an affective response"[55]—its association with reality and its attendant cultural status crucially distinguishes it from its fictional counterpart, and has significant implications for how it was able to act upon its eighteenth-century audience.

"Travel writing," Pamela Cheek observes, "could, by the second half of the [eighteenth] century, be celebrated for the edifying connection to the panorama of the real that it offered."[56] In an attempt to counter the accusations of falsification leveled at travel writing since the fantastical travel narratives of the past centuries, eighteenth-century travel writers established their credibility by emphasizing the factual nature of their observations. In his 1775 travelogue, Nathaniel Wraxall clearly distinguishes between past and present travel texts to establish the genre's credibility: "The age of imposition on one side, and of credulity on the other, seems now to be over: truth and sound knowledge are introduced into subjects where formerly they scarce ever intruded."[57] George Dekker attributes this new commitment to truth—or, at least, this performance of truth-telling—to the genre's classification as an educational resource. He argues that the intensified scrutiny and subsequent evolution of the travelogue was intimately related to "the importance of travel literature as a source of information about foreign peoples for such pioneering social theorists as Montesquieu and Adam Smith."[58] The Scottish philosopher Dugald Stewart wrote in 1793 that even the "casual" observations of travelers served as a valuable resource for historians and philosophers.[59] "The detached facts which travels and voyages afford us," he declared, "may frequently serve as landmarks to our speculations."[60] Travelogues were also used as a source of political information as travelers could provide firsthand accounts of international political developments. For example, Alexander Schaw's travel report on North Carolina was sent to Lord Dartmouth in 1775 to assist the British government in determining an appropriate course of action in regard to the rebellion in the Carolinas.[61] That the travelogue was valued for its exposition of empirical data—political, economic, geographical, cultural, and social—is further evident from the importance that eighteenth-century reviewers attach both to its veracity and to its educational quality. In a review of Jemima Kindersley's 1777 travel narrative, a critic for *The Monthly Review* is quick to assure those "who read for information" that "these letters are not . . . the manufacture of a hireling, but the production of a real Traveller."[62]

It is precisely its association with fact rather than fiction that furnished the travelogue with social approbation; whereas eighteenth-century society worried that the fictional scenarios presented in novels would corrupt young readers by instilling a dangerous disregard for the exigencies of reality, travel writing was promoted on the basis of its injunction to reflect rather than to alter reality.[63] In their conduct books directed toward young women, both Hester Chapone (1773) and Rev. James Fordyce (1766) discourage the reading of novels due to their pernicious ability to "inflame the passions of youth" (Chapone)[64] but encourage the perusal of travelogues based on their instructive quality, or their ability to "open and enlarge the mind" (Fordyce).[65] Whereas novels implant "the expectation of extraordinary adventures . . . and the admiration of extravagant passions and absurd conduct" (Chapone),[66] travelogues "remind us that we are citizens of the universe; they show us how small the part that we fill in the immense orb of being" (Fordyce).[67] According to these arguments, fiction was dangerous not just because it displaced readers from reality, but because in doing so it fostered contempt toward traditional customs and values. The travelogue was an acceptable form of entertainment because it firmly grounded its audience within their world and shaped their perception and practice of citizenship. This notion of the travelogue's comparative value as a source of positive instruction is repeated in reviews of genre throughout the eighteenth century. Writing a few years earlier than Chapone and Fordyce, a writer for *The Critical Review* argues that whereas the novel "generally croud[s] [the mind] with images that, even allowing them to be innocent, we ought to banish," the travelogue "will always entertain and improve the understanding."[68] As Nigel Leask notes, even if travel writing challenged social conventions, "inasmuch as it represented a 'literature of fact' . . . it was considered to be at least potentially improving in a way that no purely fictional narrative could be."[69]

The travelogue's instructive quality not only made it safe reading, but also invested it with a form of authority denied the novel in the eighteenth century. Susan Lamb argues that the "tremendous power and authority" apportioned to the travelogue in this period were fundamentally related to its association with both knowledge acquisition and knowledge generation.[70] "Tourism," she asserts, "was one of the eighteenth century's primary modes of producing, confirming, and interpreting knowledge . . . about human relationships of all kinds."[71] The genre's comparative authority (compared, that is, to fiction) is reinforced by travelers, who repeatedly point to the discrepancy between fiction and reality. In order to validate her own firsthand account, Janet Schaw frequently draws attention to the inconsistencies and/or omissions in narratives about America written by armchair travelers; she underscores the cultural influence of the eyewitness in her statement that her audience "know[s] nothing of the power of this country, nor will you believe it till you find it with a witness."[72] Samuel Johnson similarly emphasizes the superiority of information gained through the act of witnessing, stating that the "use of travelling is to regulate imagination by reality, and instead of thinking how things may be, to see them as they are."[73] His distinction between an armchair traveler and an authentic one suggests that knowledge acquired through indirect means is a poor substitute for direct experience. Despite constant (and often merited) suspicions regarding the factuality of travelogues, they were nonetheless understood as predominantly nonfictional accounts of a traveler's actual experiences and, as such, the firsthand information provided by travelers could be integrated into networks of knowledge.

Sterne's fictional adaptation of the travelogue in 1768 married the affective power of the sentimental novel to the cultural and intellectual authority of the travelogue. Crafting a genre that equally appealed to the sentiments and to the intellect, this innovation helped to shift both who could author the travelogue and the ways in which the genre could act upon its audience. As travel writers, women became recipients of the genre's significant sociopolitical franchise. In appropriating the influence afforded the eyewitness and inheriting the panoply of discourses available within the travelogue genre, they became legitimate producers of knowledge—providing their British audience with raw data that could subsequently circulate through the nation in various forms of knowledge. As specifically *sentimental* travel writers, they were given the license to infuse their observations with emotional and moral substance. Female sentimental travel writers both provide their readers with useful information about their own and other nations through empirical observation *and* manipulate their readers' emotions regarding this material through sentimental representation. In the words of an eighteenth-century reviewer, they establish "both what they saw and what they felt" to guide the manner in which the foreign and familiar are integrated into the British nation's political perceptions and practices.[74]

POLITICAL CONTEXTS: REVOLUTION, WOMEN, AND THE SENTIMENTAL TRAVELOGUE

The sentimental travelogue's dual work of imparting fact and feeling becomes particularly potent during revolutionary epochs, when feeling functions as both a motivation and an instrument of political change. By focusing on the politics of revolution in sentimental travelogues written by women during the 1770s and the 1790s, *Political Affairs of the Heart* recovers these women's contributions to revolutionary discourse and explores the emancipatory potential in the triangulation of sentimentality, revolution, and travel. It should not, perhaps, be surprising that the birth and flourishing of the sentimental travelogue coincides with a period of terrific political upheaval in Britain, which Linda Colley has called one of "the most formative periods in the making of the modern world and—not accidently—in the forging of British identity."[75] The raucous emotionality of sentimental literature corresponds with the political intensity that characterized Britain in the latter half of the eighteenth century, punctuated as it was by two spectacular political revolutions.[76] Yet it would be a mistake to assume that the sentimental form was simply the by-product of its particular political environment—an outlet, as it were, for venting the excessive feeling pervading the period. It was also a tactical response to political crises that sought to influence civic debate and, ultimately, to shape the changing contours of British identity. Thomas Holcroft—a British supporter of the French Revolution—bluntly dismisses the idea that "nations are governed by their laws." He insists that the "laws have indeed their influence, and do essential good or harm; but the great governing power is opinion. . . . The code of the nurse is the morality of the child; and he that would reform nations must reform their opinions." Holcroft's persuasion that opinions rather than laws are the "the great governing power" manifests the influence of Enlightenment interpretations of feeling and illustrates the relevance of sensibility for revolutionary moments.[77] Sensibility and its attendant practices—particularly as they were associated with personal and collective transformation in Enlightenment moral philosophy—become overtly politicized as legitimate grounds for political action in revolutionary moments, as evidenced by the simultaneous appeals to and fear of individual and social feeling expressed by British society during the American and French Revolutions. "Collective sympathy," Mary Fairclough explains, "operates as a medium not only of emotions but also of opinions and ideas, and therefore, at moments of political crises or unrest, it assumes an explicit and highly contested political significance in a wide range of discourses."[78] This book brings attention to the sentimental travelogue as one such discursive field that pressed sensibility into the political service of reinforcing or altering British opinions during the American and French Revolutions, and one that offered unique opportunities for women's political expression.

Revolutionary moments suspend and/or radically alter normative social codes, allowing (even if briefly) new ways of being in society. Flatley's description of political revolutions as "world-altering moments where new alliances, new enemies, and new fields of action become visible and urgently compelling" captures the combined sense of possibility, innovation, and zeal that accompanies revolution and has the power to open up alternative modes of structuring self and society.[79] For some eighteenth-century women, the American and French Revolutions created a momentary aperture in social organization and expectations that allowed for their greater inclusion in national politics—a "field of action" from which they had been aggressively excluded. The past four decades have seen a shift in the evaluation of both the American and French Revolutions to include the history of women, with scholars uncovering the extent of women's participation in both revolutions and assessing the impact of these political events on women's lives. Scholarly explorations of colonial women's involvement in the American Revolution tend to emphasize the liberating and empowering experience of the revolution for women, and particularly for female patriots. Rosemarie Zagarri, for example, has traced the transformation of colonial women during the American Revolution from "political ciphers" to "political beings who had the capacity to influence the course of war, politics, and history," arguing that the immediacy and the ideology of the revolution allowed women exceptional access to politics during the revolutionary period.[80] Scholars studying British women's contributions and responses to the French Revolution consistently suggest that the politically charged atmosphere of the 1790s acted as a catalyst for women's vigorous political activity throughout the decade. The documents written by these women, as Adriana Craciun and Kari Lokki observe, "testify to the urgency with which women of a wide spectrum of political persuasions felt compelled to respond to the moral and political questions raised by the wars with Revolutionary and Napoleonic France, despite societal taboos against such intervention."[81] The extent to which this sense of urgency politicized women is taken up in the work of Orianne Smith and Emma Major, whose investigations of the apocalyptic language used by women writers in the 1790s suggest that both radical and conservative women felt divinely licensed to supersede gendered expectations in light of their duty, as Smith puts it, "to articulate God's will in a time of social and political crisis."[82]

In the four women's travelogues examined in this book, political crises intersect with travel to broaden the grounds of their political participation. "As soon as travelers set out," Ulrike Brisson observes, "they become embedded in political structures."[83] This political embeddedness only intensifies during revolutionary moments, when the personal becomes visibly political. Paul Theroux's characterization of political crisis as "a gift to the traveler" on account of its revelatory ("nothing is more revealing of a place to a stranger than trouble") and empowering ("it transforms the traveler into an eyewitness") properties suggests the license and authority to be derived from political revolution for the female traveler.[84] For women who found themselves in the midst of revolution such as Janet Schaw and Helen Maria Williams, their proximity to the political drama both demands and validates their participation; the politicized environment in which they move spontaneously confers political identities and roles upon both women. Schaw and Williams find themselves drawn into various political dramas while also acting the part of foreign correspondents relaying important political information to their audiences in Britain. For the anonymous Lady of *A Journey* and for Mary Morgan, the pressure of revolution transforms the national landscape into political terrain and invests their representations of the domestic space with political meaning. The eruption of revolutionary politics within their travelogues mirrors the sense of compulsion described by Smith to explain eighteenth-century women's "disregard for ordinary gendered expectations in extraordinary times."[85] Both the anonymous Lady and Morgan often frame their political reflections as uncontainable emotional responses to their revolutionary moments; as the Lady of *A Journey* demurs, "I was led irresistibly to these consequent reflections; let this plead my excuse."[86] Working in the liberating space produced by the conflation of sentimental travel and political revolution, these female travel writers feel authorized to write political texts shot through with emotional appeal.

OUTLINE OF THE BOOK

Political Affairs of the Heart takes as its starting point the publication of Sterne's *A Sentimental Journey* and moves into a consideration of the work of four British female travel writers whose travel narratives are either designated as sentimental by the authors or whose representational mode manifests the characteristics of the sentimental traveler. Part I, entitled "Mobile Feelings: Mapping the Sentimental Traveler," outlines the genric parameters that inform my reading of eighteenth-century women's travel texts through an analysis of Sterne's sentimental travelogue and its literary impact. Chapter 1, "'Altogether of a Different Cast': The Development of the Sentimental Traveler," both builds a definition of the sentimental traveler according to the description given in Sterne's text and developed by his imitators, and delineates the possibilities and the difficulties Sterne's prototype posed for female travel writers.

Janet Schaw's *Journal of a Lady of Quality* and an anonymous female author's *A Journey to the Highlands of Scotland* comprise the two case studies found in Part II, "Divided Sympathies: Female Sentimental Travel Writers and the American Revolution." In Chapter 2, "'I Am Sure You Will Share My Feelings': Janet Schaw's *Journal of a Lady of Quality*, Imperial Desire, and the American Revolution," I argue that Schaw masters the selective deployment of sympathy in her representations of British colonialism in the West Indies and of the incipient rebellion in America. Informed by David Hume's and Adam Smith's theories of sympathetic exchange, she understands sympathy as a fluid, malleable quality that can be manipulated through rhetoric and representation. Eager to protect her economic and ideological investments in Britain's empire, Schaw justifies an aggressive military response to the colonial crisis in America by strategically generating sympathy for British loyalists and interrupting sympathetic identification with the American rebels. She continues to carefully manipulate the power of sympathy when it comes to gender. Her deeply sympathetic portrayal of women has clear political dimensions: Schaw perceives women as superior colonizers based upon their exceptional moral strength and national integrity, and argues for their greater inclusion in colonial governance to mitigate the refractory impulses of men.

In Chapter 3, "The Ties That Bind: Sentimentalizing Colonialism in *A Journey to the Highlands of Scotland*," I show how the anonymous English author of *A Journey* problematizes the limited sympathy of Tory conservatives like Schaw. Her rigorous censure of Samuel Johnson's damaging appraisal of Scotland in *A Journey to the Western Islands of Scotland* (1775) condemns a practice of "Britishness" that is defined by insularity and exclusivity, and one that she sees operating in the British government's violent reprisals against the rebellious American colonists. Her own extension of sympathy to the Scottish nation (and, significantly, to its past political rebels) supplies an example for how the British government should approach the American rebels, promoting a conciliatory response that she believes will redeem the relationship between the colonists and their *patria*. The author's critique of exclusivity extends beyond ethnic and into gender relations. She aligns herself with Britain's marginalized populations by suggesting that women are equally victims of the unsympathetic and exclusionary practices that she observes in Britain's patriarchal leaders. Her modeling of an alternative, inclusive form of British national identity and her enshrining of sympathy as an essential national quality jointly articulates that women possess qualities that equip them for political participation.

Part III, "Sensibility in Distress: Female Sentimental Travel Writers and the French Revolution," analyzes the use and development of the sentimental mode in Mary Morgan's *A Tour to Milford Haven* and Helen Maria Williams's *A Tour in Switzerland* during a period that witnessed the rapid demise of sensibility as a cultural phenomenon and as a political quality. Both Morgan and Williams defend sensibility as a vital component of political systems, positing that the absence of sympathy within political relations invites destructive impulses in the government and its citizenry. In Chapter 4, "Revitalizing Sensibility: Mary Morgan's Defense of Emotional Engagement in *A Tour to Milford Haven*," Morgan is shown to interpret the flourishing of incendiary activity across Britain as a symptom of the disintegration of traditional loyalties between Britain's landed and lower classes. Although the British government was aggressively stifling revolutionary activity to protect Britain from a similar political upheaval as France, she suggests that it is the cultivation of sympathy rather than the suppression of dissent that ensures traditional political loyalties. Her travel letters participate in the revitalization of sympathetic bonds within the nation through both her modeling of sympathetic feeling and her observations on "right" relations between the landowners and tenants that she encounters through her country house tourism. Morgan's belief in the power of sympathy to unify the nation is fundamentally linked to her appeal for the greater inclusion of women within public political roles. She postulates that women's exceptional ability to cultivate sympathetic relationships indicates their aptitude for establishing collectivity—a particularly expedient quality during a time of national fragmentation.

Chapter 5, "'A Renovation of Existence': Helen Maria Williams's *A Tour in Switzerland* and the Renewal of Political Vision," explores Williams's attempt to harness British sympathy to France's aggressive exportation of republicanism across Europe throughout the 1790s. Williams's sympathy with the dispossessed rather than with prevailing power structures determines the radically different shape of her political agenda. She seeks to disrupt the traditional loyalties upheld by Morgan and to reshape the political contours of Britain and Europe by exposing the toxic dimensions of asymmetrical power relations. Rewriting the French assault on Switzerland as an act of liberation rather than oppression, Williams appeals to her British audience's hearts in the hope that they will begin to sympathize with the new Directory's political motives—accomplishing the suspension of international hostilities and the political regeneration of Britain. Although Morgan's and Williams's political visions are fundamentally different, Williams shares Morgan's conviction that national regeneration could be expedited through the political empowerment of women. She portrays the exclusion of women from public political life as a symptom of corrupt political systems with roots in political despotism, and warns that perfect republicanism cannot be accomplished without the participation of women.

All four female travelers ultimately engage with the culture of sensibility in two related but distinct ways: as political rhetoric and as political praxis. Their performances of sensibility model right feeling, shaping their readers' sympathies and directing them toward what they perceive as right action. The calculated disclosure of their emotional judgments exploits the transformative power of feeling to produce an emotional alignment between the authors and their audience, creating a space in which both British national identity and the place of women within the nation can be renegotiated. As well as, or due to, their engagement with sensibility as a rhetorical form, they are invested in establishing and defending sympathy as political praxis. The gradual alienation of feeling and politics that reached its zenith during the French Revolution had roots in the moral objections leveled against sensibility in the 1770s. Thus, threaded through each of their narratives is an argument for the political value of feeling in the face of endemic prejudice and/or the diminishing franchise of sensibility. By reinforcing the political legitimacy of sensibility, all four female sentimental travel writers defend a way of imagining and participating in political society. Following in the ideological footsteps of Sterne's protagonist—whose sentimental orientation implicitly endorses the political value of sympathy in the operation of national and international relations—female sentimental travel writers advocate the assimilation of feeling and politics, arguing for what they interpret as a humane politics (understood in either radical or conservative terms) that ameliorates the injustices created by Britain's uneven power relations. In doing so, they simultaneously defend the tenuous grounds of women's political participation.

This book advances the sentimental travel narrative as an important repository of eighteenth-century women's political discourse. It addresses the questions of why and how women used the sentimental travelogue's productive melding of the discourse of sensibility with the variety of discourses available within the travelogue genre to participate in the dialogues emerging from the two political revolutions that rocked Britain in the eighteenth century. By proposing a way of reading their sentimental travelogues that is sensitive to the political nuances contained within their emotional gestures, sentimentalized encounters, affective bodies, and the literal and figurative navigation of their emotional environments, my broader aim is to assist in the recovery of the eighteenth-century female political voice—so often submerged to the point of being indistinguishable *as* political—and to consider how women sought to shape British national identity during periods of political rupture and, in the process, to alter the gendered parameters of political participation. Although their political convictions are diverse and often at odds, the women included in this book are unanimous in their dissatisfaction with their marginalization within the British nation. During a period when the British national character was increasingly imagined as masculine, these female travel writers staked a visible place for women within the national space and projected a national identity defined by both feminine and masculine principles.

Part One

MOBILE FEELINGS

Mapping the Sentimental Traveler

1

"ALTOGETHER OF A DIFFERENT CAST"

The Development of the Sentimental Traveler

IN HIS SERMON "THE PRODIGAL SON" (1764), Laurence Sterne (under the pen name of Mr. Yorick, the popular parson from *The Life and Opinions of Tristram Shandy, Gentleman* [1759–1767]) uses the biblical story of a disastrous journey to offer practical advice for young men preparing to embark on their first Grand Tour. It is significant that Sterne does not use the prodigal son's ill-fated journey to expound upon the folly of travel and to inculcate his audience with a fear of the foreign. Although he acknowledges the dangers presented to young and inexperienced travelers in foreign countries, Sterne emphasizes the value of an immersive travel experience. "Order it rightly," he encourages, "[and] the advantages are worth the pursuit."[1] Sterne is quick to clarify that by "order it rightly" he does not mean "order it rigidly." He cautions against valuing efficiency above experience, warning young travelers and their parents against hiring tutors who are motivated by "profit" rather than by "knowledge" (124). Under the guidance of "some general undertaker, who will perform the journey in so many months" (124), the young traveler will return economically secure but intellectually and culturally bankrupt: "He will learn the amount, to a halfpenny, of every stage from Calais to Rome;—he will be carried to the best inns, instructed where there is the best wine, and sup a livre cheaper than if the youth had been left to make the tour and the bargain himself. Look at our governor! I beseech you:—See, he is an inch taller as he related the advantages—And here endeth his pride, his knowledge, and his use" (124). The traveler motivated by fear and occupied with the bottom line closes himself off from the valuable knowledge gained through experience; as the "undertaker" comparison suggests, Sterne associates this type of travel with deprivation rather than with enrichment. He does not approve of the prodigal son's reckless debauchery, but his alternate parable of the cautious traveler's intellectually and culturally barren tour demonstrates that they ultimately return as impoverished as the prodigal son.

Published four years after "The Prodigal Son," Sterne's *A Sentimental Journey through France and Italy* (1768) features Yorick practicing what he preaches, and provides a more detailed illustration of how travel might be ordered "rightly." Sterne's fictional travelogue fuses the form of a traditional travel narrative with the plot of a sentimental novel, allowing him to explore the emotional rather than the purely material dimensions of travel. The result is a mode of travel and travel writing that emphasizes interpersonal relations and introspection over the more mundane details of stages and inns, good wine and cheap food. Yorick models an alternative approach to the highly efficient "undertaker" method by immersing himself in French society. He treats foreigners as potential sources of knowledge rather than as potential threats, and through his sympathetic exchanges he is rewarded with insights about himself and the world at large. Sterne's method of ordering travel sharply differed from conventional travelogues, and his alterations to the genre changed both the *way* travels were publicly documented and *who* could document their travels.

This chapter outlines the various ways in which *A Sentimental Journey* revolutionized the travel writing genre, focusing on how Sterne's changes both to the structure and to the content of the travelogue created a distinct—and distinctly sentimental—form. To clarify further what I mean by the "sentimental travelogue," I will bring together Sterne's original text and his numerous imitators to build a definition of the form as it developed in the eighteenth century. The last sections of the chapter examine how Sterne's revisions democratized a genre formerly dominated by erudite male writers and opened the door for middle-class women writers, while also acknowledging that the sentimental mode's objectification of women ultimately posed a unique set of challenges for female sentimental travel writers. Emboldened by the form's structural accessibility yet limited by its institutional misogyny, female sentimental travel writers were compelled to modify further the sentimental travelogue to assist their own inclusion. Their modifications had clear implications both for women's participation in the genre of travel writing and for the representation of women within eighteenth-century society, opening a space for women to articulate the female experience of traveling and to portray themselves in real, multidimensional ways that frequently defy eighteenth-century gender classifications.

A SENTIMENTAL JOURNEY: INNOVATION AND IDEOLOGY

In a review of a later sentimental travelogue, *The Monthly Review* credits Sterne as "the first who had sense and taste enough to quit the beaten pack-horse path" of the "dull details of post-stages, and churches, and picture-catalogues, with which books of travels heretofore chiefly abounded."[2] Sterne himself has his protagonist announce the innovative nature of his fictional travel narrative in the text's embedded preface, deliberately drawing attention to his generic revisions. Yorick, a minister by trade and a man of feeling by nature, admits that his style of travel and travel writing is unusual enough to merit a new classification that he labels "The Sentimental Traveller."[3] "I am well aware," he states, "[that] both my travels and observations will be altogether of a different cast from any of my fore-runners" (66). Yorick's itinerary (or lack thereof) shatters the well-established template of the Grand Tour. As Susan Lamb explains, "In *A Sentimental Journey* . . . [Sterne] celebrates the tourist's subjective responses at the expense of everything that contemporaries used to justify both touring and publishing a tour."[4] Rather than travel for intellectual and aesthetic enlightenment, Yorick travels to receive an emotional education by engaging in "sentimental commerce" (64). He explicitly dismisses the conventional itinerary of the Grand Tourist, stating that he will not rush to see "the Palais royal—nor the Luxembourg—nor the Façade of the Louvre," nor will he fill his time cataloguing must-see "pictures, statues, and churches" (137). Rejecting the typical points of interest, Yorick presents and treats sentimental encounters as tourist attractions. "'Tis a quiet journey of the heart," he explains, "in pursuit of NATURE, and those affections which rise out of her, which make us love each other—and the world, better than we do" (137–138). The result is an introspective document that emphasizes emotional response and interpersonal connections over intellectual judgment and technical details. Yorick essentially "feels his way across Europe"[5] and accordingly chronicles "the weaknesses of [his] heart" (70) as an indication of his progress.

Yorick criticizes conventional attitudes toward travel through the stereotypes of Smelfungus and Mundungus, both of whom he faults for their self-centered rather than other-centered approaches to travel. Smelfungus is traditionally thought to be a caricature of Tobias Smollett, whom Sterne encountered in Montpellier during his own travels and whose nonfictional travelogue *Travels through France and Italy* (1766) is characterized by an insular form of English nationalism that manifests itself in his unrelenting critique of foreign nations. "The learned SMELFUNGUS," Yorick disparagingly observes, "travelled from Boulogne to Paris . . . but he set out with spleen and jaundice, and every object he pass'd by was discoloured or distorted—He wrote an account of them, but 'twas nothing but the account of his miserable feelings" (82). Sterne represents Smelfungus as a traveler incapable of *sympathetic* feeling due to his preoccupation with his own *physical* feeling. Yorick's observation suggests that the ailing author—oriented both inward and toward criticism—suffers from emotional myopia, unable to see beyond his self and his ingrained prejudices. Mundungus appears to be a parody of the typical aristocratic Grand Tourist, guided by established itineraries and intent upon checking off all the necessary attractions (not dissimilar from the "undertaker" figure in "The Prodigal Son" [124]). "Mundungus," Yorick continues, "made the whole tour . . . without one generous connection or pleasurable anecdote to tell of; but he had travell'd straight on looking neither to his right hand or his left, lest Love or Pity should seduce him out of his road" (83–84). Rigorously goal-oriented, the Grand Tourist views the foreign through hyperopic eyes, seeing only what lies far ahead and ignoring his immediate environment. The result of both approaches is the same: neither Smelfungus nor Mundungus actually *see* the places they visit, and therefore fail to acquire a genuine understanding of their foreign environments. Sterne, through his character of Yorick, presents an alternative approach to travel that corrects the compromised vision of conventional tourists; an orientation toward sympathy expands the traveler's vision beyond him or herself and beyond prescribed ways of seeing. "He who interests his heart in everything," he insists, "who, having eyes to see, what time and chance are perpetually holding out to him as he journeyeth on his way, misses nothing he can fairly lay his hands on" (81). Seeing with his heart rather than his head, Yorick contends that he is endowed with a depth of insight unavailable to British tourists shuttered by prejudice or convention.

By revising the purpose of travel and the genre of the travelogue, Sterne was not simply providing an alternative itinerary but providing an alternative way of viewing the foreign. As *The Critical Review* notes in a review of a travel guide, a "good sensible traveller . . . should know, not only *what*, but likewise *how* to see."[6] The reviewer is suggesting that it is as important for a traveler to establish his ideological and aesthetic framework prior to departure as it is for him to structure an informed itinerary, as his attitude will ultimately determine his experience of the objects, places, and people he encounters. The political dimensions of the sentimental travelogue are hidden within this dynamic relationship between perception and feeling. In his examination of American sentimental novels, Philip Fischer observes that "sentimentality often marks precisely the point within accepted patterns of feeling and representation where radical revision is taking place."[7] According to Fischer, it accomplishes this by conceptualizing particular objects or individuals as worthy of feeling, and implicitly urges its audience to feel and act accordingly.[8]

In their incisive discussions regarding the national politics of *A Sentimental Journey*, Katherine Turner and Frank Felsenstein both argue that Sterne's use of the sentimental mode was a politically motivated decision designed to reshape Britons' perception of themselves and their presence within the world. Turner contends that Sterne's illustration of "the traveller's capacity for sympathy abroad" revises the political narrative of international relations and British national identity by expanding "the boundaries of international tolerance" and allowing the narrator the freedom to craft "a narrative identity appropriate to his particular version of British nationality."[9] Felsenstein argues that this identity—understood on both a personal and national level—is defined by a commitment to "peace and peace-making" rather than a xenophobic commitment to maintaining difference through hostility.[10] Yorick (and, by extension, Sterne) teaches his British audience an alternative way of seeing their stereotypically reviled Gallic neighbors; by changing their vision, he also seeks to modify their feelings to reflect the "spirit of reconciliation" that he espouses.[11] An old French officer expresses Yorick's sentimental agenda when he asserts that "the advantage of travel . . . was by seeing a great deal of both men and manners; it taught us mutual toleration; and mutual toleration . . . taught us mutual love" (115). However, as the writer for *The Critical Review* clarifies, *how* one perceives these "men and manners" determines whether or not "mutual love" is achieved. *A Sentimental Journey*'s provision of a sentimental lens through which to view unfamiliar cultures teaches its audience how to see in order to manipulate how they feel and, ultimately, how they act.

YORICK'S LEGACY: THE DEVELOPMENT OF THE SENTIMENTAL TRAVELER

Sterne's mock travelogue was a commercial success that triggered a deluge of imitators that transformed the travelogue genre. J.C.T. Oates observes that "to judge from the book-lists and magazines, all England and most of Europe during the last thirty years of the eighteenth century were infested with sentimental travellers," and Percy G. Adams concurs that Sterne's text "inspired a huge school of sentimental travel accounts."[12] Oates and Adams both argue that unlike later readings of Sterne's text, his eighteenth-century audience read *A Sentimental Journey* as a travelogue rather than as a novel—treating Sterne's fictional protagonist as an actual person and attempting to re-create his journey.[13] Turner notes that even critics "reviewed *A Sentimental Journey* as a travel narrative, rather than a novel, and admired the games Sterne played with the conventions of the genre."[14] It is not surprising, then, that the impact of his innovative approach is particularly apparent in the production of nonfictional travel texts post-1768. The first imitator appeared so quickly after Sterne's publication that its author, Samuel Paterson, attempted to convince his audience that *Another Traveller!* (1768) was not an imitation of *A Sentimental Journey*.[15] By the time it reviewed Paterson's publication,

The Monthly Review had already seen a sufficient amount of evidence to happily declare that "Sentimental Travels seem now to be coming into vogue."[16] Just over a decade later, in 1779, the same journal reversed its initial excitement, complaining of saturation: "*Trips*, and *Tours*, and *Excursions*, and *Sentimental Journeys*, are become so much the *ton*, that every rambler, who can write (tolerably or intolerably), assumes the pen, and gives the Public a journal of the *occurrences* and *remarks* to which his peregrinations have given birth."[17] *The Critical Review* had evinced disenchantment with the form a year earlier, facetiously stating that "in time we may expect to see sentimental stage-coaches and diligence advertised, to any part of his majesty's dominions."[18] These complaints from weary reviewers indicate the transformative impact of Sterne's text on the travel writing genre; although *A Sentimental Journey* may have been "altogether of a different cast" (66) when it was first published, within ten years it had become a well-used mold.

The sentimental travelogues published in the late eighteenth century occasionally identify their provenance directly within their titles, accomplished by indicating their desultory mode of traveling (*A Short Ramble through Some Parts of France and Italy* [1781]), suggesting their anecdotal literary style (*Travelling Anecdotes through Various Parts of Europe* [1785]), or specifying their textual emphasis on sensibility (*Travels for the Heart* [1777]; *A Sentimental Tour through Newcastle* [1794]). However, many of the travelogues that can be classified as "sentimental" are subtler in their attribution. The genre as it developed in the period after the publication of *A Sentimental Journey* lacks clear definition; eighteenth-century sentimental travel writers, their contemporary reviewers, and more recent scholars all understand the sentimental travelogue as a distinct category within the genre of travel writing, yet the basis of their distinction is often unclear.[19] This lack of clarity can be traced back to Sterne's resistance to defining the sentimental traveler due to the mode's fundamental emphasis on fluidity. Yorick performs rather than describes his new mode of traveling, and the real-life sentimental travelers that followed in his footsteps similarly enact rather than define their understanding of sentimental travel. Despite this textual resistance to classification, a perusal of eighteenth-century sentimental travelogues (categorized as such either directly by the author, contemporaneous critics, or current scholars) reveals a number of similarities that can be marshalled into a loose definition.[20] Although most travel writers inspired by Sterne's text did not wholly espouse Yorick's purely people-based itinerary or excessive performances of sensibility (except for a handful whose imitation verges on plagiarism—Samuel Jackson Pratt and John Barnard come to mind[21]), their travelogues share three key characteristics: an introspective approach to observation that privileges emotional response, an emphasis on sociability and an orientation toward sympathy, and an anecdotal style that often mimics the desultory nature of the journey.

The primary characteristic of sentimental travelers is their privileging of emotional response: their immediate feelings either take precedence over or are liberally incorporated within their scientific, sociopolitical, and aesthetic assessments.[22] They proclaim the heart as their guide and often as their aim, and stress the emotional dimensions of the objects, landscapes, and people encountered. Thus Pratt declares that every page in his travelogue "was written in the ardour of relating some event, which really happened; and the true impressions *of the heart* are given in every sentence"; Helen Maria Williams excuses her revolutionary fervor as "as an affair of the heart"; and Janet Schaw accounts for any discrepancies in opinion or fact by explaining that "every subject will be guided by my own immediate feelings."[23]

Intimately connected to this emphasis on feeling is the second distinguishing feature of sentimental travelers and their texts, which can be described as an emphasis on sentimental sociability or an orientation toward sympathy. Sentimental travelers, as Carl Thompson observes, "were especially concerned to identify, in themselves and others, a 'natural' tendency to benevolence and sympathy."[24] The sentimental traveler assumes (rhetorically, if not always in practice) an attitude of open-mindedness that manifests itself as an interest in the social dimensions of their environments and in a professed repudiation of prejudice, described by Paterson as a "disposition to be pleased."[25] Sentimental travel writers register their difference from other travel writers by accusing their counterparts of unfair representations grounded either in prejudice or in an unfeeling heart (the former often being attributed to the latter). Cornelius Cayley grounds his unfailingly positive assessments of foreign nations in his Christian duty to love and urges his British audience to "judge for themselves" rather than circulate narrow-minded "hear say."[26] The sentimental traveler's/travel writer's motto might be summed up in Jean-Baptiste Mercier Dupaty's grand statement that "humanity itself is the light that guides us."[27]

The third characteristic—the inevitable consequence of their sociable and sympathetic orientation—is the digressive nature of both their itineraries and their texts. Sentimental travelers either entirely dispense with traditional itineraries or incorporate "mishaps" that momentarily disrupt their trajectory. Accordingly, they emphasize anecdotes over facts, frequently interspersing their observations on "post-stages, and churches, and picture-catalogues" with fragments of conversations, stories, and personal reflections.[28] John Barnard, author of the series *A Sentimental Journey* that appeared in *The Lady's Magazine* from 1770–1777, distinguishes the "historical" from the "sentimental" traveler based on the flexible organization of their texts: "The historical traveller . . . is confined to his route, as much as a horse in a team. . . . The sentimental traveller is not confined to such narrow limits; he ranges over a whole district in the twinkling of an eye, and can shift the scene from one country to another with the same ease and velocity as we find it done every night during the representation of a pantomime."[29] Sentimental travelers frequently assert that the organizing principle of their physical journeys and/or their written observations is emotional prerogative rather than material objectives. Pratt explains that "all that is allied to the movements—stops and meanders of the heart, shall attract us on the way,"[30] while Mary Wollstonecraft places responsibility for the "desultory" style of her travel letters on her determination to relate "the effect different objects had produced on [her] mind and feelings, whilst the impression was still fresh."[31]

Sentimental travelers cite the ultimate advantage of their sympathetic orientation and rambling peregrinations as the attainment of superior insight. They frequently claim that their approach reveals the genuine face of the countries they visit, hitherto unobserved due to prejudice and ignorance. Yorick's proclamation that "[he] who interests his heart in every thing, and who, having eyes to see . . . misses nothing he can *fairly* lay his hand on" (81) is echoed by a parade of sentimental tourists, from an anonymous travel writer's assertion that she "had noticed several things worthy of being made public, which more laborious travellers . . . had neglected, or overlooked" to Pratt's defense that his attention to seeming "trifles" is more incisive than the conventional tourist's focus on "the might, the marvelous, and the magnificent" because "these very trifles . . . more forcibly mark a character, develop an action . . . and serve as a clue to unfold the mazes of the heart."[32] Neither myopic due to prejudice nor hyperopic due to a slavish dedication to convention, sentimental tourists profess to own a fresh and authentic vision. Claiming insight that can penetrate to the very heart of individuals and entire societies, they assert the authoritative nature of their accounts. Other travelogues may provide the measurements, but their sentimental counterparts provide the meaning. Paterson states that the overriding "intention" of his sentimental travelogue is to "diversify this short travel as much as possible—to make it narrative, descriptive, and sometimes allegorical—always with a little meaning, and seldom without a moral."[33]

"INSIGNIFICANT OBJECTS OF DESIRE": WOMEN AND THE SENTIMENTAL TRAVELOGUE

It is not a coincidence that the rise of women's nonfictional travelogues corresponds with the publication of Sterne's *A Sentimental Journey*. *The Monthly Review*'s complaint regarding the ubiquity of sentimental travelogues—that "every rambler, who can write (tolerably or intolerably), assumes the pen, and gives the Public a journal of the *occurrences* and *remarks*, to which his peregrinations have given birth"[34]—irascibly suggests that Sterne effectively democratized a genre previously dominated by erudite scholars, intrepid explorers, and accomplished writers—the majority notably male. By emphasizing personal experience over technical details and scholarly erudition, Sterne created a form of travel writing not only accessible to women writers, but also tailored to their socially sanctioned strengths.

That women possessed a greater natural capacity for sensibility than men had become a truism in the eighteenth century, and was propagated and confirmed in everything from medical treatises to conduct literature. Medical treatises on the human nervous system suggested that women's nerves were naturally more delicate, imbuing them with greater sensitivity.[35] "Herein consists the indescribable superiority of the female organization," Pratt poetically rather than medically describes: "Every artery, about them, is hung more airily; the avenues which nature hath opened to the heart, though perhaps more involved in mazes, are yet so like a wilderness of sweets, that we have more inducements to clear the way, and examine them: add to this that certain voluptuous particles swim along the beautiful labyrinths that are formed by the veins, and always fit them for a spirited proposal at a moment's notice."[36] Pratt's interpretation of women's bodies as repositories of sensation is indebted to eighteenth-century medical explanations linking women's unique physical composition to emotional sensitivity. Enlightenment philosophy built upon this physical rationale and enshrined women's superior sensibility as an essential component of progress and civilization. Francis Hutcheson determined that the "tender bonds" of marriage "chiefly civilize and unite men in society,"[37] and Lord Kames agreed that "the gentle and insinuating manners of the female sex tend to soften the roughness of the other sex."[38] The fictional narrator of Barnard's series *A Sentimental Journey*—introduced above—evinces the influence of Enlightenment conceptions of women when she proudly declares, "How much does our sex refine the nature of the male! . . . Like rough diamonds they have an intrinsic worth; but it is owing to us that they sparkle and are polished."[39] Sentimental novels like Samuel Richardson's *Pamela* (1740) and Sarah Scott's *Millenium Hall* (1762) centered their plots on the reforming influence of women's refined sensibility, illustrating how the exercise of female sympathy could effect individual and social transformation. Conduct literature such as Rev. James Fordyce's *Sermons to Young Women* (1766) and Dr. John Gregory's *A Father's Legacy to His Daughters* (1761) confirmed women's superiority in the realm of feeling and attempted to convince them that the heart rather than the head was their area of specialty. "It is not the argumentative but the sentimental talents," Fordyce proclaims, "which give you that insight and those openings into the human heart, that lead to your principle ends as Women."[40] Sterne's *A Sentimental Journey* reflects this belief in women's superior capacity for feeling; Yorick imputes greater sensibility to women and seeks sentimental encounters with them in order to refine his emotional faculties. "I could wish," he fervently proclaims, "to spy the *nakedness* of [women's] hearts, and through the different disguises of customs, climates, and religion, find out what is good in them, to fashion my own by" (137). Yorick essentially desires to "soften his roughness" through his interactions with women, and is conspicuously proud of the moments when his emotional pitch renders him "as weak as a woman" (75).[41]

It stands to reason that if the sentimental traveler is evaluated by their ability to feel, and if the goal of the sentimental journey is the exercise and expansion of sympathetic feeling, then women—as delineated by medical, philosophical, and cultural authorities—could legitimately claim a certain amount of expertise in this mode of travel and travel writing. Mary Wollstonecraft's derogatory observation that "a man, when he undertakes a journey, has, in general, the end in view; a woman thinks more of the incidental occurrences, the strange things that may possibly occur on the road" could be appropriated by female sentimental travel writers as an asset.[42] In a form shaped around digressions and invested in the incidental, their stereotyped propensities were perfectly adapted to the expectations of the sentimental travelogue. Moreover, women's accomplishments as sentimental novelists had already established them as doyennes in the literature of feeling, as Jery Melford admits in Smollett's *The Expedition of Humphrey Clinker* (1771): "That branch of business [novels] is now engrossed by female authors, who publish merely for the propagation of virtue, with so much ease and spirit, and delicacy, and knowledge of the human heart, and all in the serene tranquility of high life, that the reader is not only enchanted by their genius, but reformed by their morality."[43] Melford's comment certainly contains a touch of facetiousness, but the fact that women's talent as sentimental novelists could be parodied demonstrates the extent to which their involvement in the production of sentimental fiction had become a cultural commonplace. By transferring value from the traveler's erudition to their emotions, Sterne shifted the travelogue into an area ceded to women on the basis of their biology and into a literary territory already well traversed by female authors. In so doing, he provided a new way for women writers to justify their engagement in a literary field traditionally dominated by men. Women became, as Turner notes, "beneficiaries . . . of the changing scope of the travel narrative, away from erudite classical traditions in favour of more sociological, affective, and miscellaneous preoccupations."[44]

Yet despite its apparent accessibility to women writers, the genre as developed by Sterne is inescapably gendered. As revealed by Yorick's proclamation that he is "as weak as a woman" (75), the power that he allots to the female sex as models of sensibility is paradoxically predicated upon their weakness. Yorick's statement that "he has a fellow-feeling for whatever is *weak* about them" (137) is corroborated throughout the text; his travelogue consistently features women in moments of weakness or vulnerability, which collectively construct an idea of women as inherently fragile. His fixation on female weakness is particularly evident in his portrayals of Madame de L*** and Maria of Moulines, two women with whom he shares intense emotional exchanges. Yorick's initial attraction to Madame de L*** is premised upon her "unprotected look of distress" (73). He glories in the idea of witnessing her tears and imagines "what an exquisite sensation is there still left, in wiping them away from off the cheeks of the first and fairest of women" (97). His later encounter with Maria provides him with the opportunity of participating in a similar spectacle of emotional vulnerability. Yorick has been previously informed of Maria's tragic tale of loss and subsequent mental breakdown through the account of his friend Tristram Shandy,[45] and he deliberately seeks her out to personally witness her mental and emotional disintegration. It is precisely Maria's overt exhibition of weakness that marks her as desirable. "Affliction," he notes approvingly, "had touch'd her looks with something that was scarce earthly" (168). The emotional vulnerability of both Madame de L*** and Maria actuates Yorick with a possessive desire masquerading as protection; he fantasizes about shielding Madame de L*** in his arms and "cherish[ing]" (73) her, and he imagines drawing Maria into his cottage and "shelter[ing]" (167) her. That these women's purported weaknesses demand their protection or possession clearly demonstrates the continuity between Yorick's celebration of female weakness and eighteenth-century gender hierarchies that naturalized women's subjugation on the basis of their mental and physical inferiority.

Yorick's (always unrealized) impulse toward possession suggests the objectification of women accomplished through his admiration. His admission that his journey is motivated by the voyeuristic desire to "spy the *nakedness* of [women's] hearts" (137) may position them as models to be imitated, but it concomitantly reduces them into consumable objects. He compares his "thirst" for women to the passion "which inflames the breast of the connoisseur" (137), and like a connoisseur of art, he is eager to access, analyze, touch, and even pay for the opportunity of consuming the objects of his desire. Commenting on Yorick's "unorthodox itinerary of sights," Chloe Chard observes that he "displace[s] the monuments and works of art designated as sights by discourses such as classical scholarship and art criticism by a sequence of women, poised to yield up to the enquiring traveller the secrets of their hearts."[46] Indeed, from distressed ladies to French grisettes to unbalanced maids, Yorick's itinerary is dominated by his encounters with women.

His rapid consumption of these "fair being[s]" effectively commodifies them, remaking women into tourist sites akin to the "Palais royal," the "Luxembourg," and the "Façade of the Louvre" (137). Although his sentimental portrayal of women mystifies their objectification, his orientation as a tourist generates an acquisitive inclination that relegates women to static attractions and his exchanges with them to souvenirs.

The objectification of women—and particularly the erotic objectification of female vulnerability—becomes a standard trope in the narratives of male sentimental travel writers. Paterson litters his travelogue with observations on females in various stages of distress—anonymous women exhibiting signs of grief, persecuted female saints, and immured nuns are of particular interest.[47] Nathaniel Wraxall's frequent effusions upon the beauty of Northern women in his *Cursory Remarks Made in a Tour through Some of the Northern Parts of Europe* (1775) caused a contributor to *The Gentleman's Magazine* to exclaim with exasperation, "Could he be prevailed on to strike out all mention of every woman that he would have us believe reigned the sovereign of his affections for an hour, in very rapid succession . . . [his *Cursory Remarks*] would appear to much greater advantage."[48] Wraxall's tastes tend toward the passive female subject, as spectacularly evidenced by an episode of necrophilia in Bremen where he finds himself entranced by the perfectly preserved 250-year-old corpse of an alleged English countess.[49] Addressing his *Sentimental Letters on Italy* (1785) to his wife, Jean-Baptiste Mercier Dupaty is careful to constrain the majority of his robust descriptions of the female form to their representations in statuary and painting. However, he cannot resist waxing poetic on lovely but consumptive English ladies, half-clothed Roman matrons escaping burning buildings, and beautiful though unconscious maidens[50]—all either distressed or undressed but rendered innocuous due to their unattainability. "It is generally said," he sighs, "that there is something of the woman in whatever we love."[51] John Gabriel Stedman's detailed account of life within the Dutch colony of Surinam in *The Narrative of a Five Years Expedition against the Revolted Negroes of Surinam* (1796) is liberally punctuated with personal anecdotes recounting his doomed love affair with Joanna, a young biracial enslaved woman. Stedman is drawn to Joanna's "youth and beauty,"[52] but it is her vulnerability as a female slave that motivates his involvement. "Female virtue in distress," he asserts, "must ever claim protection."[53] Although descriptions of women had a long history in the travelogue genre—it was expected that travel writers would address the appearance, customs, and behavior of foreign women in their accounts—the details recorded by Yorick and his successors diverge from convention. The male sentimental tourist's interest in the vulnerable female body is more of the erotic than the ethnographic or even the moral kind. Rather than classifying women according to proto-ethnographic methods or studying them in order to assess a foreign society's sociocultural evolution, they generally aim to collect a series of intimate (though always "innocent") experiences for personal as opposed to public edification.[54]

Manifest in this sentimental fixation with distressed women is what Robert Markley identifies as "a masculinist complex of strategies designed to relegate women to the status of perpetual victims."[55] The trope of the afflicted, innocent female positions women at the center of the narrative, yet effectively relegates them to the margins of society by emphasizing their physical and emotional fragility. The attention to mad, mourning, sickly, or otherwise physically vulnerable females found in the pages of male sentimental travel writers suggests the victimization of women accomplished by sentimentalism: their glorification is contingent upon their impotence. Both Claudia Johnson and Ingrid Horrocks address this paradox found in sentimental and Romantic literature, and suggest that the figure of the distressed woman often functions as an object designed either to display male affect (Johnson) or absorb male anxieties (Horrocks).[56] The effect of their objectification, as Markley observes, is that women are ultimately constrained to "sociopolitical docility"—unable to act as dynamic, empowered subjects due to their narrative purpose as objects to be acted upon and their textual representation as inherently weak.[57] Both Yorick's and Stedman's impulse to literally "shelter" the objects of their affections not only reinforces the trope of female fragility, but it also suggests that women must be kept "safe" within the protracted space of the domestic sphere. References to women within Adam Smith's *The Theory of Moral Sentiments* exemplify the extent to which their association with exquisite feeling could justify the exclusion of women from public political life. Smith repeatedly genders weakness and strength, referring to various displays of weakness as "womanish" and defines expressions of strength as evidence of "manhood." His fear that "delicate sensibility" will inevitably corrupt the nation's "masculine firmness of character" implicitly suggests that women have no place within the business of the nation.[58] Smith's gendering of weakness as feminine quietly yields to and supports the prevailing idea that women were too emotionally volatile to be trusted with the demands of active citizenship.

Wollstonecraft targeted this disturbing side of "the culture of the heart" in *A Vindication of the Rights of Woman* (1792), arguing that her culture's construction of women as "creatures of sensation" effectively produced and secured their subordination.[59] Explaining the relationship between sensibility and subjection, she contends, "To their senses, are women made slaves, because it is by their sensibility that they obtain present power. And will moralists pretend to assert, that this is the condition in which one half of the human race should be encouraged to remain with listless inactivity and stupid acquiescence? Kind instructors! what were we created for? To remain, it may be said, innocent; they mean in a state of childhood."[60] The power women gain through their superiority in the realm of feeling is contingent upon their physical and intellectual powerlessness; paradoxically cultivating fragility to acquire power, they are ultimately made dependent upon and subordinate to men. The "soft phrases, susceptibility of the heart, delicacy of sentiment, and refinement of taste" that Wollstonecraft believes are "synonymous with weakness" are the very things that male sentimental travelers find so irresistible in the women they portray.[61] By reifying the female qualities that manifest weakness, they implicitly condemn them to the position of "perpetual victims,"[62] if not perpetual childhood.

THE FEMALE SENTIMENTAL TRAVEL WRITER

The eighteenth-century female travel writers examined in this book all, to some extent, adopt Yorick's sentimental model of travel and travel writing, manifesting his influence in their conspicuous deployment of the main characteristics of the sentimental traveler: an emphasis on emotional responsiveness, an acknowledged orientation toward sympathy, and a conversational writing style that liberally incorporates anecdotes. Where they radically differ from Sterne is in their displacement of women from the perceived to the perceivers—a shift that has significant implications for how femininity is defined and treated within these texts. Eighteenth-century female travel writers composing within the sentimental vein inevitably faced the problem of working within a form adapted to their designated strengths yet one that naturalized their objectification, eroticization, and stasis. The (nonfiction) women writers who followed in Yorick's footsteps confronted the form's gendered assumptions in their very act of appropriation; by transitioning from the sentimental object to the sentimental subject, they fundamentally challenged the form's construction of femininity.

Through both their portrayal of themselves and the women they encounter, female travel writers strategically modify the gendered formula of sentimental narratives. The figure of the female sentimental travel writer pits the image of the traveler and author (vigorous, mobile, authoritative) against the image of the sentimental female (weak, inert, passive). Their negotiation of these two competing positions exposes and questions the matrix of gender assumptions at work within both sentimental narratives and eighteenth-century society as a whole. The stereotype of the inherently fragile woman—whose physical vulnerability both demands and justifies women's restriction to the domestic sphere—is contested by female travelers through their physical movement through challenging foreign environments. The demanding realities of eighteenth-century travel reveal the physical strength of the female travel writers examined herein, while the intellectual conventions of the travelogue genre allow them to demonstrate their mental acuity. They stoically endure the rigors of travel by land and by sea, surviving harrowing sea storms and unforgiving landscapes; they also immerse themselves in nature, gladly hiking over hills and clambering up to glaciers. The anonymous Lady of *A Journey to the Highlands of Scotland* goes as far as to encourage the practice of hiking among women, deriding displays of feminine delicacy as unnatural: "I know you will join me in despising the affectation of those females who think, because indulgent Fortune has thrown a coach in their power, they are not to make use of the gifts Nature has bestowed."[63] The physical strength displayed by these female travelers is matched by their intellectual vigor; their astute observations demonstrate their keen intellect, political awareness, and knowledge in fields that were traditionally denominated as masculine. Mary Morgan roundly dismisses those who believe that women's intellectual activity should be confined to "dress" and "domestic drudgery," asserting that "so many of my sex have shewn they are capable of the most admirable compositions on the most important subjects."[64] By enlarging the sphere of female ability and activity, these writers craft an alternative or more multifaceted model of femininity that celebrates women's strengths rather than their weaknesses.

Additionally, their representations of the women they encounter subtly undermine the portrait of women offered in male sentimental travel narratives and in the whole spectrum of sentimental literature. The erotic objectification of women is supplanted by a more nuanced representation of women as complex, self-determining subjects. Janet Schaw praises the moral strength that she finds in colonial women; the anonymous Lady highlights and encourages Scottish women's physical fitness; Mary Morgan features women in leadership roles and advertises the various literary accomplishments of female bluestocking intellectuals; and Helen Maria Williams recovers the heroic contributions of women to Switzerland's military efforts.[65] Indeed, the two unattached women included in this study—Schaw and the anonymous Lady—deflect their society's attempts at matchmaking and circumvent their own sexual objectification by happily advertising their inability to fit within their society's standards of beauty.[66] The emphasis on female beauty found in the travelogues of male sentimental travel writers is replaced by an emphasis on the diversity of women's capabilities, avoiding the tendency of sentimental narratives (and eighteenth-century society at large) to locate women's particular value in their physical desirability.

Female sentimental travel writers' engagement with sentimental discourse is as complex and dynamic as their portrayals of gender. Rather than portraying women as victims of their feelings, they confirm women's expertise within the realm of feeling while simultaneously demonstrating their ability to master their emotions and, ultimately, to guide the emotions of others. Their deployment of sensibility and sympathy is discerning and deliberate; these female writers recognize and develop the political potential inherent in Sterne's manipulation of perception and feeling. They harness the emotional power of sentimental discourse in service to their social and political agendas, using their demonstrations of sentiment to influence and educate their audience. As Lynn Festa explains, sentimental authors' focus on emotional responsiveness—both demonstrating and inciting it—often serves a sociopolitical purpose by "train[ing] the many in the 'proper' reactions [and] becoming the means by which to create (and potentially dominate) the collective."[67] Feeling their way through foreign environments, female sentimental travel writers present their emotional responses as edification rather than as spectacle. The biases they impose on their foreign environments and the feelings that these spaces engender coalesce within their travelogues to create emotionally invested accounts that contribute to shaping Britons' feelings toward the countries, events, and people described within their travelogues. Whereas a cartographer establishes how Britons comprehend the physical parameters of the world, female sentimental travel writers directly influence how Britons *feel* about their own expanding nation and those outside British borders—they effectively shade in the immaterial, affective aspects of the nations and territories they traverse. According to Hume's and Smith's theories of sympathy, it is precisely this emotional labor that ultimately determines the political contours of the nation.

Part Two

DIVIDED SYMPATHIES

Female Sentimental Travel Writers and the American Revolution

2

"I AM SURE YOU WILL SHARE MY FEELINGS"

Janet Schaw's *Journal of a Lady of Quality*, Imperial Desire, and the American Revolution

ON OCTOBER 25, 1774, A SINGLE, upper middle-class Scottish woman by the name of Janet Schaw began a remarkable journey across the Atlantic to the West Indies and North Carolina, eventually returning to Scotland via Portugal in 1776. Schaw could not have anticipated that her stay in North Carolina would throw her into the midst of an accelerating colonial rebellion, threatening the lives and property of both herself and her loved ones and transforming this "lady of quality" into an active political player. Her politicization over the course of her journey is portrayed as a response to her colonial and revolutionary environments, suggesting the liberating possibilities of both physical mobility and political instability for women in the eighteenth century. Her correspondence demonstrates that travel is inherently political as border crossings and contact zones are inescapably politicized spaces of national, cultural, and economic negotiation, while revolution penetrates every facet of society, blurring the already imprecise demarcations between private and public spaces.[1] Schaw's travel letters document her emerging political consciousness and become the means of her active political intervention; by positioning herself as a witness to colonial realities and to revolutionary events, her personal experiences are transformed into political information.

Schaw's integration of feeling and observation produces a sentimentalized politics that derives power from the operation of sympathy. Her understanding of the nation as a "Social Circle"—its parameters defined by affection rather than by geography or biology—suggests the political importance of feeling both within eighteenth-century culture and within her travel letters.[2] She would agree with Edmund Burke that "in the immense and diversified mass of human misery . . . the mind must make a choice. Our sympathy is always more forcibly attracted towards the misfortunes of certain persons, and in certain descriptions: and this sympathetic attraction discovers, beyond a possibility of a mistake, our mental affinities, and elective affections."[3] Her strategic manipulation of sympathy demonstrates a similar conviction both in the instrumentality of emotions and in the selective quality of sympathy. During the period in which Schaw was writing, Britons were forced to choose between two equally suffering parties: American rebels and British loyalists. That the direction of their affections would determine the shape of their political actions is evident from Allan Ramsay's contention that definitive action for or against America would be impossible until the colonists' "true relation to Great Britain is accurately known."[4] Schaw engages with sensibility as political rhetoric, painting the misfortunes of those with whom she sympathizes using broad sentimental strokes intended to shift her British audiences' sympathies to align with her own. Her adoption of a sentimental persona for political effect reveals the possibilities and the limitations of both sentimental travel and sensibility as political praxis when situated within real and volatile sociopolitical contexts. Laurence Sterne's idyllic representation of universal love in *A Sentimental Journey* breaks down under the pressure of colonial and revolutionary politics, where sentimental encounters become complicated by political commitments, economic realities, and ethnic affiliations. Schaw's form of sentimental travel demonstrates an affinity with Burke's opinion that "in the immense and diversified mass of human suffering . . . the mind must make a choice."[5] Her sentimental travel narrative ensures that her British readers will make what she believes is the right choice.

JANET SCHAW: CONFESSIONS OF A SENTIMENTAL IMPERIALIST

Little is known about Schaw besides what is disclosed in her travelogue. However, her own story and the sparse details of her life preserved in the historical record reveal a self-possessed woman who was a product of the Enlightenment culture in which she was raised and of the British Empire upon which she and her circle were profoundly dependent. Schaw was likely born sometime between 1739 and 1744 and raised in the Lauriston suburb of Edinburgh, the daughter of a customs official.[6] Her eloquence, frequent allusions to literature, excellent knowledge of botany and agriculture, and personal connections suggest a woman who is educated, well-positioned within Edinburgh society, and integrated into its vibrant intellectual and cultural life. She realizes with humor that her text of choice during a particularly harrowing storm is Lord Kames's *Elements of Criticism* (1762) rather than the Bible. "We discovered," she laughs, "we were meeting death, like philosophers not Christians" (45). Her bedside copy of Kames's theoretical contemplation of aesthetics is suggestive of her familiarity with and interest in Enlightenment thought, while her warm memories of the "evening Conversations . . . I have feasted on" (21) conjure up images of the convivial intellectual milieu that characterized eighteenth-century Edinburgh. Schaw's connections along her journey and her casual references to acquaintances in Scotland indicate the impressive circles in which she moved; her network of friends included noteworthy politicians, Scottish aristocrats, wealthy planters, and successful professionals.

In October 1774, Schaw joined her brother aboard the *Jamaica Packet* as a travelling companion on his voyage to the West Indian colony of St. Christopher to secure a position as a customs official. Her journey would also include a visit to an older brother on his plantation in North Carolina and an unexpected detour to Portugal on her premature trip home in January or February 1776. She also went as the unofficial guardian of the three Rutherfurd children—Fanny, Jack, and Billie—who had been sent to Scotland for their education and were returning to their father's plantation in North Carolina after a lengthy absence. It is unclear whether Schaw traveled to the Atlantic colonies as a tourist or as a colonist; she assures her Scottish correspondent that "time will restore me to you" but then more ambivalently states that time will "*perhaps* [restore me] to my Native land" (21–22). Her expressions of relieved astonishment at being able to return to Scotland following the breakdown of colonial relations in America suggest that she had intended to remain with her brother in St. Christopher: "Shall I really see you and dear Scotland once more? My head turns giddy at the thought. I am ready to faint. Oh my God! 'tis a sort of feeling I have long been a stranger to" (214–215). Following the abrupt conclusion of her letters in Portugal, Schaw disappears into obscurity; one of the few indications of the type of life she led upon her return home is a fragment of an address and date inscribed on one of the three existing copies of her travelogue: "St. Andrews Square, March 10, 1778."[7] It seems that she temporarily settled into one of the choicest addresses in Edinburgh, making her home in the center of its New Town—the city's posh new addition that had been built with the profits of empire and where she would have called David Hume her neighbor. According to Schaw's family, she eventually left Edinburgh to live with her brother's family in the bustling English port city of Plymouth, where her brother was employed as the Principle Ordnance Storekeeper at the Gun Wharf in the Royal Dockyards and where, as family legend would have it, she met and dined with the Royal family during their visit to the Royal Dockyards in 1789.[8] Her final known residences once again suggest her integration within Britain's cultural, intellectual, and political elite, as well as the extent to which her life was enmeshed with the fortunes of the British Empire.

Her travelogue purports to be a compilation of the letters she intermittently sent to a close friend in Scotland throughout her voyage. Schaw's account of the journey is separated into four distinct parts: the seven-week voyage to the West Indies, her sumptuous progress through the sugar islands of Antigua and St. Christopher, the terrifying experience of revolution in North Carolina, and her brief stop in Portugal prior to returning to Scotland. Once settled back in Edinburgh, Schaw transcribed her original letters into at least three different polished manuscripts, which remained the form in which her travel narrative was circulated until Charles McLean Andrews and Evangeline Walker Andrews found one of the manuscripts in the British Museum and finally published Schaw's travelogue in 1923. Although the manuscripts maintain the appearance of a private correspondence, the sophisticated presentation of Schaw's letters, her evident concern with literariness, and the urgency of her political concerns suggest that her text was written (or rewritten) with a wider audience in mind.

The scale of Schaw's audience and the intended reach of her political intervention are admittedly difficult to assess given the unofficial nature of manuscript circulation and the regrettable absence of information regarding the *Journal*'s original audience and reception. Despite this lack of historical confirmation, scholars have repeatedly suggested that Schaw's correspondence was intended for a broad audience; these claims are largely based on the remarkably polished appearance of her manuscripts and on the communal nature of both epistolary correspondence and manuscript circulation in the eighteenth century.[9] The fact that Schaw reproduced at least three manuscripts provides compelling evidence that she intended her original correspondence to be received by a relatively large readership. In her study of seventeenth- and eighteenth-century manuscript culture, Margaret Ezell has cautioned against the tendency of contemporary scholarship to conflate "private" with "personal."[10] She argues that unpublished texts by women served a "'social' function" and often enjoyed extensive circulation—occasionally more extensive than their published counterparts.[11] "By collapsing 'public' into 'publication,'" she warns, "we seriously misconstrue the literary practices of such women."[12] The presence of multiple copies of Schaw's travelogue indicates that her text did, indeed, serve a social rather than a strictly personal purpose. Katherine Turner notes that Schaw's practice of deliberately omitting names throughout her manuscript "suggests that she envisaged a readership far beyond the circle of her family, and may even have been considering publication."[13] Considering her unvarnished and controversial opinions on colonial politics, it certainly may be the case that she ultimately decided to retain a measure of control over the circulation of her text. It equally may be the case that her pointed observations were specifically aimed at influencing the powerful Edinburgh elite that formed her inner circle of friends.[14] Schaw would have been aware of the political value of her eyewitness account given the delivery of her younger brother's letters to Lord Dartmouth, the secretary of state for the colonies. In an effort to convince Lord Dartmouth to send a suitable supply of weapons to the colony, the governor of North Carolina persuaded Schaw's brother to record his impressions of the colony's political situation and to personally convey his written account and additional political documents to Lord Dartmouth and his circle of associates.[15] It is possible that Schaw's letters had a similar political motivation, but were intended for a more diffuse—but no less politically invested—Edinburgh audience.

In her excellent chapter on the Atlantic voyage and West Indian sections of Schaw's travelogue, Katrina O'Loughlin argues that "throughout the *Journal*, feeling is accorded a primary role in the mind's assembly of experience, and is made a critical aspect of communicating that experience to others."[16] O'Loughlin's study of the language of feeling in Schaw's text convincingly treats her sensibility as constitutive of transatlantic sociability; my reading prioritizes the formative influence of the sentimental travelogue on Schaw's literary sentiment, and contextualizes her literary sensibility as a strategic political response to the upheaval in the American colonies. Schaw identifies her travel persona as sentimental within the first few pages of her travelogue by freely declaring the emotional character of her observations. "Every subject," she states, "will be guided by my own immediate feelings" (20). She explains that the form of her letters will be adapted to reflect her sentimental orientation. Echoing Yorick's assertion that his travelogue will offer an account of "the weaknesses of [his] heart in this tour" rather than the usual catalogue of sites,[17] Schaw forewarns her correspondent that she will not "inform you of what you know so well already" but will compose "a journal of my own thoughts, ideas and apprehensions, where every thing is new to me" (217). She is not primarily concerned with calculations and categorization but with her own emotional response to the foreign environment. Schaw reinforces her affective disposition throughout her account, repeatedly gesturing toward her "feeling heart" which, she assures her reader, "is not composed of very hard materials" (33). Near the conclusion of her travelogue, she asserts the merits of a sentimental orientation by criticizing the work of Richard Twiss—author of *Travels through Portugal and Spain* (1775)—using the same language found in Yorick's appraisal of the "splenetic traveler." "Mr Twiss says a great deal," she observes, "but his travels seem only a journal of his own bad humours, prejudices and mistakes, for I believe he would not willingly tell a falsehood, but I am at a loss to think where he found the dirty scenes he describes" (250). Schaw recycles the sentimental traveler's oft-repeated defense: unencumbered by common prejudices and egocentricity, the sentimental traveler achieves a clarity of vision that ensures the truth of their observations. Although she admits that her feelings directly affect her judgment, confessing that her "opinions and descriptions will depend on the health and the humour of the Moment"

(20), she repeatedly demonstrates that her feelings—oriented toward sympathy—ultimately *clarify* rather than *cloud* her judgment. Schaw's frequent alignment of tyranny with a lack of feeling (she refers to tyrannical individuals or collectives as "without heart or feeling" [23] or "hard-hearted" [34]) suggests that sympathetic feeling ultimately serves as a moral compass that directs individuals toward right action. Given this correlation between feeling and morality—a correlation well established within Scottish Enlightenment philosophy—the audience is directed to read Schaw's expressions of emotional responsiveness as moral judgments rather than as spectacles of self-indulgence.

The spontaneity and intensity of Schaw's emotions work both to justify her political engagement and incite what Hume refers to as "like passions and inclinations" within her distant readers.[18] As a woman of feeling, she cannot help responding to the spectacle of her nation's trauma during the beginning stages of the American Revolution; her emotional convictions demand to be articulated for the amelioration of her national community. Despite the appearance of spontaneity, however, her sentiments are carefully structured responses to political realities that provide a framework for thinking about distant Britons. Through her strategic deployment of sympathy, she polices the circulation of feeling between colonial and metropolitan populations; her extension of sympathy identifies those worthy of emotional investment. Schaw's assurance of her audience's affective complicity—"I am sure you will share my feelings" (33)—indicates her confidence in the power of sympathy.

The transformative power of Schaw's sentimental gaze is established in an early episode involving a community of Highlanders smuggled aboard the *Jamaica Packet*. Her immediate reaction to the unexpected passengers is revulsion, and she likens the Highlanders to the filthy, brutish Yahoos that Jonathan Swift invents in *Gulliver's Travels* (1726). Hume's theory that the absence of similarity impedes emotional transactions helps to enlighten Schaw's response in this episode;[19] her perception of the Highlanders' bestiality effectively obstructs sympathetic identification on the basis of radical difference. However, Schaw's opinion of her fellow passengers is quickly reversed upon witnessing their outpouring of emotion at the sight of their former home (the Orkney Islands). The Highlanders' display of sensibility contributes to their transformation into sentimental subjects as their suffering demands and activates a sympathetic response from Schaw's "feeling heart" (33). Her instinctive response to their suffering corroborates Hume's and Adam Smith's theories of human sociability. According to Hume, the immediate perception of another's grief instigates the "motions of the tenderest compassion and pity" due to the susceptibility of the human heart; Smith similarly asserts that compassion operates as an instinctive response to misery "when we either see it, or are made to conceive it in a very lively manner."[20] The Highlanders' transformation into members of the sentimental community to which Schaw belongs is completed by her response to their suffering. Her apostrophe to pity establishes the transformation effected by sympathy: "Pity, thou darling daughter of the skies, what a change do you produce in the hearts where you vouchsafe to enter. . . . What a change has she wrought on me since my last visit to the deck. Where are now the Cargo of Yahoos? they are transformed into a Company of most respectable sufferers, whom it is both my duty and inclination to comfort, and do all in my power to alleviate their misfortunes, which have not sprung from their guilt or folly, but from the guilt and folly of others" (36). The mutual transformation accomplished by sympathy—Schaw shares the sentiments of the steerage passengers, while they conform to her standards of human—ultimately enables the formation of community within the microcosmic world of the ship.

Schaw's lived experience of emotional conversion confirms Hume's and Smith's theories of sympathetic exchange, revealing her Enlightenment understanding of sympathy as a powerful tool of personal and collective transformation. It is a tool she continues to use throughout her letters, governing her British readers' relationships with their colonial populations by deploying or withholding sympathy according to political exigency. Her account actively intervenes in British society's perceptions of Scots, Americans, and women. The alternate versions that she provides through her observations on how all three groups function within colonial or foreign environments contest and/or consolidate their positions within the British Empire. Schaw's sympathetic representations of both her nation and her gender advocate for their greater inclusion within the British polity, while her failure to sympathize with the American colonists (or, to be more specific, *their* failure to elicit sympathy) ultimately justifies their oppression under British rule. Throughout her travelogue, sentimental discourse interacts with imperialist ambitions to exploit the transformative power of feeling and obscure the violent practices that her political commitments require.

"WHAT, IN THE NAME OF GOD, SHALL WE DO WITH IT?": THE AMERICAN CRISIS

In order to fully understand Schaw's intervention in the political debates of her day and to clarify her political motivations, it is necessary to first contextualize her position within the political dynamics and sociopolitical forces that defined Anglo-American and Anglo-Scottish relations during the early years of the American Revolution. That Schaw was at least marginally aware of the increasingly fraught relationship between Britain and its American colonies is evident both from her active intellectual life and from the tone of anxiety that pervades her text. Given that she had assiduously prepared herself for her journey by reading "all the descriptions that have been published of America" (151), she could not have been ignorant of the fact that she was traveling to a troubled part of Britain's empire. In addition to the coverage the colonial situation received in pamphlets, books, and periodicals, her close connections both in the West Indies and in North Carolina would have presumably informed her of the fragile political situation in the American colonies. Although she dismisses her Bostonian supercargo's revolutionary pronouncements as "silly," her hope that "what this fool says may not prove at last too true" (65) contains a note of insecurity that suggests her concern with the rapidly disintegrating relationship between Britain and America. By the time Schaw left Scotland in October 1774, an internecine war between Britain and its American colonies had become a real possibility. In his study of the coverage of the American Revolution in the British press, Troy Bickham finds that by late 1774 the press was busily estimating the potential costs of a war and speculating about Britain's chance of success against its colonies.[21] Although Parliament was still working toward a peaceful resolution with the colonies—with conciliatory proposals drafted by Lord North, Edmund Burke, and Lord Chatham in the late months of 1774 and the early months of 1775—Lord North's administration was simultaneously preparing for war. Evidence of Britain's militarization is found in Schaw's travelogue: in December 1774, the *Jamaica Packet* passed a "King's ship of seventy four guns" with "troops on board for Boston" (64). She could not have foreseen that the troops abroad the *Boyne* would go on to fight in the first battles between Britain and the colonies—Lexington, Concord, and Bunker Hill.[22]

In his final formal proposal for conciliation between Britain and its American colonies in March 1775, Burke succinctly states the question that had plagued the British government and populace since the first signs of American resistance. "The question is," he opines, "not whether their [fierce spirit of liberty] deserves praise or blame; [but] what, in the name of God, shall we do with it?"[23] Parliament had alternately attempted to appease and reprimand their recalcitrant colonies in an attempt to avoid an all-out war while maintaining at least the appearance of authority. Burke blamed the escalating crisis on the government's uneven approach to their colonies. "What woeful variety of schemes have been adopted," he laments, "what enforcing, and what repealing; what bullying, and what submitting . . . what shiftings, and changes, and jumblings of all kinds of men at home, which left no possibility of order, consistency, vigor, or even so much as a decent unity of color in any one public measure."[24] The lack of unity and uncertainty that Burke perceives in the parliamentary approach to the colonial crisis was mirrored in British popular opinion. Similar to their indecisive and divided leaders, the public's response to the question of what was to be done with the rebellious colonists was by no means unified or coherent. James E. Bradley's analysis of the pro-war addresses and anti-war petitions sent from all corners of Britain to Parliament in 1775–1776 exposes the national schism produced by the American war. While he found that the addresses outnumbered the petitions, the numbers of signatures on the anti-war petitions ultimately outnumbered those on the pro-war addresses.[25] What this demonstrates, as Stephen Conway observes, "is not the preponderance of one side or the other, but the deep division over the justice and necessity of the conflict."[26]

The question of what should be done with the American colonists was fundamentally problematized by their complicated status as British citizens. Dror Wahrman believes that "the whole problem of the American war in a nutshell" came down to the question of "whether this was a civil war among Englishmen or a war with aliens . . . masking themselves as Englishmen."[27] Allan Ramsay, then employed as George III's principal painter, certainly blamed Britain's lack of direction on the colonists' split or slippery identity. Neatly dividing the world into the categories of "Englishmen" and "Foreigners,"[28] he explains, "There has lately started up to view in America a new class of men, who will be found upon examination to belong to neither of those two classes; who for that reason, give great perplexity both to the Government and people of England, and must ever continue to perplex them till their true nature, and their true relation to Great Britain is accurately known."[29] Ramsay imputes both the government's vacillations and the political schism within British society to the colonists' heterogeneous identity as both "Englishmen" and "Foreigners"—not altogether British, yet not officially foreign. He stresses that "a suitable mode of proceeding" in regard to the crisis is impracticable until the colonists' identity is clarified.[30] How Britons perceived the American colonists ultimately impacted political decisions, a reality that Ramsay acknowledges in his assertion that the colonists' slippery identity was hindering effective action.

American sympathizers maintained the view that the colonists were inescapably British, and emphasized the genealogy between the inhabitants of the British Isles and those in North America, referring to the colonists as their "children" (John Erskine), "brethren" (Richard Price), and "kindred" (Edmund Burke).[31] Emphasizing the shared heritage between Britain and its American colonies served the purpose of justifying the Americans' resistance as a fundamentally British act while simultaneously representing parliamentary aggression as suspiciously authoritarian. Asserting the kinship ties between Americans and Britons further complicated efforts to mobilize British support for aggressive action against the colonists. Anti-war petitioners stressed that this was not a war that pitted the British against easily othered foreigners, but an internecine struggle that pitted the British against themselves. Projecting horror, John Erskine exclaims, "Shall the friend, the brother, the father, the son, imbrue their hands in the blood of men, by the tyes of nature, esteem, or gratitude, dear to them as their own souls?"[32] American sympathizers endorsed conciliatory action as the means to restore the colonists' loyalty and to ensure the continuation of important transatlantic trading networks. John Knox attempted to convince his British audience that the stability of the nation's empire could only be ensured through the cultivation of sentimental ties between Britain and her colonies. "Politically speaking," Knox mused, "clemency . . . proves an irresistible victory over generous minds, and its charms frequently reaches even the most stubborn heart, which it unhinges, softens, and qualifies for the duties of society. It is this, more than the conquering swords, which raises petty states to mighty empires, as the opposite reduces mighty empires to insignificant states."[33] Invoking the ruin of the "great empires of antiquity,"[34] Knox ascribes their downfall to the violent means through which they secured and maintained their territory. By acknowledging Americans as brethren and treating them as such, American sympathizers hoped that a form of familial affection would "once more *unite* both sides of the Atlantic . . . upon a basis more durable than the precarious and the expensive security arising from any army of mercenaries stationed among them, to enforce obedience."[35]

The government and its supporters, however, preferred a more hardline approach that favored the intimidation of an "army of mercenaries" to Knox's ephemeral ties of affection. Their rhetoric tends to project unsavory images of Americans as unscrupulous rebels, intent on appropriating power to satisfy their selfish, materialist desires. Ramsay argues that Americans should not be perceived as equals, but as natural inferiors with suspect motivations. He accuses Americans (and, indirectly, American sympathizers) of pulling at the heartstrings of Britons by calling themselves "*Fellow Subjects*" and labeling the conflict a "*civil war.*"[36] "But all this juggling," he clarifies, "must lose its effect upon Englishmen, whenever they come to be distinctly informed, that the Americans are not their fellow-citizens, but their subjects."[37] Constructions of Americans as self-interested rebels rather than as conscientious objectors—traitorously plotting the ruin of their magnanimous government—suggest the criminality of their actions and effectively justify aggressive intervention. In his argument for war, Adam Ferguson contends that American colonists are oriented toward destruction rather than justice. He confidently proclaims that "a war, thus undertaken in the support of our constitution . . . ought to be promoted, and carried on with united vigor on our side, till rebellion is convinced, that her erroneous destructive principles have been the detested cause of the profusion of so much blood."[38] Lord North's administration and its supporters demonized the colonists to validate their conviction that coercive measures were necessary and just. Americans, they argued, were not acting as Britons through their rebellion and were actively destroying British principles.

There was also a small but vocal minority of Britons who favored the complete emancipation of the American colonies for purely economic reasons. The incredible expense involved in securing Britain's North American colonies during the Seven Years' War (1756–1763) weakened arguments regarding the financial value of empire. Josiah Tucker, who had been agitating for American emancipation since the conclusion of the Seven Years' War, ostensibly felt that support for his cause had gained popularity in the 1770s. "The Proposal for separating totally from *North-America*," he confidently asserts, "is observed to make Converts every Day."[39] Bickham's research finds that Britons' *were* deeply anxious about the financial costs of another war, and this anxiety may have fueled the desire to simply excise the troublesome colonies. By late 1774, newspapers were estimating that war with the colonies would cost Britain £14 million per year—a total, Bickham notes, that "substantially exceeded the accepted value of annual trade with the mainland colonies."[40] Considering the significant costs of maintaining the American colonies against the comparatively minimal financial gains, Adam Smith concluded that Britain would be wise to pursue American emancipation. He closed his 1776 publication *The Wealth of Nations* by casting aspersions on the economic benefit of Britain's Atlantic colonies:

> The rules of Great Britain have, for more than a century past, amused the people with the imagination that they possessed a great empire on the west side of the Atlantic. This empire, however, has hitherto existed in the imagination only. It has hitherto been, not an empire, but the project of empire; not a gold mine, but the project of a gold mine; a project which has cost, which continues to cost, and which, if pursued in the same way as it has been hitherto, it likely to cost, immense expense, without being likely to bring any profit. . . . If the project cannot be completed, it ought to be given up.[41]

Smith's message to his British audience was that the fantasy was over: the American war had revealed the bleak reality of empire. Exposing the gap between Britain's imperial ideal and the lived experience of imperialism, the American Revolution raised uncomfortable and ultimately divisive questions regarding the tenability of empire.

THE TIES THAT BIND: ANGLO-SCOTTISH RELATIONS AND THE BONDS OF EMPIRE

Janet Schaw came from a population whose status within the nation underwent a similar process of being alternately contested and consolidated throughout the eighteenth century. The relationship between Scotland and England remained fraught following the Act of Union in 1707. Two Jacobite rebellions and the virulent racism of John Wilkes and his supporters during the earl of Bute's tenure as prime minister exacerbated the deep cracks within the façade of political unity. While the Act of Union attempted to neutralize tensions, the early attempts of Scots to achieve independence and the mid-century efforts of Wilkes's followers to preserve a specifically English identity for Britain reveal the mutual suspicions and animosities that continued to plague the relationship between the two nations. However, as Linda Colley argues, the paranoid Scottophobia of the Wilkite movement may also be taken as an indication of the political integration of Scotland and England by the latter half of the century. "In reality," Colley suggests, "[Wilkite virulence against the Scots] was a testimony to the fact that the barriers between England and Scotland were coming down, savage proof that Scots were acquiring power and influence within Great Britain to a degree previously unknown."[42] The Act of Union allowed Scots previously unprecedented access both to England and to its colonial markets, an opportunity of which ambitious and/or beleaguered Scots took full advantage. From 1750 onward, Scotland's overseas commerce increased by 300 percent—far exceeding England's 200-percent commercial expansion.[43] Significant numbers of Scots left their native country to seek their fortunes in Britain's Atlantic colonies; David Dobson has estimated that 150,000 Scottish emigrants left for North America prior to 1785, and Douglas J. Hamilton has estimated that 17,000 Scottish emigrants left for the West Indies between 1750 and 1799.[44]

For the English, the loyalty of their Scottish neighbors ensured a measure of security against foreign invasions and a ready supply of manpower necessary for the expansion and maintenance of their burgeoning empire. The participation of Scottish Highlanders in the Seven Years' War and Scottish colonists' resistance to the American Revolution indicates the links forged between the nations by the demands and assets of the British Empire. "Such changes," Leith Davis argues, "were due to the work both of the Scots, who were anxious to present a more positive view of Scotland to ensure their participation in the British economic market, and of the English, who were equally anxious to create a unified national identity in the face of international unrest and competition in Europe and North America."[45] In the three decades between the last Jacobite Rebellion in 1745 and the beginning of the American Revolution in 1775, Scots had gone from presenting a threat to Britain's stability to becoming its bulwark. In 1775, Governor Josiah Martin had enough confidence in the loyalty of North Carolina's Highland population to believe that he could raise a regiment of 3,000 Highlanders to march against the American revolutionaries.[46] It is certainly significant that the second-in-command of this loyalist regiment (ultimately composed of 1,500 soldiers) was the husband of Flora MacDonald—the Jacobite heroine who infamously assisted Bonnie Prince Charlie's escape and was briefly imprisoned for her rebel sympathies. Thirty years later, she was an active opponent of the American Revolution and her husband was eventually imprisoned by the Americans for his loyalty to the British government. Regarding this seemingly remarkable shift in Anglo-Scottish relations, Hamilton argues that "the majority of Scots, whether in Scotland or in the colonies, saw themselves as partners in the empire as part of the metropole, rather than as subordinate provincial associates like North Americans."[47] Hamilton's language of partnership suggests that Scots felt a sense of ownership over the British Empire; having a stake in its success, their energetic defense of the empire is perhaps better understood as a defense of their own economic investments than as a patriotic defense of the British nation. As in so many eighteenth-century marriages of convenience, economics preceded affection as the impetus for cooperation.[48]

The colonial crisis threw into sharp relief the problematic dynamics of the British Empire, challenging the fundamental tenets of British national identity and compromising the traditional solidarities that shaped the nation. Schaw's travelogue is written in reaction to these pressures. Politicized by her immediate experience of both the British Empire and the American Revolution that threatened to break it apart, she uses her eyewitness account to zealously promote the empire that supported her family and financed Scotland's economic flourishing in the eighteenth century. She establishes empire as foundational rather than peripheral to British national identity and fiercely advocates for the expansion and defense of Britain's imperial interests. Her travelogue negotiates the position of both the American colonies and Scotland within the British nation according to their contributions to the empire. Schaw does not appear to harbor traces of the bitterness that motivated both the 1715 and 1745 Jacobite Rebellions but embraces the union between England and Scotland as a mutually beneficial partnership. She emphasizes the significant contributions of Scots to the development and defense of the British Empire in an effort to overcome the latent suspicions that dogged Anglo-Scottish relations. Schaw's comparatively negative treatment of Americans as "foreigners"—to use Ramsay's category and understanding of the term—is consistent with her political agenda. Her hostility toward the American colonists is a reaction to the threat they pose to the empire upon which her family is profoundly dependent. Witnessing the aggressive militarization of the colonists and motivated by the economic dispossession of her loyalist friends and family, Schaw voices her support for coercive action against the rebellious colonists to protect British imperial interests. Through her representations of the colonists and colonial relations, she attempts to clarify Scots' and Americans' "true nature" and "true relation to Great Britain" in a manner that supports Britain's expansionist designs and her own imperial vision for the nation.[49]

BRINGING THE WEST INDIES HOME TO BRITAIN

Schaw's magnificent five-week sojourn in the West Indies forms an important counterpart to her stay in the American colonies. Her direct experience of the British Empire in Antigua and St. Christopher shapes her vision of model colonial relations and generates ideas about nationality, race, and ethnicity that subsequently inform her interpretation and representation of America. Schaw's immediate affinity for the West Indies is perhaps predictable given the density of its Scottish population, but the sense of home that she feels while in Antigua and St. Christopher is also staged for a particular political effect. With the American crisis raising questions about the function of empire and suspicions regarding the character of colonists, Schaw embraces both the West Indian landscape and its inhabitants to generate enthusiasm for the grand scheme of empire and to underline the exemplary work of Scottish colonists. Eager to overcome the detachment produced by distance, she attempts to imaginatively collapse the expanse between Britain and the West Indies through her sentimental representations of West Indian society. She familiarizes her British audience with their distant colonists by describing her emotional experience of both the people and the place, projecting a sense of continuity between Britain's metropolitan and colonial populations in an effort to strengthen Britons' sympathetic attachment to their West Indian investments.

Schaw's immediate sense of familiarity in the West Indies significantly diverges from common eighteenth-century representations of West Indian culture as conspicuously foreign. West Indian colonists occupied a liminal position within British society; while the colonial population in the Caribbean fiercely maintained their Britishness, the people back home were inclined to perceive them as a distinct cultural (and even racial) group. "West Indian planters," Steven Thomas argues, "had to insist repeatedly that they shared a common heritage, a common economic future, and even a 'common nature' with England."[50] Schaw emphasizes the colonists' loyalty to Britain in her consideration of the rampant absenteeism in Antigua and St. Christopher, blaming the ongoing exodus of British West Indian planters on the "longing they have to return to Britain" (92).[51] However, as she goes on to suggest, Britons were more ambivalently disposed toward their prodigal countrymen. Schaw describes the reception of showy West Indian planters in London as cold at best: "They are, either entirely overlooked or ridiculed for an extravagance, which after all does not even raise them to a level with hundreds around them" (92). Her comment suggests that West Indian returnees were regarded with suspicion within London society; despite (or due to) their newly accumulated wealth, they remained outsiders. British representations of absentee planters reveal that domestic culture did, indeed, perceive them as fundamentally different from their native countrymen. Although Richard Cumberland's wildly successful play *The West Indian* (1771) stages a sympathetic portrait of Belcour—the play's West Indian protagonist—it also reinforces the sense that West Indian colonists were distinctly foreign. Belcour's ignorance of British customs quickly situates him as the victim of scheming Londoners, his foreign mannerisms single him out as an object of ridicule, and his incongruity is staged for comic effect. The eponymous West Indian admits that he must learn how to be British, explaining to his love interest, "New to your country, ignorant of your manners, habits, and desires, I put myself into your hands for instruction; make me only such as you can like yourself."[52] That Belcour must be taught how to be British marks the protagonist as foreign, and demonstrates metropolitan society's suspicion of West Indian colonists.

Belcour's attribution of his integral difference to the shaping effects of the West Indian climate ("O my curst tropical constitution! Wou'd to Heaven I had been dropt upon the snow of Lapland, and never felt the blessed influence of the sun, so I had never burnt with these inflammatory passions!") reveals the extent to which metropolitan Britons othered West Indian colonists.[53] Anthropological studies like Lord Kames's *Sketches of the History of Man* (1774) and Adam Ferguson's *An Essay on the History of Civil Society* (1767) posited a link between hot climates and inflamed passions,[54] fueling suspicions that the West Indian environment had a transformative effect on colonists. Edward Long's description of Jamaica's British planters in his 1774 travelogue *The History of Jamaica* clearly demonstrates this belief:

> The native white men . . . are in general tall and well-shaped . . . their cheeks are remarkably high-boned, and the sockets of their eye deeper than is commonly observed among the natives of England; by this conformation, they are guarded from those ill effects which an almost continual strong glare of sun-shine might otherwise produce. . . . The effect of climate is not only remarkable in the structure of their eyes, but

> likewise in the extraordinary freedom and suppleness of their joints, which enable them to move with ease. . . . Although descended from British ancestors, they are stamped with these characteristic deviations. Climate, perhaps, has had some share in producing the variety of features which we behold among the different societies of mankind, scattered over the globe.[55]

Long describes the Jamaican colonists as if they are a different race; his ethnological interest in their physical "deviations" and his reference to the influence of climate on the human body suggests that they are evolving into a unique racial group.

While Long limits the influence of climate to the purely physical, others worried that the tropics effected a *moral* change in colonists. Almost seven decades prior to Long, Hans Sloane toured the West Indies and reported his findings in his comprehensive travelogue *A Voyage to the Islands Madera, Barbados, Nieves, S. Christophers and Jamaica* (volume 1 was published in 1707 and volume 2 in 1725). Sloane eschews environmental theories, but notes that he finds West Indian colonists significantly "more debauch'd than in *England*."[56] In his extensive list of medical conditions unique to the West Indies, he frequently identifies excessive living (heavy drinking, sexual promiscuity, and hard partying) as the cause of the diseases he encounters—regardless of gender. Salacious reports like Sloane's did not help the integration of West Indian returnees into British society. Andrew O'Shaughnessy notes that the well-oiled absentee planters that poured into Britain were subject to "moral censure" for their luxurious lifestyles and, increasingly, for the slave economy that underwrote their wealth.[57] In *The History of George Ellison* (1766), novelist Sarah Scott contrasts the ethical behavior of the recently emigrated eponymous hero with that of his morally bankrupt Creole wife.[58] Whereas the selfless Ellison acknowledges the humanity of the enslaved population on his plantation and treats them accordingly, his Creole wife is happy to perpetuate their inhumane treatment. Scott's comparison between the British born and educated Ellison and his West Indian wife suggests the disintegration of British values that could occur within the exotic environment.[59] Kathleen Wilson confirms that eighteenth-century stereotypes of plantation society commonly associated the West Indies with moral inversion: "The fabulously wealthy Caribbean planter that emerged in fact and fiction came to represent the West Indian uncouthness, backwardness and degeneracy that inverted the acclaimed standards of English civility and culture."[60] Hume's theory that distance impedes sympathetic identification is demonstrated in the perception and construction of difference between mainland Britons and their West Indian colonists. For Britons, it seems, absence did not make the heart grow fonder; separation from the mother country compromised the national integrity of the colonial subject.

In light of this common conflation of distance and difference, Schaw's emphasis on the West Indies' familiarity rather than on its foreignness is striking. Her departure from conventional representations suggests her political motivations. She strives to familiarize the foreign in order to overcome the alienating effects of distance and to assist a transatlantic exchange of sympathy. Schaw's attempt to rectify Britons' perceptions of the West Indies and its colonists is evident from her initial impression of Antigua. After detailing the island's natural features, she ruefully concludes, "Will you smile, if after this description, I add that its principal beauty to me is the resemblance it has to Scotland, yes, to Scotland" (74). Her unlikely comparison of the lush tropical hills of Antigua to the naked heaths of Scotland performs the opposite function of the alienation effect that she first applied to the Highlanders: rather than make the familiar strange, here Schaw attempts to make the strange familiar. She carefully moderates the exoticism of Antigua with what she perceives as its thorough domestication. The hills have been neatly ordered into rows of sugarcane, the shorelines have been tamed into shaded pathways designed for leisurely walks, and both the outcroppings high above the ocean and the valleys beneath serve as platforms for sumptuous plantation houses and army barracks (74–75). The level of domestication the colonists have achieved is summarized in her later observations on St. Christopher, which she compares to the highly structured British gardens popular in the seventeenth and early eighteenth centuries: "I was surprised at the complete cultivation I met every where. The whole Island is a garden divided into different parterres" (130). According to Schaw's description, the colonists have transformed unruly nature into an orderly and productive landscape; the Leeward Islands appear to have been remodeled into an exotic version of Britain.

Schaw is particularly careful to stress the transformative activity of the colonists; she repeatedly clarifies that both Antigua and St. Christopher have been actively *shaped* into a domestic idyll by their British (and specifically Scottish) colonists. After itemizing the "delightful confusion" (126) of fruit trees, cotton plants, and coffee shrubs that line the banks of a river in St. Christopher, she is quick to note that the native plants are "generally raised in cultivated plantations, for tho' they are all indigenous, they are much the better of culture" (127). Her ensuing discussion details the agricultural practices of planters, which she describes as enriching the already productive soil in order to increase the yield of crops (127). In both instances, British industry and skill are shown to improve nature; the colonists have introduced order to the landscape and have engineered its increase. Similarly, her approbation of an acquaintance's carefully arranged gardens indicates that the Antiguan landscape has been infinitely enhanced—or even corrected—through the application of British aesthetics. "His plantation," she observes, "which is laid out in the greatest taste, has a mixture of the Indian and European. If your eye is hurt by the stiff uniformity of the tall Palmetto, it is instantly relieved by the waving branches of the spreading Tammerand, or the Sand-box tree" (101). It becomes apparent that the sense of familiarity Schaw purports to feel in the West Indies is due to the effective management of its colonists, and their industry redounds to their credit. Her portrayal of the responsible stewardship practiced by the predominantly Scottish colonists with whom she associates ultimately reinforces the value of Scotland within the British Empire. In their literal and figurative enrichment of the empire, the Scottish colonists are shown to be invested in its success. Schaw enacts the process of accommodation by proxy that Smith describes as necessary to the sympathetic exchange; in order to be considered as objects of sympathetic consideration, the colonists must "accommodate and assimilate" their "sentiments, principles, and feelings" to those from whom they seek sympathy.[61] She sculpts an identity for the colonists that appeals to her metropolitan audience's sense of propriety, facilitating a transatlantic exchange of sympathy that ultimately strengthens both the bonds of empire and the Anglo-Scottish union.

The manifestation of British aesthetics and the evidence of British industry in Antigua and St. Christopher further articulate an important message regarding the nature of the colonists: that they are busy changing their environment signifies that their environment has not changed them. The Scottish population in the West Indies has preserved their Britishness; the "longing they have to return to Britain" (92) serves as evidence of the primal connection they retain to their mother country. Schaw's description of her intimate interactions with the Scottish inhabitants of the Leeward Islands differs considerably from the ethnographical descriptions of West Indian populations in the travelogues of Long and Sloane. Her portrayal of colonists as friends rather than as objects of scientific curiosity establishes connections between metropolitan and colonial Britons; she does not find foreigners when she arrives in the West Indies but "a whole company of Scotch people, our language, our manners, our circle of friends and connections, all the same" (81). Despite the distance from Britain, the people are "the same" and provide an immediate sense of home for Schaw and her companions. "We were intimates in a moment," (82) she declares after only a few hours on shore. This instant connection that she experiences in the company of Scottish transplants repudiates the Belcour-like stereotype of West Indian colonists as inherently foreign—possessing different manners, customs, and even different physical features. Her comfort among her new hosts indicates the national integrity of West Indian colonists.

Schaw's appraisal of the colonists' appearance and conduct largely reinforces this sense of continuity between metropolitan and colonial Britons. Her description of their morals and manners counters negative West Indian stereotypes and disavows the degenerative effects of climate. The qualities that she ascribes to the West Indian male colonists of generosity, gallantry, and honesty (111–112) repudiate their caricatured traits of "uncouthness, backwardness, and degeneracy."[62] Her particularly detailed account of Colonel Martin's benevolent leadership indicates the preservation of British identity and values within the foreign plantation culture of the West Indies. As both a longtime commander of the Antiguan militia and as a plantation owner, Martin is a leader in both public and private areas of colonial life. As an officer he is loyal to his nation and committed to the maintenance of British order; despite his advanced years, "he says with his usual spirits, if his country need his service, he is ready again to resume his arms" (109). Schaw is later acquainted with his third son, Josiah Martin, who does, indeed, battle against the American rebels in his role as the governor of North Carolina. As a plantation owner Colonel Martin exercises a form of benevolent paternalism that Schaw believes ensures the loyalty and affection of those he has enslaved. As she explains, "[His estates] are cultivated to the height by a large troop of healthy Negroes, who cheerfully perform the labour imposed on them by a kind and beneficent Master, not a harsh and unreasonable Tyrant. Well fed, well supported, they appear the subjects of a good prince, not the slaves of a planter" (104). Her fiercely whitewashed account of Martin's plantation counteracts abolitionist narratives of cruel West Indian plantation owners and their desperate slaves. Anti-slavery texts such as Thomas Bicknell and Thomas Day's poem *The Dying Negro* (1773) paint colonial slave owners as "pallid tyrants" with "a soul unus'd to pity or to feel,"[63] and other West Indian travel narratives like John Singleton's *A Description of the West-Indies* (1767) regard planters as "revengeful lord[s]."[64] Schaw's grossly sentimentalized portrait of Martin and his plantation can be interpreted as a direct response to abolitionist literature that emphasized the moral impoverishment of slave owners. Her comparison of Martin's leadership style to "a kind and beneficent Master" and "a good prince" rather than to a "harsh and unreasonable Tyrant" suggests a model of authority that is particularly British in character.

Corresponding with her vindication of West Indian landlords is her rehabilitation of the image of West Indian female colonists, who were frequently portrayed as morally suspect due to their susceptibility toward the effects of heat and luxury. Ferguson's theory that heat unleashed "burning ardours, and the torturing jealousies of the seraglio and haram" manifested itself in the figure of the selfish, unbridled Creole woman that remained in currency all the way up to and beyond Charlotte Brontë's creation of Bertha Mason—Rochester's insane and insatiable Creole wife in *Jane Eyre* (1847).[65] Schaw's description of the community of Scottish women in the West Indies as veritable nuns casts doubt on the stereotype of the intemperate West Indian female colonist. She specifically clarifies that the sun does *not* cause women to let loose in the West Indies but appears to refine their sense of propriety. "The women," she describes, "are modest, genteel, reserved and temperate. . . . The truth is, I can observe no indulgence they allow themselves in" (113). Her depiction of Lady Isabella Hamilton as her plantation's resident Virgin Mary reinforces the purity of the West Indian female colonist. "There were several of the boilers condemned to the lash," she explains, "and seeing her face is pardon. Their gratitude on this occasion was the only instance of sensibility that I have observed in them" (129). This bizarre, quasi-religious ceremony in which Lady Hamilton acts the part of the saint suggests the role West Indian female colonists play as their colonies' moral conscience. Their ability to maintain British values within distant environments recommends them to a metropolitan audience accustomed to images of the Creole woman abandoned to her passions.

In order to sanitize the image of West Indian society and to harmonize the character of colonists with that of their fellow citizens across the Atlantic, Schaw recognizes that she needs to address the issue of slavery beyond its glossy portrayal in Colonel Martin's plantation. The slave economy that underwrote West Indian wealth had become an increasing source of division and differentiation between Britain and its Atlantic colonies. Schaw left Scotland one year after the historic Somersett Case, in which Lord Mansfield ruled that enslaved peoples could not be forcibly taken from British soil to be sold abroad. Considering that she held Lord Mansfield as a close acquaintance (89), Schaw no doubt would have been very familiar with his celebrated ruling and with the furor of abolitionist activity spurred by his decision. The anti-slavery material that emerged from this period frequently relies on the language of sentiment to encourage sympathy for enslaved peoples and to direct their audience toward right action. In his study of early Scottish abolitionist poetry, Corey E. Andrews finds that "much Scottish poetry from the eighteenth century sought to redress the sufferings of slaves by appealing to core emotions in its audience, producing as a result a body of political writing that powerfully imagined the painful experience of slavery."[66] Bicknell and Day's aforementioned abolitionist poem *The Dying Negro* takes as its subject an enslaved man driven to suicide after being forcibly separated from his beloved and his home and driven into a life of brutal labor. The authors assert in the preface that they "delineate the feelings of [those enslaved]" to provoke moral outrage in their audience.[67] This focus on the feelings of those enslaved deploys what Brycchan Carey identifies as a common "sentimental argument" within abolitionist literature: that enslaved peoples' equal ability to feel demanded their equal treatment.[68]

By asking their readers to sympathize with those enslaved, abolitionists like Bicknell and Day simultaneously invite them to deplore the masters who orchestrate their suffering. They preface their anti-slavery poem by stating, "They who are not more inclined to sympathize with the *master*, than the *servant*, upon the occasion,—will perhaps not be displeased at an attempt to delineate the feelings of the latter."[69] Sympathy is directed away from unfeeling West Indian masters toward the victims of their cruelty. To facilitate the movement of sympathy between her British audience and the slave owners condemned within abolitionist literature, Schaw interrupts the sympathetic gaze cast upon suffering enslaved peoples by denying them the very thing emphasized by abolitionist writers: feeling. In both Smith's and Hume's theories of sympathy, the presence of feeling is requisite for a sympathetic exchange to occur. In Hume's version of the sympathetic exchange, we are infected by the feelings of those with whom we interact; in Smith's adaptation, the agent responds to the subject's expressions of feeling. That Schaw understands the necessity of mutually expressed feeling for the operation of sympathy is seen in her interaction with the Highland emigrants; their expression of feeling triggers Schaw's recognition of their common humanity and instigates her sympathetic response. Indeed, her first impression of enslaved peoples in the West Indies mirrors her impression of the Highland emigrants. Like the emigrants, she describes the enslaved peoples she encounters as simian-like by deliberately confusing Black children with monkeys (77). However, Schaw refuses to humanize the enslaved population in the West Indies through sympathy as she did with the Highland emigrants. Her entrenched racism forms a stark contrast to the abolitionist message found in much sentimental literature—including Sterne's *A Sentimental Journey*[70]—and reveals the naked politics of Schaw's sentimentalism. She wields sympathy as a political tool, using it to mark of parameters of communal belonging in order to accommodate her political and economic investments in the Atlantic slave trade.

In order to maintain her sentimental persona, Schaw absolves herself from the imperatives of sympathy by placing the blame for her lack of feeling squarely on the shoulders of those enslaved. When first confronted with a visual reminder of the violence that underwrites slave economies (whip marks upon the bodies of laboring enslaved peoples), Schaw demonstrates her sympathetic nature by suggesting her "horror"; however, she informs her audience that her feelings were misplaced, and prevents her readers from similarly transitioning to sympathy by asserting the fundamental absence of feeling in those enslaved: "When one comes to be better acquainted with the nature of the Negroes, the horror of it must wear off. It is the suffering human mind that constitutes the greatest misery of punishment, but with them it is merely corporeal. As to the brutes it inflicts no wound on their mind, whose Natures seem made to bear it, and whose sufferings are not attended with shame or pain beyond the present moment" (127). It is here that the dark potential of the eighteenth-century understanding and practice of sympathy is revealed with horrifying clarity. Schaw distinguishes between emotional and physical pain, asserting that enslaved peoples are immune to the deeper and more lasting repercussions of emotional pain while insinuating that their experience of physical pain is mitigated through their particular biological composition (note the modifiers "*merely* corporeal" and "*present* moment," as well as her observation that their "Natures seem made to bear it"). Schaw explains that the enslaved peoples' lack of feeling renders sympathy theoretically impossible and justifies their exclusion from the community of sensible individuals. Her justification of slavery appropriates the sentimental abolitionist argument and turns it on its head: since enslaved peoples *do not* feel the same way they *should not* be treated the same way. Schaw's disturbingly racist representation of the enslaved population in the West Indies contains strong hints of the polygenist arguments advocated by Long and favored by both Hume and Kames, all of whom accounted for the distinctions between European and African populations by suggesting that they were composed of different species.[71] Whether or not Schaw espouses a polygenist point of view, she certainly posits that the affective capacities of White and Black populations are fundamentally different, and it is this difference that enables her to situate enslaved peoples outside of systems of sympathetic exchange.[72]

By obstructing sympathetic traffic between her British audience and the enslaved population in the West Indies, Schaw removes the potential emotional blockages between metropolitan Britons and West Indian colonists. Her sentimental treatment of the islands' Scottish communities distinguishes them as the proper objects of feeling, effectively routing her reader's sympathy toward the masters rather than those they have enslaved. Schaw draws on sentimental tropes to engage her audience's emotions: she traces the benevolent character of the elderly Colonel Martin, at whose parting her "heart felt a pang like that which it sustained when I lost the best of fathers" (106); she describes the joy with which she reunites with Lady Isabella Hamilton and the heartbreak with which they part (124, 132); and she mourns the slow decease of the young Miss Milliken and Miss Acres, both of whom suffer from consumption and latter of which she pitiably depicts as preparing for marriage and death simultaneously (124). "They are a people I like vastly," she concludes, "and were there nothing to make me wish otherwise, I would desire to live for ever with them" (130). Through her carefully drawn sentimental portraits of West Indian colonists, Schaw invites her metropolitan readers to sympathize with these distant Britons. Her friendships provide her audience with a concrete structure for imagining relations with this seemingly foreign society. Schaw's use of sentiment to consolidate imperial relations demonstrates Lynn Festa's assertion of the symbiotic relationship that existed between sentimental literature and the project of empire. "In an era in which imperial reach increasing outstripped imaginative grasp," she contends, "sentimental fiction created the tropes that enabled readers to reel the world home in their minds. By designating certain kinds of figures as worthy of emotional expenditure and structuring the circulation of affect between subjects and objects of feeling, the sentimental mode allowed readers to identify with and feel for the plight of other people."[73] Although Schaw does provide an abstract of West Indian society near the conclusion of her stay in Antigua, she clarifies that she does so to satisfy the demands of her correspondent (who is obviously well-versed in the conventions of the travelogue), and she explicitly resists the biological examination of the colonists favored by travel writers such as Long. Her overall representation of West Indian society removes the colonists from their abstract form and carefully develops them into fully realized citizens with whom her audience can form vicarious connections.

THE AMERICAN REVOLUTION AND THE "LABOR OF UNFEELING"

Schaw's sympathetic depiction of British colonial society in the West Indies provides two important precursors to her American narrative: it establishes her as a sentimental rather than a splenetic traveler—intuitive to her surroundings and sympathetic toward her local hosts—and it provides her British audience with a model society that demonstrates the benefits that accrue within a well-managed and loyal colony. It follows that her negative reaction to the American colonies cannot be attributed to spleen; nor can it be unproblematically used to illustrate the drawbacks of empire. The structural and rhetorical relation between the West Indian and American sections of Schaw's travelogue necessitates their equal consideration. The political motivations undergirding her insistently Edenic portrait of the West Indies are clarified when placed within the context of the American Revolution, and the process by which she demonizes or, more appropriately, dehumanizes the American colonists is illuminated by an examination of her careful manipulation of sympathy within her West Indian account. The two sections together demonstrate how sympathy could be simultaneously deployed as an inclusionary and exclusionary force within eighteenth-century culture, equally capable of figuratively contouring bodies to fit or not fit within the national mold.

Alerted to the advantages to be gained from empire after her stay in the West Indies, Schaw experiences the American Revolution as a direct threat to both her personal investments and national coherence. Thrust into a revolutionary context increasingly threatening the stability of Britain's Atlantic empire, she believes that

Britain must take substantive action to protect its valuable colonial assets. During Schaw's residence in North Carolina, Governor Josiah Martin was urging the British government to send sufficient supplies and troops to quell the burgeoning rebellion. While in March 1775 he was confident that a shipment of arms and ammunition would impede the progress of rebellion,[74] by October of the same year he increased his request to include two battalions of troops.[75] The intensification of Governor Martin's demands indicates the quickly deteriorating situation in North Carolina over the period of Schaw's stay (she arrived in February 1775 and left in September or October 1775). The British government's failure to meet his requests is alluded to repeatedly throughout Schaw's letters. Witnessing Martin's escape in the spring, the increasing persecution of loyalists under the newly inaugurated Committee of Safety, and the organization of locals into rebel militias throughout the summer, she shares the governor's conviction that Britain must act quickly and fiercely. While her younger brother is furtively sent to Britain carrying messages from the governor—never to return to his promised post in St. Christopher—Schaw throws herself into the work of changing British perceptions through her letters in order to hasten the military defense of the colonies. Her representation of the American colonists is calculated to interrupt sentimental identification between Britons and Americans (what Festa refers to as the "labor of unfeeling") and to redirect her readers' feelings toward more deserving objects—namely, the colony's beleaguered Scottish loyalists (what Carey refers to as "sentimental diversion").[76] Ramsay's strict classification of "Foreigners" as "enemies" and "Englishmen" as "friends" is instructive here.[77] Schaw clearly shares the belief that Americans must be sufficiently othered in order to be understood and treated as legitimate enemies by the British nation. She transmutes Americans into objects of terror—inherently foreign and hostile—by emphasizing their rejection of British values and by expressing her own sense of alienation within their culture. Schaw concomitantly portrays the loyalist faction as the appropriate objects of sympathy. Made to suffer for their national integrity, they embody the eighteenth-century sentimental trope of "virtue in distress."

FEAR AND LOATHING IN THE AMERICAN WILDERNESS

Schaw could not have left the idyllic shades of the West Indies for a more different place than North Carolina. Settlement of the colony had only begun in earnest approximately fifty years prior to Schaw's arrival,[78] and her descriptions of the primitive conditions that exist in North Carolina indicate that the colony was still in its early stages of development. According to a certain Scotus Americanus in 1773, "This colony [North Carolina] is but in a manner in its infancy, and newly settled in respect to its neighbouring ones."[79] Fifty years after settlers began streaming into the Cape Fear region, the majority of British commentators writing on the American colonies still profess to know very little about this relatively new colony. Writing in 1779, Alexander Hewatt laments the paucity of information regarding the Carolinas: "The southern provinces in particular have been hitherto neglected, insomuch that no writer has favoured the world with any tolerable account of them."[80] Indeed, Schaw notices that despite her extensive reading, she "meet[s] every moment with something I never read or heard of" (151). The few publications that did consider North Carolina tend to emphasize the opportunities available in the young colony.[81] Americanus—purportedly an emigrant from Islay in Scotland—describes North Carolina as a land of "liberty and plenty" where "each may sit safe, and at ease, under his own fig tree."[82] Targeting a specifically Highland audience, he assures prospective emigrants that "Highlanders are kindly received, and sumptuously entertained" and that "they may live as well and happy as lairds at home."[83] North Carolina is represented as an improved version of Britain: the people are freer, the soil is richer, the inhabitants are kinder, and the food more plentiful. His idealized depiction of the colony aligns with a well-established literary tradition of imagining America as a present-day golden age, a representation dating back to fifteenth- and sixteenth-century travel accounts that depicted America as the new Eden, for obvious political reasons.[84] That this conception was alive and well around the time that Schaw was writing is evident in the fictional representations of America in Arthur Young's *The Adventures of Emmera, or the Fair American* (1767) and Frances Brooke's *The History of Emily Montague* (1769). Both epistolary novels—one set on the shores of Lake Ontario in America and the other set in Canada—represent North America as a pastoral paradise untouched by the corruptions of urbanization and luxury.

Americanus's text is a typical example of early boosterism: eager to attract British colonists, he represents North Carolina as a veritable utopia in which desperate Highlanders will prosper. Schaw's goal of attracting the British military to North Carolina's shores requires an opposite approach: she represents the colony as a place that *requires* rather than *extends* help—as a dystopian rather than utopian space. Needless to say, she does not encounter an "abundantly inviting" and "safe" (Americanus) place upon arriving in February 1775.[85] Her initial description of North Carolina's landscape forms a marked contrast to her first impression of the West Indies; her nod to the political unrest suffusing America suggests the motivation underlying her bleak description. "At last America is in my view," she heavily states. "A dreary Waste of white barren sand, and melancholy, nodding pines. In the course of many miles, no cheerful cottage has blest my eyes. All seems dreary, savage and desert; and was it for this that such sums of money, such streams of British blood have been lavished away? Oh, thou dear land, how dearly has thou purchased this habitation for bears and wolves. Dearly has it been purchased, and at a price much dearer still will it be kept. My heart dies within me, while I view it" (141). Whereas the thriving appearance of British plantations on Antigua's manicured hills warm Schaw with thoughts of Scotland, the lack of a tangible British presence marks America as a palpably foreign space. The eventual sight of Fort Johnston ultimately augments rather than alleviates her anxiety. If the solid army barracks and red-coated officers in Antigua offered the appearance of British order (75), here the meager façade of the military quarters on North Carolina's coast augur disorder. "In figure and size this fort resembles a Leith timber-bush," she mocks, "but does not appear quite so tremendous, tho' I see guns peeping thro' the sticks. If these are our fortresses and castles, no wonder the Natives rebel; for I will be bound to take this fort with a regim[t] of black-guard Edinburgh boys without any artillery, but their own pop-guns" (141). The fragile appearance of the fort suggests the equally fragile state of British order in the American colonies, and the wild landscape imbues Schaw with a real sense of fear that she communicates to her audience. While her description of Antigua prepares her audience to be emotionally receptive to the people who have created such flourishing and familiar surroundings, her first impression of North Carolina grooms her audience to be wary of the people who inhabit such a foreign and hostile environment.

Schaw's initial description of the American landscape as a barren wasteland contains shades of John Mitchell's scathing account of North Carolina in *The Present State of Great Britain and North America* (1767). Mitchell, whose account is based on hearsay rather than on firsthand experience, characterizes North Carolina as a "*pine-barren*, or sandy desart," and blames the colony's unfruitfulness on its poor soil, swampy landscape, and inhospitable climate.[86] Although Schaw's first impression of North Carolina bears the marks of Mitchell's influence, her subsequent experience of the colony convinces her that its apparent barrenness is due to its inhabitants rather than to its environment. She challenges Mitchell's opinion that the southern colonies are "hardly worth cultivating" by emphasizing the potential capital to be gained from North Carolina's abundant natural resources.[87] Schaw feeds her culture's appetite for imperialist accumulation through her descriptions of plenty: "the cotton is in plenty growing every where for the wick"; "the berries hang to the hand, and seem to beg you to gather them" (203); "wherever you see the peach trees, you find hard by a group of plumbs so fit for stocks, that nature seems to have set them there on purpose" (163); "noble trees that might adorn the palaces of kings are left to the stroke of thunder"; "the banks [are] so constituted by nature that they seem formed for harbours" (159). "I do assure you," she stresses, "that every gift of nature is here. Not Italia, Spain, or Portugal produce an Article that might not be had in higher perfection" (174–175). This emphasis on the colony's resources directly contests Mitchell's conclusion that the British government should focus its efforts on the more promising areas of Ohio and Mississippi, and also contradicts the idea popularized by Tucker and developed by Smith that it was in Britain's best interest to emancipate the Americans because the cost of maintaining the colonies exceeded their worth.

Schaw makes it abundantly clear that the issue is not with the colony's scarcity of resources but with the character of the colonists. She clarifies that the "dreary, savage" (141) scenery that she first encounters demonstrates the colonists' negligence rather than land's deficiency. "Tho' I may say of this place what I formerly did of the West India Islands," she explains, "that nature holds out to them every thing that can contribute to conveniency, or tempt to luxury, yet the inhabitants resist both, and if they can raise as much corn and pork, as to subsist them in the most slovenly manner, they ask no more" (153). Unlike West Indian colonists, Americans are not interested in enriching Britain through the cultivation of its colonies. Their subsistence living is a rejection of the mutually beneficial, reciprocal relations of the British Empire. Although personified nature appears to be pleading for cultivation—berries "beg" to be gathered (203) and pine trees "seem to lament that they exist for no purpose" (159)—the products of empire lie fallow in the land, waiting for the active hand of cultivation. "One is really grieved," she asserts in frustration, "to see so many rare advantages bestowed on a people every way so unworthy of them" (174). Schaw's "grief" in this passage is directed toward the environment and the empire; both are ultimately victims of the colonists' negligence. She carefully sows seeds of suspicion within her metropolitan readers by implying that the Americans' disregard for the land directly translates into a disregard for their mother country. The colonists' refusal to appropriately care for their nation's imperial investments ultimately marks them as conspicuously alien; they are "unworthy" of the benefits of empire precisely because they have rejected the duties (quite literally, in this case) of British citizenship.

The foreign quality of the American colonies is further clarified through Schaw's profound sense of alienation within North Carolina. During her trek to Schawfield (her brother's plantation), her party is hindered by the "impenetrable darkness" (147) and difficult terrain of their American surroundings. "The idea of being benighted in the wilds of America," Schaw shudders, "was not a pleasing circumstance to an European female. . . . All I had heard of lions, bears, tigers and wolves now rushed on my memory, and I secretly wished I had been made a feast to the fishes rather than to those monsters of the woods" (146–147). The precarious position of the specifically "*European* female" within this foreign environment suggests the tenuous status of Britishness within the American colonies. Schaw's unease is in response to the perceived foreignness of the American landscape: it is impenetrable, unfamiliar, and brimming with latent violence. The contested status of Britishness within America is reiterated in another episode where Schaw finds herself navigating the coarse streets of Wilmingtown: "There was no object on which my own ridicule fixed equal to myself and the figure I made, dressed out in all my British airs with a high head and a hoop and trudging thro' the unpaved streets in embroidered shoes by the light of a lanthorn carried by a black wench half naked. No chair, no carriage—good leather shoes need none. The ridicule was in the silk shoes in such a place" (154). Schaw portrays herself as both visibly out-of-place and distinctly vulnerable within the American environment; in each scenario, her European or British identity renders her conspicuous. Unlike their West Indian counterparts, Americans have failed to effectively modify the colonial landscape along British lines. Schaw's image of trudging through the "unpaved streets" with a "black wench half naked" forms a suggestive contrast with her Antiguan experience of fashionable carriages and gallant male escorts, where "no Lady ever goes without a gentleman to attend her" (87). That Schaw's "British airs" are an object of ridicule rather than respect within America communicates that its colonists are not British but decisively American—or, to use Ramsay's categories, they are not "Englishmen" but "Foreigners."[88]

Through her depiction of their unaltered environment, Schaw seriously questions the imputed British character of the colonists. The West Indian scenario is here reversed: that they have not changed their environment suggests that their environment has fundamentally changed them. She provides confirmation of the colonists' (d)evolution through her detailed sketch of the typical American male. "Their appearance," she begins, "is in every respect the reverse of that which gives the idea of strength and vigor. . . . They are tall and lean, with short waists and long limbs, sallow complexions and languid eyes, when not inflamed by spirits. Their feet are flat, their joints loose and their walk uneven" (153). Schaw applies ethnological description to American colonists to assert their difference; she alleges that Americans are physically differentiated from Britons to refute the idea of their common nature. Indeed, her representation of American colonists suggests their essentially animalistic character: their long limbs, flat feet, and loose joints bear a striking resemblance to contemporary descriptions of monkeys and to Swift's characterization of the monkey-like Yahoos.[89] Schaw's surprise at meeting an American with humanlike characteristics—he "spoke with a voice that seemed humanized and entered into conversation very much like a rational being" (81)—reinforces her implicit assertion that Americans are closer to beasts than humans (it should come as no surprise that she later learns that this remarkably sensible American is actually a recently emigrated Scot). By suggesting the brute nature of Americans, Schaw deploys the same distancing technique she applied to Highlanders and to the enslaved population in the West Indies. Her insinuation that they have evolved into a distinct racial group aggressively defamiliarizes (by dehumanizing) the colonists in an effort to block the channels of emotional traffic that connected Britons with their Atlantic colonists.

NOT ALL IN THE FAMILY: "UNLAWFUL BRETHREN" AND "TRUE OBEDIENT SONS"

Through her representation of the American landscape and society as ineffably foreign—and, more significantly, as noticeably hostile—Schaw interrupts the circulation of sympathy encouraged by British pro-American activists who characterized Americans as close relations. She deliberately eschews the language of brotherhood and the idea of a shared identity, estranging her subjects from her readers by emphasizing the distinct lack of familial resemblance between the two populations. Her intervention in Britons' perceptions of their American colonists accomplishes the work of differentiation that Ramsay believed was necessary for the protection of the British Empire in America. However, it is not enough for Schaw to convert Americans into foreigners—she must also transform them into legitimate enemies. Alienating British affections from American colonists may inhibit the exchange of sympathy, but it does not follow that her metropolitan readers will feel compelled to instigate violent reprisals. Smith and Hume are quite clear that distance in and of itself simply ensures indifference. "When I am a few miles from home," Hume observes, "whatever relates to it touches me more nearly than when I am two hundred leagues distant."[90] Smith posits that animosity implies care—we must have feelings for something in order to develop animosity against someone. We adopt the antipathies of our friends and are animated by expressions of hatred against our communities.[91] Schaw attempts to activate her readers' animosity against Americans by deploying both of these principles. She directs her audiences' sympathies toward the victimized loyalists and clarifies the rebellious colonists' hatred of the British.

Responding to the preponderance of sentimental imagery in the literature of the American Revolution, Sarah Knott observes that there was "a tangible instrumentality in sensibility's wartime logic."[92] American sympathizers churned out sentimental images of suffering colonists throughout the 1770s that framed the American experience as "virtue in distress"—deliberately drawing on the popular eighteenth-century scenario of the innocent victim (America) molested by a corrupt aggressor (Britain). Schaw seeks to reverse her audience's emotional commitments by rewriting the narrative of the colonial crisis as a struggle between malevolent Americans and virtuous loyalists. There is Governor Martin who is forced to flee from his home, hastily send his young family away to an unknown fate, and move to a miserable military ship (186–187)—all but abandoned by the British nation that he is attempting to protect. Schaw portrays him as a "worthy man by all accounts" (156) whose "situation is every way to be pitied . . . he must submit, as he has not power to do otherwise" (173). Governor Martin's young Scottish assistant, Archibald Neilson, is similarly styled as a sympathetic figure. Made literally sick with fear for his employer (197, 206), threatened by unruly rebels for his loyalty (209), and divested of the opportunities he had come to America to pursue (188), his suffering serves as an indictment of the power exercised by American rebels. "When one considers the fate of this young fellow," Schaw states, "it is impossible not to be greatly affected. Had this unlucky affair not happened, he had been in as fine a way as any man in the province" (188). The persecution of the Scottish merchants and planters who dominated North Carolina's economy further exemplifies the suffering experienced by British loyalists in revolutionary America. Schaw details the arrest of eleven merchants and planters (seven of whom were Scots) who refused to declare allegiance to the Continental Association.[93] She transcribes their intrepid words after being threatened by their captors with further violence: "'And we will suffer every thing,' replied one of them, 'before we abjure our king, our country and our principles'" (192). Their devotion stands in stark contrast to the British nation's seeming abandonment of its loyal subjects. In each of these cases, suffering functions both as a sign of loyalty and as a condition for sympathy; Schaw's representation of British loyalists as political martyrs invokes sympathy by appealing to nationalist feeling.

Schaw is careful to guide her audience toward the appropriate response in each scenario—prohibiting itinerant emotions from adhering to the "wrong" objects—and she directly condemns her British readers for their negligence or their aberrant affections: "Oh Britannia, what are you doing, while your true obedient sons are thus insulted by their unlawful brethren; are they also forgot by their natural parents?" (192). Her identification of loyalists as "true obedient sons" and of American rebels as "unlawful brethren" performs a serious rewriting of the colonial narrative as composed by American sympathizers such as Burke, who characterizes the colonists as Britain's legitimate offspring. While Burke interprets the American rebels' desire for independence as a sign of their British ancestry,[94] Schaw interprets the same desire as a sign of their inherent difference. While loyalists demonstrate their parentage through their filial obedience, American revolutionaries equally demonstrate their corrupted lineage through their rebellion. Schaw's message is clear: by treating all American colonists as brethren, Britons are perversely supporting the suffering of their legitimate children. Her pointed observation that "the *Loyal* party are all as one family" (193) functions as an indictment of metropolitan Britons whom she represents as absconding their familial obligations. Drawing from her opponents' bag of sentimental tricks, she manipulates Britons' sense of paternal responsibility to encourage her readers to protect their "insulted" (192) children from those attempting to steal their inheritance—redirecting her audience toward what she considers to be appropriate objects of feeling.

That American rebels should not be considered as kin is exposed in their abuse of the land and of loyalists; that they should be treated as enemies is revealed through their barefaced animosity toward Britain. Schaw insists that the rebels' violence toward Britain's "obedient sons" (192) should be considered as violence toward the nation as a whole. She suggests that political conciliation is not only contributing toward the ruin of Britain's "obedient sons" but contributing toward damaging Britain through the collapse of its Atlantic empire. Observing the rapid development of a revolutionary infrastructure within North Carolina, Schaw warns her audience that they are effectively nurturing these rebellious "schemes" through their "mistaken mercy to a people, who have a rooted hatred at you and despise your mercy, which they View in a very different light" (149). She dissembles confidence in the political power of clemency by asserting that the colonists perceive Britain as an enemy nation rather than as their mother country. In an effort to convey the dangerous nature of the colonial rebels, Schaw repeatedly represents them using violent imagery. "They are of that sort of figure," she shudders, "that I cannot look at them without connecting the idea of tar and feather" (154). Americans embody violence; the threat they represent to her British body is so palpable that she can only see them in terms of her own physical destruction. Schaw's comparison of American colonists to an alligator further indicates the danger they pose to the British body. Having earlier established the "amazing strength" (150) of a full-grown alligator in a riveting scenario where two men attempt to kill the dangerous creature, she later uses the creature as a metaphor for the American colonists: "You at home know nothing of the power of this country, nor will you believe it till you find it with a witness. I yesterday killed an Alligator with my foot that in six months hence would be able to devour me. Six months ago a very little force would have done here, and even yet a proper exertion would do much towards resettling peace in these Southern parts" (189). Imagining the colonists as this wild beast, Schaw underscores their menacing nature and suggests the futility of mercy. The colonists cannot be tamed through conciliatory methods but must be crushed through more aggressive means. "Gentle methods," she warns, "will not do with these rusticks" (156–157).

Prior to her hasty departure from North Carolina, Schaw addresses the complicated identity of the American colonists in an effort to clarify their relationship to Britain. "Surely you folks at home," she provocatively suggests, "have adopted the old maxim of King Charles: 'Make friends of your foes, leave friends to shift for themselves'" (189). Schaw's reference to Charles II's covert treaty with France in 1670 clearly aligns the American rebels with Britain's traditional enemy and answers Ramsay's call to reveal the colonists' "true nature, and their true relation to Great Britain."[95] Positioned as a witness to that of which she speaks, Schaw warns her British audience that their mistaken interpretation of all American colonists as their "friends" may lead to the violent dismemberment of the British Empire. Echoing her earlier warnings, she pleads, "I wish to God those mistaken notions of moderation to which you adhere at home may not in the end prove the greatest cruelty to the mother country as well as to these infatuated people" (157). Her documentation of the rebels' (somewhat shambolic) military organization and her frequent assertions of their rapidly increasing strength together illustrate the importance of acknowledging the American rebels as legitimate "foes" and of acting with swift and potent military intervention. "A few months ago the task would have been easy," she says in frustration. "It is still possible, but (God make me a false prophetess) it will not be long so" (197). As history shows, Schaw's prophetic insight proved only too correct. Only months after she left, Governor Martin gathered together his Highland army with half the numbers he expected and no external support. They were slaughtered at the Battle of Moore's Creek Bridge by an organized rebel army, and North Carolina subsequently belonged to the American revolutionaries.

"A REBEL TO CUSTOM": SCHAW'S PERSONAL REVOLUTION

Women form the exception to Schaw's unsympathetic treatment of American colonists; she remains consistent in her sympathetic treatment of colonial women throughout her travelogue, regardless of their nationality. "For Schaw," Elizabeth Kim observes, "political needs dictate the mode of othering."[96] Indeed, her disparagement of American colonists is ultimately complicated by her uncompromising commitment to her own sex. While aggressively othering Americans, she is always quick to mitigate her criticism of American women. She is happy to discover "amiable and agreeable acquaintances amongst the Ladies; many of whom would make a figure in any part of the world" but is not surprised that "few of the men who are natives of this country . . . rise much above my former description" (154). Her commendation of American women clearly reveals that in the matrix of loyalties and animosities that form her political ideology, gender and nationality share a complex relationship. Her interest in the position of women within the British Empire is a dominant theme in her text; as a woman attempting to fortify her precarious speaking position and to justify her political intervention, Schaw is deeply invested in advocating for the greater inclusion of women within Britain's political life. In order to be heard, she must first shift her culture's assessment of her gender.

In the midst of detailing what she believes is an appropriate response to the colonial crisis, Schaw stops to acknowledge the extent to which her circumstances have politicized her: "I am no politician, as yet at least, tho' I believe I will grow one in time, as I am beginning to pay a good deal of attention to what is going on about me" (157). Her own identification as a (potential) politician abjures the eighteenth-century axiom that femininity and politics are incompatible. She loosely defines a politician as an individual who takes an active interest in politics and suggests that women can occupy this customarily male domain given the opportunity to engage in politics in real and vital ways. In the hyperpoliticized environment of revolutionary America—where daily activities and associations assumed major political significance—Schaw is *compelled* to engage in politics. Accordingly, she is able to imagine occupying a conventionally masculine role because traditional social structures are undeveloped or compromised within both colonial and revolutionary contexts. Schaw's indication of her political potential forms part of her message that women are not limited by inherent difference, but by sexist ideologies designed to keep women powerless. Her issue with prescribed gender roles is demonstrated in her frustration with Antiguan women's apparently unwholesome practice of abstaining from alcohol. The ladies' explanation that "it was custom" prompts Schaw to briefly rage against restrictive social conventions: "What a tyrant is custom in every part of the world. The poor women, whose spirits must be worn out by heat and constant perspiration, require no doubt some restorative, yet as it is not the custom, they will faint under it rather than transgress this ideal law" (81). She sets out both to demonstrate the loss society sustains by repressing women's diverse abilities and to model an alternative model of femininity that openly transgresses the restrictive "laws" so diligently heeded by the women she encounters.

Schaw's pointed comparisons between colonial men and women expose her belief that British women merit greater inclusion in the political life of the nation. Her representation of female colonists suggests a position for women within the empire that reaches beyond their passive role as simply "the emblems and proxies of the whole male enterprise of colonialism."[97] In her comparison of West Indian colonial men and women, Schaw reveals the superior moral character of the female colonists by sacrificing her overall idealization of West Indian men. She gingerly divulges and criticizes the reality of miscegenation among West Indian colonial men, suggesting that their sexual activities compromise the stability of colonial power. Schaw argues that miscegenation jeopardizes the already tenuous power structure between plantation owners and those they have enslaved and drains the financial resources of the plantation economy by compromising enslaved populations (112–113). The restraint of British women in the face of male excess displays their comparative fitness for the business of colonialism. Schaw suggests that whereas men have difficulty maintaining British protocol within foreign environments, women develop a heightened sense of propriety that manifests itself in impeccable morality—becoming "modest, genteel, reserved, and temperate" (113). Unlike their metropolitan counterparts, female colonists shun alcohol, despise scandal, are unacquainted with jealousy, and are deeply religious (113–114). Displaced from the metropolitan center, British women remain impervious to the attractions and freedoms of their foreign environments and are capable of maintaining British culture. Although Schaw derides West Indian women's obsessive maintenance of their White complexions, this physical preservation of whiteness also serves to signify their role as the keepers of cultural and racial distinction within colonial society (114–115). "Certainly," Deirdre Coleman observes, "Schaw's narrative strongly reflects the view that the future of the colony's British race lies in the sexual purity and virtue of its white women. . . . While the men endanger racial purity and cultural identity by interracial mixture, the women uphold white prestige and are the safekeepers of colonial morality."[98]

The surprising difference she finds between American men and women is once again attributed to her gender's greater immunity to the transformations wrought by the foreign environment. As Schaw explains to her reader, "The mothers took care of the girls, they were train'd up under them, and not only instructed in the family duties necessary to the sex, but in those accomplishments and genteel manners that are still so visible amongst them, and this descended from Mother to daughter. As the father found the labours of his boys necessary to him, he led them therefore to the woods. . . . But a few generations this way lost every art or science, which the fathers might have brought out" (155). The women preserve British values by instilling them in the younger generations, whereas the men have forgotten their ancestral ways by neglecting to instruct their sons in British "arts and sciences." Matriarchal governance is represented as both more effective and more reliable than patriarchal governance. Schaw's suggestive comparison of American men and women indicates the latter's competency as colonial subjects and proposes the wisdom of expanding women's participation in Britain's imperial endeavors.

Despite her praise of the moral propriety and domestic virtues of female colonists, Schaw carefully differentiates herself from these women. While Creole ladies staidly drink water, she raucously throws back "bumpers" of wine with her approving landlady (80); while they avoid physical exertion, she proudly hikes up mountains (83, 125); while they cover their faces to avoid the sun, she revels in her "brown beauty" (125)—a feature that physically distinguishes her from the pale-skinned ladies who dominate West Indian society and that visibly signifies her disregard for convention. Elizabeth Bohls argues that this contradiction between what Schaw says and what she does exposes an "unstable tension" within the text "between explicit homage to conventional femininity and an unstated resistance against it."[99] This tension reveals Schaw's incisive recognition of women's problematic position within eighteenth-century British society. In order to assert their fitness for imperial duties, she must establish their strict adherence to British standards. However, Schaw also registers discomfort with prescribed gender roles in her stated frustration with custom and her personal rebellion against it. She is profoundly aware that conventional definitions of femininity and its attendant practices circumscribe women's sphere of influence and condemns them to weakness. She takes issue with the colonial female custom of abstaining from alcohol because it protracts physical weakness and criticizes their obsession with pale skin because it similarly undermines their physical strength ("They only want colour to be termed beautiful. . . . This I am convinced is owing to the way in which they live, entirely excluded from proper air and exercise" [114]). In both cases, Schaw demonstrates that adhering to gender norms literally enervates women. Yet to demonstrate the depth and diversity of women's abilities through the colonial women she encounters would undoubtedly invite the accusation that their environment has changed them—that their unconventional behavior is the unfortunate result of the climate or the seductions of foreign cultures. As a result, Schaw places the weight of demonstrating difference upon her own person, proclaiming her intention to be "a rebel to a custom that did not appear founded on reason" (81). As a female traveler positioned outside of the traditional female roles of wife, mother, housekeeper, or romantic object, she has greater freedom to embody an alternative model of femininity. Although she briefly finds herself in one romantic entanglement with a certain Mr. Baird, she offers a distinctly unsentimental representation of her suitor as both aged and ugly, and comically emphasizes their mutual lack of physical attraction in order to obviate sentimental objectification (82). Her refusal to be pigeon-holed into traditional female roles opens the opportunity for her to explore and exemplify the range of women's abilities beyond the sentimental templates of distressed virgins; adoring wives, and long-suffering mothers, while her rejection of what she describes as "custom that did not appear founded on reason" (81) poses a direct challenge to eighteenth-century constructions of femininity.

Schaw establishes the depth of her abilities by resorting to the same strategy she uses to represent the strength of colonial women: she juxtaposes her character with that of a man—that of Archibald Neilson, Governor Martin's assistant, to be exact—in order to disrupt the gender hierarchy that justified the marginalization of women on the basis of their natural inferiority. Her initial description of Neilson aligns him with the physically fragile and alarmingly pale White women in the West Indies. "His wan meagre looks disgusted me," she recollects. "His white hands gave me great offence, as I could not help thinking he displayed them ostentatiously" (181). Neilson's delicate, feminine appearance forms a visible contrast to Schaw's "brown beauty" (125) and robust physical condition (83, 125), subverting eighteenth-century theories that rationalized male dominance by conflating physical and mental strength. According to Lord Kames, the physical and mental vigor of men designates them for leadership, while the relative weakness of women naturally circumscribes their abilities to the domestic sphere: "The man, naturally more robust, is fitted for severe labour and for field-exercises: the woman for sedentary occupations. . . . The man, as a protector, is directed by nature to govern: the woman, conscious of inferiority, is disposed to obedience. Their intellectual powers correspond to the destination of nature: men have penetration and solid judgment to fit them for governing: women have sufficient understanding to make a decent figure under good government."[100] By representing herself as Neilson's physical superior, Schaw disrupts Kames's gendered equation; her subsequent comparison of their "intellectual power" further problematizes the logic of Kames's hierarchy. Neilson quickly assumes authority over his female companions upon their arrival in Portugal, naturally adopting the status of the "protector" based on his gender rather than on his actual leadership qualities. "I plainly see he is to take such a charge of us," Schaw sighs. "Lord help him" (221). His attempts at governance quickly become an inside joke between Schaw and her reader as the narrative reveals Neilson's incompetence as a leader; he presupposes his female companions' weakness in his appropriation of authority, but it is Neilson who is ultimately exposed as the weak link.

While Schaw describes herself as "perfectly easy" with the vagaries of travel and "more inclined to laugh than cry at the little accidents we meet on this journey" (221), Neilson's incessant anxiety becomes troublesome. "I am often vexed at his anxiety," she complains, "for as he is hurt by our smallest inconveniency, he is for ever uneasy" (226). Her comparative fortitude and her gentle criticism of Neilson's fastidiousness disparage the gender ideology that informs his misdirected concern with the well-being of his female companions. Schaw's underlying message that women are limited by convention rather than by nature is repeated in a scenario where Neilson refuses to allow Schaw and Miss Rutherford to ride pack-saddles. Although the women are delighted by the prospect of riding a donkey, his strict adherence to convention prevents them from taking advantage of the opportunity. "What! Miss Rutherford and me on pack saddles!" Schaw playfully mimics. "Be it ever so easy a method, he would not submit to see us in such a style" (227). Neilson's conventional interpretation of femininity imposes limits upon Schaw and Miss Rutherford that constrains them to "sedentary occupations" despite their physical ability and inclination.[101] Schaw's ensuing comical portrayal of Neilson's dismal attempt at riding a packsaddle pointedly underscores that masculinity does not translate into superiority (230–232).

Having first indicated Neilson's relative weakness, her subversion of Kames's gender hierarchy is complete upon revealing that it is Neilson who ultimately requires Schaw's protection; she rescues him from the suffocating embraces of a particularly amorous Portuguese landlady by masquerading as his wife. She relates with delight that "he is quite afraid of her" and explains that "I am to take him under my protection" (222). The image of Neilson cowering under Schaw's protection (from a woman, no less!) offers a direct contrast to Kames's parallel image of women scuttling under the protection of men. The exigencies of travel and the stress of reality exposes Schaw as the individual endowed with true leadership qualities and ridicules a system that enshrines women's weakness at the expense of progress and improvement. Marching at the head of a night watch while in North Carolina, she revels in her newfound freedom from the constraints of social convention: "Oh! I shall make a glorious knapsack-bearer. You have formed a very wrong idea of my delicacy; I find I can put it on and off like any piece of dress" (201). Schaw reveals eighteenth-century femininity to be a set of socially constituted practices that are just as superficial as clothing. Like her rehabilitation of the West Indian colonists and her reinterpretation of American colonists, Schaw's depiction of women corrects common stereotypes and asks her readers to dispense with their uninformed ways of seeing and to consider the genuine nature of women.

TRAVEL AND SYMPATHY

Prior to embarking on her journey, Schaw offers this contemplation on the meaning and definition of "nation": "I had long taken root in my native Soil, yet it is not the spot of Earth that gave me being I call my Country. No! it is the Social Circle of such friends, as few can boast their brightest hours of prosperity were enriched with, it was these that constituted my happiness" (21). Schaw's articulation of the nation as a social construct recalls Hume's argument that national formation is the direct product of humankind's propensity for sympathy.[102] She is reassured by the idea that her sense of home is the consequence of shared sympathies rather than of shared topography; if national belonging is demarcated by relational rather than by physical parameters, then she is capable of extending her sense of home to the exotic climes of the West Indies and North Carolina. However, as Eve Tavor Bannet observes, Schaw discovers that "political allegiances based on the natural tie to friends with a common culture could, in these crucial years, easily go either way."[103] Her experience in America reveals the fragility of a national identity built on sympathetic attachments; the transient and impressionable nature of feelings could lead to errant political connections capable of destroying the "royal first-rate vessel" (211) to which she belongs. Indeed, while describing the qualities of two men vying for leadership within the rebel army, Schaw asserts that what makes Colonel James Moor a particularly frightening choice (frightening, that is, to Britain) is his ability to inspire affection. "A virtuous life," she states, "has gained him the love of every body, and his popularity is such that I am assured he will have more followers than any other man in the province" (167). Yet it is this recognition and experience of the affective basis of national identity that empowers Schaw to intervene in the national debates regarding the function of empire, the American Revolution, and the place of women within the polity. She writes with the intention of targeting her audience's feelings in order to manipulate the highly malleable "fashionable evolutions of opinion" (Burke) that threatened to dissolve the British Empire.[104] Schaw attempts to access people's convictions through their emotions in order to influence the formation of a national circle that sustains her in ways not dissimilar from her much smaller "Social Circle." Her conviction that sympathy can indeed transform individuals into a nation indicates that her "feeling heart" (33) functions as a political tool throughout her travel letters; her performance of feeling is more a political act than an expression of self.

Schaw's mobility is often overlooked in contemporary scholarship, yet her physical movement through the colonial terrain invests her feelings with particular power. Not only does travel associate her feelings with truth, but Schaw's circulating body and letters also act as proxies between Britain and its colonial populations, alternately overcoming and reinforcing the constraints posed by geography. The hospitality or harm proffered her British body in the diverse colonial spaces through which she moves articulates what Ramsay calls the "true relation" between Britain and its various colonies.[105] Reading Schaw's letters connects her British audience to their colonial populations; her textual representation of cultural (dis)connection allows her readers to vicariously enter into relationships with West Indian and American colonists. That she characterizes her letters as a substitute for actual encounters suggests the relational work accomplished by her correspondence. "Tho' it be a hundred to one you never see these letters," she comments, "yet as they give an idea of conversing with you, they afford myself infinite satisfaction" (36). As her readers' imagined relationships with their colonial populations are filtered through her personal experience, Schaw maintains control over the ways in which Britons imagine these relationships by modelling right relations for the British nation.

This representation of personal interactions as templates for political relations is redeployed by the anonymous English Lady whose sentimental travelogue is the focus of Chapter 3. She also uses her circulating body and letters to weave emotional connections and a sense of national unity between Scotland and England, contributing to the work of reconciliation that Schaw promotes in her travelogue. However, whereas Schaw's exposure to the realities of colonial life and political revolution demonstrate the potential dangers of sympathy, the Lady locates the threat to national unity in the absence of sympathy. She aggressively condemns the practice of selective sympathy, arguing that exclusive affections inhibit the emergence of a unified Britain given the nation's multiethnic, racial, and cultural composition. She suggests that it is precisely the inability of people like Schaw to sympathize with difference that created the intercultural hostility that was quickly escalating the American crisis from a national skirmish into a civil war.

3

THE TIES THAT BIND

Sentimentalizing Colonialism in *A Journey to the Highlands of Scotland*

JANET SCHAW'S HASTY DEPARTURE from America coincided with the more leisurely arrival of a certain English "Lady" to Schaw's much-beloved Scotland. Although the two travelers share similarities, their journeys and political positions could not be more different. Both women evince an interest in imperial politics and exploit their extradomestic experience and exposure to Britain's diverse populations to intervene in the divisive political debate inaugurated by the American Revolution. However, the Lady's pacifist leanings advance a very different political argument than Schaw's sanction of war; whereas Schaw finds evidence in America's revolutionary landscape for the necessity of violence, the author of *A Journey to the Highlands of Scotland* finds evidence in Scotland's past and confirmation in its present for the inadequacy of violence in achieving political stability.[1] In her study of eighteenth-century women's participation in the equally violent enterprises of war and empire, Kathleen Wilson concludes, "British women's engagement with the romance of war and empire generated possibilities for both complicity with and resistance to the nation-state's injunction to militarism. Equally important, their involvement created conditions that construed the terms and iconography of national belonging, circulating competing notions of nation, liberty, and political identity."[2] The conflicting positions on war and empire presented in the travel letters by Schaw and this unidentified English Lady bear out Wilson's assertion of women's diverse experiences of and involvement in the British Empire, as well as the opportunity for political engagement opened by the ideological fissures created under the pressure of conflict. Their adoption and adaptation of the sentimental mode and its attendant theories of sympathy further demonstrate the nuanced ways that feeling could be manipulated for political effect; a comparison of their travelogues reveals that sentimental discourse could be used to support radically different political ends and contradictory visions of the British nation. The anonymous author of *A Journey* problematizes the limited sympathy demonstrated and encouraged by pro-war pundits such as Schaw, proposing that culturally- or ethnically-specific sympathies create dichotomies that weaken the structure of the British Empire by inhibiting the formation of national unity.

TRAVELING "*SENTIMENTALLY*": THE POLITICS OF PERSONA

The slim volume of travel letters entitled *A Journey to the Highlands of Scotland. With Occasional Remarks on Dr. Johnson's Tour: By a Lady* appeared on the market in 1777. The text is the work of an anonymous female author who assiduously compiled and published eighteen letters ostensibly written during her tour of Scotland, with each letter alternately addressed to two women and one man: Lady Mary B—, Miss—(the author's sister), and the Earl of C—. The letters reveal the author as a playful, opinionated, and inquisitive individual with a romantic streak and a knack for self-effacing humor. Like Schaw, she is a single woman who appears to be accompanied by a traveling party. Together with her companions, she spends four months touring the Scottish landscape from Edinburgh, to Inveraray, and all the way up to Banff, completing what was referred to as the "Short Tour" of Scotland.[3] The resulting text never saw a second printing, and was quickly dismissed by reviewers as "[not] sufficiently curious and original to merit the public's attention."[4] Although the Lady's travelogue may appear unexceptional, her place both in the history of tourism and in the travelogue genre invests her text with historical interest. Scottish tourism was certainly becoming more common by the mid-1770s, but the Lady's trip to the Highlands was still relatively novel for the time period and characterizes her as an intrepid tourist.[5] Martin Rackwitz argues that when Thomas Pennant traversed and recorded the length and breadth of Scotland in 1769—only six years prior to the Lady's trip—there was "hardly anything known about the Highlands of Scotland and their population," and that it was not until the 1780s and 1790s that travelogues about Scotland began to be published in earnest.[6] Indeed, the publication of *A Journey* was the first of its kind from a female pen; travelogues by women were still in scant supply by 1777. As both a tourist and a female author, she is more "original" than *The Monthly Review* gives her credit for.

Although reviewers denigrate her attention to what they perceive as "frivolous subjects," they unanimously commend her "agreeable" and "lively" style.[7] *The Monthly Review* goes as far as to recommend her text as a cheerful alternative to Samuel Johnson's moody Scottish travelogue: "[These letters] give a lively and pleasing view of the country, which may serve as a counter part to the picture which Dr. Johnson has drawn with his *sombre* pencil."[8] The critic indirectly attributes the difference in tone and style to the author's gender, manifesting the cultural expectation that a woman's observations would be "lively and pleasing" as opposed to intellectually rigorous. Recent scholarship tends to reinforce this reading of the author's playful voice as a deliberate performance of gender. In her analysis of the Lady's travelogue in *Tourists and Travellers: Women's Non-Fictional Writing about Scotland, 1770–1830* (2010), Betty Hagglund interprets her distinct stylistic register as an "endeavor to create a different 'feminized' discourse."[9] While it certainly may be true that the Lady is emphasizing her gender to differentiate her text within the masculine field of travel writing, her expressive authorial style is also closely modeled on Sterne's sentimental traveler. She identifies her sentimental mode as the primary difference between her text and those of previous travel writers, and is careful to state her travel orientation in the preface: "I did not suffer the postilion to indulge his professional passion, to pass briskly through any parts of cultivated country, or rattle rapidly over the pavement of towns, that were fertile of remark, but ordered him to go *sentimentally*."[10] By labeling her style of travel "sentimental," the Lady associates herself with the category of the "sentimental traveler" as defined within Sterne's text and developed by his various imitators. Her reference to the postilion in the preface ensures that her readers will recognize the literary connection; her injunction to the postilion to travel at an appropriately sentimental tempo alludes to Yorick's wish for his postilion to have "stolen off with [him] in something like a pensive pace" rather than "clattering like a thousand devils."[11] The Lady proceeds to incorporate the definitive markers of the sentimental travelogue: espousing a sympathetic approach to otherness, emphasizing feeling over judgment, and adopting an anecdotal form. She is openly critical of "*literary* travellers" who "travel not with the intent to give the world a fair account of manners and customs, but merely to exaggerate the bad and sink the good" (23). The Lady enters Scotland's unknown terrain with a sentimental traveler's sympathetic disposition, ready to be delighted by its people and places. "I am convinced," she announces, "that virtue is the growth of every clime!" (43). She acknowledges the emotional source of her observations through frequent poetic outbursts, statements of inexpressibility, and reflections on her sentimental nature. Her assertion that "my sentiments always flow from my feelings" (35) echoes Yorick's declaration that he will describe his experiences "with the same simplicity, with which I felt them."[12] In each statement as in each travelogue, feeling is cited as the inspiration for the written reflections.

As an inexperienced writer and as a woman following the pathway trod by a series of men with towering reputations, the Lady finds both justification for her endeavor and authority for her voice in Sterne's fresh approach to travel writing. The anonymous author directly informs her audience of the value of her sentimental orientation: "I . . . noticed several things worthy of being made public, which more laborious travellers, and some of those who absolutely journeyed *ex officio*, had neglected, or overlooked" (4). She is likely alluding to three of her distinguished predecessors in this statement: Thomas Pennant, Samuel Johnson, and Daniel Defoe.[13] The "laborious travellers" are presumably Pennant and Johnson; Pennant's travelogues were praised for their exhaustive documentation of Scotland, and the Lady frequently mocks Johnson's travelogue for its "great scrupulosity of minute investigation" (18). The reference to travelers who "journeyed *ex officio*" refers to Daniel Defoe, whose *A Tour thro' the Whole Island of Great Britain* (1724–1727) was written based on travels undertaken on official business. Her comment on her predecessors' ultimate deficiencies as travelers and as travel writers recalls Yorick's ridicule of Smelfungus and Mundungus—the two stock travelers whose refusal to cultivate meaningful connections within their foreign environments compromises their perception (see Chapter 1). The Lady similarly connects the gaps in her predecessors' accounts to their materialist or unsympathetic approach to Scotland. She singles out Johnson for particular censure, asserting that his "contracted sentiments" (43) result in a "false representation of a very worthy set of people" (22). The Lady suggests that by traveling sentimentally—with the intention of feeling rather than cataloguing or judging—she is able to discern details missed by those travelers who objectify Scotland. She does not view the prospect only to declare "'tis barren";[14] rather, she claims that traveling sentimentally "not only made amends for those occasional glooms which seemed to breathe the spirit of melancholy, from the surrounding barrenness, but gave to the whole that sort of *chequer-work*, which inevitably mixes with every business, and every pleasure" (4). The implication, of course, is that the sentimental traveler—who possesses expansive rather than "contracted" sentiments—produces a comparatively reliable travel account because their disposition allows for authentic connections.

The Lady's sentimental orientation provides more than a justification for her literary endeavor: it also provides both the façade and the framework for a penetrating political critique. Her publisher, Fielding and Walker, published *A Journey* alongside numerous political works on the American Revolution, ranging from political verse like Richard Brinsley Sheridan and Israel Pottinger's *The General Fast; A Lyric Ode* (1776) to political sermons like John Witherspoon's *An Address to the Natives of Scotland Residing in America* (1778) and political essays like *The Delusive and Dangerous Principles of the Minority, Exposed and Refuted. In a Letter to Lord North* (1778).[15] Sold amidst these warring political pamphlets, the Lady's breezy, sentimental travelogue appears to be a reprieve from the wartime concerns that populated her publisher's catalogue in the late 1770s.[16] But appearances, as we know, can be deceiving: her chosen travel persona *is* her political statement. The sympathetic orientation of the sentimental traveler provides her with an interpretive framework that corresponds with her vision of British national identity. The Lady's travel text is invested in redefining Britain's national character according to a sentimental model that imagines a British politics and imperial policy rooted in sympathy and characterized by benevolence. Her sentimental engagement with the Scottish landscape and its people allows her to demonstrate how Britain should structure its imperial relations to ensure the stability of its empire. For the author of *A Journey*, Scotland provides the ideal platform for considering the current revolution. Although the Lady does not directly address the American Revolution, her experience of traveling through a once rebellious territory provides her with the opportunity to reflect on issues relevant to the contemporary colonial crisis. Despite obvious differences in terms of its contemporary political representation and past political history, Scotland's post-Union status as a "stateless nation" within the British Empire and its history of rebellion against English rule offered compelling parallels with the American colonies.[17] Political commentators had already made explicit connections between the past Scottish and present American rebellions. In his 1776 pamphlet, *Remarks on Dr. Price's "Observations on the Nature of Civil Liberty,"* Scottish historian Adam Ferguson draws on the similar positions of Scotland and America within the British Empire to justify the war against America. He argues that by quelling the American rebellion, the English government is simply repeating the imperial strategy that they successfully implemented against the two most recent Scottish rebellions. "The one case," Ferguson claims, "is equally applicable as the other."[18] The Scottish soil's imprint of rebellion thus organically introduces the reality of political insurrection, but the Lady's sentimental method of journeying suggests an approach to intercultural relations that precludes war as an appropriate response to conflict.

Johnson's *A Journey to the Western Islands of Scotland*, published just two years before the Lady's travelogue in 1775, presents another occasion for the Lady to consider and critique conventional ways of structuring imperial relations. She takes Johnson to task on what she perceives as his deeply prejudiced perception of Scotland's people and landscape. Her condemnation of Johnson's interaction (or lack thereof) with this part of the British nation develops into an impassioned argument against a practice of Englishness characterized by insularity and exclusion. The danger that she locates in Johnson's Smelfungus-like approach to otherness is that it ultimately reinforces emotional barriers between England and its peripheries, leading to dangerous fractures within the British Empire that threaten both its unity and its progress. The Lady combats the pro-war argument disseminated by the Tories and illustrated within Schaw's text by insisting upon the cyclical nature of violence and positing a version of the biblical maxim that those sustained by violence will perish by the same means. With America questioning the ideological foundations of Britain's imperial prerogative and demonstrating the fragility of their political bond, the Lady seeks to reform her nation's imperial politics and strengthen the connective fabric between England and its peripheries by encouraging the development of affective ties. Deploying her sentimental orientation as a model, she attempts to establish sympathy as the medium through which all imperial relations should be understood and conducted. Using the language of sentiment, she articulates that an empire stitched together by the threads of affection is far stronger than an empire bound by the iron chains of fear; friendships endure, but prisoners will always try to escape.

ACTS OF PASSION: THE MARRIAGE ACT AND THE AMERICAN REVOLUTION

The author of *A Journey* opens her travelogue by immediately discussing the motivations for and realities of rebellion. However, the rebels she conjures are far more benign in their national impact than either the Scottish Jacobites or the American revolutionaries: these rebels are lovers, not fighters. Traveling on the infamous road to Gretna Green—Scotland's premier destination for clandestine weddings—the Lady cannot help but comment on the rebellious young lovers who frequent this well-trodden path seeking independence from their parents and freedom from England's strict marriage laws. "Nothing need to be said of the road between England and this place," she begins, "it being so universally known, since the legislature thought fit to form an act which hath rendered it so usefully fashionable to the happy race of Hibernian heroes and English *misses* longing to throw off the leading-strings of parental restraint" (5). The "act" to which she refers is undoubtedly Lord Hardwicke's Marriage Act of 1753, which further extended parental and state authority over marriage contracts and severely curtailed the ability of underage youths to freely enter marital unions. This direct reference to the controversial act—along with her suggestive language of liberty and restraint—alerts her readers to the political nuances of her ensuing consideration of a clandestine marriage. Although the parallels between reckless young lovers and heady American revolutionaries might be lost on twenty-first-century readers, the Lady's contemporary audience would have been attuned to the similarities between the political debates over the Marriage Act and the American Revolution. In *By Birth or Consent: Children, Law, and the Anglo-American Revolution in Authority* (2005), Holly

Brewer argues that both debates were entangled in the same struggle of defining the basis and extent of political authority. As such, Brewer asserts, the opposition to the passage of the Marriage Act and its subsequent repeals "invok[ed] some the same arguments used to justify the American Revolution."[19] The Marriage Act's regulatory laws create a compelling parallel to the contested regulatory laws imposed upon the American colonies following the Seven Years' War (primarily the Stamp Act of 1765, the Townshend Acts of 1767, and the Coercive Acts of 1774). Although the contents of the laws obviously differ, their intentions (specifically the protection of property and the increased regulation of society) are similar, providing an opening for the author of *A Journey* to consider questions of parliamentary authority, individual liberty, and the relationship between freedom and constraint. Although the Lady's satirical portrait of rebellious young lovers suggests her criticism of the American revolutionaries, her related portrait of sympathetic authority registers her discomfort with Britain's decision to wage war against its American colonists and suggests a different, more liberal approach to governance that emphasizes care over control.

When Lord Hardwicke's Marriage Act was introduced in 1753, it instigated an avalanche of debate that continued through the various repeals of the act in 1765, 1772, and 1781.[20] In an effort to restrict clandestine marriages, the act instituted a more stringent approach to marriage rites: banns had to be published or licenses obtained several weeks (or three Sundays) in advance of the marriage, marriages had to take place within a church and presided over by an authorized clergyman, and parental consent had to be obtained before the age of twenty-one or the marriage would be rendered void. Severe penalties could be incurred if couples or participating authorities failed to comply with any part of the procedure. The vigorous debates surrounding the passage of the act in 1753 and the repeals over the next three decades reveal that more was at stake than simply the restructuring of marriage rites. The debates themselves tied the issue of clandestine marriage to questions of property, social mobility, and civil liberties, among other weighty political concerns. Of all the objections to the act's provisions, the issue of parental control and contractual consent seems to have particularly captured the public's imagination. Support for either parental (and particularly paternal) restraint or for the rights of minors articulate two divergent national ideologies: one defined by social hierarchy and patriarchal authority and the other by individual rights and freedoms.[21]

Supporters of the act contended that it contributed toward the social stability of the nation by safeguarding property and that it protected the vulnerable (i.e., impressionable minors) from exploitation. Henry Gally, a vociferous supporter of the Marriage Act, asserted that its reinforcement of parental authority would preserve "the Peace and good Order of Society" by protecting both "Liberty and Property."[22] He predictably interpreted parental restraint as a valuable protective measure, observing that "in the Case of clandestine marriages the Parties themselves are benefitted by the Restraints, which are put upon them. For the Laws made to prevent them are founded upon the many bad Consequences, with which such Marriages are, by Experience, generally found to be attended."[23] Richard Brinsley Sheridan—a rather unlikely supporter of the act given his own rakish elopement, and perhaps even more surprisingly given his consistent advocacy for individual rights and freedoms—agreed with Gally's alignment between restraint and liberty. In a parliamentary speech responding to the 1781 repeal of the Marriage Act, he opposed Charles James Fox's proposal to lower the age of consent on the basis that both sexes may be "prevailed upon to make an imprudent match" and find themselves contractually bound within an unhappy marriage.[24] He argued that the temporary restraint of impressionable youths preserves their freedom of choice when they are fully capable of making a rational decision. This idea—that legally constituted state authority *preserved* rather than *compromised* personal liberty—was a fundamentally conservative one that reified traditional authority as a bulwark against individual ambition.

Opponents of the act countered by arguing that the law fundamentally undermined individual rights and freedoms by privileging parental authority over individual choice; in doing so, it appeared to shift English politics toward a dangerously authoritarian system that emphasized obedience and obligation over liberty and consent. This line of argument can be seen in Fox's sardonic rebuttal to Sheridan's opposition, in which he claims that Sheridan "had so much ingenuity of mind, that he could contrive to give an argument what turn he pleased; he considered not, therefore, when what he said was really in support of domestic tyranny, he should ground it on a wish to preserve liberty."[25] The anonymous author of *Reflections on the Marriage-Act* (1764) similarly suggests that the act is reminiscent of a form of tyranny inconsistent with England's commitment to liberty: "We have so long been fettered, and shackled with all the forms and restrictions of this most impolitic law: to [Scotland] people have hurried, as to the land of liberty. . . . It is to be hoped the period is near at hand . . . when the inhabitants of England, shall no longer be obliged to fly to Scotland, to regain these natural rights which every subject, in every part of the kingdom, ought at all times enjoy."[26] The author reinterprets Gally's innocuous "restraints" as imprisoning "shackles," and asserts that the very fact that young English citizens must escape their country in order to gain freedom divests England of its proud designation as the "land of liberty."

The anonymous author of *Reflections on the Marriage-Act*'s questioning of English liberty on the basis of its repressive laws demonstrates the potential for concurrence between the debates on the Marriage Act and on the American Revolution. Those who argued in support of the revolution likewise suggested that the colonists' resistance to the "oppressive" restrictions and demands placed upon them demonstrated their admirable commitment to the principles of liberty and positioned America as the new "land of liberty." In Thomas Paine's explosive revolutionary document, *Common Sense* (1776), he explicitly relocates liberty to the American colonies in order to suggest the tyrannical nature of England's imperial policies. "This new world," he avers, "hath been the asylum for the persecuted lovers of civil and religious liberty from *every part* of Europe . . . and it is so far true of England, that the same tyranny which drove the first emigrants from home, pursues their descendants still."[27] The intersection of the Stamp Act and the repeal of the Marriage Act in 1765 clearly exposed their shared political genealogy and geography. The author of *Reflections on the Marriage-Act* specifically draws attention to the issues linking the newly-introduced Stamp Act to the Marriage Act: "Amidst . . . the discussion of civil rights and constitutional prerogative, it cannot but afford great pleasure to every thinking mind, to see the attention of the legislature once more recall'd to a question, which involves . . . our most invaluable rights as men."[28] As this alignment indicates, the arguments instigated by the colonial crisis essentially retraced the contours of the arguments that had long been used to justify or vilify the Marriage Act. The definition of liberty was particularly germane to both arguments, as was its delicate interplay with authority. Both political debates asked: What are the features of individual liberty within society? Does authority without the consent of the governed (children or American revolutionaries) compromise liberty? Is freedom without restraint properly considered liberty, or does its sanction of individual desire form a fundamental threat to liberty?

The debate over the American Revolution transferred these questions of parliamentary authority and individual liberty from children to colonists (although the colonists were often styled as the "children" of their imperial parent).[29] The public debate conducted between Richard Price and Adam Ferguson on the issue of civil liberty as it pertained to the colonial crisis illuminates the similarities between the debates on the Marriage Act and the revolution; their competing definitions of liberty and subsequent interpretations of the American colonists resonate with the issues and images already circulating through the Marriage Act debate. In his 1776 pamphlet *Observations on the Nature of Civil Liberty*, Price explores what he interprets as the defining characteristics of civil liberty in order to provide a justification for the colonists' grievances and their desire for independence. Price defines liberty as the "[freedom] to be guided by one's own will."[30] He believes that Americans exhibit a profound grasp of liberty in their opposition to the British government, whom they recognize as imposing a system of slavery upon them by abrogating their constitutional right to representation. Similar to the author of *Reflections on the Marriage-Act*'s characterization of the legal restraints placed upon minors as "fetter[s]" or "shackle[s],"[31] Price interprets the various non-consensual regulatory laws placed upon the American colonists as a form of captivity. "To be guided by the will of another," he claims, "is the characteristic of servitude."[32] Recalling the fears of "domestic tyranny" expressed by opponents of the Marriage Act,[33] Price depicts Britain as a tyrannical parent unnaturally attempting to dominate its fully grown children: "We should have been gradually relaxing our authority as they grew up. But, like mad parents, we have done the contrary; and, at the very time when our authority should have been the most relaxed, we have carried it to the greatest extent, and exercised it with the greatest rigour."[34] Price's metaphor posits that the relationship between authority and its subordinates must be based on reciprocity; without the consent of the governed, authority devolves into despotism.

In Ferguson's immediate response to Price's pamphlet, *Remarks on Dr. Price's Observations on the Nature of Civil Liberty* (1776), he counters Price's definition of liberty with his own, asserting that liberty should be understood as "regulated freedom, not an anarchy of acting agreeably upon passion."[35] Ferguson shares Gally's belief that civil liberty is ensured through the ideal balance of consent and restraint. He contends that both Price and the Americans possess a mistaken understanding of liberty that confuses it with the absence of restriction: "The vulgar think that their liberty is infringed, if they receive the least curb of legal restriction: unrestrained by morality, a lawless conduct, unchecked, is the only idea they possess of liberty."[36] Like Sheridan's fear that "imprudent matches" would arise from the unrestricted freedom of immature youths,[37] Ferguson predicts that the absence of salutary British checks and balances will render America vulnerable to tyranny: "Ambition in every one of them would lead some artful individual to place himself at the head; and opposition, that sprung from a mistaken sense of liberty, would end in despotism."[38] Parliamentary authority, according to Ferguson, ultimately safeguards civil liberty; consequently, he interprets Britain's war against the colonies as a battle for liberty rather than as an act of domination. Not surprisingly, Ferguson turns Price's familial metaphor on its head, finding madness within the violent colonial "children" rather than the benevolent imperial "parent." "Cruel must that disposition be," he accuses, "who after rising to manhood, by the protecting wing of an indulgent guardian, wishes to plunge a dagger in his breast."[39]

The author of *A Journey* exploits the rich philosophical similarities between the Marriage Act and the American Revolution by fabricating a fanciful elopement narrative that can be read as a cautionary tale for reckless young lovers *or* rash revolutionaries. Given the shared political geography of both debates, and the pervasiveness of the analogy between the nuclear family and the nation-state in revolutionary rhetoric, the Lady's imaginary tale of elopement can be read as a fictional parallel to actual political events. Her fictional scenario begins by imagining the initial flight and considering the motivations of the rebellious young women who frequent the road to Gretna Green. "The glowing females of the present generation," she observes, "are not to be tyed down by either prudish or prudential duties, to fathers or mothers, or any such antiquated doctrines—No, forsooth, liberty! Dear liberty is the TON" (5). The Lady takes full advantage of Gretna Green's fraught associations with rebellion and independence to consider her culture's current preoccupation with defining, claiming, and enacting liberty. Although her exclamation is contextualized within the Greta Green elopement narrative, it is tempting to read this declaration as an allusion to the Americans' desire for liberty from their fiscal "duties" and from the control of the "parental" authority of the British government. Her playful reference to "liberty" and her critical portrayal of the liberated "English *misses*" (5) absconding parental protection suggests an oblique criticism of the colonists' ideals and actions. Her lighthearted description of elopement as "usefully fashionable" and liberty as "the TON" (5) belies a serious critique. By labeling liberty as "fashionable," she is also saying that the desire for liberty can be driven by entirely superficial reasons. Rather than arising out of actual oppression, the pursuit of liberty may be motivated by a transitory but infectious cultural fixation. She was not alone in her sense that the rebels' fascination with liberty was superficial: Ferguson likens the Americans' current aspirations to an "infatuation" and declares them to be motivated by a heady mixture of "restlessness," "giddiness," and "illusion";[40] and Janet Schaw characterizes the American rebels as an "infatuated people."[41] The Lady's derisive portrayal of those pursuing this political trend—the infatuated English females—reinforces the sense that she is constructing a pointed critique of the reckless pursuit of independence. The starry-eyed lovers' desire for liberty is founded on nothing but thoughtless rebellion; they long "to throw off the leading-strings of parental restraint" (5) simply to indulge their fleeting passions.

The situation in which these young women subsequently find themselves is tragically comical: the "sighing pair" (5) are linked together by none other than a businesslike, unsentimental blacksmith who fuses people with the same facility as he fuses iron. "Though they who visit our Vulcan," she explains, "go, now and then, upon the wings of passion, the blacksmith himself makes it, uniformly, a mere matter of business" (5). The Lady shatters the illusion of romance surrounding the idea of liberation; although the fantasy of freeing oneself from constraint and flying off on the "wings of passion" appears alluring, the reality is undeniably prosaic. Her specific characterization of these eloping couples as "Hibernian heroes and English *misses*" (5) references the bumbling elopement attempt between a young Irishman and his English intended in Tobias Smollett's *The Expedition of Humphry Clinker* (1771) and further invests her own fictional portrait with an additional layer of cynicism. The Lady's gesture to Smollett's fictional scenario suffuses her depiction of "the glowing females of the present generation" (5) and their desire for liberty with the absurd, and ensures that her audience will recognize the irrationality of their actions.[42] Similar to Ferguson's critique of Price's definition of liberty, the Lady represents the idea of liberty espoused by these impassioned women as a profound misunderstanding of the concept. They imagine liberty as the freedom to do whatever they want—the freedom "to be guided by [their] own will."[43]

However, as Ferguson warns the American revolutionaries and their supporters, the ignorant pursuit of what appears to be independence may result in a stricter, more profound bondage. The Lady can be read as echoing a similar concern for the young American colonies by providing an ambiguous conclusion to her fanciful narrative of youthful rebellion. Her portrait of a hasty Gretna Green elopement ends with the following ominous image: "When the conjugal *work* is brought to [the blacksmith's] anvil, he always strikes the iron while it is warm, and often proves himself, alas! but too able an artificer, at connecting the *links* of the matrimonial *chain*" (5). The abrasive language used to describe the marriage—striking, iron, links, chains—evokes images of incarceration rather than of matrimonial bliss. The young women's pursuit of liberty ends with them fused to their husbands by a permanent "matrimonial chain" that is far more binding than the comparatively slight "leading-strings" (5) of parental supervision.[44] The obvious contrast between the two types of ties emphasizes the tragedy in the young brides' new circumstances. Considered within the Marriage Act debate, the Lady's portrayal of flighty young women turned chained wives aligns with Sheridan's fears of the permanent bondage that awaited duped young brides. Extended to the debate surrounding the American Revolution, it recalls Ferguson's conception of equally flighty American colonists turned disillusioned subjects of a tyrant. Ferguson's sense that American independence may devolve into arbitrary power was a fear shared by Britons and Americans alike. During the nascent years of the revolution, Francis Hopkinson—eventually one of the signatories of the Declaration of Independence—expressed anxiety that an independent America would be vulnerable to the machinations of ambitious individuals. Deploying a familial metaphor similar to the Lady of *A Journey*, he argues, "Should the Colonies, with base ingratitude, attempt to throw off all dependence on the mother country, they would put themselves in a situation of a silly girl, who leaves the guidance and protection of a wise and affectionate parent, and wandering away exposes herself to ruin by the artful insinuations of every wicked and designing stranger."[45] What the Lady's naïve girls have in common with Ferguson's eager colonists and Hopkinson's "silly" Americans is that all misinterpret protection as oppression; the message shared across these different narratives is that legal and constitutional restraints ultimately act as a safeguard. Just as the "leading-strings of parental restraint" can prevent the "matrimonial chain" (5) from binding young women to conniving opportunists, the "strings that moved the wheels of government" ultimately prevents the "despotism of the most artful."[46]

However, the Lady's support of a more conservative politics that enshrines parliamentary authority as both necessary and incontrovertible does not also act as a defense of Britain's war against its American colonies. She carefully avoids Ferguson's and Schaw's approbation of disciplinary action against America by representing benign parental figures whose benevolent "restraint" (5) does not shade into aggression. Her image of the tender "leading-strings of parental restraint" (5) recalls Benjamin Franklin's description of the British Parliament's former and, according to his interpretation, salutary relationship with its American colonies. Standing before the House of Commons in 1766, he stated, "[The American colonists] were governed by this country at the expense only of a little pen, ink and paper: *they were led by a thread*."[47] The similarity between the two images of authority offered by the Lady and by Franklin is not coincidental. The circulation of the same image within the debates over the American Revolution suggests a political reading of the Lady's depiction of parental authority, one which affirms a form of constitutional governance characterized by limited authority. She does not champion the disciplinary tactics defended by Ferguson and Schaw, but implicitly endorses a noncoercive version of authority that balances the demands of consent and restraint through a commitment to civil liberties, evocatively illustrated by Franklin's picture of the colonists being "led by a thread" and by her own sentimental image of parental "leading-strings" (5).[48]

ROMANTICIZED REBELS: THE 1745 JACOBITE REBELLION AND THE AMERICAN REVOLUTION

The political analogy buried in the Lady's narrative of romantic rebels is further developed in her observations on a set of increasingly romanticized rebels—the Jacobites of the 1745 rebellion. Like her experience on the road leading to Gretna Green, the Lady's journey into the Highlands allows her the opportunity to tread in the footsteps of rebellious subjects, providing her with yet another occasion to contemplate the nature of liberty and the legitimacy of political rebellion. In both cases, physical location and the demands of her sentimental orientation furnishes the author with the means to delve into political issues. She concludes her observations on the 1745 Jacobite rebellion by claiming the combined effect of contiguity and emotional susceptibility: "Being on the spot, which at that period, set all England in a tremor; I was led irresistibly to these consequent reflections; let this plead my excuse" (22). Her efforts to justify her incursion into political argument reveal the more nakedly political nature of her reflections on the Scottish incendiaries. The Lady's assessment of the rebellion and its participants clarifies the importance of sympathy within human relations, firmly advocating for the establishment of an empire that functions as a sentimental union of hearts.

Wandering along "the track of the rebel army" (21) between Falkirk and Sterling, the Lady switches from landscape description to political disquisition, contritely but urgently launching into a discussion of Britain's last political rebellion. She seeks to discover why Prince Charles Edward Stuart gained such popular support in 1745, which constitutes a particularly pertinent line of inquiry given Britain's immersion in a new rebellion. Based on her knowledge of the Scots' "life and manners," she concludes, "Their so easily gaining followers, and possessing themselves of these towns, is not at all surprising; since those who were well-affected to government, were so few, in comparison to the ignorant multitude, which run with the stream, and are one moment ready to join the Pretender's standard, and the next, on sight of our troops to discard their new-acquired friends and throw up their bonnets for KING GEORGE" (21). Her criticism of the Jacobites resonates with her previous treatment of the impetuous young girls escaping to Gretna Green: she suggests that the rebels' fight for liberty was rooted in ignorance and impulse. Their rebellion is essentially a mechanical response to a powerful stimulant; the superficiality of the rebels' conviction is revealed in the alacrity with which they switch sides. The Lady's portrayal of the Scottish rebels as mindlessly drifting with the current recalls a similar image used by Ferguson to represent the American rebels: "The cry of freedom, that never-failing word, that incendiaries make as subservient to their designs, and which always sets the multitude in an uproar, inflamed some; while others, *carried by the current*, unintentionally aided the rebellion."[49] Similar to the Lady's treatment of the Jacobites, Ferguson denigrates the American revolutionaries by suggesting that they lack authentic conviction—their rebellion is the product of impulse rather than of principle. The impact of this strategic representation is twofold: it demystifies the rebels by depicting them as scarecrows—intimidating on the outside but without substance—and defends the existing political order by asserting that the rebellion is motivated by licentiousness rather than by liberty.[50]

Ferguson's observation further suggests that the *idea* of liberty is often exploited as a means to power; incendiaries harness the appeal inherent in the "cry of freedom" to accomplish their base designs. Whereas Price is convinced that "ENGLAND should venerate the attachment to Liberty amidst all its excesses,"[51] Ferguson believes that an "attachment to Liberty" may be counterfeit; what appears to be a desire for liberty may conceal a desire for control. In her commentary on the '45, the Lady reveals a similar pessimism toward the "cry of freedom." Inserting a (mis)quotation from a John Dryden play, she suggests that the idea of liberty is often used as a manipulative tool:[52]

> Some popular Chief
> More noisy than the rest, but cries halloo,
> And in a trice the bellowing herd come out;
> And one and all is the word;
> They never ask for whom, or what they fight,
> But turn 'em out, and shew 'em but a foe;
> Cry liberty, and that's the cause of quarrels. (*A Journey*, 21)

Liberty becomes the "cause of quarrels" rather than the objective; the "bellowing herd" is incited by the cry of liberty rather than by its principles, oblivious to the actual basis of their dispute. The herdlike rebels resemble the eloping young girls in their ignorance of the true nature of liberty: neither party is fully aware of what they are pursuing or whom they are embracing. However, the image of the chained brides conveyed on the first page of the travelogue indicates that the costs of ignorance are high. The Lady is careful to clarify that the Scottish rebels were effectively fighting to maintain what she characterizes as an oppressive political hierarchy administered by chieftains who reigned like "absolute monarchs" or "oriental potentate[s]" (40). "It very frequently happened," she asserts, "that, a chieftain would involve his slavish subjects in the calamities of public contest, to gratify his private ambition, his envy, or his avarice" (40). According to this representation of Scottish society, what may have seemed like liberation from the English in '45 would have resulted in the establishment of a genuinely oppressive government. Similar to the parents with their protective "leading-strings" (5), the English government ultimately safeguards liberty by protecting the rebels from their rapacious chieftains; it is the English who extend "a proper proportion of liberty to the commonality" (40), not "some popular Chief" (21).

Although the American Revolution remains an unspoken reality in the author's reflections on the '45, the similar nature of the political events organically invites comparison. In her detailed study of *A Journey*, Marie E. McAllister also notices the immediate political implications of the Lady's observations on past hostilities between Scotland and England and argues that "the temptation to read this as a comment on liberty in general, in a period of American unrest, is irresistible." She goes on to assert that the Lady's rhetoric ultimately "permits the interpretation."[53] Indeed, by using Dryden's statement on a past political crisis to articulate her opinion on the Jacobite rebellion, the Lady demonstrates that Britain can gain wisdom from its former contests and use this knowledge to interpret the present. Her examination of Britain's former rebellions posits a reading of the American Revolution that defends British interests and dismantles arguments that favor American independence. In her version of events, genuine liberty is located within England. It is the English who, through "the many wise acts since passed" (40), successfully liberated the Scottish people from their archaic practices. Reinforcing England's image of itself as the seat of liberty makes a significant political statement during a period when this image was being aggressively disputed by Britons on both sides of the Atlantic. "A nation," Price reprimanded Britain, "once the protector of Liberty in distant countries, and the scourge of tyranny, [is] changed into an enemy of Liberty, and [is] engaged in endeavoring to reduce to servitude its brethren."[54] The Lady's loaded examples of the calamitous fates awaiting rebellious subjects suggest that sympathy for the American cause may be, in fact, fundamentally unsympathetic. According to her rendering of rebellion, those who defy the safeguard of benevolent authority find themselves vulnerable to predatory individuals eager to exploit the lure of autonomy in order to confiscate it. By reminding her audience that constitutional governance functions to protect rather than to undermine personal liberty, the Lady counteracts the criticism of detractors like Price. Her sympathetic depiction of authority—both parental and political—reinforces the British government's position at a time when its legitimacy was being questioned from both within and without.

To be clear, the author of *A Journey* is not attempting to instigate contempt against either the Scottish rebels of days past or against Britain's current rebels across the Atlantic. By cultivating sympathy toward the British government, she does not (like Schaw) simultaneously withhold sympathy from those who have threatened and are threatening its authority. The Lady dismantles revolutionary discourses in order to preserve the unity of her nation, but she maintains a sympathetic attitude toward rebellious subjects that emphasizes their vulnerability rather than their animosity. Price's support of American independence and Ferguson's conservative defense of war both imperil Britain's cohesion; the Lady seeks to find a middle ground that successfully negotiates the prerogatives of government and the rights of its citizens. The complex negotiations required "to make authority and liberty compatible" or "to find surer ground for obligation and obedience than 'the fear of the rod'" was, as Jay Fliegelman argues, "the great challenge of eighteenth-century politics, familial and national."[55] Through her contemplation of rebellion in both familial and political contexts, the Lady attempts to harmonize authority and liberty by supporting a form of benevolent authority that protects individual liberty. The "surer ground" in which this relationship is rooted is sympathy. Her understanding of sympathetic governance is partly contained in the image of the "leading-strings of parental restraint" (5), which visually communicates that the exercise of authority should apply itself in the protection rather than in the oppression of the governed. The Lady's criticism of the chieftains who operate according to a personal rather than a communal consciousness—prioritizing "private ambition" (40) over the good of the community—partners nicely with Adam Smith's argument for the necessity of sympathy within the organization of society. Smith contends that private desires must be regulated to establish a correspondence of sentiments that contributes to the cohesion of society; unmitigated desires introduce a disharmony that fractures relationships.[56] Taking a page out of Smith's book, the Lady suggests that structures of authority must adopt a communal consciousness in order to construct an ethical society bound by the reciprocal imperatives of sympathy. For the author of *A Journey*, war represents a radical absence of sympathy; her delineation of the disharmony introduced by warfare and her corresponding argument for the necessity of sympathy within the functioning of the nation is where we must now turn.

"BLINDNESS OF HEART": MILITARISM AND THE ABSENCE OF SYMPATHY

The author of *A Journey* acknowledges that discussing one political rebellion while Britain is stifling another strays onto sensitive political ground. While discussing the '45, she suddenly avers, "But a truce with politics, they ill become a woman's pen" (22). Her "truce" is deceiving: it appears to convey a temporary cessation of political argument, yet the Lady's self-effacing statement simply diverts attention away from the political undertones of her ensuing observations. While her reflections on rebellion—both personal and political—indirectly dismantle the arguments for independence, her portrayal of Scotland and her biting criticism of Samuel Johnson's travelogue jointly construct a case for why the colonies must be retained and a method by which Britain can ensure their loyalty. The Lady's observations on Scotland reveal her conviction that colonization is essential to national prosperity and progress; her travel letters detail the economic and cultural benefits of political integration for both the center and its peripheries. Like Schaw, her paean to colonization implicitly refutes the argument that Britain should acquiesce and sacrifice its largest collection of colonies. However, unlike her aggressively Tory counterpart, she perceives militarism as an inherently destructive approach to rebellion; her denunciation of war in regard to past Anglo-Scottish hostilities heavily discourages military action as an appropriate response to internecine conflicts. The Lady's sympathetic engagement with Scotland's landscape and its people constructs a model for colonial relations both by demonstrating how Britain should interact with its colonies and by providing an ideological framework for effective colonization. She advocates for the implementation of sensibility as political praxis, suggesting that the form of gentle paternalism that she portrays in her Gretna Green narrative should characterize Britain's transactions with its colonies. By attacking Johnson's response to Scotland, she dismantles what she interprets as an exclusionary politics characterized by the failure of sympathy, cautioning that the alienation of non-English British citizens ultimately weakens the foundations of the British Empire. Her criticism of Johnson suggests that Britons must pursue a politics of inclusion and widen the restricted circumference of British national identity in order to accommodate their rapidly expanding territories and the diversity of their inhabitants.

Following the commencement of military action in the spring of 1775 between the American rebels and the troops on board the ship that Schaw encountered on her Atlantic crossing, the issue of war became central to the debates regarding the American Revolution. Whereas Schaw is heartened to hear of the British victory in the Battle of Bunker Hill just prior to her escape from America,[57] Britons' reaction to the outbreak of war was seriously fractured. Parliament was flooded with both anti-war petitions and pro-war addresses, and pamphlets grappling with the American crisis increased exponentially during this period of political uncertainty.[58] In his 1776 pamphlet "Taxation No Tyranny," Johnson professes to be uncomfortable with the reality of bloodshed, but adopts the particularly Tory argument that punitive measures are necessary to discourage the colonists from further rebellion: "Nothing can be more noxious to society, than that erroneous clemency, which, when rebellion is suppressed, exacts no forfeiture, and establishes no securities, but leaves the rebels in their former state. Who would not try the experiment which promises advantage without expense?"[59] American sympathizers perceived the war either as evidence of their government's increasingly authoritarian personality or as a disastrous political move that would irretrievably alienate the colonies. Criticizing Johnson's pro-war stance in "Taxation No Tyranny" (and his baffling title), Samuel Estwick condemns war against the colonists as distinctly anti-British: "Dictionary Johnson, cries out for fleets and for armies for America; and, treating the body politic, as the French doctors do the body natural, maintains, that the best cure for a fever is to bleed the patient into consumption. This method of cure I had like once to have experienced myself, and therefore may venture to pronounce it a practice ill suited, at least, to an *English constitution.*"[60] Estwick's metaphor conveys the message that British aggression is both reminiscent of French tyranny and perverse given the self-destructive quality of civil war. John Erskine similarly laments the perverse nature of internecine conflict, and argues that reconciliation is only possible through benevolent action: "It is only by gaining the heart, that destroys all inclination to revolt. No victories have such irresistible, happy, and abiding effects, as victories gained by clemency and condescension."[61] The author of *A Journey* subtly intervenes in this popular discussion through historical analogy. As the Lady wanders through ancient Scottish castles and the ruins of the 1745 Jacobite rebellion, she pauses to consider the drawbacks of militant societies, arbitrary power, the consequences of civil conflict, and the advantages of benevolent governance. Her disquisitions on traditional Scottish society steadily build a critique of militarism and her observations on the 1707 Act of Union remind contemporary society of the libertarian principles and sympathetic methods that she believes defined them in the past.

Writing the Earl of C—from an old castle in Dalvey with her Highland adventures behind her, the Lady spends the length of a letter reflecting on the history of violence suggested by the architecture of the castle. "All the castles of this country," she explains, "are built for defence; which precaution was but too necessary in times of civil commotions amongst themselves" (39). The structure's sturdy fortifications "naturally" lead her into a discussion on the nature of the society that built these defenses, and she uses her observations on the castle's aesthetics to launch into a lengthy polemic on the evils of militant societies and arbitrary power. She asserts that pre-Union clan culture was characterized by excessive violence motivated by the unchecked exercise of power. Painting Highland society with a broad brush, she observes that it was "their great delight to harass and distress one another" (36) and attributes this incessant hostility to a hierarchical clan system that enshrined the power of the chieftains. "Every chieftain was absolute monarch," she explains, "by virtue of this authority, however originally obtained, or with whatever tyranny carried on, these chieftains, could with all the supremacy of an oriental potentate, lead forth their slaves to battle" (40). According to the Lady, war was not motivated by the "justice of the cause" or the "propriety of the bloody engagement" but was primarily instigated to "gratify [the chieftain's] private ambition, his envy, or his avarice" (40). Embedded in her condemnation of the clanship system is a trenchant criticism of war. Whereas the Tory administration and pro-war apologists such as Schaw were confident that military action would effectively terrify the colonists into submission and preserve the unity of the British Empire, the author of *A Journey* implies that militancy breeds rather than alleviates aggression. "As is the common practice of war," she pointedly suggests, "to have the power to distress, and the inclination to use that power, [is] exactly one and the same thing" (40). The Lady establishes that war fundamentally produces divisions rather than unity, the evidence of which is manifest in the fortified castles littering Scotland's landscape. "It appears that they were always altercating," she observes, "so that nothing but arms, and structures almost impregnable, could render their persons or property to any degree secure" (39). The impenetrable structures suggest the division accomplished by "civil commotions" (39): the physical barricades symbolize the emotional barricades built by the practice and expectation of violence. Her evocative illustrations suggest that nations built upon violence inevitably self-destruct as communication and connection are unfeasible in the midst of hostility.

Her assessment of the social repercussions of war is reminiscent of Edmund Burke's criticism of civil war in his 1777 pamphlet *A Letter to the Sheriffs of Bristol*. He states, "War suspends the rules of moral obligation, and what is long suspended is in danger of being totally abrogated. Civil wars strike deepest of all into the manners of the people . . . By teaching us to consider our fellow citizens in a hostile light, the whole body of our nation becomes gradually less dear to us. The very names of affection and kindred, which were the bond of charity whilst we agreed, become new incentives to hatred and rage, when the communion of our country is dissolved."[62] The Lady's bleak depiction of clanship society illustrates Burke's belief that civil war creates irreparable schisms by inhibiting sympathy. According to the author of *A Journey*, the chieftains' sense of "moral obligation" to their own community is compromised by their enthusiasm for violence; their "slavish subjects" are reduced to cannon fodder, whom the chieftains recklessly "involve . . . in the calamities of public contest" (40) without regard for their welfare. The Lady's praise of the changes instigated by the Act of Union makes her case for the importance of sympathy in national governance: "Union with England regulated the power, and put an end to the inhospitable bickering of these petty princes, and chieftains. Add to which, the many wise acts since passed, have given a proper proportion of liberty to the commonalty. Industry, civilization, and plenty, are the natural consequence of such political, public measure" (40). In the Lady's clearly whitewashed rendering of the Anglo-Scottish Union and the later Heritable Jurisdictions Act of 1746, England interrupted the cycle of violence perpetuated by the Scottish chieftains by restricting their authority and empowering the people. Her rendition suggests that English governance is characterized by sympathy; unlike the Scottish chieftains, England's leaders prioritize the well-being of their subjects by guaranteeing the security of the "commonalty." The "natural consequences" of a political system grounded in sympathy is "industry, civilization, and plenty" (40).

Whereas the Scottish clan system is described in terms of its insular and destructive qualities, the Lady attributes collaboration and progress to sympathetic governance. Not surprisingly, modern architecture becomes a symbol of the overall improvement produced by the practice of sympathy; she asserts that the "fair and open temper of the times" is reflected in the exposed aesthetic of modern buildings, forming a contrast to the "inhospitality" (12) of the enclosed buildings belonging to a harsher political period. "Everything is now sufficiently displayed," she observes, "and, whatever charges may be brought against the moderns; neither moralist, critic, or cynic will, I believe, reproach them for concealing their possessions" (12). With the protection of property secured by the English government (rather than threatened by arbitrary power) and the emergence of a more sentimental politics reflecting the general flourishing of sympathy within social relations, possessions need not be concealed nor persons protected by physical fortifications. Historical precedent verifies that sympathy as a political practice—other-centered rather than self-centered, outwardly rather than inwardly inclined—is morally, economically, and politically sound.

By 1777, Burke was of the opinion that the British government and its people had abandoned the principles that the Lady describes in her rendition of the Union. "In most of the late proceedings," he laments, "we see very few traces of that generosity, humanity, and dignity of mind which formerly characterized this nation." He blames the growing clamor for war on the "blindness of heart" that "arises from the phrenzy of civil contention."[63] In the midst of this warmongering, the Lady subtly reminds her nation that "generosity, humanity, and dignity of mind" are key to the British government's success as showcased by the stability of the Union. "I dare say there are none," she claims, "who do not rejoice at the friendship which subsists between the two countries" (40). In the political context of 1777, her particular narrative of the Anglo-Scottish Union reads as a call for clemency in Britain's current contest. In the past, the English Parliament focused on neutralizing hostility, or "inhospitable bickering," and extending a "*proper* proportion of liberty to the commonality" (40, emphasis added). Her reflections on the Union serve as a reminder that generosity is an effective political tool. What she interprets as the English government's sympathetic measures ultimately overcame the Scots' initial hesitation ("it was a good while before either the higher or lower degrees of the Scots, could be taught to consider the union of the two kingdoms as either constitutional or salutary" [40]) and yielded a productive friendship. Viewing Fort George near the conclusion of her travels, she reasserts her discomfort with war through her aversion to the armory: "I never can conceive much pleasure in beholding so many instruments of destruction to my fellow-creatures" (44). Her statement emphasizes the human aspect of war: the proudly displayed machines are destroying "fellow-creatures." Her emphasis on the stark reality of violence reminds her readers of the horrors of war in an effort to counteract the "blindness of heart" (149) that grieves Burke.

"SURER GROUND": SYMPATHY AS POLITICAL RESPONSE

The Lady's discomfort with militarism is apparent in her observations on the violence embedded in clan culture and manifest in her reaction to weaponry, but it is in her rigorous criticism of Johnson's 1775 travelogue, *A Journey to the Western Islands of Scotland*, that she most clearly advocates sympathy as a powerful political alternative. As the subtitle of her work suggests (*A Journey to the Highlands of Scotland. With Occasional Remarks on Dr. Johnson's Tour*), the Lady's travelogue is almost as much a disquisition on Johnson's moral failings as it is a reflection on Scotland. Her travelogue is written in the manner of a corrective: lengthy passages enumerating Johnson's errors in judgment, speculating on his malicious motivations, and suggesting his disreputable character are littered throughout the text. The Lady's recorded impressions of Scotland deliberately amend Johnson's interpretation of the northern nation; she even indicates that her travelogue was motivated by a deep-seated desire to vindicate Scotland from those "illiberal aspersions under which they have too long labored" (43). Addressing the Lord of Seaforth, she states, "The intention of the following work, is, to give a just representation of [your] country" (2). Her trenchant criticism of Johnson has served as a focal point for scholars, who interpret her engagement with his travelogue either as a smart commercial move or as a comment on gender. Zoë Kinsley suggests that the Lady's text "is carefully constructed to exploit current reader interest in both the Highlands and in Johnson, and demonstrates an astute understanding of the way in which the literary marketplace works."[64] Marie E. McAllister, on the other hand, perceives a more gendered motivation behind the Lady's criticism, asserting that she is "trying throughout her account to counter the male voice of travel established by generations of male writers before her."[65] I would like to suggest that the juxtaposition the Lady constructs between Johnson and herself acts as a political allegory: the contrast between the two travelers forms a comparison of two competing approaches to imperialism and cultural difference. Careful scrutiny of her condemnation of Johnson and her attempt at reparation through her own observations reveals a profound concern with the prejudicial and imperious attitude that underlies Johnson's judgments. By critiquing Johnson's conduct and correcting his vision, the Lady is condemning an insular form of Englishness that manifests itself as xenophobia. She models an alternative approach to otherness that cultivates connection rather than creates alienation, ultimately proposing an imperial character that extends moral sentiments to those outside of England's reified borders.

Although Johnson's travelogue is not unremittingly unsympathetic toward Scots, his observations do tend to emphasize their weaknesses and failings.[66] The landscape is repeatedly characterized as gloomy, desolate, and unproductive—a "wide extent of hopeless sterility . . . incapable of form or usefulness."[67] He infamously fixates on Scotland's dearth of trees as an indication both of its sterility and of its inhabitants' negligence, declaring that "few regions have been as denuded as this, where many centuries must have passed in waste without the least thought of future supply" (6). The Scottish people are frequently portrayed as incompetent or philistine, their lack of sophistication manifested in their "rude" (83) language, their "incommodious" (14) dwellings, their "mediocr[e]" (119) education, and their uncultivated landscape. Johnson's portrayal of Scotland perpetuates the sense of threat (both economic and political) that England had long associated with its neighbors. In his explicit and implicit comparisons between Scotland and England, the latter is consistently confirmed as the exemplar; Scotland remains uncomfortably foreign for the English traveler.

It is precisely Johnson's perpetuation of this English/Scottish hierarchy that infuriated Scots and even a certain number of Englishmen and women. Discussing the reaction to Johnson's travelogue, Katie Trumpener claims that "the *Journey* was read with bitter indignation by several generations of Scottish readers, for whom it marked the lowest point in Anglo-Scottish relations and served as a lightning rod for nationalist anger."[68] For Scots, Johnson's text epitomized England's attitude toward Scotland; his sense of natural superiority and his criticism of various aspects of Scotland's culture and landscape were taken as an index of England's disdain. Evan Gottlieb observes that Johnson's narrative identity as an objective spectator merely made him appear to his hosts as "yet another overbearing, proto-colonial, southern overseer."[69] Rather than contribute to the fusion of the two nations, Johnson exacerbated Scotland's deep-seated animosities toward England by approaching Scotland with what Gottlieb labels as "a fundamentally superior subject position."[70] As one anonymous Scottish critic bitterly put it, "The flame of national rancour and reproach has been for several years but too well fed—you too have added your faggot, and well deserved the thanks of your friends."[71]

In light of the antagonistic reception of Johnson's text, the Lady's rigorous criticism of Johnson and her own sympathetic portrait of Scotland's landscape and culture read as an act of reparation. Her reference to the "chorus of ironical approbation for the edifying remarks of the great D. J—" (18) demonstrates her knowledge of the hostility with which Johnson's travelogue was received.[72] She willingly joins this "chorus," accusing Johnson of abusing Scottish hospitality by publishing a derogatory account of Scotland intended to affirm England's sense of superiority. "What shall be said of a person," she vents, "who, after many printed confessions of kindness, goes deliberately through an extensive track of country, drinking your drink, eating your bread, reposing on your bed, and then, with premeditated malignity, dipping his goose-quill in gall, and returning to his own country, merely to swell her triumph over that, which cherished him?" (23). The Lady alleges that Johnson deliberately misrepresented Scotland in order to augment English pride, and insists that "those who go on the same road, will soon be convinced, how false an account he has given of a country, to the hospitality of whose inhabitants he owns himself so much obliged" (23). By criticizing what she perceives as Johnson's duplicity, the Lady enters into a sympathetic relationship with the affronted nation; she validates their sense of betrayal and shares their antipathy toward Johnson. Her adoption of Scottish grievances against Johnson evokes a specifically Smithian notion and practice of sympathy. "As we sympathize with the sorrow of our fellow-creature whenever we see his distress," Smith contends, "so we likewise enter into his abhorrence and aversion for whatever has given occasion to it. Our heart, as it adopts and beats time to his grief, so is it likewise animated with that spirit by which he endeavors to drive away or destroy the cause of it."[73] The Lady demonstrates her sympathy by expressing "abhorrence and aversion" toward the source of the Scots' distress; imagining their sense of betrayal, she adopts their resentment and becomes animated by the desire to redress the injuries they have endured. She identifies her text's intervention in nationalist discourse in her bold statement that "nothing but justice for the opprest, could have obliged me to have spoken my sentiments of Dr. J—'s historical *Ramble*; and, for that I have, though a woman, fortitude enough to stand any attack from the pens of *such* critics, in the defence of *our mountainous neighbors*" (48).

Her attempt at reparation does not stop at the condemnation of Johnson's travelogue but is further pursued in her own description of Scotland. The Lady is determined to produce a "just representation" (2) of the nation that gives due recognition to its positive qualities and endeavors to redeem its putatively negative characteristics. She suggests that her consciously sympathetic orientation allows her both to see past the "occasional glooms which seemed to breathe the spirit of melancholy" and anticipate the "gayer and fairer complexion of country [that] always succeeded" (3–4). Distinguishing herself from Johnson and other "literary travellers" who "ever look on the black side of the prospect" (23), the Lady demonstrates an alternative approach to tourism, travel writing, and cross-cultural interaction marked by positivity ("virtue is the growth of every clime!" [43]). Her endorsement of sentimental travel has political implications that extend beyond the individual journey: she is proposing a way of *seeing* the foreign that transforms both the perceiver and the perceived, generating a mutually beneficial relationship that allows for the growth of both national and international relations.

The author of *A Journey* intentionally divests the Highland landscape of its hostility, desolation, and infertility by rewriting it as an Arcadian paradise—the "Elysium of Caledonia" (38), in fact. Under her pen, the Highlands become fecund and pleasing to the cultivated English eye. Nature is abundant in her gifts; the land easily and profusely yields its fruits to its Scottish inhabitants. Describing the landscape near Taymouth, she observes, "This favored spot seems to enjoy every benefit of the boasted South. Nature having poured out her blessings with the hand of profusion; everything appears to grow with the greatest luxuriance" (30). The road between Dunkeld and Blair is "one of the most agreeable [she] ever travelled" and boasts "cornfields, woods of natural oaks, [and] plantations of fir trees" (35). Indeed, the crops she sees in Scotland may even "rival the boasted production of the English soil" (39), and the villages she visits "[are] not inferior to the most cultivated village in England" (38). Her admiration of Scotland's natural wonders—its "noble rivers" (22), the "splendor" of Loch Lomond (16), the "formidable grandeur" of its numerous waterfalls (30), its "Arcadian scenes" (14)—certainly suggests that the landscape may even exceed England in terms of aesthetic beauty. The Lady's descriptions of luxuriant farmland, plentiful trees, and natural wonders are undoubtedly meant to discredit Johnson's portrayal of Scotland—and specifically the Highlands—as a barren wasteland "dismissed by nature from her care and disinherited of her favors, left in its original elemental state" (27). According to this female traveler, the Scottish landscape appears neither foreign nor unproductive. After viewing greenhouses successfully growing exotic plants, she suggests that it is prejudice—not mediocre soil, laziness, or an unmanageable wilderness—that has prevented cultivation: "It is nothing but prejudice which can make us suppose any reason why, with proper care, the plants of all countries may not thrive here as well as in England" (49). Blinded by prejudice, Johnson is unable to perceive the possibility present within the Scottish landscape; his assumption of Scotland's inferiority fundamentally compromises the validity of his observations. The Lady indicates that her comparatively sympathetic orientation opens her eyes, like those of the Scots in recent years, to the "degree of improvement their country [is] capable" (4).

Like her description of the Scottish landscape, the Lady's sketch of its inhabitants is similarly sympathetic and calculated to counter Johnson's portrayal of Scottish society. She removes the threatening and/or foreign features of the Scottish people by portraying them as accomplished, civil, and ultimately similar or superior to the English. The inhabitants of a hut she visits receive her with "untaught good nature and hospitality" (27). Comparing her reception at the hut with her reception at the houses of the "genteel and polished" (28) in English society, she condemns the latter's generosity as often duplicitous; the genteel "smile, and smile, and murder while they smile" (28),[74] while the goodwill of the Scottish peasants is authentic and restorative. Her comparison effects an interesting reversal of cultural stereotypes, locating real personal danger within upper-class English society rather than within Highland communities, so often portrayed as "lawless, primitive and barbaric."[75] The Lady continues to repudiate negative Scottish stereotypes by emphasizing their peaceable society. "There is hardly ever such a thing heard of," she states, "as a Highland robber; their roads are not, like ours, infested by those pests to society" (42–43). She attributes this absence of crime to the superiority of the Scottish legal system, whose judicious administration effectively prevents criminal behavior: "Your purse and your person are equally secure; nor do their news-papers, like ours, shock humanity every month. . . . Their laws are too wisely calculated for the good of the community in general" (43). Her praise of their institutions extends to the organization of their churches, whose ethical administration she claims to be worthy of emulation. Contrasting the deeply hierarchical structure of the Church of England with the Scottish Kirk, she explains that "their church is under most excellent regulation" (43) due to the egalitarian structure of the Presbyterian Church. "Here," she pointedly states, "the clergy are upon an equality" (43).

It is significant that she praises the two institutions that remained under Scottish administration following the Act of Union; she suggests that where the Scots have been allowed a certain amount of self-government, they have surpassed similar English institutions. The Lady infers that the excellence of the courts and the Kirk is ultimately due to the Scots' remarkable natural capabilities. Unlike the South with its addiction to "softening luxuries" (19), Scots are distinguished for their "general habit of œconomy, which, from the highest to the lowest order of men is here characteristic" (20). In addition to their economically and morally sound habits, the Lady is quick to praise their intellectual and cultural talents, which she presents as advantageous to the British nation as a whole. "No country," she confidently claims, "has produced men, more capable of making a shining figure than *Scotland*; as indeed our Senate, our Army, and our Courts, both of justice and politeness can witness" (43–44). Although the Act of Union may have provided the condition of possibility for improvement, the Lady argues that the Scots have been assiduous in their own cultivation. Her final impression of Scotland is that the nation is "making large strides to equal us" and that, speaking both metaphorically and literally, "this once naked country [will] become a towering forest" (49). Whereas Johnson dispiritedly equates the possibility of cultivating the Highlands to seeing the deaf successfully taught arithmetic—challenging, but possible given "courage" (121)—the Lady not only emphasizes that cultivation is *already* underway, but that the Scots have *themselves* undertaken the process of self-improvement. They are neither a threat nor a burden to England, but essential to Britain's progress as a commercial and imperial nation. She carefully establishes a reciprocal rather than hierarchical relationship between the two nations. England may have set the precedent, but Scotland now provides its southern neighbor with lessons in matters economic, moral, social, cultural, and intellectual.

The Lady is certainly not unequivocally positive in her assessment of Scotland, raising objections to clan culture, bagpipes, occasional landscape features (or lack thereof), the peasantry's lack of shoes, and the aesthetics of plaid. Yet despite these objections, she is consistent in her desire to liberate the Scots "from those illiberal aspersions under which they have too long labored" (43), both through her criticism of prejudiced travelers and her comparatively sympathetic description of Scotland. The danger of these "snarlers" is that they "travel not with intent to give the world a fair account of manners and customs, but merely to exaggerate the bad and sink the good" (23). This impulse toward deliberate misrepresentation is a symptom of a greater problem, which the Lady identifies as a lack or circumscription of sympathy in her country's imperial administration. She proposes that Johnson is part of a "set of men, whose prejudices are such, that they think wisdom and worth confined to one spot only, and that spot without doubt, they think *their own*" (43). The "contracted sentiments" (43) of these men have the toxic effect of inhibiting the cultivation of meaningful connections, the repercussions of which threaten the British Empire's very foundations. Focusing on what Scotland lacks, English travel writers have been prevented from seeing the wealth of resources apparent to the sympathetic perceiver. The Lady strategically quotes and agrees with Johnson's own self-assessment that he "cannot but be conscious that my thoughts on national manners are the thoughts of one *who hath seen but little*," and she asserts that with these words Johnson "condemns himself" (48, emphasis added). Her choice of quotation indicates that Johnson's fault lies within his circumscribed vision; the shutters of prejudice have obscured Scotland's potential from his perception. The Lady complains that Johnson and his type—these "querulous gentlemen"—do not grasp that "if the face of the earth was naturally uniform; if destitute of that diversity, which it derives from the hill and valley, the barren heath, the blooming garden, there would neither be any motive to excite the curiosity of the traveller, nor, perhaps, any incentive for one country to connect itself *commercially* with another" (22). Her message is clear: difference is productive, but sympathy is required to perceive value in the foreign and unfamiliar. Echoing Smith, she argues that sympathy has a transformative impact on vision. Moving within the medium of sympathy, Smith's perceiver is able to transcend his particular feelings and perceptions and provisionally feel and perceive in accordance with the object of his sympathy.[76] In *A Journey*, as in *The Theory of Moral Sentiments*, sympathy allows the perceiver to *see* differently. The ultimate advantage of this changed perception is the cultivation of reciprocity; Smith's participants establish social harmony through their emotional and perceptual transformations, while the Lady emphasizes the specifically *commercial* connections enabled by a worldview informed by sympathy.

"INDUSTRY, CONTENT, AND OPULENCE": THE ECONOMICS OF SYMPATHY

The author's connection between sympathy and commerce decisively reveals the politicoeconomic commitments underlying her endorsement of the extension of British moral sentiments. A comparison of Glasgow and Edinburgh early in the text first indicates her investment in the economics of sympathy: "[Glasgow] is, by far, the greatest commercial town in the kingdom, and that very mercantile spirit, produces those effects in the appearance of the people, which commerce never fails to bestow,—industry, content, and opulence; whilst in Edinburgh, there is poverty, and a sort of northern misery in the very feature of the commonalty—*here*, on the contrary, they appear happy, and debonair" (9). Glasgow, she states, is a "modern" (9) city. While Edinburgh's "contracted" design bespeaks and perpetuates a detrimental insularity reminiscent of ancient times, Glasgow's "liberal scale" (9) evinces a generous receptivity to the world characteristic of modernity. Edinburgh's "dirty, dismal, and irregular" (9) design effectively resists incursion; its streets are "narrow" (7) and difficult to navigate, the height of its buildings obscures the sun, and its looming castle appears "impregnable" (8). In contrast, Glasgow's "broad and well paved" streets, "architectural uniformity," and the "spacious" (9) arrangement of buildings creates a hospitable environment for visitors.

The corollaries of Glasgow's openness to and involvement in the world are the twin blessings of happiness and wealth. "Such will ever be the benefits," the Lady promises, "arising from the seats of trade, to every part of mankind" (9). Her comparison of the two cities correlates insularity and inertia, openness and progress; these associations are repeated throughout her travelogue—most notably in her attack on the clan system—building an argument for reciprocity in the socioeconomic progress of the nation. In light of her economic theory, the Lady's criticism of Johnson and the English traveler he typifies suggests itself as a condemnation of an insular definition and practice of "Englishness" that alienates other members of the British nation. Trade is imperative to Britain's progress, but the "contracted sentiments" (43) of Englishmen, like Edinburgh's "contracted" design, ultimately repel outsiders and inhibit growth. Alternatively, openness to difference—manifested in Glasgow's "liberal" composition and demonstrated in the Lady's sentimental orientation—successfully establishes vital connections that stimulate progress.

Glasgow's success had been built on its commercial connections with the Atlantic trading network. The city was the center and direct beneficiary of the tobacco and tar trade, commodities that were almost exclusively produced in the southern American colonies.[77] Scottish merchants dominated the tobacco trade in the years leading up to the American Revolution, with Scotland receiving 52 percent of all British tobacco imports by 1769.[78] Streets and houses named after American colonies and powerful tobacco merchants ("Virginia Street," "Virginia House," "Buchanan Street," "Ingram Street") served as reminders of the American source of Glasgow's success.[79] Whether or not the Lady was consciously aware of the financially beneficial relationship between Glasgow and America, her enumeration of the benefits the city accrued through trade certainly implies the importance of Britain's Atlantic trading networks. Her glowing depiction of Glasgow's wealth illustrates why Britain should accommodate its colonies: to maintain the economic partnership that has generated Glasgow's "opulence," "happ[iness]," and "content" (9). Her emphasis on the importance of trade relations and on a spirit of liberality as opposed to illiberalism in national relations suggests that the British government would do well to once again extend a "proper proportion of liberty to the commonalty" (40). Her comparison of Edinburgh and Glasgow on the basis of their relational character and commercial activity poses a question to her British audience: Which example shall the nation follow?

"INDELICATE CREATURES": RESISTING SENTIMENTAL FEMININITY

Given *A Journey*'s condemnation of damaging stereotypes that preclude those targeted from full participation within the nation, it is perhaps unsurprising that its female author also challenges the misrepresentation of women within eighteenth-century culture. The Lady's travelogue is not only invested in defining Britain's national character and positioning Scots within the nation, it is also actively involved in (re)defining femininity and querying the place of women within the nation. Her text shows an acute awareness of what eighteenth-century society deemed to be feminine and unfeminine. She introduces her letters with a long justification of her foray into the unfeminine territory of Paternoster Row, a center of the London publishing trade. The Lady assures her audience that her travels did not divorce her from the domestic sphere; indeed, her mind remained "untravelled," clinging to the "domestic circle" (3) she left behind. Accordingly, she suggests that her original letters from Scotland should be interpreted as physical manifestations of her connection to home rather than as threatening symbols of her mobility. She explains that the publication of her correspondence is the result of the intervention of an eager friend, who secured an offer of publication by furtively submitting the Lady's original letters into the hands of a "literary gentleman" (4). Her account of the publication process insists that *A Journey* is the product of obedience (an admirable feminine trait) as opposed to ambition (an unequivocally unfeminine trait). The apologetic undertone of the Lady's preface acknowledges that both her mobility and her literary production come dangerously close to transgressing gender boundaries; she distances her physical and literary adventures from a politics of dissent by repeatedly acknowledging and affirming proscribed gender roles. Thus, after criticizing Scottish political dissidents, she apologizes to her reader for her politically inflected outburst, demurring that "politics . . . ill become a woman's pen" (22) and promising that she will subsequently refrain from broaching political controversy. "I know not a more ridiculous figure," she continues, "than a petticoat pedant, or politician" (22). The Lady disassociates herself from the figure of the female politician in her readers' imaginations by drawing explicit attention to the comic nature of the "petticoat pedant." She acknowledges gender boundaries to deflect suspicions that she is participating in similarly transgressive behavior, appeasing her audience by creating a distinction between herself and the manifestly political woman.

Yet by announcing the incompatibility of women and political conflict, she effectively draws attention to the fact that she is engaging in political discourse; and although she apologizes for her political tangent, *she does not omit it.* Despite her resistance to the figure of the female politician, she posits that moral exigency and sentiment both demand and justify her political involvement. The Lady asserts that her feelings "irresistibly" (22) led to her political reflections on the Jacobite rebellion. The spontaneous and inexorable nature of her emotions vindicates their expression, she informs her audience: "When a woman *sets her heart upon any thing* . . .'tis not in nature, or argument, to make her easy" (9). Likewise, she excuses her political intervention in Anglo-Scottish relations by insisting that her involvement is impelled by a sense of moral responsibility. "I have, though a woman," she contends, "fortitude enough to stand any attack . . . in the defence of *our mountainous neighbors*" (48). She characterizes her intervention as an ethical imperative rather than as political dissidence; to ignore her responsibility toward an injured people would be tantamount to participating in their abuse. Becoming a "petticoat politician" in order to defend Johnson's victims is the lesser of two evils, comparatively less questionable than ignoring their suffering in the name of propriety.

That her sensibility demands and justifies her political intervention ultimately complicates her mockery of the female politician; the Lady's theoretical affirmation of contemporary gender roles is contradicted within her own practice. By configuring sensibility as a political praxis that assists in the administration and integration of the British Empire, she is able to propose the particular fitness of women within imperial politics. Her self-positioning in relation to Johnson suggests her comparative facility both for the work of sociopolitical analysis demanded by the travelogue genre and the complex negotiations demanded by national and imperial politics. It is Johnson who ultimately cuts a "ridiculous figure" (22) rather than the female author who dares to address politics; he is "totally unfit for the task he undertook" (48), while the Lady's fitness for the task of political mediation is implied through her ability to correct Johnson's lapses in judgment. The superiority she demonstrates within the province of national and imperial relations calls into question her laughter at the "petticoat pedant" and suggests its function as a clever literary mechanism for obscuring her own political purposes. Her mockery of politicized women capitulates to her society's standards of femininity, yet her own actions ultimately resist those standards and suggest the broader faculties of women. Sensibility becomes the tool of her empowerment rather than the source of her marginalization; by establishing the relevance of the feeling heart beyond the domestic sphere, she also establishes the relevance of women outside of the home.

Her subtle derision of gender expectations throughout her text obliquely indicates her own personal objections to restrictive definitions of femininity. After using the word "horticulture," she teases "surely I may in *my* journey, my dear, be allowed one hard word" (13), and, prior to using the word "extravagantly," she pronounces—tongue-in-cheek—that she will now use a "woman's word" (14). The Lady's playful contempt of the gender expectations inscribed in language suggests her skepticism of eighteenth-century definitions of femininity. Like Schaw, she also deplores the affectation of female weakness, censuring women who internalize their socially constructed helplessness. Admiring the exertion of a "Scotch woman" who walked twelve miles in a day, she declares, "I think I hear some fine lady amongst my own countrywomen, who affect to be tired with a couple of turns in the Mall, exclaim, Oh! What horrid, indelicate creatures must those women be that could *form* such a plan, much less *execute* it! But I know you will join me in despising the affectation of those females who think, because indulgent Fortune has thrown a coach in their power, they are not to make use of the gifts Nature has bestowed" (16). These moments reveal that her attitude toward femininity is not as conventional or as unambiguous as she would have her audience believe. She balks at the intellectual and physical limitations both imposed upon and perpetuated by women, and her resistance suggests the inaccuracy of contemporary definitions of femininity.

The Lady's self-exclusion from the typical sentimental categorization of women as objects of pity or desire contributes to her suggestion that women as well as Scots are laboring under specious representations. Mobile, single, childless, and with no romantic attachments or aspirations, she cannot be neatly grouped into any of the conventional sentimentalized images of women. She carefully wards off her possible objectification as an object of desire by emphasizing her relative unattractiveness in comparison to other females: "The ladies here are the great *sublime in beauty*, most of their favourite toasts being five feet eight, or even nine. Methinks, I hear you laugh, and say, what chance stands my little lively friend? Why, they look at me with as much wonder as did the Brobdignags at Gulliver, and spare me, I suppose, out of compassion to my diminutiveness: in my turn I am content, their beaus being much too *high*, to raise in me an aspiring expectation" (8). The Lady further reminds her correspondent—who appears to be inquiring into her romantic life—that her "province is to make *remarks* not *conquests*" (39). Similar to Schaw, she subverts the objectification of women within sentimental literature by assuming the position of the subject rather than the object; as an eyewitness and a producer of knowledge, she occupies a position of authority that challenges a gender hierarchy based upon the presumed inferiority of women. In a text that repeatedly condemns divisive cultural hierarchies and exclusive social practices, it seems possible that the Lady's alternate performance of femininity offers a rebuttal to the distortions that justify the exclusion of women from various facets of public life.

POINTS OF CONNECTION

The Lady's mobility is key to her political project; her movement across and narration of the nation impacts the manner in which her readers imagine Britain. She enacts on a national scale Thomas Gisborne's injunction to women to foster "ties of connection" within their local communities.[80] Travel extends her sense of community—the "domestic circle" (3) of which she speaks—to encompass her Scottish neighbors, and extends her conciliatory role beyond the local to the national. I close this investigation of *A Journey* with a final example to clarify how the Lady's act of travel and her political ideology intersect to promote her vision of a unified nation.

The Lady marks her entrance into Scotland with a seemingly innocuous comment on the Great North Road: "Nothing need to be said about the road between England and this place, it being so universally known" (6). Penny Fielding's explanation of the symbolic significance of the Anglo-Scottish border and of the Great North Road as "the principle topographic figures on which the social geometrics of the nation rest" suggests that the Lady's focus on the road rather than the border can be read as a political statement.[81] "The road and the border," Fielding argues, "provide a visible shape to the nation. . . . The border marks the distinction between England and Scotland while the Great North Road traces their union."[82] The Lady's focus on points of connection (the road) rather than points of division (the border) between England and Scotland distinguishes her work from that of her predecessors and could be interpreted as part of her effort to shape the British nation into a unified space. Both Daniel Defoe and Thomas Pennant specifically emphasize their act of border crossing and invest their movement between England and Scotland with a sense of transition rather than of continuity. Defoe's description of the Anglo-Scottish border accentuates the cultural gulf between the two nations. "When we entered upon the *Scotish* Borders," he writes, "the first Town we came to is almost as perfectly *Scots*, as if you were 100 Miles North of *Edinburgh*; and there is very little Appearance of any thing *English* there."[83] A generation later, Pennant reinforces this image of Scotland as a distinctly foreign space. He observes that, compared with the English landscape which precedes it, "the entrance into *Scotland* has a very unpromising look"[84] and likens the appearance of Scotland to "the work of a new colony, in a wretched impoverished country."[85] The Lady's comparative silence on the experience of "crossing over" suggests both geographical and cultural continuity, which indicates that the space between England and Scotland lacks the visible contrast noted by Defoe and Pennant. By minimizing her act of border crossing, she effectively diminishes the sense of difference between the two nations; her alternate emphasis on the road rather than on the border spatially configures Scotland as part of the national space. "Roads homogenize the nation," Fielding argues, "reducing the difference between centre and periphery, urban and rural; they facilitate 'carriage' and the circulation of commodities and capital in continuous motion."[86] The Lady's sentimental journey maps Britain in terms of its points of connection rather than division, a configuration that disrupts the violence enabled through the reification of cultural barriers.

Not long after the Lady published her travelogue, Burke conceded that reconciliation between Britain and its American colonies seemed increasingly unlikely given the division that had grown between the two nations. "But," he stated, "this we know with certainty, that though we cannot reclaim them, we may reform ourselves. If measures of peace are necessary, they must begin somewhere; and a conciliatory temper must precede and prepare every plan of reconciliation."[87] Burke's statement articulates directly what the author of *A Journey* expresses indirectly in her sentimental travelogue. She uses her narrative identity, representation of Scotland, criticism of Johnson, and subtle revision of femininity to weave a complex argument for a reformed British national identity that mirrors her sentimental orientation and urges her audience to develop a national character that is open to the diversity encompassed by Britain's expanding borders. Following in the philosophical track of Adam Smith, she quietly argues that sympathy is necessary to establish a stable, harmonious society. Smith warned his eighteenth-century audience that the absence of sympathy in social relationships creates irreparable fractures through the breakdown of communication: "If you have no fellow-feeling for the misfortunes I have met with," he states, "or none that bear any proportion to the resentment which transports me, we can no longer converse upon these subjects. We become intolerable to one another. I can neither support your company, nor you mine."[88] The Lady's criticism of xenophobia manifests a belief in the necessity of sympathy that mirrors Smith's contention: if the English approach their peripheries without a "conciliatory temper,"[89] they risk alienating those to whom they are "so much obliged" (23). The high cost of colonial alienation was being demonstrated across the Atlantic as she wrote her reflections. In the absence of sympathy, Britons and Americans were becoming "intolerable" to one another, and the Lady evinces a specific concern with the economic implications for the empire if Britain does not adopt the "conciliatory temper" urged by Burke and espoused within the Lady's travelogue. With the British increasingly favoring intimidation over sympathy in their response to their American colonists, the Lady chooses to critique forms of authority that assert themselves through physical or emotional violence. She strategically suggests the moral failure and the destructive consequences of an imperial politics that establishes itself upon the exclusion and/or subjugation of another people. Her criticism argues for a constructive approach to otherness that cultivates fusion rather than friction, connection rather than division. Surveying the landscape of the once rebellious Scottish nation, she finds evidence for Burke's belief that sentimental ties "though light as air, are as strong as links of iron."[90]

The redefinition of Britain according to shared sympathies rather than geographical boundaries is continued in the work of Mary Morgan, whose 1795 travelogue is the subject of Chapter 4. However, the decades between the Lady's Scottish tour and Morgan's Welsh excursion saw a shift in the political climate away from the culture of sensibility, and the female sentimental travel writers publishing in the final decade of the eighteenth century were forced to navigate a culture that was increasingly suspicious of sentimental forms of expression. The Enlightenment interpretation of humans as reservoirs of emotion was not denied by late eighteenth-century society, but it was reconceived as a potentially fearful property as sensibility was increasingly aligned with socially destructive desires. Emotions became a facet of one's character to be overcome or disciplined into submission. Katherine Turner argues that, given the hostility toward the culture of sensibility in the 1790s, British travel writers (particularly those writing about Europe) shied away from Sterne's emotionally flamboyant style and increasingly turned toward "a narrative persona which [was] textually and ideologically bland enough to function as a representative of the newly defensive variety of British common sense."[91] Yet despite the politically suspect status of sentimentalism, a steady stream of sentimental travel writers seeps through the cracks of political conformity throughout the 1790s, for some of whom emotional expression still functioned as a powerful method of political persuasion (which is, of course, one of the reasons it was feared in the combustible final decade of the eighteenth century) and for others feeling still registered as a necessary correlative of politics. Morgan falls into the latter category; despite a rather fashionable distaste for excessive sensibility, she evinces a profound concern with the increasing alienation of feeling from politics in the 1790s. Like the Lady of *A Journey*, Morgan's sentimental persona forms part of her political statement; she resists the pressure to fashion an emotionally neutral character, instead articulating the dangers associated with the *absence* of sensibility within a culture precariously balancing on the knife-edge of political revolution.

Part Three

SENSIBILITY IN DISTRESS

Female Sentimental Travel Writers and the French Revolution

4

REVITALIZING SENSIBILITY

Mary Morgan's Defense of Emotional Engagement in *A Tour to Milford Haven*

MARY MORGAN'S *A Tour to Milford Haven, in the Year 1791* (1795) was published during the escalation of a new revolution—this time located in France rather than America—the events of which instigated a period of political volatility within Britain generated by the dangerous interplay between revolutionary fervor and political repression. Although Morgan and the anonymous author of *A Journey to the Highlands of Scotland* traveled in different periods and under the threat of different revolutions, the circumstances and the ideological motivations of their travels are similar: Morgan, as with the mysterious Lady, leaves England's tumultuous urban center for its rural retreats, searching for vestiges of a harmonious Britain during a period marked by sociopolitical turmoil. While drawn to the equally appealing prospects of sublimity and stability promised by Britain's Celtic fringe, both travel writers implicitly conceptualize their journeys and letters as political acts; their movement through and re-presentation of the national space participates in binding the disparate communities that constitute Britain in what Benedict Anderson refers to as a "deep, horizontal comradeship."[1] Their sentimental appeal to the idea of a nation bound by ties of affection and experienced as a symbiotic relationship counteracts what they perceive as the revolutionary and reactionary impulses toward national fragmentation. Like her anonymous predecessor, Morgan does not write her travelogue as an escape from political reality; rather, her exposure to Britain's social, political, and historical landscape enables her to construct an informed response to the spectacle of national disorder occurring at the time of her peregrinations and publication.

However, whereas the anonymous author of *A Journey* attempts to foster sympathetic relations between England and its colonies, Morgan's political aim is more localized. Given that the revolutionary threat against the British establishment was largely emanating from Britain's disenfranchised middle and working classes, Morgan's text focuses on strengthening what Vicesimus Knox, an apologist for British political reform, refers to as "the sentiment of affection" between Britain's ruling class and those subject to its power.[2] "Loyalty seems, in its common acceptation," Knox observes, "to include in it also a sentiment of affection. It is the obedience of love, and anticipates compulsion. It is a sentiment which all men will feel, when they live under a good government, honestly administered."[3] Morgan shares Knox's political persuasion that social cohesion is the responsibility of the ruling class. She places direct responsibility for the preservation of Britain's hierarchical structure upon the conduct of the aristocracy, whom she charges with the maintenance of sympathetic relations among the various classes. Her travel observations provide a salient critique of Britain's aristocratic governance by identifying the fault lines within court government and culture—namely, a marked tendency toward materialism, social detachment, and a defensive posture that was readily apparent in the British government's politics of terror throughout the 1790s. Morgan's disapproval of aristocratic corruption participates in the late eighteenth-century conservative campaign to reform the manners of the elite in order to ensure their preservation. The 1780s saw the flourishing of what Joanna Innes calls a "comprehensive programme of moral reform" that culminated in King George III's Royal Proclamation for the Encouragement of Piety and Virtue, and for the Preventing and Punishing of Vice, Profaneness and Immorality in 1787 and the subsequent formation of the Proclamation Society, whose purpose was to translate the king's proclamation into action.[4] Although the campaign was focused on the moral reformation of the poor, there was also a significant push for the reformation of the manners of the elite, as their behavior set the precedent for the rest of society.[5] The French Revolution politicized the campaign in new ways; in particular, the intense scrutiny under which the British aristocracy found themselves in the face of France's egalitarianism underscored the importance of polishing their image. M. O. Grenby claims that "the disquieting recognition that corrupt aristocracy lay behind the Revolution . . . underlay the new urgency added to the campaign for the reform of the corruption of the elite in the 1790s."[6] Morgan's strategic condemnation of aristocratic decadence and detachment demonstrates the sense of urgency that Grenby describes; her observations regarding Britain's hierarchy suggest that change must come from within the aristocracy before it is enforced from without.

Morgan's late eighteenth-century context presents an additional challenge in the form of an emergent culture of anti-sentimentalism that threatened the cultural capital of sensibility and the sociopolitical value of sympathy. Similar to Edmund Burke's conservative defense of Britain's political system in *Reflections on the Revolution in France* (1790)—a book with which Morgan was familiar[7]—she perceives and portrays the nation as a collection of interconnected relationships extending from the primordial to the political. Accordingly, she believes that national instability is the direct result of social, economic, or political ideologies and practices that destroy the affective ties that facilitate Britain's social hierarchy. She attributes the erosion of these affective ties in 1790s Britain not only to the aristocracy's abandonment of their socially conciliatory duties, but also to the diminishing sociopolitical value of sensibility. Fundamental to her project, then, is a defense of sensibility as both a social value and a political praxis at a time when sensibility and its attendant practices were being unceremoniously pushed to the margins of society.

Morgan's adoption of the then increasingly unfashionable persona of the sentimental traveler in *A Tour to Milford Haven* announces her commitment to sensibility and allows her to advertise its valuable properties. Her travels and travelogue are a testament to her rich social and emotional life; her journey is motivated by the promise of renewing old relationships, her letters are both products and affirmations of the sentimental connections she shares with her friends, and their publication demonstrates the productive power of friendship. Whereas other eighteenth-century travel writers tend to locate the motivations for their Welsh journeys in more academic interests such as botany, geography, antiquarianism, and ethnography,[8] the purpose of Morgan's four-month trip from her home in Ely, England, to her husband's birthplace in South Wales is explicitly social and sentimental. "We have two things in view in this journey," she explains, "the first is, to visit friends we have long wished to see, and the next, to enjoy the prospects of a much-admired and picturesque country, without hurry or interruption" (4). The travelogue's form supports the relational nature of her journey. The hefty volume is comprised of sixty-two letters to twelve different correspondents, enabling Morgan to write in a personal register that both suggests and creates intimacy. In turns gossipy and reflective, and teeming with literary quotations and flights of fancy that reveal a deeply romantic sensibility, her letters read as a warm conversation with her close circle of friends. Morgan attributes the publication of *Milford Haven* to these friends, explaining that her foray into print was made possible through their personal encouragement and financial investment: "They all separately desired to have my *Tour* complete," she notes, "they also proposed, that I should publish by subscription, that their names might give a sanction to my appearing in print" (viii). She portrays both her journey and her publication as communal endeavors, representing the nation as an extended community and reminding her audience of the beauty and benefits of sentimental connections.

Responding to a culture that she suspects is becoming increasingly alienated through the disintegration of sentimental ties, Morgan strives to transform her personal knowledge of the positive effects of fellow feeling into political argument. She observes the impact of emotional deadening in the violent actions of the French mob, the unscrupulous thievery of pillagers on the Welsh coast, the appetite for war in Britain's military leaders, and even in her culture's active repression of women. Throughout *Milford Haven*, Morgan gathers evidence for the importance of sensibility within social relations by witnessing the repercussions of its presence or absence on the microcosmic societies found inside the estates that define Britain's landscape. By interpreting Morgan's travelogue through her personal context of her elite Anglican circle, her immediate political context of the British reaction to the French Revolution, and her cultural context of the trenchant anti-sentimentalism pervading Britain in the 1790s, her detailed observations on Britain's modern country homes and ancient ruins emerge as studies of the sociopolitical systems, practices, and behaviors that maintain or disrupt community. She submits the revitalization of sensibility as a corrective to the cycle of violence that she sees operating in Britain's past and threatening to reemerge in its present—the impulse to "pull[] down others" (418) in an effort to arrogate or maintain power.

MARY MORGAN: A "HEART . . . TOO FULL OF SENSIBILITY"

Morgan's linked commitments to Britain's receding culture of sensibility, its traditional social order, and to the active participation of women within this order were undoubtedly shaped by the intersecting cultures of conservative politics, bluestocking intellectualism, and Anglicanism that constituted her elite society. Although the details of her life are scant, a few telling particulars can be gleaned from her obituary and from the three texts that she published during her lifetime. The politically conservative character of the largely Anglican circles in which Morgan circulated is evident from the details of her social milieu sketched out in the subscription list that fronts *Milford Haven*: the list is replete with members of the gentry, aristocracy, and Anglican clergy—many of whom had a vested interest in preserving Britain's hierarchical structure. The impressive caliber of the subscription list caught the attention of a critic in *The Monthly Review*, who notes with approbation that "the list is a very handsome one."[9] Her husband, Rev. Caesar Morgan, was a high-ranking member of the Anglican clergy whose published sermons advertise his commitment to preserving the social hierarchy that protected his privilege. His publications generally coincide with major political events and preach active patriotism and due regard for authority in the face of political unrest.[10] However, like Mary Morgan's travelogue, his publications betray a concern with what he perceives as a toxic tendency toward profligacy and dissipation in Britain's upper ranks; his sermons frequently serve to remind Britain's ruling class of their duty to model responsible citizenship and to pursue social amelioration through philanthropy. Rev. Morgan's politically conservative ideology is indicative of his wife's political leanings, and Mary's support of conservative politics is further confirmed by her personal friendship with and keen support of Matthew Montagu (née Robinson)—a Tory Member of Parliament who was also Elizabeth Montagu's nephew and heir. Matthew Montagu was resolutely pro-establishment and anti-revolution in his political views,[11] and Mary makes her affinity with his politics known through her written praise of his political work. To one of her many correspondents in *Milford Haven*, she says that he was "deserving of more than I venture to say of him" (16) and proceeds to thank her correspondent for sending copies of Matthew Montagu's most recent parliamentary speech.

Morgan's avid interest in parliamentary politics demonstrates her sense of women's significance as agents of transformation (or reformation); as she declares in her travelogue, "I would not . . . have them stand by unconcerned spectators of what is passing in the world" (286). Her travel letters consistently emphasize women's abilities rather than their weaknesses, and her obituary celebrates rather than diminishes her own intellectual achievements, listing her "vigorous understanding" and "brilliant genius" alongside her publication of *Milford Haven* (it fails to mention her chapbook *Mary, the Osier-Peel, a Simple but True Story*, published in 1798, and her editorial work on a putatively ancient poem, *The Knyghte of the Golden Locks*, published in 1799).[12] Her belief in the sociopolitical efficacy of women can be traced to her integration within the bluestocking circle, which provided her with a supportive environment that affirmed her sense of women's powerful potential and aided her intellectual pursuits as both author and editor.[13] "Through friendship and patronage," Elizabeth Eger states, "bluestocking women formed their own distinctive intellectual networks, or 'circles' of learning, as a means of overcoming some of the prejudices and constraints they experienced."[14] The emboldening influence of this invigorating network of both male and female intellectuals can be seen in Morgan's defense of female authorship. Dismissing the idea that women are "formed merely to dress and be admired, or for domestic drudgery," she firmly retorts that "these notions have long ago been exploded by people of polite manners and liberal education" (ix). Her own publications were not only inspired by the liberating bluestocking belief in "freedom of enquiry irrespective of nature or gender,"[15] but were also generously endorsed by her relationships within the bluestocking community. The subscription list for *Milford Haven* reveals that two prominent bluestocking hostesses, Elizabeth Montagu and Frances Boscawen, both ordered editions of the travelogue, with Montagu ordering a rather extravagant ten copies. Morgan's editorial work on *The Knyghte of the Golden Locks* was aided by her friendship with Ellis Cornelia Knight's family, in whose library she purports to have first discovered her love for ancient poetry.[16] Morgan's travelogue is, in turn, an expression of her investment in the practice and promotion of female intellectual and creative development. "As a female," she argues in her preface, "I have certainly no occasion to excuse my temerity, so many of my sex have shewn they are capable of the most admirable compositions on the most important subjects" (ix). She supports this assertion throughout her travelogue, commending Elizabeth Montagu's scholarship (42, 48), endorsing Ellis Cornelia Knight's and Sarah Scott's novels (15, 38, 112), and praising Anna Laetitia Barbauld's and Sarah Trimmer's children's literature (321).

While Morgan's immersion within the bluestocking circle fostered her sense of women's value, her specifically Anglican religious context further provided her with a deep sense of women's moral obligation to virtuous action. The extent to which this belief both sanctioned and consecrated the involvement of women in public life can be seen in Morgan's obituary, which positions her intellectual activity as a form of faithful labor.[17] "Her conduct through life," the author muses, "conspicuously shewed what a grace, what an odour of sanctity, the practice of domestic virtues, and the duties of religion and humanity, diffuse over a vigorous understanding, a brilliant genius, an elegant taste, and a lively wit."[18] The interweaving of Morgan's religious and intellectual activity in her obituary speaks to the ways religious duty could be used to validate female intellectual activity. Morgan contextualizes her act of publication within religious motivations, asserting that "there is no reason why I should not depicture scenes that have so often elevated my ideas, and awakened in me a thousand moral and religious sentiments" (x). Perhaps more importantly, however, the moderating effect that Morgan's religiosity serves within her obituary extends beyond her intellectualism to her sensibility. That her sense of moral obligation was fundamentally intertwined with an active, intuitive sympathy is evident from the inclusion of one of Morgan's poems that reflects upon the pain associated with possessing a "heart . . . / Too full of Sensibility."[19] The obituary goes on to emphasize the impact of her sympathetic nature within her community, noting that "the lamentations of the rich and poor at the time of her decease, bore unequivocal testimony to her affectionate disposition towards her friends, and her attentions to the wants of the distressed."[20] Karen O'Brien's observation that eighteenth-century Anglican female intellectuals "came to understand benevolence not as a delusion of egotism . . . but as the main business of a virtuous, socially purposeful life" helps to illuminate the ways in which Morgan (and the author of her obituary) understood a sensitive *emotional* constitution as inextricable from a *moral* constitution.[21]

Morgan's "heart . . . / Too full of Sensibility" is on full display in *Milford Haven*, and the sentimental voice she adopts in her travelogue recalls the social personality and emotional vitality of Laurence Sterne's sentimental traveler. Her interest in the interpersonal and anecdotal (derided by her critics as "trifling and common incidents"[22]) and the contemplative pace of her travels (she states her intention to travel "without hurry or interruption" [2]) contain shades of Yorick. Morgan's orientation toward sympathy is manifested in her professed commitment to cultural sensitivity; in her preface, she immediately asserts her "difference of opinion" from those who characterize the Welsh "to be an ignorant and uncivilized set of people" (xiii) and is relatively consistent in her positive portrayal of the Welsh—liberally complimenting their language (151, 254, 366) and culture (255–264). Similar to Yorick's contention that sentimental travel permits the discovery of authenticity,[23] Morgan locates the benefit of a sentimental orientation in its ability to perceive truth rather than perpetuate stereotypes:

> Travelers, who only run through a country, perfect strangers to every body in it, take their notions of people from inn-keepers, and, with a degree of arrogance and folly hardly to be conceived in persons who set up for delineators of manners, positively set a place down for good or bad, for polite or uncivilized, just as the inns at which they stop happen to be comfortable or not, or the landlord obliging, or the contrary. To discover the genius, disposition, and natural bent of a people, requires a much longer acquaintance with them than a night's stay at an inn. (xiv)

Her censure of the disengaged traveler mirrors Yorick's critique of Mundungus—who "travell'd straight on, looking neither to his right hand or his left lest love or pity should seduce him out of his road"[24]—and likewise suggests sympathy not only as a precondition for true knowledge but also as the true purpose of travel. Morgan attributes her sympathy to a responsive sensibility, and it is her admission and performance of a sentimental disposition that most clearly categorizes her as a sentimental traveler. "I never remember that time in my life," she claims, "when I could laugh at the sufferings of a fellow-creature, whether deserved or undeserved, real or imaginary. However, I took great care to conceal these emotions, taking it to be a great defect in my nature, that I should be ready to weep at what diverted every body else" (433–434). As this statement reveals, she does not attempt to "conceal" her emotions within her travelogue but rather demonstrates her emotional sensitivity to confer value onto a quality that was being increasingly derided within British culture.

The newly suspect nature of sensibility in the tumultuous 1790s is apparent in the reviews for *Milford Haven*, all of which take some issue with her travelogue's sentimental style. Both *The Gentleman's Magazine* and *The British Critic* criticize the subjective nature of Morgan's observations. The reviewer for *The Gentleman's Magazine* complains that "[she] has made the most of her book by trifling and common incidents, and now and then a marvelous story,"[25] while the reviewer for *The British Critic* dismissively states that "very trifling events are interesting to the parties concerned, but the mass of readers are very little affected by 'the joys or sorrows of a chaise and one.'"[26] *The Monthly Review* is far more generous in its appraisal of Morgan's text; the travelogue's subjective style, so disparaged by *The Gentleman's Magazine* and *The British Critic*, is the quality admired by the reviewer in the *Monthly Review*. The critic commends Morgan's "great sensibility of temper and disposition," applauds her episodes of sympathetic identification (they do "honour to her feelings"), and invests her personable/personal style with the power of persuasion ("Mrs. Morgan has a vivacity and good humour in her manner, which engage the attention and frequently interest the heart of the reader").[27] Yet the review ends by cautioning that the "natural and easy style" espoused by Morgan shades into "that affectation of sentiment and flippancy of language which of late years have infected many of our good writers of travels."[28]

That all three reviews of *Milford Haven* evince varying degrees of antipathy toward her sentimental orientation is indicative of the increasing social condemnation of sensibility in the eighteenth-century's final decade. Katherine Turner suggests that the shift away from sentimental travel writing in this period is "symptomatic of the extent to which affective terminology (especially 'sensibility') is increasingly associated within dissidence during the 1790s."[29] The moral threat associated with sentimental fiction in the 1780s quickly became a political one following the eruption of the French Revolution in 1789 and its escalation under the leadership of Maximilien de Robespierre and the Jacobins. Britons at opposite ends of the political spectrum alternately accused one another and the French revolutionaries of lacking sensibility or of possessing it in spades; feeling became simultaneously entangled with revolutionary excess and with reactionary regression. Although contemporary scholarship continues to struggle over the meaning and status of sensibility in the 1790s, the majority of scholars tend to agree that the culture of sensibility that dominated British society in the last half of the eighteenth century eventually retreated under the pressure of political events. "By the end of the century," Chris Jones argues, "the concept [of sensibility] and its associated vocabulary were virtually unusable except for the purposes of satire."[30] Yet it would be a mistake to assume that sensibility and its associated concepts failed to exert an influence in the eighteenth-century's troubled final decade; indeed, the controversy regarding sensibility formed a central component of what became known as the "Revolution Debate."[31]

THE REVOLUTION DEBATE AND THE POLITICS OF SENSIBILITY

The language of feeling dominated early responses to the French Revolution; conservatives and radicals alike put sensibility and its attendant practices in the service of their disparate political agendas. In Edmund Burke's *Reflections on the Revolution in France*, the former defender of the American cause flagrantly draws on sentimental tropes and language to excoriate the French Revolution and to shore up Britain's hierarchical system. Reacting to Britons' early enthusiasm for the revolution and to the reignited push for parliamentary reform instigated by France's political transformation, Burke defends Britain's constitutional monarchy by naturalizing sentimental attachments to prevailing power structures and by demonizing the French revolutionaries as dangerously *un*sentimental. "In England," he asserts, "we preserve the whole of our feelings still native and entire. . . . We have real hearts of flesh and blood beating in our bosoms. We fear God; we look up with awe to kings; with affection to parliaments; with duty to magistrates; with reverence to priests; and with respect to nobility. Why? Because when such ideas are brought before our minds, it is *natural* to be so affected."[32] Burke sanctions loyalty to traditional structures of authority by claiming the organic nature of these hierarchical relations; his statement that "no cold relation is a zealous citizen" (198) encapsulates his idea that national loyalty is simply a natural extension of private affections. Burke casts aspersions upon the French Revolution by accusing its leaders of emotional vacuity; they are men unnaturally constituted of "cold hearts and muddy understandings" (77) who have "perverted in themselves, and in those that attend them, all the well-placed sympathies of the human breast" (65). He exposes the danger of France's new system and its callous disciples in his infamously sentimental depiction of Marie Antoinette's near assault at the hands of the angry French mob and the royal family's forcible removal from Versailles. The desecration of the domestic space (the queen's bedchamber), the assault on the innocent and vulnerable (the queen and her children), and the debasement of authority (the royal family) suggest the social chaos that ensues following the disintegration of traditional structures of feeling (71–72). Situating sensibility rather than reason at the core of social relations, Burke posits that civic order is fundamentally compromised by the removal or alteration of traditional social bonds.[33]

Various political radicals, notably Helen Maria Williams and John Thelwall, challenged Burke's early appropriation of sensibility for the conservative cause. Williams's sentimental representation of the French Revolution in her series of travel letters from France yoked the values of sensibility to radical politics (see Chapter 5). In the first of her *Letters Written in France*, published the same year as Burke's *Reflections*, Williams mobilized British support for the French Revolution by framing its events within a sentimental narrative meant to appeal to her readers' hearts. She represents those victimized under the oppressive ancien régime as the proper objects of feeling as opposed to Burke's glittering Marie Antoinette. "Must I be told that my mind is perverted," she retorts, "that I have become dead to all sensations of sympathy, because I do not weep with those who have lost part of their superfluities, rather than rejoice that the oppressed are protected?"[34] Countering Burke's defamation of the French revolutionaries as unsentimental rationalists, she insists that the leaders of the revolution are men "well-acquainted with the human heart" and that their sensibility is manifest in France's emerging system of government and evident in the "universal joy" pervading the nation.[35] Similar to Burke's "natural" sympathy with power, the emotional alignment that she experiences with the revolution's energy and aims serves as the ultimate evidence of its legitimacy. "It is very difficult . . . to avoid sympathizing with general happiness," she argues. "My love of the French Revolution, is the natural result of this sympathy, and therefore my political creed is entirely an affair of the heart."[36]

Radical appropriations of sensibility lingered throughout the 1790s, one notable example being Thelwall's mock-travelogue *The Peripatetic* (1793). In his walking tour around the English countryside, Thelwall's protagonist creates an argument for the "finest susceptibilities of nature" against the "maxims of cold-blooded apathy."[37] He stresses the revolutionary rather than the conservative quality of sensibility by linking emotional responsiveness with a reformist agenda, insisting that true sensibility cannot help but be actuated by the "picture[s] of oppression" populating Britain's landscape.[38] "The subject of our political abuses," he declares, "is so interwoven with the scenes of distress so perpetually recurring to the feeling observer, that it were impossible to be silent in this respect, without suppressing almost every reflection that ought to awaken the tender sympathies of the soul."[39] Drawing on Williams's strategy, Thelwall asserts that it is difficult to avoid sympathizing with general *un*happiness; his heart ultimately directs his actions toward those whom he sees as the victims of Britain's asymmetrical power relations.[40]

These early powerful appeals to sentiment on both the conservative and radical sides of the political spectrum ultimately condemned the discourse of sensibility to sociopolitical ignominy. Both the radical backlash against Burke's sentimental attack on the French Revolution *and* the conservative reaction to the revolution's bleeding-heart radicals excoriated the sentimental discourse operating at each end. On the side of radical politics, Mary Wollstonecraft and William Godwin produced some of the most critical responses to Burke's *Reflections*, attacking his political manipulation of sensibility and exposing the irrationality of his sentimental methodology.[41] Wollstonecraft's prompt response to Burke in *A*

Vindication of the Rights of Men (1790) takes the politician to task over his sentimental defense of institutionalized inequality. "Sensibility is the *manie* of the day," she observes, "and compassion the virtue which is to cover a multitude of vices, whilst justice is left to mourn in sullen silence, and balance truth in vain."[42] Wollstonecraft repeatedly yokes sensibility and corruption, suggesting that—*pace* Burke—instinctive feelings obscure rather than reveal immutable truths. In the first edition of *An Enquiry concerning Political Justice* (1793), Godwin similarly rejects Burke's argument regarding the connection between primordial affective ties and responsible citizenship, contending that emotional attachments counteract the "general good" as they incline individuals to the personal rather than to the universal.[43] Godwin interprets both the disturbing turn toward violence in the French Revolution and the conservative commitment to hierarchy as products of sensibility, concluding that unregulated feeling leads society to choose wrong actions or constrains it to inaction. Both Wollstonecraft and Godwin place reason above sensibility as the appropriate foundation of moral and political action, effectively rescuing rational idealism from its dubious status as a "barbarous philosophy" (77) in Burke's *Reflections*.

The attack on sensibility was not confined to radical polemicists; while radicals associated it with political and moral corruption (exemplified by Burke), conservatives worked to align sensibility with moral and political disorder (exemplified by Jean-Jacques Rousseau and the Jacobins). "As a result," observes Nicola J. Watson, "attacks on the debilitating effects of the 'cant' of sensibility are often hard to assign to any particular political standpoint."[44] In George Canning's prototypically conservative rendering of sensibility in *New Morality* (1798), the poet imagines sensibility as a young woman corrupted by her association with Rousseau and radical politics. "Sweet child of sickly Fancy!," he addresses the now-contaminated quality,

> From her loved France Rousseau to exile bore;
> . . . .
>
> Taught her o'er each lone vale and Alpine steep
> To lisp the story of his wrongs, and weep
> . . . .
>
> —Taught by nice scale to mete her feelings strong,
> False by degrees, and exquisitely wrong;—
> —For the crush'd beetle *first*,—the widow'd dove,
> . . . .
>
> *Next* for poor suff'ring *guilt*;—and *last* of all,
> For Parents, Friends, a King and a Country's fall.[45]

Canning's representation of sensibility emphasizes its worrisome vulnerability; its obvious misdirection and easy conversion to radicalism marks it as a fundamentally volatile quality. The morally suspect character of sentimentalism is further expressed by Maria Edgeworth, whose criticism of sensibility in *Practical Education* (1801) encapsulates the conservative reaction to emotional responsiveness by the end of the eighteenth century. "Experience," she states, "does not teach us, that sensibility and virtue have any certain connexion with each other. No one can read the works of Sterne or of Rousseau, without believing these men to have been endowed with extraordinary sensibility; yet who would propose their conduct in life as a model for imitation? That quickness of sympathy with present objects of distress, which constitutes compassion, is usually thought a virtue, but it is a virtue frequently found in persons of abandoned character."[46] Edgeworth's alignment of radical sensibility with moral transgression became commonplace by the latter half of the decade, spurred by the flagrant violence of the Reign of Terror and the scandalous revelations concerning the personal lives of several prominent radical figures. Contaminated by its associations with political radicalism and moral transgression, sensibility became a questionable quality and was confined to only the most regulated and disciplined contexts.

THE CONSERVATIVE POLITICS OF AN "AFFECTIONATE HEART": AN APOLOGY FOR SENSIBILITY

Whether feeling was being appropriated or excoriated, it was undeniably and intensely political in the 1790s. Jones argues that these debates over sensibility were fundamentally debates about politics, and that what has been called the "problem of sensibility" [47] must be explored in order to understand the terms of the political arguments that rocked the period: "The debates of the 1790s were characterized by a politicizing of issues raised within the school of sensibility to the extent that one's stand on matters such as the conduct of the private affections, charity, education, sympathy, genius, honour, and even the use of the reason, became political statement, aligned with conservative or radical ideologies. Under the suppression of direct political expression, these issues became a code in which conservative and progressive thinkers proclaimed their allegiances and work out terms of accommodation."[48] Marilyn Butler stresses that these debates were primarily concerned with the structure of British rather than French society. "The effect," she asserts, "is not that of a protracted university seminar, dedicated to studying events overseas, discussion centres instead on British society, what it is like and what it ought to be like."[49] Mary Morgan inserts herself into this national debate simply by adopting a sentimental persona; choosing to write within the school of sensibility was not a neutral act, and it implicates her text in the politically freighted discussions regarding the sensible self and the social affections.

In order to separate her sentimental orientation from the radical ideologies espoused by Williams and Thelwall, Morgan uses her preface to establish the conservative nature of her sensibility by critiquing the emotional excess associated with radical politics. "In an age," she states, "which abounds with idle, not to say licentious productions, and when the press groans with a species of novels, replete with what a Reviewer very significantly terms 'sentimental profligacy,' if in such an age an observer of nature can induce his readers to 'look from nature up to nature's God,' his work may not only prove amusing but beneficial" (x–xi). Morgan's condemnation of "sentimental profligacy" illustrates Jones's contention that British writers encrypted their political loyalties within their discussions of sensibility and its associated concepts. The phrase she quotes is likely drawn from Rev. Thomas Rennell's published sermon *The Connexion of the Duties of Loving the Brotherhood, Fearing God, and Honoring the King* (1792), in which he accuses Jean-Jacques Rousseau of subverting the morals of a generation by promoting radical sociopolitical ideologies in the guise of sensibility: "The mischief done to morality and religion by Rousseau are beyond all calculation. The passions, in their worst excesses, are painted by him in the garb of virtue; and, by these means, the progress made to vice is most artfully rendered imperceptible to the unwary mind. . . . The purest philanthropy is the profession of this writer; but the real purpose and effect of his writings is, to diffuse a principle of sentimental profligacy."[50] Rebuking the radical sensibility associated with Rousseau by invoking Rennell's severely conservative and very loud defense of "SOCIAL SUBORDINATION and RELIGIOUS PRINCIPLE,"[51] Morgan clearly aligns herself with conservative politics and strategically distances her work from the subversive tendencies found within the culture of sensibility.

However, her rebuke of "licentious productions" is not a disavowal of feeling per se, but of a particular emotional orientation associated with sociopolitical radicalism—unregulated, self-indulgent, and leveling. Morgan is invested in rescuing sensibility from the notoriety of Jacobinism; her text gradually reveals itself as a defense of feeling within a culture that was increasingly hostile to sensibility and its attendant practices. Morgan's reproof of "sentimental profligacy" creates a distinction between her affective prose and the more suspect emotionalism found in sentimental fiction; she accrues moral credit by asserting that her sensibility is rooted in religious rather than sensual feeling. "There is no reason," she states, "why I should not depicture scenes that have . . . awakened in me a thousand moral and religious sentiments" (x). Morgan posits a spectrum of sensibility bracketed by "sentimental profligacy" at one end and "moral and religious sentiments" on the other. Unlike the degenerative nature of Rousseau's "artfully rendered" sentiments,[52] Morgan's moral sentiments encourage her audience to "'look from nature up to nature's God'" (x). She interpolates her sensibility and her religious practice to remind her audience that sensibility can produce spiritual and social regeneration. Her performance of conservative sensibility illustrates O'Brien's argument that Anglican female intellectuals carefully maintained the social value of sensibility throughout the eighteenth century; although they were careful to avoid "sentimental irrationalism," they consistently defended sensibility as a core component of religious feeling and the social affections and thus as a "source of moral normativity in society."[53]

It is precisely as the source of morality and religious devotion that Morgan recuperates sensibility as foundational to national stability. Similar to Burke's understanding of the organic connection between the sensible self and the veneration of authority ("We have real hearts of flesh and blood beating in our bosoms. We fear God; we look up with awe to kings; with affection to parliaments; with duty to magistrates; with reverence to priests; and with respect to nobility" [86]), Morgan's fusion of her innate sensibility and her reverence for religious authority suggests that a lively sensibility can organically sustain Britain's hierarchical political structure.[54] As such, she perceives political radicalism grounded in philosophical rationalism as one of the primary threats to Britain's national stability, as revealed in her dedication to the Countess of Winterton: "There is nothing more mortifying to an affectionate heart, than to be restrained, through fear of the world, or of giving offence to the delicacy of a friend, from expressing the dictates of its regard. Yet, according to the present system of things, every mark of attention to a superior rank is so liable to be construed into adulation, that real affection is often obliged to be silent" (iv). Her reference to the suspect nature of "adulation" is an allusion to the politically radical proposal offered in Richard Price's infamous sermon *A Discourse on the Love of Our Country* (1789), whose criticism of traditional social affections as both conservative in nature and oppressive in practice influenced the complementary critiques offered by Wollstonecraft and Godwin. In his provocative address—given on the anniversary of the Glorious Revolution and on the eve of the French Revolution—Price condemns what he refers to as the "idolatry" of authority figures,[55] arguing that the veneration of superiors participates in creating relationships of exploitation. "Adulation," he contends, "is always odious, and when offered to men in power it corrupts *them* . . . and it debases those who offer it, by manifesting an abjectness founded on improper ideas of *themselves*."[56] Price criticizes political relationships defined by hierarchy and argues that "adulation" upsets the appropriate balance of power between subjects and their monarch by enabling those with authority to "consider themselves as possessed of an inherent superiority, which gives them a right to govern."[57] He lauds the French Revolution for restoring right relations between the people and their leaders by instituting a contractual relationship based on rights and responsibilities rather than on traditional hierarchies and their related affects, glorying in "the dominion of kings changed for the dominion of laws, and the dominion of priests giving way to the dominion of reason and conscience."[58]

Price's denunciation of traditional social affections clearly threatened entrenched sociopolitical relationships, and it is this threat that Morgan finds so menacing. Her fear suggests her ideological affinity with Burke, whose vigorous defense of traditional social affections and critique of what he labels the "mechanic philosophy" (77) of radical politics was prompted by Price's speech. Burke accuses Price of replacing instinctive affections with an artificial construct that suppresses human nature. "As things now stand," Burke observes, "with everything respectable destroyed without us, and an attempt to destroy within us every principle of respect, one is almost forced to apologize for harbouring the common feelings of men" (80). Morgan's comment to the Countess of Winterton that "real affection is often obliged to be silent" (iv) directly echoes Burke's statement on the newly suspect status of sympathy with the privileged; in the same vein as Burke, she suggests that the egalitarian demands of political radicals such as Price effectively stifle the operation of "real affection" (iv). That the countess is revealed to be Morgan's cousin at the conclusion of her dedication serves to emphasize the perversion of Price's mechanistic system: despite the familial relation between Morgan and the countess, her cousin's social position nevertheless renders the feelings of an "affectionate heart" (iv) questionable according to the exigencies of egalitarianism. The conflation of private and public affections in the figure of the countess speaks to Burke's concern that radical politics ultimately threatens the cohesion of society by attacking all domestic, social, and political relationships. Analyzing the potential political impact of Price's "barbarous philosophy," Burke cautions, "On this scheme of things, a king is but a man; a queen is but a woman; a woman is but an animal; and an animal not of the highest order. . . . Regicide, and parricide, and sacrilege are but fictions of superstition" (77). By demanding equality, political radicals effectively reduce humans to mere objects and expunge their humanity by denying the "common feelings" of humankind. That violence was feared to be the consequence of this political philosophy is suggested by Burke's immediate shift to national, domestic, and religious chaos.[59]

Morgan similarly connects the absence of sympathy with social chaos in a dramatic retelling of a pillaging incident off the coast of Wales. According to Morgan's version of the events, a laboring ship was besieged by rapacious pillagers who willfully ignored the distress of the imperiled passengers and ravished the vulnerable ship of its contents. In the frenzy that ensued, one of the looters—consumed by greed and incited by "unthinking wantonness" (207)—set fire to the plundered gunpowder, killing or maiming all those within the circumference of the explosion. Morgan attributes the mercenary behavior of the pillagers to a deficiency of sympathy, observing that they "do not . . . feel all that sympathy for the distresses of ship-wrecked mariners, which naturally arises in the breasts of those, who are less habituated to such scenes of woe" (208). Her narration of the pillagers' selfish actions demonstrates that the demands of desire overcome those of duty and humanity in the absence of sympathy. The consequence—as Burke both prophesied and feared—is unmitigated social chaos as senseless violence consumes both passengers and pillagers. Her nightmarish representation of the unruly destruction of the beleaguered ship forms a parallel to Burke's equally horrifying representation of the French mobs demolishing the "edifice" (51) of their traditional political structure. Morgan amplifies the revolutionary connotations of the pillagers' act in a later comment on the equally destructive actions of the French mobs: "Let any one who pretends to despise titles and dignity, and affects to call stars and ribbons baubles, say, whether it is not better to be a statesman, a general, a counselor to princes, a patronizer of merit, and a friend to the learned and elegant, than to grovel in obscurity, and have no way to raise themselves from their native meanness, but by pulling others down, and railing at those talents and those honours which they can never hope to emulate, or by any *honest* means obtain" (418–419). The revolutionary image of subordinates "pulling others down" to arrogate power mirrors the equally violent conduct of the peasant thieves ripping apart a ship for fleeting personal gain. Both sets of actions derive from a pronounced deficiency of sensibility and the attendant dictates of sympathy; the avaricious incendiaries and pillagers are immune to the "natural" feelings so powerfully felt by Morgan. Her message is clear: retributive, cyclical violence is the outcome of sociopolitical systems that excoriate sensibility and expunge traditional ties of affection.

Morgan's criticism of radical political philosophy and her "awe and veneration" (418) of political authority clearly advertise her commitment to the preservation of rank for which William Pitt the Younger's government stood. However, although she fears the consequences of Price's rational egalitarianism, Morgan is equally critical of the measures the British government instituted in order to inhibit revolutionary activity within Britain. In the years following the inauguration of the French Revolution, Pitt's administration responded to the threat posed by France's radical ideology by becoming progressively authoritarian and threatening violence against subversives. In addition to engaging France in the Revolutionary Wars, the British government established surveillance operations to monitor its citizens and introduced repressive measures to stifle both real and imaginary threats to Britain's political stability. The aggressive repression of radical activity reached its peak in the mid-1790s with the much-publicized Treason Trials of 1794, the concurrent suspension of habeas corpus, and the introduction of the Treasonable Practices Act and the Seditious Meetings Act in 1795. These external and internal pressures created what John Barrell describes as an "atmosphere of suspicion" that effectively policed the British public through the pervasive threat of violence.[60] Surveying the British nation in 1793, Thelwall represents the public as conspicuously terrified; buffeted by a "torrent of popular delirium" he observes, "the tranquility of every district in the kingdom has been so artfully disturbed."[61]

Morgan's travelogue is profoundly skeptical of the use of violence as a governing tool, and her repeated suggestions of the inherently anti-social nature of violence ultimately registers as a quiet critique of both reactionary and radical politics. Her discomfort with the use of violence as a means of domination can be seen in her surprising alignment between military and mob violence at the conclusion of her tale of the Welsh pillagers. "Ye naval and military officers," she pronounces, "who rejoice at the rumour of war, in which thousands and ten thousands must perish . . . be not too severe in your strictures upon the inhospitable temper of these untutored rustics" (208). Her provocative parallel between the actions of Britain's military leaders and those of unscrupulous pillagers suggests that Britain's institutionalized violence is born out of a similar absence of sympathetic feeling, and that the zealous attitude with which military leaders accept the annihilation of "thousands and ten thousands" is productive of the same process of dehumanization manifest in Price's egalitarianism. Morgan's subtle alignment of what she sees as the equally damaging agendas of the British Parliament and Price indicates that both repression and revolution create cultures of violence that compromise the traditional ties of affection that she believes are responsible for the political stability of the British nation. In order to ensure that Britain avoids France's fate, Morgan proposes that the working of sympathy rather than the operation of fear will ensure the stability of Britain's sociopolitical framework. Her travel letters participate in the revitalization of sensibility within the nation through both her modeling of sympathetic feeling and her observations on right relations between the different sectors that constitute British society. In her pointed comparisons between Elizabeth Montagu's and the Duke of Marlborough's estates, Britain's feudal past and its enlightened present, Welsh and British landowners, and communities of women and patriarchal societies, Morgan promotes an approach to governance that purposely cultivates rather than silences affection through the inclusive practice of sympathy. In contrast to the disruptive political agendas of Price and Pitt, she situates the maintenance of relationships at the core of her political vision—endorsing a top-down ethics of care that will produce a national community interfused by what Vicesimus Knox calls "the obedience of love."[62]

SANDLEFORD, BLENHEIM, AND THE (E)STATE OF THE NATION

Morgan's British itinerary implicitly announces her political commitments. Turner notes that home tours multiplied in the 1790s due to the twin constraints of political unrest abroad and the conservative demand for patriotism at home.[63] Domestic tourism, as Carl Thompson explains, could be "easily constructed as a patriotic exercise, in keeping with a self-image that identified the middle classes as the moral and economic heart of the nation."[64] Traveling abroad increasingly invited accusations of bolstering foreign economies, contracting foreign contagions, or of implicitly conveying a belief in British cultural, political, or aesthetic inferiority. However, domestic tourism was not always synonymous with political conservatism, as demonstrated by Thelwall's mock travelogue. His particular interest in the dwellings of the poor rather than in the country houses of the rich enables him to highlight the conditions of oppression that demand reform. Whereas Thelwall emphasizes the *evils* of property to encourage political revolution, Morgan reinforces the *benefits* of property to divert revolutionary energies. Her itinerary revolves around the splendid estates of the rich, which she represents as emblems of national rather than of private prosperity. Since the estate was often considered, as Gary Kelly notes, as a "metonymy and metaphor for the larger state of the nation,"[65] Morgan's attention to and description of country houses can be read as political allegory. The tradition of conflating the private space of the propertied gentleman with the broader compass of the nation extends back to—and well beyond—the country-house panegyrics of the seventeenth and early eighteenth centuries. In her study of the country house and its literary representations in eighteenth-century culture, Virginia C. Kenny observes that British writers were actively involved in "modifying the symbol of the country-house ethos as an interpretive image of the right use of the wealth, power and knowledge now available to civil society."[66] Morgan draws on this tradition to communicate her political (re)vision of the state. Her position as a tourist allows her the opportunity to access a variety of country homes and to compare and contrast their qualities in the evaluative manner anticipated of the travel writer, and she is eager to parlay her eyewitness perspective into political currency. Morgan's detailed descriptions of and comparison between the very different estates of Sandleford and Blenheim form the crux around which she carefully develops her political vision for the British nation. Her brief stay at Montagu's estate in Berkshire comes early in the text, and subsequently becomes the standard against which both the larger estate of the British nation and all other private estates are weighed.

In 1755, Elizabeth Montagu wrote the following observation to Gilbert West: "If every Gentleman and lady that live in the Country would allow their poor neighbours to apply to them for relief in necessity, for advice in difficulties, for consolation in affliction, what an effect would it have on the common people! The desire of being in favour with such persons would keep them regular, make them industrious, and prevent the crimes, the follies and misfortunes that attend a dejected or a fearless state of mind. How glorious to be the visible providence of a Country!"[67] Montagu's fantasy of socially responsible governance and her desire to be "the visible providence of a Country" was fulfilled in the management and design of the Berkshire estate over which she had full control after her husband's death in 1775. Through her actions and words, she cultivated an image of herself as a benevolent landlord and of Sandleford as a sentimental community sustained by the kind of reciprocity she imagines in her letter to West. Montagu established her benevolence through her many charitable acts, which ranged from employing the infirm and unemployed to subsidizing food and livestock for her tenants.[68] Throughout her extensive redesign of both the house and its grounds from the 1780s onward, Montagu carefully maintained the appearance of social responsibility by stressing the financial sustainability of her project. In contrast to her spectacular city dwelling in London, she stipulated that Sandleford's improvements must conform to her comparatively modest budget. "We shall not erect temples to the gods," she declared, "build bridges over humble rivulets, or do any of the marvelous things suggested by the caprice, and indulged by the wantonness of wealth."[69] Despite hiring Lancelot "Capability" Brown—whose landscape parks were synonymous with the practices of enclosure and emparkment—Montagu confidently asserted that the comprehensive redesign of the estate effectively fostered rather than ruptured her connection with the local community as it created economic opportunities for laborers.[70] Her efforts appear to be directed toward establishing Sandleford as a real-life counterpart to the female utopia created within *Millenium Hall* (1762), the novel written by her sister, Sarah Scott. *Millenium Hall* describes a productive, peaceful community presided over by a female collective who govern according to altruistic principles. Montagu's country house allowed her to implement the philanthropic ideals championed within the bluestocking circle and to bring to life the moral economy fantasized by Scott.

The tense political atmosphere of the 1790s only served to amplify Montagu's desire to obviate the increasingly threatening repercussions of a "dejected and fearless" populace.[71] Emma Major argues that Montagu's philanthropic activity during the 1790s can be understood as a distinctly political "anti-revolutionary practice."[72] Her philanthropic initiatives, Major claims, "become defined by a Protestant patriotism that sees the best refuge from the French, and the best rebuttal to their revolutionary principles, in piety and charity, and an Anglican respect for law, order, and the preservation of rank."[73] Peter Denney agrees with Major that Montagu's philanthropic initiatives "must be regarded as an attempt . . . to diffuse unrest"[74] but further problematizes her exercise of charity by specifically focusing on the class politics that it enshrines. Denney imputes Montagu's charity to the classist desire to "promote deference and industry in the poor, not their upward mobility or material comfort."[75] His assessment of Montagu's philanthropy participates in a critical discussion of her charity—extending from contemporary opinions to modern scholarship—that interprets her very public charitable acts as motivated by self-aggrandizement rather than by benevolence. These suggestions of egotism are perhaps nowhere as blatantly stated as in James Woodhouse's damaging portrayal of Montagu in his autobiographical poem *The Life and Lucubrations of Crispinus Scriblerus* (written in the 1790s but not published until 1896), in which he directly addresses her philanthropic works and estate management. Woodhouse—who worked as Montagu's land bailiff and house steward—berates Montagu by attributing her altruism to vanity and criticizing Capability Brown's fashionable "improvements" of Sandleford as an act of profligacy and as a gesture toward exclusion.[76] "To administer more food for Pride," he mocks, "With ornaments [she] bedeck'd the fair outside, / Where she might show her Wealth."[77] Woodhouse's revolutionary energies are precisely what Montagu feared and attempted to placate by actively courting the goodwill—or, more equivocally, the "gratitude"[78]—of her rural community.

As Zoë Kinsley observes in her reading of *Milford Haven*'s Sandleford episode, Morgan's glowing appraisal of Montagu's philanthropic initiatives acts as a defense of Montagu by suggesting that her charity is motivated by selfless virtue rather than by selfish vanity.[79] However, Morgan's positive assessment does more than act as a personal defense of Montagu: it also promotes her "piety and charity" as an effective antidote to revolutionary fervor.[80] Morgan shares the classist motivations of Montagu's philanthropy, and she interprets her implementation of philanthropic ideals as an advisable approach to assuaging discontent and to safeguarding Britain's hierarchy. She clearly elides some of the problematic elements of Montagu's landscape redesign (particularly her participation in enclosure and emparkment) by moralizing Montagu's aesthetic decisions as an example of responsive and responsible landlordism. "[Montagu's] whole behaviour," she enthuses, "gives you a perfect conception of what is meant by possessing 'the milk of human kindness.' . . . [She] is always thinking of some great or good work, which tends to the encouragement of genius, or the promotion of plans for the benefit of her species" (42–43). Her characterization of her host carefully emphasizes the importance that Montagu places upon sympathetic social relationships, which Morgan indicates is achieved within Sandleford through the operating principles of functionality and inclusivity—both of which serve to maintain the relational function of the country estate as both the economic and the social heart of the community. She suggests that Montagu's nature and actions are fundamentally oriented toward community and stand in direct contrast to the twin menaces of British stability in the 1790s: the equally solipsistic figures of the mercenary Jacobin and the self-serving aristocrat.

Morgan and her husband visited Sandleford at the invitation of Montagu, with whom she was previously acquainted and whose family she counted as close friends. Her eagerness to visit Montagu's country estate is evident in her declaration that "I was as full of expectation, as a young beauty going to be introduced at court; but without the anxious fear of not being able to shine as much as I wished" (32–33). She goes on to say that she felt "sufficiently gratified that a great portion of genius is possessed by my sex, and I was entirely void of dread or envy" (33). Morgan's comparison of Sandleford to the royal court positions Montagu as a leader of national import but avoids attributing the more suspect connotations of court culture to Sandleford by suggesting that this is a different kind of sociopolitical space—one defined by inclusivity rather than by exclusivity, and by moral seriousness rather than by frivolity. These qualities are immediately confirmed in Morgan's initial impressions regarding the entrance to the estate. As the liminal space connecting public and private, the entrance functions as an important symbolic space that immediately defines the relationship between those inside and outside the manor. In *Grammars of Approach* (2019), Cynthia Wall explains that the shifting scenes that shaped the approach to the eighteenth-century country house "were not simply of house and grounds but *about* house and grounds, about subject and object, center and periphery."[81] Morgan's description of the natural corridor leading to the manor house establishes the socially responsible design of the estate. "The approach to the house is a fine lawn," she approvingly notes, "with sheep feeding upon it. This gives you an idea of beauty blended with utility, which always produces agreeable sensations in the mind" (33). Her description of the main building's entry signals the host's hospitality and suggests the values of functionality and inclusivity governing the estate: "The carriage draws close up to the front door, by which comfortable circumstance we avoided running the gauntlet up a high flight of steps in view of the windows, to which people are often subject, when they visit at great houses. No such distress awaits you at Sandleford, when you alight you enter a small hall, for Mrs. M—has not spoiled her house in order to make a grand vestibule" (33). The entrance to the manor house rebuffs architectural features designed to display the power and status of the proprietor; the emphasis on comfort clearly invites fellowship rather than worship. In a letter to Hannah More, who was a fellow bluestocking and conservative religious author and activist, Montagu states that she intended the estate's gothic entrance to convey precisely what Morgan senses: that "ancient simplicity and hospitality resided there, and a homely and sincere reception awaited them, if they would do the mistress of the mansion the favour to walk in."[82] The "ancient simplicity and hospitality" of the entrance advertises Montagu's (symbolic if not always actual) commitment to preserving the traditional socioeconomic function of the estate; the simplicity of the design suggests an emphasis on functionality, and its gesture toward hospitality hints at a social milieu defined by inclusivity.

Morgan's further survey of the Sandleford's outdoor spaces provides additional evidence of Montagu's benevolent governance. Her initial impression of the estate is confirmed in the design of the landscape and in the treatment of the estate's employees. Although she clearly admires Capability Brown's aesthetic improvements to the landscape, Morgan is careful to focus on the estate's functional qualities and to gloss over the more controversial aesthetic aspects of Brown's design. Her description of the estate's practical features participates in the larger socioeconomic discussion that debated the wisdom of dispossessing Britain's yeomanry and rupturing the traditional relationships between landowners and their tenants for aesthetic and/or economic reasons. The ruin of local economies due to landlords enclosing their property for profit or pleasure and divesting the land of its social function had been subject to criticism for decades, and the disturbing progress of the French Revolution lent renewed urgency to the discussion. As Woodhouse's trenchant condemnation of Sandleford's redesign indicates, Brown's extensive landscape parks—with their large swaths of sterile turf and careful segregation of gentlemen's seats from rural labor—were subject to particular criticism. As Denney explains, "Isolating the country house from the working countryside, parks accordingly became signs of how landlords were abandoning public duty for private pleasure."[83] Indeed, Uvedale Price—a landowner and the author of the influential *Essay on the Picturesque* (1794)—criticized the "solitary grandeur" of the Brownian landscape, arguing that "he who destroys dwellings, gardens, and inclosures, for the sake of mere extent and parade of property, only extends the bounds of . . . dreary selfish pride; but contracts those of variety, amusement, and humanity."[84] Price's land agent, Nathaniel Kent, detailed the economic devastation caused by the trend toward divorcing the land from its agricultural uses. Discussing the removal of working dairies from estates, he observes, "From the great farmers dropping their dairies the markets of Yarmouth and Norwich are so ill supplied with butter, that it is become a matter of favour to be able to obtain enough for common consumption, notwithstanding the price, within a very few years, is increased from 8d. to 16d. the pint."[85]

Both Price and Kent feared the political repercussions of the various forms of economic dispossession caused by emparkment and urged landowners to maintain the social function of their land. In *Thoughts on the Defence of Property* (1797), which was published as a response to a possible French invasion, Price associates inclusive land use practices with national stability, contending that the welfare of the laboring classes serves as an antidote to revolution. "Vast possessions may give ambitious views" he observes, "and ambition destroys local attachments; but even the cottager, with a few acres which he has tilled and manured . . . has at least as much attachment to his little spot, as the greatest lord to his immense domain."[86] Kent shares Price's conviction regarding the political wisdom of an integrated landscape, arguing that the laborer who is assured property "is always a faithful servant to the farmer who employs him; he has a stake in the common interest of the country, and is never prompt to riot, in time of sedition, like a man who has nothing to lose; on the contrary, he is a strong link in the chain of national security."[87] Both Price and Kent identify the breakdown of sentimental attachments—between landlord and tenant, tenant and land—as the real danger posed by land enclosures and the development of fashionable parks. In the absence of a social attachment to the landowner and a material attachment to the land, the laboring classes are unlikely to form attachments to their nation at large. As the riots in Britain and the mobs in France had recently demonstrated, the failure of landowners to recognize and mitigate the real, concrete effects of depravation could have significant repercussions.

The emphasis Morgan places on the functional and inclusive aspects of Montagu's estate suggests that she would agree with Price's and Kent's endorsement of land use practices invested in social reality. Indeed, she voices her disapproval of the practice of land enclosures at a later point in her travelogue, observing that "the gentlemen in Wales have not adopted the custom of throwing several little farms into one great one, by which the small farmer . . . is deprived of the means of subsistence, and must perhaps become the menial servant of one who has hired his cottage over his head, or starve" (270). Although Brown's redesign of Montagu's estate predictably relocated the more utilitarian structures to the margins in order to provide an unimpeded view of the park, Morgan's portrayal of the landscape reintegrates these marginalized outbuildings into the prospect.[88] She effectively performs a revision of the Brownian landscape, placing the realities of agrarian life back into the visual frame in a way that aligns with her overall portrayal and understanding of Montagu's relational, community-oriented approach to governance. She notes the use of land for pasturage (33), observes that "the farm and the dairy are not omitted" (40), and includes the appearance of cultivated fields in her description of the prospect (36). Morgan deftly manages the thorny issue of Montagu's support of and participation in enclosure and emparkment by claiming that the grounds have been developed both to delight the owner and to serve the community—carefully balancing the dictates of beauty and utility, desire and duty. "The whole of the place," she commends, "suggested to me the idea of a Roman villa. There is everything for use as well as beauty" (40). According to Morgan's impression of the landscape, Montagu's estate stands in contrast to the aestheticized barrenness of fashionable pleasure grounds; by integrating both practical and aesthetic considerations, the landscape signals her rejection of the solipsistic trend of divorcing the country retreat from rural labor and the landlord from their larger community.

While the physical structuring of Montagu's grounds suggests an ethics of care, her sympathetic governance is most effectively displayed in her management of the estate. Morgan represents Montagu as a conscientious landlord, carefully detailing her maternal, sympathetic, and perhaps unorthodox treatment of her employees: "When walking in the grounds, I observed an extraordinary degree of cleanliness and decency in the men, who were at work upon them. Upon enquiry I found they were all fed and cloathed by her hand. I perceived too that many of them had some great defect, occasioned by age, natural infirmity, or misfortune, being either blind, deaf, dumb, or lame, yet she had so paired them, and fitted their employments to their several faculties, that the remaining senses of the one served to supply the deficiency of the other" (39).[89] As a result of Montagu's sympathetic initiatives, she remakes marginalized individuals into "useful and happy members of society" (39). Her redemptive role is further supported through Morgan's rather over-the-top comparison of Montagu to Christ: "I hope it is not prophane to say [that] she has made the blind to see, the deaf to hear, the dumb to speak, and the lame to walk" (39–40). By attributing (miraculous) healing capacities to Montagu, Morgan establishes the transformative power of sympathy; Montagu wields sympathy as an agent of transfiguration, "convert[ing] things ugly and uncouth into beauty and uniformity" (40). Morgan carefully avoids framing Montagu's charitable acts as self-interested by pointing out that her philanthropy is not materially remunerated. "Though she does not get so much work done," she explains, "as she would by stronger and abler men, she has the heartfelt satisfaction of making those happy and useful members of society . . . who, but for her, must be dependent upon a parish for an idle and scanty subsistence" (39). The economic benefit is to the laborers and to the larger community; the benefit that

Montagu accrues through her social initiatives lies equally in her own "heartfelt satisfaction" and in the reciprocal happiness of her employees.

It is precisely this atmosphere of social contentment that advertises the potential political benefits of sympathetic governance. Given the atmosphere of sociopolitical discontent pervading Britain in the 1790s, the peaceful community that Morgan witnesses within Sandleford posits Montagu's relational leadership as an effective mode of governance. To Montagu's nephew, Matthew Montagu, Morgan writes: "I cannot help comparing [your aunt] to a loadstone, which has not only the power of attraction, but communicates some of its virtue to everything that approaches it" (209). Montagu's sympathetic character is both appealing and transformative; as a result, she does not need to resort to force or intimidation to secure obedience. Morgan's suggestion of the transformative value of sympathy recalls both Adam Smith's and David Hume's ideas regarding the ability of sympathy to convert atomistic individuals into like-minded communities. "The man," Smith notes, "who associates chiefly with the wise and virtuous, though he may not himself become either wise or virtuous, cannot help conceiving a certain respect at least for wisdom and virtue."[90] Smith's emphasis on propinquity illuminates the political dimensions of Morgan's endorsement of Montagu's socially engaged landlordism; Montagu's integration of the estate with the community fosters loyalty grounded in respect. The representation of Sandleford sketched in *Milford Haven* ultimately bears out Uvedale Price's contention that it is the practice of benevolence rather than the operation of force that obviates revolution. "Attentive kindnesses," he states, "are amply repaid by affectionate regard and reverence; and were they general through the kingdom, they would do much more towards guarding us against democratical opinions, 'Than twenty thousand soldiers arm'd in proof.'"[91] Montagu's cultivation and maintenance of relationships produces a community that demonstrates in reality what Price proposes in theory: that benevolence is a far more effective antidote to disorder than fear.

Morgan's visit to the magnificent palace of George Spencer, the fourth Duke of Marlborough, almost immediately follows her stay at Sandleford, creating a narrative structure that not only invites comparisons between the two estates but also parallels the contrast created in Sarah Scott's *Millenium Hall* between a fictional feminocentric community and its neighboring, distinctively masculine estate. Morgan admired Scott's novel, and the familial relationship between Scott and Montagu must have created an evocative comparison in her mind.[92] In her novel, Scott directly contrasts the ladies' flourishing estate with a contiguous manor facing disintegration due to neglect by a series of selfish and materialistic male proprietors. The contrast between the two estates explicitly advertises the communitarian values governing the women's thriving community. "How directly were we led," the male narrator states, "to admire the superior sense, as well as transcendent virtue of these ladies."[93] The structural affinity between Scott's comparison of Millenium Hall and its neighboring estate and Morgan's comparison of Sandleford and Blenheim forms a suggestive allusion that implicitly frames the Duke of Marlborough's magnificent palace as the aesthetic and ideological foil to Montagu's comparatively modest country seat.

Blenheim by its very nature invoked the issue of aristocratic profligacy and raised questions regarding the right use of power and wealth. Built largely from public funds awarded to John Churchill (1650–1722), the first Duke of Marlborough, in recognition of his military achievements, the ostentatious palace quickly became enmeshed in controversy. Churchill's decision to appoint John Vanbrugh as the architect signaled his grand aspirations for the estate; Vanbrugh had a reputation for flamboyant baroque designs, and together he and Churchill planned a structure characterized by extravagance. Although the initial cost of Blenheim was estimated to amount to £100,000,[94] the final figure came to approximately £300,000—a princely sum that remained unsurpassed in the eighteenth century.[95] Further money was expended on the estate's features under the ownership of George Spencer, Churchill's great-grandson, in the late eighteenth century. Spencer evidently shared his great-grandfather's grandiose vision and invested large sums of money in modernizing and further embellishing the estate; his alterations and additions included Capability Brown's extensive redesign of the grounds and the construction of William Chamber's Temple of Diana.[96]

Blenheim's theatrical architecture and its associated cost came to represent the socially enervating effects of luxury; the first Duke of Marlborough's detractors, Kenny observes, denigrated the building as "a useless show-place."[97] In Alexander Pope's 1714 poem, "Upon the Duke of Marlborough's House at Woodstock," he underscores the uselessness of the palace through his wry observation that it was unsuited for domestic use:

> Thanks, Sir, cried I, 't is very fine,
> But where d'ye sleep, or where d'ye dine?
> I find by all you have been telling
> That 't is a house, but not a dwelling.[98]

John Loveday, an English antiquarian and travel writer, decried what he described as Blenheim's "plain" or impractical gardens in his travel memoir *The Diary of a Tour in 1732* (1732), lamenting the erasure of traditional responsibilities and relationships represented by the estate's artistic rather than agrarian landscape.[99] Three decades later, Brown's modern restructuring of the estate's grounds simply exacerbated the issue of the landscape's showy rather than functional quality by replacing the traditional gardens with unending turf and by flooding over a hundred acres of land to create a magnificent lake. Indeed, Montagu's declaration she will not "erect temples to the gods, or build bridges over humble rivulets, or do any of the marvelous things suggested by the caprice, and indulged by the wantonness of wealth" could be taken as a thinly veiled criticism of Blenheim's ostentatious grounds, particularly as it developed under the guidance of the fourth Duke of Marlborough.[100] Her instructions that Brown's plan for Sandleford heed both the "character of the place" and her "purse" creates a clear distinction between Sandleford and Blenheim, and communicates to Brown that his design must be both socially and fiscally responsible.[101]

Although Blenheim's showy quality attracted criticism, it also attracted curiosity; the palace became a must-see tourist attraction by the 1790s and constructed an entire industry around the demand. "The flow of human traffic into the house and park," Carole Fabricant explains, "was carefully controlled and monitored at the same time that it was actively (indeed, aggressively) promoted."[102] Morgan describes the packaged feel of the tour, recounting her sense of being herded through the palace: "Through that house, which would take a week to survey, you are dragged in an hour, and, perhaps, as it was our fate, to be obliged to follow a party, whose numerous absurd questions to the person who conducts you prevents even the agreeable ideas you might have in that short stay" (69). The grand scale of Blenheim overwhelms, while the combined sense of coercion and exclusion that she professes to feel provides a notable contrast to the hospitality she experiences at Sandleford. Her veiled criticism of Blenheim pivots on its flamboyant materialism and lack of hospitality, which she slowly exposes as the products of a disturbing solipsism that reveals itself in the design of the estate. Just as Montagu's virtue is manifested in the character of Sandleford, the more questionable nature of the Marlborough dynasty is suggested through Blenheim's aesthetic.

Morgan's elaboration of the significant aesthetic differences between the two estates begins with her observations on the approach to the palace. After passing through a "prodigious grand triumphal arch" (67), she is overcome by the estate's sumptuousness: "I seemed transported into a new world, such a magnificent scene presented itself all at once to my ravished sight. The palace, the park, the canal, the bridge, and a hundred other objects, struck upon my senses in a moment" (69). The approach to Blenheim is extravagant and overwhelming, which forms a sharp contrast to the simplicity and utility that characterizes the approach to Montagu's manor. Morgan's initial impression of the estate's extravagance is augmented by her further survey of the palace and its grounds; her account abounds with statements regarding her inability to adequately summarize the estate, which cumulatively suggest Blenheim's material excess. The house "would take a week to survey" (69), the ornaments are "too numerous to mention" (70) and "too numerous . . . to describe" (83), the furnishings are "impossible to remember" (73), and to detail the paintings "would take more time than I had for seeing them, or have now for writing" (73). The entire experience leaves her with "eyes tired of seeing" (86). Although she is appropriately awed by the display, Morgan ultimately finds the *dulce et utile* of Sandleford superior to the purely ornamental splendor of Blenheim. Whereas in Montagu's estate "nothing is gaudy or superfluous" (42), the Duke of Marlborough's palace is "too gay and too gaudy to be real" (76).

Her disapproval of Blenheim's gaudiness reprises the long-standing criticism of the estate's apparent uselessness. That the Dukes of Marlborough have eschewed utility for spectacle visibly indicates their repudiation of the traditional, socioeconomic function of the land. Morgan's specific representation of Blenheim as unreal further suggests that the Marlborough dynasty has created a world deliberately divorced from immediate reality, which—as Uvedale Price's and Nathaniel Kent's connections between inclusive land use practices and national stability indicate—was a dangerous quality at a time when sociopolitical realities threatened the very foundations of aristocratic privilege and power. Vicesimus Knox directly blamed Britain's mounting political instability on the aristocracy's segregation from material reality in his 1795 publication *The Spirit of Despotism*. According to Knox, the aristocracy's pursuit of "sordid and vain-glorious purposes" demonstrates their disregard for the "real, substantial happiness of the governed."[103] In serving themselves rather than the national community, the aristocracy's political utility is compromised and their reformation (or, more radically, their removal) is ultimately justified. "Degenerate aristocrats," M. O. Grenby contends, "threatened revolution every bit as much as levellers . . . since in not fulfilling the duties incumbent upon them by virtue of their station they deprived the hierarchies of the nation of their very raison d'etre and therefore of their sustainability."[104] Morgan's disapproval of Blenheim's superficiality is more than just an aesthetic judgment; her negative assessment gestures toward the sociopolitical threat inherent in the the combined effects of aristocratic profligacy and indifference. Without cultivating real, lived relationships with their local community, the aristocracy risked alienating the British public through their displays of gaudiness.

The fourth Duke of Marlborough's continued investment in show rather than in substance does not merely segregate the estate from the surrounding community, but it also forms a statement on his approach to governance. Morgan's immediate response to the estate's architecture draws attention to the power dynamics suggested by its design. Blenheim imposes itself upon Morgan's consciousness in a particularly aggressive manner ("my ravished sight," "struck upon my senses" [69]); her sense of being overwhelmed upon entering the estate suggests that it is designed to advertise the power of its owner and to instill an awareness (or, to use Morgan's earlier phrase, "anxious fear" [33]) of inferiority within the spectator. William F. Mavor, who wrote the definitive guide to the palace in 1789, remarks that its appearance reflects the militaristic legacy of its first owner: "Its massy grandeur, its spacious portals, and its lofty towers, recal the ideas of defence and security."[105] Although Mavor approves of this nod to the building's genesis, his observation that Blenheim's façade conjures up images of ancient fortified castles is indicative of the building's intimidating and insular aspect—forming a significant contrast to Sandleford's appeal to "ancient simplicity and hospitality."[106] Consequently, whereas the design of Sandleford's entrance both invites community and invokes the idea of community by drawing in visitors through a succession of welcoming gestures, the very architecture of Blenheim's entrance manufactures distance between those inside and those outside by conjuring the specter of violence. Morgan's sensation of being immobilized, or "tranfixt" (69), by the estate's image suggests that the architecture fulfills its intention. Her description of the two different entrances illustrates two approaches to power: while Montagu maintains her authority through the cultivation of community, the Duke(s) of Marlborough appears to favor a form of power premised upon intimidation.

That the estates embody two different modes of governance becomes clear in a later and more explicit comparison between Blenheim and Sandleford. "Having before described Sandleford to you," Morgan confides to her correspondent, "I cannot help observing, that it is a striking contrast to Blenheim. But it is such a one, as when the eye, dazzled with gazing at the sun, falls on the soft green of a beautiful lawn, upon which it may rest for ever without satiety or weariness. At S—the mind is gratified with every thing, that can render life rational and happy. At B—it is fatigued with contemplating objects, that seem like a golden dream" (76). Morgan carefully negotiates the minefield of political critique in the tense atmosphere of the 1790s by submerging her political commentary in the language of aesthetics. Her comparison directly paraphrases a passage from Burke's *A Philosophical Enquiry into the Origin of Our Ideas of the Sublime and the Beautiful* (1757) in which he discusses the tranquil appeal of the beautiful as opposed to the terror of the sublime. To use his precise words, "It is rather the soft green of the soul on which we rest our eyes, that are fatigued with beholding more glaring objects."[107] Morgan's use of Burke's analogy loosely allies Sandleford with his definition of the beautiful and Blenheim with his definition of the sublime, investing the two divergent estates with the aesthetic qualities and the political dimensions manifest in Burke's categories. According to his theory, the innocuous nature of beauty elicits love, whereas the threatening nature of the sublime induces terror. As a result, beauty is productive of society because it is naturally attractive. "I call beauty a social quality," Burke explains, "for where women and men . . . give us a sense of joy and pleasure beholding them . . . they inspire us with sentiments of tenderness and affection towards their persons; we like to have them near us, and we enter willingly into a kind of relation with them."[108] Although the sublime provokes respect, it is an admiration grounded in fear and therefore fundamentally anti-social; Burke argues that we intuitively distance ourselves from that which elicits terror out of a sense of self-preservation.[109] The political applications of Burke's aesthetic theories become evident in his rough alignment of the beautiful with a form of British libertarianism and the sublime with "despotic governments."[110] The former secures obedience through affection, garnering loyalty through the dispensation of "reliefs, gratifications, and indulgences"; the latter acquires power through fear, obviating "mischiefs" through the threat of "dangers, punishments, and troubles."[111]

Montagu's sympathetic governance operates according to the dictates of the beautiful, procuring love (or at least loyalty) through acts of social amelioration. The association that Morgan draws between Blenheim and the sublime suggests that the Duke of Marlborough represents a more authoritarian approach to governance that achieves submission through the spectacle of power—a suggestion that is reinforced both in her characterization of Blenheim as a "monument of . . . martial achievements" (74) and in her sensation of being incapacitated by the estate's presence.[112] Her elaboration of Burke's "glaring object" into the scorching sun and the nightmarish experience of inhabiting a world gone slightly mad underscores the terrifying experience of the sublime as described by Burke,[113] indicating the negative impact of Blenheim's aesthetics and the politics enshrined therein. Morgan attempts to convey that Montagu's relational approach to power and attention to social realities produces a society that is both contented ("the mind is gratified") and sustainable ("upon which [the eye] may rest for ever without satiety or weariness"), while the Duke of Marlborough's spectacle of wealth and naked display of power fosters disillusionment ("too gay and too gaudy") and is ultimately unsustainable ("dazzled with gazing at the sun"). Given the critical juncture at which Britain found itself in 1795, Morgan asks her audience to examine the principles ensuring the social harmony of Montagu's estate and to seriously consider their implementation on a national scale. Her comparison of Montagu to a "loadstone" (209) in her correspondence with Matthew Montagu not only suggests the magnetic quality of sympathy but also identifies his aunt as a compass both for the Tory politician and, more broadly, for a nation struggling to find its way amidst the push and pull of revolutionary and reactionary forces.[114]

RUINED CASTLES AND MODERN IDYLLS: WELSH LANDOWNERS AND THE EVOLUTION OF BRITISH GOVERNANCE

Morgan's pointed comparison between authoritarian and sympathetic approaches to governance is further developed in the contrast she builds between ancient Welsh ruins and modern Welsh estates, and specifically between medieval and modern leadership practices. Long hailed as the birthplace of the British nation, Wales provides Morgan with ample opportunity to investigate her nation's genesis and political evolution. The Arthurian legends that Morgan collects and the ruins she is so eager to discover are invested with national significance: by exploring Welsh history, she is simultaneously tracing the emergence of British national identity. Although she is fascinated with British history and is interested in its preservation, she is also deeply critical of the past and harbors a suspicion of romanticizing history and turning to the past for a vision of the ideal future. Her seemingly contradictory impulse both to preserve and improve embodies Burke's argument for balancing the dictates of tradition and innovation in *Reflections*. "A good patriot and a true politician," he asserts, "always considers how he shall make the most of the existing materials of his country. A disposition to preserve, and an ability to improve, taken together, would be my standard of a statesman" (157–158). For Morgan, the past is important as an indication of Britain's progress rather than as a model for how the nation should function. She rejects the Whig interpretation of British political history as a devolution away from ancient freedoms, understanding freedom as a relatively modern achievement acquired through the efflorescence of sensibility. Her ambivalence toward the past is imbricated with her disapproval of systems that perpetuate themselves through sublime terror, and her criticism of the factionalism and the feudalism in Britain's past doubles as a condemnation of the divisive politics of radical reformers and of the aggressive policies of the British government in the present.

Entering into Wales, Morgan is struck by the plethora of ancient ruins: "Every town and every village, through which we have passed, from Hay hither, has a castle in it, and all of them in ruins. These carry the mind back to other times, and bring to its view haughty barons and feudal tyranny, the croisades, the age of chivalry, bloody battles, paynim knights, distressed damsels, gallant lovers, haunted towers, ghosts, fairies, and inchantments" (146). She is drawn to these ancient remnants for their evocative quality, equally fascinated by their romantic associations as she is repelled by their history of violence. Yet despite her occasional indulgence in romantic reveries, Morgan refuses to allow Britain's actual history ("haughty barons and feudal tyranny") to be eclipsed or palliated by a romantic version of British history ("the age of chivalry"). She consciously avoids idealizing

Britain's past to prevent the perpetuation of its evils into the present. Similar to the anonymous Lady's reaction to Scottish ruins described in Chapter 3, Morgan adopts what Malcolm Andrews refers to as a "political" response to Welsh antiquities, which considers "the ruin as an image of Nature's levelling of haughty tyranny."[115] Her political approach to these fragments of the past is demonstrated in her statement on the contemporary condition of Welsh peasants: "There are no remains of that subjection, to which their free-born necks were unwillingly bowed down, when a stately castle over-awed every village. Those castles, now in ruins, serve only to remind them of the happy change that has taken place" (270–271). The ruined castles serve as symbols of Britain's political evolution; they are a material reminder of the unsustainability of political systems predicated upon fear and oppression.

The physical fragmentation of ancient buildings further suggests the political fragmentation of ancient Britain. Surveying the landscape from the vantage point of hindsight, Morgan reminds her audience that these romantic ruins reveal a violent history of political schism. Her representation of ancient Britain as a series of disconnected communities gestures toward the former division of the British Isles: "They lived in solitary dignity, hemmed in on all sides by mountains and precipices, having a little principality within their own jurisdiction, and lording it over the poor simple peasant, their humble tenants and neighbours. This mode of living in voluntary seclusion from the society of their equals, was by no means peculiar to Wales, but prevailed over every part of this island" (132). Morgan's initial portrayal of the "solitary dignity" of feudal societies suggests a romanticized reading of the past that is then disrupted by her negative appraisal of this "voluntary seclusion." Casting a side-eye toward Rousseauvian primitivism, she asserts that the absence of social feeling—indicated by the oppression of the peasantry and the "*voluntary* seclusion" of ancient Britons—engenders violent behaviors that ultimately obviate the formation of community.[116] The nation's fraught history of internecine violence is illustrated in a lengthy excerpt that recounts the life of King Arthur, which Morgan professes to have collected from various oral storytellers. She confesses that the "marvelous and poetical" elements of ancient texts are suited to her sentimental tastes but finds the "opinions and manners of remote times" (160) to be perverse rather than exemplary. She guides her audience's reading of the legend by prefacing it with the following statement: "I know not whether it be most mortifying or pleasing to observe, how little can be attributed to our boasted natural understanding, when left to itself, uninformed by education, and unenlightened by revelation" (160). Morgan's ambivalence appears to be at least partially directed toward the brutality that characterized ancient life; the version of the Arthurian legend she presents is a catalogue of slaughter among the diverse nations that comprised medieval Britain. Although Jacqueline Pearson believes that the popularity of the Arthurian legend during the revolutionary 1790s and the subsequent Napoleonic Wars was "accelerated by its political usefulness in defining an idealized, stable and virtuous English nationalism,"[117] Morgan appears to interpret the legend differently—not as a celebration of Britain's founding principles, but as an index of Britain's progression from its primitive roots. Britain's monuments and myths present a legacy of violent factionalism that provides further evidence for the instability of governing systems that achieve and retain power through violence.

Indeed, Morgan clarifies that it is only after social feeling developed and sympathy mitigated the exercise of power that the British Isles could cohere and emerge as a nation. "What a happy change has this kingdom undergone since those times!" she exclaims. "Now the nobility and gentry find a rational pleasure in the society of those, who can either do them service or communicate information. They look upon their tenants and neighbours as men and brothers, and are happy, by the urbanity of their behaviour, to set them an example. . . . In return, they receive sincere affection and friendship, instead of fear and servility" (132–133). The cohesive and conservative implications of sympathy are clearly advertised in this image of contemporary British unity. The development of social feeling among the aristocracy progressively eliminated the "bloody wars" (146) generated by endemic factionalism, while the formation of sympathetic bonds between landowner and tenant established a society characterized by the exchange of mutual ministrations. Loyalty, then, arises organically from the reciprocal action of sympathy; the contemporary Welsh communities that Morgan describes are firmly bound through ties of affection rather than through fear of retribution.

This idealized version of Britain that she professes to find in eighteenth-century Wales is represented as an antidote to the sociopolitical ills threatening the health of the British nation.[118] The connection that Morgan creates between sympathy and social stability in her observations on Montagu's estate extends to her description of the modern estates she encounters in Wales, progressively building an argument for the political value of sympathy. She is careful to note the Welsh landlords' sympathetic management of their tenants, and the corresponding well-being and loyalty of the Welsh peasantry. She marvels at the "healthiness, cleanliness, and ease in the countenance of a Welsh peasant" and suggestively observes that "they are much better fed and clothed than ours are" (261). Her description of the Welsh peasantry echoes her description of Montagu's employees, who are likewise characterized by "an extraordinary degree of cleanliness and decency" and all "fed and cloathed by [Montagu's] hand" (39). Given this clear parallel, it is unsurprising that Morgan is quick to attribute the physical and emotional fitness of the Welsh peasantry to the benevolent governance practiced by Welsh landowners: "Men of fortune have a number of tenants . . . but I believe they never exercise the least degree of tyranny. They rather consider them as under their protection, than as their vassals. It seems to be the land of perfect liberty" (270). She finds the same values governing Welsh estates as she found governing Sandleford: these modern landowners manage their communities using benevolent rather than coercive practices, protecting rather than threatening individual liberties. She underlines her argument by noting the decorous behavior of the Welsh peasantry, which she attributes to a genuine affection for authority: "There are no marks, in either the looks or manners of the Welsh peasantry, which indicate a greater degree of subjection to superiors, than the due order of society requires. They have certainly more civility in their behavior than the boors in England; but it seems to be the result of a generous disposition, not of fear" (272). Her reference to the "boors in England" is reminiscent of Burke's derogatory classification of the lower classes as a "swinish multitude" (79) and invokes the mob activity that spread through Britain in the mid-1790s due to political unrest and food shortages. Morgan's pointed juxtaposition of the orderly Welsh peasantry with the disorderly English peasantry suggests that the source of their difference lies in social rather than biological factors. That they have been shaped by the structures of power under which they labor is indicated by her observation that the Welsh aristocracy "set . . . an example" (133). Welsh landowners model "civility" and "genero[sity]" (79) through their leadership practices; their sympathetic behavior is mirrored back to them in the form of "sincere affection and friendship" (133). Through Morgan's application of the golden rule to political relationships, she suggests that the English peasantry's boorish behavior has perhaps more to do with the deportment of English authority than the nature of the English peasantry.

Morgan's message is clear: fellow feeling has political dimensions. She distinctly emphasizes the reciprocal benefits exchanged between landlord and tenant within a society ruled by sympathetic governance. Read within the hostile political context of 1795—a period marked by the British government's uncompromising suppression of subversive political expression—Morgan's depiction of these idyllic landed estates suggests itself as an active questioning of what some perceived as the British government's devolution into a regime motivated by fear. The wrecks of castles littering the Welsh landscape serve as a reminder that a kingdom constructed upon oppression—or "fear and servility" (133)—is unstable and unsustainable. Her mobility performs the crucial task of enabling her to study, compare, and submit what she believes are the best examples of governance functioning within the nation. Under the pressures of revolution and war, she insists that Britain must not look for answers in the distant past or toward what radicals perceived as the future in France but consider the contemporary models of benevolent leadership quietly and successfully operating throughout the British countryside.

"THE TRANQUILITY OF A SOCIETY OF FEMALES": AN ARGUMENT FOR FEMALE POLITICAL PARTICIPATION

Fundamental to Morgan's project of national revitalization is the modification of the role women play in Britain's political culture. By reinforcing the political function of sympathy throughout her observations on Britain's sociopolitical landscape, she simultaneously opens up the possibility of women's inclusion in the nation's political life. Her representation of women—including her own self-representation—conspicuously supports the eighteenth-century construction of women as repositories of sensibility, alive to the complex emotional dynamics operating between individuals and within societies. She postulates that this heightened emotional responsiveness facilitates their critical faculties and leadership qualities; the ability of women both to perceive emotional nuances and to create sympathetic communities aligns with Burke's definition in *Reflections* of the "true lawgiver" endowed with "an heart full of sensibility" (169). Morgan builds her argument for the greater inclusion of women within the nation's political life by progressing through two rhetorical strategies: she contrasts the sympathetic nature of women against the violent impulses of men and suggests women's intellectual capacities through her representation of accomplished, diversely gifted women and through her support of female education.

Whereas Morgan repeatedly associates men with aggression, women are shown to foster community. Describing the society she encounters at Malvern Wells, Morgan finds similarities between the tourist hub and the "charming imaginary society" (113) pictured in Scott's *Millenium Hall*; the only difference between the nonfictional and fictional societies is the absence of men in the latter. "In that," Morgan wryly states, "Mrs S—shewed perfectly her knowledge of human nature, for men are terrible disturbers of the tranquility of a society of females" (112). The implications of this male disruptive quality are manifest in Morgan's ambivalent representations of war throughout her travelogue. Given her husband's contribution to the war effort in the form of patriotic sermons, it seems likely that Morgan was well versed in Britain's ongoing struggle against the French Revolutionary Army. In "A Sermon on Public Spirit" (1798), Rev. Morgan rallied public support for king and country by representing Britain's leaders as paradigms of civic virtue. "They have stepped forth at the call of their country," he asserts, "have relinquished their princely abodes . . . [and] have placed themselves in the first rank, to oppose, at the hazard of their lives, the inveterate enemies of our king and our constitution."[119] Mary Morgan's publications noticeably lack the patriotic cheerleading of her husband's sermons; in both her travelogue and in her later publication *The Knyghte of the Golden Locks*, she focuses on the destruction accomplished by masculine violence. In *Milford Haven*, her visual representations of war tend toward the grotesque rather than the glorious. Her image of the world "deluged . . . with blood" (115) coheres with her images of mutilated soldiers—few of whom ever "recover the injury done to their constitution by wounds or a great effusion of blood" or "had a limb restored when . . . dismembered" (235)—to form a particularly disconcerting picture of military conflict. This bleak emphasis shares rhetorical and ideological similarities with Vicesimus Knox's anti-war missives rather than with the more militant effusions of her husband.[120] Knox's emphasis on "the ugliness of slaughter" aligns with Morgan's representation of war, and she shares his discomfort regarding violence undertaken for personal and national profit.[121] Comparing the behavior of territorial lobsters to the war-like tendencies of men, she asserts, "Though there appears to be little worth contending for in the possession of a lobster; yet perhaps, in the eye of cool reason and philosophy, they may seem wiser than men in their quarrels. Their very existence may depend upon securing a booty of small fish, a commodious bank of land, or a piece of rock in a particular situation" (234–235). Morgan posits that the male *desire* for violence renders them more animalistic than lobsters; whereas the sea creatures are motivated by self-preservation, men are driven by personal gain or glory. Her parallel between Britain's military leaders "rejoic[ing]" (208) at the prospect of war and the Welsh peasants who greedily eye a distressed ship firmly suggests that war is often fueled by desire rather than by duty or necessity. The propensity of men to disturb rather than to pursue peace implicitly questions their socially sanctioned role as Britain's political leaders.

On the other hand, Morgan's insistence on women's ability to enable and sustain community encourages revising their political marginalization—an urgent consideration in light of Britain's national disorder. She demonstrates the female capacity for effective political leadership in her portrayal of Elizabeth Montagu and in her own roles as traveler and writer. Both Montagu and Morgan provide tangible, alternative models of femininity that underscore women's intellectual abilities. Morgan's implication that Montagu's estate management provides the best prototype for governance suggests that women are gifted with leadership qualities worthy of wider application. It is not insignificant that Montagu's exemplary estate lacks a governing male figure; the absence of masculine supervision suggests that women can not only construct well-ordered societies independent of men, but that they can construct societies *better* than men. Whereas the broader political implications of Montagu's domestic management are suggested through the conventional association between the private estate and the nation, Morgan's physical and intellectual activity renders the *extra*domestic capabilities of women visible. Her movement forms an important counterpoint to Montagu's stasis.[122] Operating within the national space rather than within the domestic sphere—forming connections between different ethnicities through her movement within nation, gaining perspective through her national survey, and imparting counsel through her sociopolitical insights—she demonstrates the ability of women to perform public political roles. Indeed, Morgan encourages the politicization of women through her argument for educational reform, through which she seeks to equip women with the tools necessary to achieve greater influence within society. "I would not," she asserts, "have [women] stand by unconcerned spectators of what is passing in the world, but acquire such a general knowledge as not to be totally ignorant of any thing that is a frequent subject of conversation" (286). Her statement expresses a desire for women to be involved citizens who exert influence both within and outside of the domestic sphere. Morgan clearly believes that women deserve a strong and visible presence within the nation, emphatically stating during a discussion of domestic roles that women should *not* "confine themselves to their nurseries" (285).

She defends her own excursions (both physically and professionally) into the public sphere by asserting the diverse capabilities of women. Her preemptive rebuttal to fogyish critics is worth quoting at length: "As a female, I have certainly no occasion to excuse my temerity, so many of my sex have shewn they are capable of the most admirable compositions on the most important subjects. I therefore am not afraid of being accused of going out of my sphere in publishing this trifling Work. To those who think a woman cannot find leisure to write, without neglecting either her person or some part of her family duty, I say nothing. They must believe, that the sex is formed merely to dress and be admired, or for domestic drudgery" (ix). Morgan's defense of her publication both asserts the intellectual equality of women and condemns the attempts of critics to stifle her work on the basis of gender. Her gesture toward the repressive measures used by patriarchal society to condemn women to "dress" and "domestic drudgery" is repeated in a deceivingly lighthearted jab at her husband's condescending treatment of her. "I see now," she declares, "how you men deceive, and treat us like children, for when you seem to be acceding to our humours the most willingly, you have something in reserve that you know must, in the end, bring us over to your own" (145). That men are represented as using condescension to force women into submission creates a suggestive parallel between their behavior and that of despotic landlords, whom Morgan describes as using similar techniques to maintain power over their tenants. Of course, whereas the power dynamics between landlord and tenant have evolved to reflect modern ideals, Morgan's rebuke of both her critics and her husband demonstrates that women remain confined within archaic standards. Her defense of women's public contributions reads as a clarion call for an evolved interpretation of the female sex that acknowledges women's multifaceted nature and expands their influence beyond the traditional roles of sexual objects, wives, and mothers. Not only is their active intervention in the life of their nation defensible, it is exigent given the political crisis facing the British nation. Morgan cautiously suggests that masculine aggression must be mitigated by, or subordinate to, feminine sensibility to create the possibility of a cohesive national community.

SYMPATHY AND UNITY

Morgan's personal interaction with the foreign and the familiar throughout her travels models sympathetic engagement and advertises the benefits of a sentimental disposition. She is critical of travelers and travel writers who approach different cultures with an attitude of suspicion or disinterest rather than with sympathy. Morgan suggests that this mode of interacting with different cultures obviates the possibility of connection; travel becomes a way to assert rather than overcome racial, cultural, and national divisions. As she explains, "I have deviated widely in my account of the manners and dispositions of the Welsh from the generality of those authors who have gone before me. . . . They pronounce them, *in the mass*, to be an ignorant and uncivilized set of people" (xiii). Morgan argues that these travelers expect to experience different cultures as inferior, incomprehensible, and ultimately not relatable: "They look upon the Welsh as foreigners, and expect to hear them speak unintelligibly, to see them dress grotesquely, and behave uncouthly . . . [when] they are in most respects like the rest of the world" (253). Their unsympathetic preconceptions prevent the formation of authentic relationships ("They only run through a country, perfect strangers to every body in it" [xiii]) and consequently reinforce rather than dispel prejudice. Morgan advertises the more productive effects of sentimental travel through her own experience: "The freedom and politeness which an intercourse with the world produces are so very captivating, they make you consider every one as your friend who pays you any civility. This casts such a universal benevolence over the mind, that you feel in perfect union with all your species, you forget that clashing interests and cruel ambition have ever set mankind at variance, and deluged the world with blood" (115). Her observation specifically underscores the sociopolitical value of emotionally engaged travel. By practicing sympathy on a national scale and by observing its repercussions on a local level, Morgan discovers that emotional exchange actively counters the violent impulses that splinter nations and ravage the international community. Writing within a context where "clashing interests" had indeed "set mankind at variance," Morgan reminds her audience of the value of sympathy at a critical juncture within British history. If clashing interests are to be smoothed over and national unity achieved, sympathy must be integral to political processes rather than disciplined and relegated.

Morgan's brief dalliance with the notion of "universal benevolence" (115)—the notion that, according to Evan Radcliffe, "benevolence and sympathy could be extended to all humanity"[123]—forms both the motivation for and message behind the final travelogue examined in this book: Helen Maria Williams's *A Tour in Switzerland*. Both Morgan and Williams participate in the vindication of sensibility. Williams understands feeling as a vital component of both private and political life, and shares with Morgan the conviction that the absence of active sensibility augurs sociopolitical degeneration. Where the two travel writers diverge is in their sentimental visions both of society and of the state, as indicated by their conflicting sympathies. Morgan's sympathy ultimately lies with power; her "real affection" (iv) works to cultivate and naturalize sentimental attachments to what she refers to as "titles and dignity" (418). Williams, on the other hand, sympathizes with the politically dispossessed rather than with prevailing power structures; her 'natural' feelings challenge the traditional hierarchies upheld by Morgan by exposing the antipathetic dimensions of asymmetrical power relations. Comparing Morgan's and Williams's travelogues illustrates the struggle over sensibility in the last decade of the eighteenth century—both the struggle to defend sensibility against the accusations of its critics, and the struggle between British conservatives and radicals to harness the potent power of sensibility to their divergent causes.

5

"A RENOVATION OF EXISTENCE"

Helen Maria Williams's *A Tour in Switzerland* and the Renewal of Political Vision

HELEN MARIA WILLIAMS ARRIVED in Switzerland in 1794, traveling under very different circumstances than Mary Morgan. Williams entered Switzerland from revolutionary France not as a tourist but as an exile; fearing Maximilien de Robespierre's retribution for her blatant criticism of his government, she fled to the Alps seeking both personal security and emotional succor. "I am going to repose my wearied spirit on those sublime objects," she states at the outset of her travelogue, "to sooth my desponding heart with the hope that the moral disorder I have witnessed shall be rectified, while I gaze on nature in all her admirable perfections."[1] Although this statement frames her tour as an *escape* from political reality, Williams's travelogue is actually an attempt to *reframe* political reality; her unconventional representation of Switzerland disrupts the political sympathies that were shaping the course of the French Revolutionary Wars and the political composition of both Britain and Europe.

Published four years after Williams's actual journey, *A Tour in Switzerland* is written as a political intervention in Britain's public opinion of France's precarious new republic and its military endeavors on the Continent. Her text is a refutation of the anti-Jacobin opinion pervading Britain and counters many of Morgan's political principles described in Chapter 4. Williams believes that the traditional loyalties and mutual dependencies hailed by Morgan as the source of national cohesion are, in fact, the basis of the internecine and international violence that both women deplore; the revolutionary feeling that Morgan interprets as breeding national disorder is embraced by Williams as a generative force that liberates individuals and nations from political exploitation. Williams attempts to colonize the same emotional terrain sought after by Morgan. Her radical argument is embedded in sentimental language, creating an emotionally engaged and engaging text that appeals to the feelings of her British audience to reverse the nation's increasingly counterrevolutionary mood. Her political project seeks to direct (or redirect) her readers' emotional investments toward what she defines as the proper objects of feeling, forging mutually transformative sentimental identifications among nations in conformity with her republican vision. While Williams and Morgan use sensibility and its associated vocabulary to accomplish very different political ends, they are united in the conviction that feeling informs the construction of a just and harmonious society. Both attribute political injustice and social dissonance to the vitiation of sensibility they perceive within their respective societies. Their shared persuasion that gendered injustice fundamentally undermines social stability is intimately connected to their shared sense that social cohesion and progress are tied to the healthy circulation of feeling within and between nations.

THE PERSISTENCE OF FEELING: WILLIAMS'S POLITICAL LOYALTIES

Williams's background evidently informed her development into one of the eighteenth century's most infamous female politicians and the most vocal apologist for the French Revolution. Born to a Scottish army officer and a Welsh mother, her combined heritage of two cultures so often marginalized within the British polity perhaps shaped her adoption of a cosmopolitan rather than strictly British identity. Her upbringing in an all-female family after the early death of her father initiated a lifelong interest in the condition of women, while her immersion in the liberal atmosphere of Britain's Dissenting circles fostered a commitment to radical politics that would later inform her enthusiasm for the French Revolution and sustain her faith in its central tenets even after she witnessed its disintegration into violence and tyranny. Williams was an established author by the time she published *A Tour in Switzerland* in 1798, having first distinguished herself as respected poet and novelist in the 1780s before reinventing herself as a controversial travel writer after moving to revolutionary France. *A Tour in Switzerland* was but an installment in her growing repertoire of published travelogues; she had already published eight volumes of travel letters that spanned the six tumultuous years following her arrival in Paris during the Fête de la Fédération, establishing the British transplant as the "leading interpreter" of the revolution by the end of the decade.[2] Her sentimental depiction of the French Revolution urged her British audience to sympathize with the radical agenda of the revolutionaries; she envisioned her letters as forging "a line of connection across the divided world"[3] and hoped that this sympathetic connection might instigate similar reforms in her native country. While her staunch commitment to the revolution's early principles earned her admiration and friendship within France, it alienated her from her British friends and readers. She visited Britain for the last time in 1792, thereafter principally remaining in France until her death in 1827. Williams's texts continued to receive widespread recognition in Britain during the last decade of the eighteenth century and into the first decades of the nineteenth century. Although her support of radical politics was increasingly controversial as the revolution descended into violence, her position as an eyewitness to the rapidly changing and sensational events in France ensured her an eager audience back home.

Williams's trip to Switzerland in 1794 was motivated by both political exigency and political curiosity. She explains that she left Paris under duress, forced to flee Robespierre's bloody campaign before she became the guillotine's newest victim. Robespierre's administration had become increasingly hostile to foreigners, and due to both her association with the deposed Girondins and her public deprecation of Robespierre in her *Letters from France: Containing a Great Variety of Interesting and Original Information Concerning the Most Important Events that Have Lately Occurred in that Country* (1793), Williams occupied a particularly precarious position in Jacobin-ruled France. "With the knife of the guillotine suspended over me by a frail thread," she describes, "I fled to Switzerland."[4] She traveled to Switzerland in the company of two British expatriates: the political radical and recently divorced John Hurford Stone, who was scandalously rumored to be her lover, and Benjamin Vaughan, a British politician who fled England after being suspected of conspiring with French and Irish revolutionaries in a plot to invade England. That Stone was reputedly traveling as a representative for the French government suggests that factors other than exigency determined their choice of destination. In its review of Williams's travelogue, *The British Critic* suspects that Stone may have been engaged in subversive activity while in Switzerland, acting on behalf of the French government as an "incendiary" and as a "spy."[5] Although the exact purpose of his political business remains unknown, Stone's previous involvement with the United Irishmen and the allegations of treason made against him during his brother's trial for sedition in 1794–1796 certainly tarnished his reputation in Britain.[6] The political events that transformed the Swiss Confederacy in the years immediately following their journey and Williams's particular attention to the revolutionary mood within Switzerland suggest the political interests and investments that the company may have been pursuing over the course of their six-month tour. Although their activity was centered in Basel, they also traversed the nation's northern, southern, and western parts in search of Switzerland's much-admired natural wonders, storied historical and literary sites, urban centers, intellectual elite, and—perhaps most importantly—to gain a sense of Switzerland's political climate.

A Tour in Switzerland was published in two volumes and appeared four years after Williams's actual journey, its contents based on a combination of her original travel journals and accounts of recent political developments. It is an engaging mixture of sentimental reverie, aesthetic contemplation, and rigorous political description, with Williams's narratives of personal and national regeneration holding the pieces together. Her explanation in the preface of the time lapse between journey and publication suggests that she had originally determined to keep her Swiss journals private, checked by the awareness that her "unfinished outline" ultimately "offered nothing new" to a public well-served with Swiss travel accounts. However, the prospect of a political revolution in Switzerland in the years following her six-month stay provided Williams with a convenient excuse to publish her original observations. "It is the present moral situation of Switzerland," she adds, "that justifies the appearance of these volumes, in which an attempt is made to trace the important effects which the French Revolution has produced in that country, and which are about to unfold a new æra in its history." The publication of her travelogue nearly coincided with the French invasion of Switzerland, causing at least one reviewer to (not inaccurately) speculate that her text "may be considered as a precursory apology for what has since happened between the french and swiss republics."[7] Williams presents her observations in a journalistic style that both reflects her source material (journals) and mirrors the approach taken by her predecessors. Her frequent references to the immensely popular Swiss travelogues of Dr. John Moore and William Coxe suggests her familiarity with their works (Moore was also a close family friend). Moore's *A View of Society and Manners in France, Switzerland, and Germany* (1779) and Coxe's *Travels in Switzerland* (1789) were considered the gold standard of travel writing; their weighty volumes were carried by travelers on their Swiss tours,[8] were exceptionally well reviewed, and had gone through multiple editions. Williams's decision to emulate their style of documentation suggests her determination to be placed among their ranks as a travel writer and for her revisionary work to be considered alongside of their productions.

Although Williams's travelogue received extensive coverage in the British press, critical reception of her work was mixed. Williams's lifestyle and political investments had irretrievably damaged her reputation in Britain; her unrelenting commitment to the revolution's ideals and reports of her affair with Stone were cited as evidence of her moral perversion. Moreover, her glowing representation of the French Revolutionary Army certainly did not gain her any favors in a nation at war against the very military she defended. Critics continue to admire her powers of description, but their condemnation of her politics is nearly unanimous. "As a Poetess," one reviewer cautiously comments, "Miss Williams attracts us much more than as a politician."[9] Their judgment is directed against what they perceive as her transgression of gender roles, her specific political commitments, and her sentimental style. *The Monthly Review* carefully questions her political orientation by casting aspersions upon her intellectual capacity, commenting that "politics seem to be Miss W.'s favorite science, but it is not the subject in which she is the best qualified to excel."[10] *The London Review* interrupts its generally favorable evaluation of her work to condemn its politics, cautioning that "her bias to the *Gallic phantom of Liberty* is too obvious, not to make us read with jealousy, and recommend with caution, [her] work."[11] Not unlike the negative appraisals of Mary Morgan's travelogue three years earlier, the dominant reproach of Williams's text is her sentimental style of narration. The reviewers' pointed criticisms of her signature blend of politics and sentiment all suggest the dangerous nature of feeling. *The Analytical Review* archly cites Williams's inspiration as James Macpherson's heavily romanticized (and fraudulent) translation of the Gaelic Ossian cycle of poems, implying that Williams's sentimental orientation compromises the veracity of her account. "Her fancy, cradled by Ossian," the reviewer suggests, "had peopled the primæval scenery of Alps, and rocks, and glaciers, with a primitive race, if not of giants, at least of patriarchal form and manners."[12] The reviewer for *The British Critic* similarly suggests that her sentimental form of expression reveals an inherent absence of judgment, characterizing her work as "more remarkable for the gaudy glare of declamation, than for sound reason or sober argument."[13] *The Monthly Review* provides a more general statement on the conflation of sentiment and politics, citing the sentimental politics of Edmund Burke and Williams as examples of the danger that comes from situating "sound over sense."[14] "Both [Burke] and Miss W.," the reviewer concludes, "afford very striking examples that poetical politicians are . . . objectionable; since all sound moral and practical reasoning, to which the science of politics eminently belongs, is totally incompatible with the giddy flights of an unrestrained and impassioned fancy."[15]

The recurrent attack on Williams's sentimental politics reflects the beleaguered condition of sensibility and its attendant practices by the late 1790s, as appeals to the heart became aligned with disordered imaginations and disorderly behavior, while the realm of politics became progressively divorced from feeling. Williams's joint identity as a doyenne of sentimental literature and as a vocal apologist for the French Revolution made her an obvious target for the late eighteenth-century backlash against the culture of sensibility. Her *Letters Written in France* is a tour de force in sentimental travel writing; as she explicitly states, "My political creed is entirely an affair of the heart, for I have not been so absurd as to consult my head upon matters which it is so incapable of judging" (91). Early reviews of her travel letters reserved warm praise for her sentimental representation of the

French Revolution. The critic for *The Monthly Review* commends the "rapturous feeling" with which she relates the events in France,[16] and the reviewers for *The Gentleman's Magazine* and *The General Magazine* grudgingly indulge what they consider to be the "enthusiasm of a sprightly writer" and the "natural, and perhaps unavoidable effusion of a young and fervid imagination."[17] The critic for *The English Review* might doubt the veracity of Williams's account, yet still admires and admittedly succumbs to her ability to "melt even a heart of stone."[18] Enshrined as the archetypical sentimental subject in Wordsworth's "Sonnet on Seeing Miss Helen Maria Williams Weep at a Tale of Distress" (1787) and in Edward Jerningham's "On Reading 'Letters Written from France, in the Summer 1790, to a Friend in England, by Helen Maria Williams'" (1790), Williams was hailed for her ability to translate personal feeling into political argument.[19] "She tries no formal refutation," Jerningham enthuses,

> Nor raves of Governments and Laws,
> For she to Nature trusts her cause;
> Makes to the heart her strong appeal,
> Which all who have a heart must feel . . .[20]

However, as the French Revolution devolved from a political phenomenon into a national threat and failed to live up to the idealistic vision championed by its supporters, conservatives and radicals alike were quick to point out the dangers of what Laetitia Matilda Hawkins described as the "heart unaided by the head."[21] Hawkins published a two-volume refutation of Williams's politics entitled *Letters on the Female Mind* (1793), which was written as an explicit condemnation of and corrective to Williams's sentimental defense of the French Revolution. "Sentimental ladies," Hawkins opined, "are not to be relied on for their opinions on subjects where the passions and affections ought not to interfere."[22] Williams's tenacious advocacy of revolutionary ideals amidst the disintegration of France was increasingly interpreted as perverse rather than charming, and her sentimental persona became an indication of the dangers posed by sensibility. Chris Jones observes that for anti-Jacobins, Williams "demonstrated too clearly the untrustworthiness of sensibility as a creed that could justify assassination and the Terror."[23] The unease with her persistent conflation of personal feeling and national politics exhibited in the reviews of her later work serves as an indication of the demise of the culture of sensibility in the final years of the eighteenth century.

Not unlike her stalwart commitment to the revolution's original principles, she remained fiercely invested in what Jones refers to as the "wider potentialities of sensibility" despite,[24] or perhaps due to, the social backlash against sensibility in its various manifestations. Her belief that the heart holds the key to both ethical and effective political reform perseveres through the atrocities she witnesses and remains a guiding principle in *A Tour in Switzerland*. The travelogue certainly lacks the youthful excitement and hopeful energy of her first travel letters, a tone that occasionally has been taken as an indication of her waning faith in the sociopolitical possibilities of feeling. Jones, for instance, reads Williams's Swiss travelogue as a failure of sympathy and as a statement on the limitations of sensibility in post-Terror Europe. "She follows a trajectory common to many radical writers," he contends, "from a relatively unthinking trust in the progressive reformation of society to a recognition that such hopes cannot rely merely on collective humanitarian feelings."[25] However, the personal context of Williams's travels is important to take into consideration; what Jones interprets as skepticism may also be interpreted as the effects of hard-won maturity or as the preponderance of grief. The space of eight years, the trauma of imprisonment, and the violent deaths of many of her close friends would certainly dampen the ardor of youth. That her sentiments are not as "sprightly" as they once were is to be expected,[26] yet it would be remiss to say that Williams abandons her faith in the transformative potential of sensibility. She believes that the impulse to divorce "sound" from "sense" is fundamentally dangerous,[27] and in her Swiss travelogue attributes the eruption of revolutionary violence to the absence rather than the excess of sensibility, emphasizing the Jacobins' unsympathetic nature (1:83, 89–91) and characterizing their administrative period as "the epocha of the worship of reason" (1:90). In the volatile period following Robespierre's execution, Williams, in *Letters Containing a Sketch of the Politics of France, from the Thirty-first of May 1793, till the Twenty-eighth of July 1794, and of the scenes which have passed in the Prisons of Paris* (1795) measures national regeneration according to the role feeling is allowed to play within society. "The love of public virtue in the people of France," she effuses with some relief, "is now blended with all the sympathies and affections of their natures" (1:258). She clearly reverses Hawkins's observation that the "heart unaided by the head is the most deceitful advisor,"[28] suggesting that the head unaided by the heart is a far more terrifying mentor. Not dissimilar from Burke's fear that the abstraction accomplished by reason reduces humans to animals,[29] Williams suggests that the absence of authentic feeling enables a process of dehumanization that both invites and justifies violence. I perceive a profound distrust of pure reason in Williams's later work and read her Swiss travelogue as a defense rather than as a denunciation of sensibility. Her experience with revolutionary violence reinforced her conviction that "collective humanitarian feelings" must participate in the redevelopment of society,[30] as it is only through the widespread cultivation of sensibility that the selfish imperatives of exploitation are inhibited.

Williams's choice to record her Swiss experience in the form of a sentimental travelogue—a form to which she had amply contributed over the years—demonstrates her continued investment in the political rhetoric and praxis of sensibility. The reviews of her work all attest to the sentimental tenor of her Swiss travel letters, and the travelogue itself exhibits the typical characteristics of the sentimental traveler. Her emphasis on emotional responsiveness, intersubjectivity, and anecdote clearly categorizes her work within the Sternian school of travel writing, and her appeals to the heart are grounded in the Yorick-like conviction that the heart is more discerning than the head.[31] Although Jones labels Williams's political project within *A Tour in Switzerland* as "anti-sentimental" given her criticism of "Swiss life and manners,"[32] her active demythologizing of Swiss culture is strategically presented as act of sympathy rather than of prejudice. She explains that she entered Switzerland with an optimistic spirit, carefully distinguishing her orientation as a sentimental rather than as a splenetic traveler: "The first view of Switzerland awakened my enthusiasm most powerfully—'At length,' thought I, 'am I going to contemplate that interesting country, of which I have never heard without emotion! . . . How delightful a transition shall I find in the picture of social happiness which Switzerland presents! I shall no longer see liberty profaned and violated;—here she smiles upon the hills, and decorates the vallies, and finds, in the uncorrupted simplicity of this people, a firmer barrier than in the cragginess of their rocks, or the snows of their Glaciers!'" (1:4–5). Williams looks to Switzerland to fulfill her elusive ideal of a society that operates according to the revolution's founding principles of liberty, equality, and fraternity. Her subsequent criticism of Swiss society is portrayed as a necessary corrective to previous travel writers' false representations—necessary because these mistaken depictions of Switzerland as a land of liberty perpetuate the oppression of its population. Similar to John Thelwall's fictional sentimental traveler who cannot help but respond to "the scenes of distress so perpetually recurring to the feeling observer,"[33] Williams's criticism is discursively presented as an irrepressible response to suffering. Interpreted as an act of sympathy—incited out of her deep feeling *for* rather than *against* the Swiss—Williams's rewriting of accepted representations of Switzerland can be firmly placed within the sentimental school of travel writing. In this travelogue as in her previous publications, she deliberately represents her politics as "an affair of the heart."

In her study of political tourism, Maureen Moynagh finds that "as tourists move across boundaries of cultural difference, apparently fixed markers of social location, of belonging and attachment, shift. Gender, race, sexuality and nationality come to mean differently . . . in the process, new terms of belonging are worked out."[34] This is precisely the political effect that Williams hopes to achieve in her sentimental travelogue. She attempts to shift her British readers' attachments from conservative ideologies to revolutionary ideals by disrupting their "fixed markers" through her own solidarity with the revolutionaries she encounters in both France and Switzerland. Her political agenda is clearly specified in *A Tour in Switzerland*. As several critics suspected in their reviews of her text, her travelogue provides a detailed apology for the imminent French invasion (ideological and physical) of Switzerland, using eyewitness authority and sentimental argument to sway a hostile British public in favor of the aims and vision of the newly inaugurated French Republic. *A Tour in Switzerland* is a carefully crafted political document intended to polish the reputation of the new French government and its military endeavors. Her description of France's total regeneration following the dramatic fall of Robespierre and her glowing recommendation of the French military as the repository of unsullied revolutionary spirit are sharply contrasted with her representation of Switzerland as a nation characterized by degeneration due to the perversion of liberty under its antiquated, oligarchic system of government. Williams's descriptions of the political oppression found in the various cantons she visits and her documentation of the inchoate desire for revolution within the Swiss population builds an argument for the desirability of France's intervention in Switzerland's affairs. In order to align the sympathies of her British public with France rather than with Switzerland, Williams draws on the principle of reciprocity established within the moral philosophies of Adam Smith and David Hume: that sympathizing with suffering individuals carries with it either the moral obligation or the impulse to mitigate their pain. The textual representation of suffering, Lynn Festa explains, "brings the wretchedness of the earth home to the reader" in a manner that moves them "not only to tears but also to right action."[35] What constitutes "right action" for Williams is the cessation of violence between Britain and France, allowing for the movement of revolution from France to Switzerland—and, perhaps, to Britain—which she presents as a solution to the suffering she witnesses in the alpine nation. Her own (political and politicizing) movement through the physical spaces of France and Switzerland contributes to readjusting Britons' ideological attachments by bringing reality to bear upon the idealized interpretations of Switzerland that had shaped Britons' perceptions of, and affiliations with, the nation for generations.

"LET US NOT RENOUNCE THE LAND OF PROMISE": THE POLITICAL REGENERATION OF FRANCE

The French government's more temperate character following the deposition of Robespierre did little to appease public opinion within Britain. The memory of the Reign of Terror and France's unrelenting commitment to the establishment of republican governments across Europe cast a permanent pall over the newly instituted Directory. In an open letter addressed to Williams and published during the height of Robespierre's rule, Anna Seward urged her friend to "fly . . . that land of carnage!—from the influence of that equalizing system, which, instead of diffusing universal love, content, and happiness, lifts every man's hand against his brother!"[36] Seward approvingly reflects upon the rapid expansion of conservatism within Britain in response to the French Revolution's violent turn, observing that radical sentiments have been replaced by "such an universal glow of loyalty, such a grateful and fervent sense of the blessings of our balanced government."[37] Her rather harrowing description of France as the "land of carnage" pales in comparison to Edmund Burke's figurative alignment of the Directory with the biblical Antichrist in his *Letters on a Regicide Peace* (1796): "Out of the tomb of the murdered monarchy in France has arisen a vast, tremendous, unformed spectre, in a far more terrific guise than any which ever yet have overpowered the imagination and subdued the fortitude of men. Going straight forward to its end, unappalled by peril, unchecked by remorse, despising all common maxims and all common means, that hideous phantom overpowered those who could not believe it was possible she could at all exist."[38] Burke's use of apocalyptic imagery recalls the monstrous creatures featured in the book of Revelation, clearly representing the new republic as the embodiment of evil.[39] His *Letters on a Regicide Peace* were written to discourage William Pitt the Younger's ministry from pursuing peace with France, based on his conviction that Jacobin principles must be annihilated in order to prevent their spread.

The cynical appraisals of France's recovery and the disturbing portrayals of its military efforts by several British travel writers assisted in the entrenchment of anti-Jacobin sentiment within Britain. Fellow British travel writer Charlotte Biggs wrote *A Residence in France* (1797) in an obvious attempt to discredit the optimistic tone of Williams's post-Thermidor *Letters from France*,[40] casting the Directory within the same mold as Robespierre's ministry. "Exaction and oppression are still practised in every shape," she declares, "and justice is not less violated, nor is property more secure, than when the former was administered by revolutionary tribunals, and the latter was at the disposition of revolutionary armies."[41] Her characterization of the Directory's aggressive dissemination of republican principles as "spreading universal ruin" is expanded upon by several British travelers who witnessed the devastation of war in the course of their Continental travels.[42] In *Gleanings through Wales, Holland, and Westphalia; with Views of Peace and War at Home and Abroad* (1796), Samuel Jackson Pratt details the atrocities committed both by the French government against its own people and by the French troops against the nations they invade. "It is not easy to suppose," he states, "the ravagers could, in so short a space of time, change *every happy circumstance to its bitterest opposite*; that they could turn, for instance, plenty into famine, health to disease, and a contented mind to an agonized, broken spirit! Yet all this had been done *by the sons of liberty*, who too truly put their threat of execution, of *carrying misery and death* into every place they visited."[43] Pratt encourages and justifies Britain's military involvement on the Continent by comparing the French Republic to a "gangrene" that must be eradicated by "fire and sword."[44] Although Ann Radcliffe is more measured than Pratt in her assessment of the French Revolutionary War in *A Journey Made in the Summer of 1794* (1796), she also expresses her disapproval of the French government's international aggression. Her disturbing descriptions of wounded soldiers, devastated landscapes, and destroyed cities construct an argument against war instigated for offensive rather than defensive purposes. In its cautious appraisal of Williams's 1798 travelogue, *The London Review* characterizes the purpose of the French Revolutionary Army as spreading "anarchy" and describes the effect of war as "destroying mankind and devastating the face of nature, under the specious pretence of asserting their inalienable rights."[45] This emphasis on the violent genesis and investments of the new republic contributes to its demonization, constructing fear as an appropriate response to the radically transformed French nation. In his overview of domestic responses to the British war effort, Philip Harling finds that "depictions of the Revolution as a system of absolute violence and destructiveness were commonplace among anti-Jacobin propagandists. They reflected as much as they shaped a widespread perception among Britons that French society and politics were engulfed in a perpetual Reign of Terror."[46]

It is this perception that Williams is addressing in her 1795 *Letters Containing a Sketch of the Politics of France* when she solicits her audience not to "renounce the land of promise" (2:88), and it is this image of France that she attempts to invalidate in *A Tour in Switzerland*. In the former, Williams openly despises Robespierre and his radical faction—whom she refers to as "ignoble usurpers" (2:214)—and attempts to create clear distinctions among the revolution's original principles, the Jacobins, and the Directory. "The last stroke has been given to that vile and degrading system," she emphasizes in reference to Robespierre's ministry. "We may now approach the altar of Liberty with confidence and hope; the hideous spectres which haunted it have fled forever; and its incense in future will rise grateful to heaven, and spread fragrance over a regenerated land" (2:214). Reifying liberty as a goddess, Williams suggests that Robespierre has desecrated her holy spaces through his twisted exploitation of her principles. She demonizes Robespierre in an effort to demonstrate that his ministry was an aberration from, rather than extension of, the revolution, countering the perception broadcasted by anti-Jacobins such as Biggs, who asserts that "all the principles of this monstrous government [Robespierre's ministry] were established during the administration of the Brissotins, and . . . the factions which succeeded, from Danton and Robespierre to Sieyes and Barras, have only developed them, and reduced them to practice."[47] Williams strategically separates the Jacobins' conduct from both the revolution's initial and current aims to preserve enthusiasm for political revolution. In an effort to counter anti-Jacobin rhetoric and feeling within Britain, she attempts both to foster sympathy for what she represents as the victimized French population and to salvage the reputation of the French Revolutionary Army by emphasizing the virtue of its leaders.

The French Revolution as Sentimental Narrative

Within sentimental travelogues, anecdotes often function to humanize experiences and places; they quite literally represent a deviation from the well-trodden path of sights and accommodations to provide information that deepens the readers' understanding of the people, places, and events that the traveler encounters. In *Letters Written in France*—recorded during the heady period following the Fête de la Fédération—Williams extends the anecdotal form of the sentimental travelogue to its limits, embedding a lengthy sentimental narrative featuring Madame and Monsieur du Fossé's harrowing tale of exile, imprisonment, and eventual rescue and reconciliation due to the timely arrival of the French Revolution. Her sentimental narrative humanizes the revolution and draws her British audience into emotional identification with the political event by illustrating its effects upon emotionally appealing subjects, and it was popular enough to be excerpted into a chapbook that was circulated in the early 1790s.[48] She reuses this strategy in *A Tour in Switzerland*, explaining the political trajectory of the revolution's rise, corruption, and regeneration through a lengthy anecdote that conflates political reality and sentimental narrative to shape the emotional orientation of her British audience toward the political events and ideologies represented within the story.

In her travels through Switzerland, Williams opportunely encounters a family of French émigrés living in humble circumstances in a small Swiss village; her lengthy account of their woeful history of seduction and betrayal clearly parallels the course of the revolution and provides a way of thinking about its development that condemns its degeneration into tyranny while enshrining its original character. The sentimental heroine is Madame C—, who is described as a woman possessed of a virtuous character, sympathetic disposition, and aristocratic lineage who embraced the first stirrings of Revolution with the same fervor as Williams. Although her husband "detested the principles of the Revolution" with a revulsion common among the aristocracy, Madame C—"exulted in that change of system which she dared not openly applaud: she had often wept over the miseries of the oppressed people, and was more disposed to rejoice in the amelioration of solid substantial wretchedness, than to lament the ideal deprivations of greatness" (1:288). Following the revolution's descent into retributive violence, Monsieur C—flees to Switzerland in order to secure a place for his young family; in the absence of his wife, he is seduced by a profligate female émigré who represents all the worst excesses of the ancien régime and of Robespierre's ministry. Selfish and voluptuous, Madame de—'s profound disregard for others is evinced through her immorality ("[She] had broken the heart of many a tender female, from whom she had alienated the affections of a beloved husband" [1:300]) and through her inhumanity ("She had been accustomed to consider [the poor] as only born for slavery and silence" [1:301]). Williams refers to her influence as "witcheries and enchantments" (1:303), rhetorically aligning Madame de—with Robespierre, whose power she characterizes as a "terrible spell which bound the land of France."[49] The apparently contradictory conflation of Madame de—with both the ancien régime and with the Jacobin's radical leader is consistent with Williams's political thought. She frequently compares the excesses of Robespierre's administration with those of the ancien régime, arguing that the Jacobins simply reintroduced political tyranny in a different form.[50] Made vulnerable by fear and grief, Monsieur C—succumbs to the "siege" of his seductress, his feelings corrupted as "virtuous love" (1:305) is supplanted by perverse desire. The distortion of Monsieur C—'s feelings mirrors the corruption of the French population, whose exploitation of revolutionary violence Williams interprets as the "powerful testimony to the depravation, not merely of manners, but of the heart" (1:42). As an allegory for revolutionary France, Monsieur C—'s infidelity suggests that France was seduced by the empty fascinations of the Jacobins during a period of political vulnerability, momentarily neglecting its original political commitments.

Monsieur C—'s realization of his wife's loyalty and suffering as a result of his actions eventually rouses him from the "hideous dream" by which he had been "been so fatally misled" (1:316). His affections restored to the right object, the prodigal—broken and broke—gradually experiences both physical and emotional healing, as well as renewed economic stability. Williams closes the tale of the prodigal husband by assuring her audience of Madame and Monsieur C—'s domestic harmony, stating that Madame C—in particular "has a mind capable of relinquishing rank and splendor without a sigh, since she has found happiness in exchange" (1:322). Monsieur C—'s restoration to his original commitments functions as a commentary on France's present sociopolitical circumstances. With Robespierre's "terrible spell" ruptured upon his execution, Williams represents revolutionary France as returning to its founding principles: "The shrieking whirlwinds, the black precipices, the bottomless gulphs, suddenly vanished; and reviving nature covered the wastes with flowers, and the rocks with verdure."[51] With the original, Girondin-led revolutionary movement encapsulated in the figure of the virtuous wife (inspired by authentic feeling to ameliorate social inequality) and both the ancien régime and Robespierre's administration encapsulated in the figure of the seductress (whose deficiency of authentic feeling and desire for domination perpetuates systems of oppression), Williams illustrates the distinction between these two different political factions. By soliciting her audience's emotional identification with the abandoned wife through her sentimental narrative, Williams simultaneously solicits their emotional identification with the once abandoned and now restored French Revolution. Loosely represented by the prodigal husband in Williams's tale, France takes on a sympathetic rather than a threatening character; it is the victim of a scheming opportunist rather than the Antichrist—the dupe of evil rather than its source.

The French Military as Sentimental Heroes

Williams, significantly, exonerates the French Revolutionary Army from the guilt of betrayal. "They alone remained pure and unsullied by the contagious guilt which overspread their country," she claims, "they alone appear to have been the true representatives of the French nation" (*Sketch*, 4:206). Throughout her *Letters from France* and within *A Tour in Switzerland*, Williams consistently upholds the French military as the repository of original revolutionary feeling; their distance from Robespierre's influence and their frontline experience of defending the republic preserves their commitment to the revolution's founding program. It certainly can be argued that her lack of direct exposure to the reality of war allows her to maintain a pristine perspective of the French army. Unlike several other British travel writers then traversing the Continent, Williams's itinerary does not lead her directly through war zones; she does not witness the bloody vestiges of battle that devastate both Pratt and Radcliffe. Yet it is difficult to believe that she was ignorant of the horrors of the battlefield; her military heritage ensured a personal interest in the French army's progress that can be seen throughout her *Letters from France.* Avoiding the reality of war may be her way of dissociating France from the images of desolation circulated by other British travel writers—she shows her readers what she *wants* them to see, creating a version of reality that aligns with her political project. By emphasizing the destruction left in the wake of the French army, both Pratt and Radcliffe (to varying degrees) associate France's international policy with violence and foster resentment toward what they represent as French aggression. "War," Radcliffe states after seeing recently wounded soldiers, "is compounded of something else, besides the glories, of which it is so easy to be informed."[52] Williams sidesteps the reality of the battlefield, instead focusing on the principles motivating France's invasion of Europe and on the admirable military leaders placed at the helm of the nation's international offensive. She divests the military of its faceless and threatening character by delineating the sympathetic personalities of Napoleon Bonaparte and Amédée Emmanuel François La Harpe—two of the French military's most prominent leaders. By depicting both men as modern heroes—successors to the acclaimed classical heroes of ancient Greece and Rome—Williams posits that they and their cause possess a universal appeal that transcends national borders. Her emphasis on the active sensibility of both men further suggests their quality as specifically sentimental heroes, while also constructing a political statement on the necessity of feeling within the realm of politics—an argument that is compounded through her attribution of unfeeling reason to "the greatest revolutionary sinners, the Jacobins" (*A Tour in Switzerland*, 1:83).

Williams launches into a consideration of Bonaparte after recounting his instrumental role in the recent liberation of the Valtellina region, portraying the Corsican general as a savior figure. She suggests that Bonaparte ultimately exceeds the heroes of old as his exploits are motivated by sympathy with the oppressed rather than by selfish desire. "The heroes meed," she states, "arises from other exploits than those of multitudes destroyed, and provinces desolated. It is not Buonaparte scaling the Alps, and chasing the imperial eagle back to its haunts . . . that claims the transport of admiration . . . it is the benefactor of his race converting the destructive lightening of the conqueror's sword into the benignant rays of freedom, and presenting to vanquished nations the emblems of liberty and independence entwined with the olive of peace" (2:55–56). This is indeed a different representation of war than the images of ruin depicted by Pratt and Radcliffe! Williams's choice of words suggests that multitudes have *not* been destroyed *nor* have provinces been desolated through his military maneuvers, creating the image of a bloodless intervention that contradicts Pratt's characterization of the French army "*carrying misery and death* into every place they visited."[53] She attributes Bonaparte's salutary influence to his finely attuned sensibility: "We [do not] wonder to find associated with such a mind . . . 'that sympathy with the elevated sentiments, the pathetic sublimity of Ossian; Ossian, the companion of his solitary hours, who seems to raise him above this terrestrial region'" (2:56–57). Williams interprets Bonaparte's connection with James Macpherson's epic poem cycle—which Dafydd Moore characterizes as manifesting "heroic sentimentality"[54]—as an indication of his capacity for feeling. It is this quality that distinguishes him from both classical heroes and the Jacobins, both of whom Williams portrays as motivated by anti-social aspirations that result in crimes against humanity. Bonaparte is written as a new kind of sentimental hero whose restorative actions—described as "unparalleled acts of pure expansive beneficence" (2:57)—are grounded in sympathy.

Williams's sentimental narrative of La Harpe's exile from Switzerland and service in the French Revolutionary Army is motivated by her discussion of the government of Berne's strict repression of revolutionary activity. Exiled under the threat of execution for organizing a celebration commemorating the fall of the Bastille, La Harpe sought refuge with the French army and achieved hero status through his service. Williams first establishes the innocuous, sociable nature of the celebration he instigated in order to emphasize the injustice of the government's ruling against La Harpe. "They had drank to the success of the French revolution," she asserts, "but without ever conjecturing that those acts could justify an arraignment before such a tribunal" (2:236). Williams clarifies that La Harpe's flight to France is not a sign of his guilt, but an indication of the government of Berne's tyranny: he fled because he had "little hope of establishing proofs of his innocence, when already persons arbitrarily arrested had, without accusation or proof, been sent to the prisons of Chillon" (2:238). She strategically places the onus on the government, arguing that La Harpe's development into a French revolutionary was a direct response to his persecution. In true sentimental style, Williams draws attention to La Harpe's disrupted domestic situation in order to condemn the actions of the government. She imagines his wife, surrounded by her six children, supplicating the government for the retention of her property in the compulsory absence of her husband (2:242). Williams's emphasis on the private suffering caused by political action aims to expose the cruelty of oppressive systems; La Harpe's fractured family illustrates that tyranny interrupts social harmony. Her subsequent account of his heroic endeavors within the French Revolutionary Army underscores his virtue, communicating the admirable nature of those who oppose tyranny and the questionable nature of systems that would demand the death of such citizens. His victories are the direct result of his "military skill and valour" (2:246); his "devotedness" (2:243) to the cause of liberty inspires his troops; and his sensibility is demonstrated through his generous treatment of Swiss prisoners (2:247). Upon his unfortunate death, Williams describes the "consternation and sorrow" (2:247) that enveloped the French military and the profound regret with which Bonaparte himself received the news. Her eulogy of La Harpe ultimately reinforces the integrity of the French Revolutionary Army; their recognition of La Harpe as a hero and their veneration of him as a "martyr" (2:243) reveals their exemplary character.

To allow sympathy to flow unimpeded between her British audience and her revolutionary subjects, Williams grounds her sympathetic portrayal of both

Bonaparte and La Harpe within a cosmopolitan context. She argues that their heroism shares a universal appeal reminiscent of traditional heroes, whose influence is not limited to the cultures from which they emerge. "The glory of Buonaparte," she contends, "belongs not exclusively to France, or her revolution; like Homer, or Newton, Buonaparte belongs to the world" (2:57). Bonaparte embodies for Williams what Gary Kelly characterizes as an "internationalized Revolution";[55] like Homer's creations and Newton's innovations, France's revolution is broadly relevant. She declares the international character of France's political revolution in a footnote on Bonaparte's eulogy for La Harpe. Noting the novelty of a Corsican eulogizing a Swiss citizen for his service in the French army, Williams observes, "It is not unworthy of remark, that, among the Generals who have rendered themselves the most illustrious in the defence of the French Republic, we find the names of Italians, English, Scotch, Irish, and Germans. . . . The friend of liberty, whatever may be his native soil, considers every free state as his country" (2:248). Allied under the auspices of a shared vision rather than shared origins, Bonaparte, La Harpe, and the army as a whole are fighting for universal freedom rather than for France. Williams challenges her audience to reimagine the French Revolutionary Wars as a struggle to extend liberty rather than to extend the boundaries of the French nation.

It follows that to do battle with the French army is not to fight against France, but to fight against liberty. Williams's conviction that shared vision rather than shared soil binds people together meshes with Hume's and Smith's theories of social cohesion. Her experience as a traveler—connecting with various national and ethnic groups—confirms the cohesive quality of sympathy. Bonaparte, La Harpe, and Williams herself are bound to the French cause and to one another by emotional rather than national or ethnic ties; her reference to the multinational character of the French Revolutionary Army indicates that shared sympathies are a far more powerful binding agent than a shared heritage. Although she approves of national attachments (for instance, she indulges in national pride when reflecting upon Bonaparte's preference for Ossian), Williams disapproves of a form of nationalism that impedes the formation of universal affections and the dissemination of liberty. Her aversion to national boundaries that translate into emotional barriers is evident in her criticism of Berne's strict border controls, which "destroy all impressions of Swiss Freedom" (2:197). She attempts to dissolve these barriers—particularly between Britain and France—through both her own transnational affiliations and her representation of Bonaparte and La Harpe as figures that transcend national borders through their commitment to liberty. Their assault on national borders is therefore not an assault on liberty, but an assault on the political barriers that inhibit the expansion of liberty. By casting the French Revolutionary Army as purveyors of liberty, Williams provides a way of thinking about the French Revolutionary Wars that allows Britons to sympathize with the "enemy" and problematizes their involvement in the war against the French Republic.

DECONSTRUCTING THE MYTH OF SWITZERLAND

The purpose underlying Williams's discussions of the French Republic's political issues in a travelogue advertised as being about Switzerland becomes clear when contextualized within the immediate political situation on the Continent at the time of her text's publication. France began its invasion of Switzerland in February 1798, and within a few months it had established a centralized state that was renamed the Helvetic Republic. Jones observes that France's conquest of Switzerland decisively turned the tide of public opinion in Britain and on the Continent against France. "The invasion of Switzerland," he asserts, "has been likened to the 1956 invasion of Hungary in its effect upon international opinion, and its 'subjugation' was . . . a crucial point of transition in public sympathies with the French."[56] One of the critics responding to Williams's travelogue indicates Britons' intense interest in the political drama taking place in Switzerland, noting that "the fate of Switzerland is the theme of general discourse and common commiseration."[57] That the reviewer describes Britons as commiserating with the Swiss indicates the general sympathy with the invaded nation in response to France's actions. Other critics are more direct in their obvious sympathies with the Swiss, with a contributor to *The Analytical Review* bemoaning "the dissolution of a friendly nation, once the cradle, domain, and barrier of liberty, endeared to us by political alliance, religious and moral analogy, and long continued intercourse."[58]

That the source of this critic's sympathy lies within the apparent similarities between Britain and Switzerland suggests one of the primary reasons for Britons' sympathy with the invaded nation. British writers had long established the political, cultural, and ideological similarities between their nation and Switzerland. Reverence for liberty united the two nations in a shared political vision and heritage emphasized by poets, travel writers, and politicians. In his poem *The Traveller,* Oliver Goldsmith characterizes the Swiss according to the image of the independent peasant, who

> Sees no contiguous palace rear its head,
> To shame the meanness of his humble shed;
> No costly lord the sumptuous banquet deal,
> To make him loathe his vegetable meal.[59]

Coxe's and Moore's popular travelogues cemented the image of Switzerland as a nation of independent citizens united under a series of democratic governing bodies. In *Travels in Switzerland,* Coxe emphasizes the liberty enjoyed by the Swiss and draws clear parallels between Britain and Switzerland: "I feel great delight in breathing the air of liberty; every person here has apparently the mien of content and satisfaction. . . . I can trace in all their manners, behaviour, and dress, some strong outlines, which distinguish this happy people from the neighbouring nations. Perhaps it may be prejudice and unreasonable partiality; but I am the more pleased, because their first appearance reminds me of my own countrymen, and I would almost think, for a moment, that I am in England."[60] He repeatedly classifies the various Swiss governments he encounters as "mild and equitable" and observes the effects of liberty in the independent bearing of Switzerland's inhabitants.[61] Moore—whose early support of the French Revolution reveals a different political orientation than Coxe's deeply conservative leanings[62]—is similarly impressed by Switzerland's political liberty. "As far as I can judge," he states, "a spirit of independency and freedom, tempered by sentiments of decency and the love of order, influence, in a most remarkable manner, the minds of the subjects of this happy republic."[63] The influence of these representations can be seen in Williams's early enthusiasm for Switzerland in "An Epistle to Dr. Moore," a 1786 poem addressed to her good friend. Inspired by the images and ideas that she finds in Moore's travelogue, she imagines Switzerland as a place where "freedom rears her humble home" and where "GREATNESS seems not quite so stern."[64] Given the tacit sense of fraternity between Britain and Switzerland, it is unsurprising that Britons reacted to France's conquest of Switzerland as an affront to themselves. Lord Carlisle appealed to the well-established parallels between Britain and Switzerland to mobilize support within Parliament for a military offensive against France: "The Swiss, in some degree, were in a similar situation with ourselves; they were opposed to the tyranny of the French nation, and they were contending for every thing that was dear to them; Switzerland and Britain were the last and only countries who had virtue and resolution enough to dispute the power and attempt to repel arms."[65] He argues that the cause of Switzerland is the cause of Britain; an attack on Switzerland is not only an assault on liberty; it also makes a similar invasion of Britain alarmingly imaginable.

Three attempts by French convoys to land on British shores in the period between 1796 and 1798 provided tangible reasons for alarm; as Lord Carlisle's speech suggests, Britons could see their fate reflected in the recent conquest of Switzerland. The developing Irish Rebellion provided the Directory with ready allies and a point of entrance into Britain. Two of the three invasion attempts were made in Ireland, and at least one resulted in a minor insurrection. Linda Colley describes the "panic" that permeated Britain during this period and details the anxious efforts of the British government to assess patriotic feeling within the nation: "The danger of a massive French invasion was so great after 1793, and so protracted, that they were compelled to establish how many Britons would take up arms in defence of their nation."[66] Written in response to the French expeditionary force that landed in Fishguard, Wales, in 1797, Uvedale Price's *Thoughts on the Defence of Property* shows how seriously Britons considered the possibility of a French invasion. He argues in favor of arming Britain's yeomanry to provide a sturdy defense against French forces, contending that the ability to defend the nation is essential in promoting patriotic spirit.[67] Johann Casper Lavater's *Remonstrance Addressed to the Executive Directory* (1798), in which the Swiss national criticizes France's invasion of and subsequent conduct in Switzerland, was translated and republished in Britain to discourage Ireland's collusion with France. "Will not Ireland," the publisher pleads in his introduction to the text, "which the French at this moment look forward to as the very next victim of their rapacity, take warning from this awful testimony, and join with one heart to save their honour, their property, their existence?"[68] The publisher's characterization of Ireland as France's "very next victim" suggests the sense of imminence with which Britons regarded the Gallic threat during the French Revolutionary Wars. The invasion of Switzerland demonstrated that no European powers were safe from the revolutionary fervor of the new French Republic, and the Directory's involvement with the United Irishmen suggested the method by which they might launch a similar attack on Britain.

Williams was well aware of France's political ambitions given both her connections in Switzerland and France and her acquaintance with the leaders of the Irish Rebellion, Theobald Wolfe Tone and Lord Edward Fitzgerald.[69] She dismantles the common stereotype of Switzerland as "one of the happiest, the most prosperous, and the best governed countries upon earth" to disrupt traditional loyalties and to effect a reversal of British sympathies.[70] That Lord Carlisle draws on the idea of Anglo-Swiss fraternity to aid his anti-Gallic agenda suggests how British sympathy with Switzerland increased hostility toward France, which manifested both in conflict abroad and in the entrenchment of conservative opinion at home. To allay the violence bred by British fears of France and its revolutionary principles, Williams deploys her eyewitness authority to counter the ingrained perception of Switzerland as a land of perfect liberty, refuting the largely complementary accounts of Goldsmith, Coxe, and Moore with which she was evidently familiar.[71] Her romantic preconceptions of the alpine nation, aided by previous travel writers, gradually unravel in the face of what she represents as reality; Switzerland as the home of liberty and the Swiss as an independent people are exposed as a carefully maintained fiction. Williams's revision proceeds on three fronts: she deconstructs the Swiss definition and practice of liberty to reveal what Jones calls "a bare idea, a construction of the mind" rather than a fully realized practice that ensures the freedom and rights of all citizens;[72] she challenges the perception of Switzerland as "one of the happiest . . . countries" by revealing the social discontent endemic throughout the nation;[73] and she aligns contemporary Swiss political rebels with the historical Swiss freedom fighters traditionally revered in Britain, rewriting the narrative of the current revolution as part of the nation's ongoing struggle for liberty. Her alternative interpretation of Switzerland's political landscape justifies France's political intervention and suggests that Britain might avoid a similar insurrection by modeling itself after France rather than Switzerland.

A Tour in Switzerland systematically debunks the popular perception of Switzerland as a model republic that operates according to democratic principles. Williams disputes this romantic stereotype by interrogating the form and praxis of power exercised by the governments within the Swiss Confederation, examining who has access to political rights, how those rights are gained and transferred, and the manner in which they are exercised. What her analysis reveals are governments characterized by asymmetrical power relations that create cultures of dependence rather than independence. In order to emphasize the actual oppression of Swiss so-called democracies, she exposes the discrepancy between the total population of each canton and the number of individuals granted political agency. Surveying a number of the smaller Swiss cantons, she asserts, "No other part of Switzerland is so unenlightened, and consequently so hostile to the spirit of true liberty, as these little Cantons, where democracy and despotism march under the same banners; for although the government is democratic, the number of those who have the right to the seat in the general assembly is inconsiderable, compared with the numbers that are excluded" (1:213). The government in Switzerland may be "democratic with respect to those individuals who make a part of the sovereignty," but "[it] is to the unprivileged inhabitants of the Cantons . . . a confirmed hereditary aristocracy" (1:214). She particularly draws attention to the political subjection suffered by the disenfranchised populations within these cantons. The inhabitants of the Valley of Levantina, subject to the Canton of Uri, have been divested of all political rights and are "the slaves of their citizen-sovereigns" (1:202). Williams describes the inhabitants of the Valtellina province as "oppressed subjects of the Grison democracies" (2:48), creating an ironic juxtaposition between their political oppression and the ostensibly democratic practice of the Grison administration. She carefully details the "abuses" (2:247) suffered by the Vaudois in their attempts to gain constitutional privileges denied them by the Canton of Berne. Her lengthy narratives of the systematic political dispossession and oppression suffered by the inhabitants in Switzerland's subject territories shatter the myth of Swiss democracy. "The history of these Cantons," she observes, "is nearly the same; the same sovereignty and the same servitude" (2:72).

The coercive means through which authority is secured—identified by Williams as economic manipulation, censorship, and violence—further emphasizes the restrictions placed upon these ostensibly independent people. She details how the economic control exercised by the burghers in various cantons results in the servitude of the lower classes; the freedom of the people is limited by taxation schemes and trade restrictions that financially benefit the burghers and financially burden the disenfranchised population. She describes the frustrations of a peasant farmer who "may cultivate his field of flax" but "has no right over the produce of his labour, no power to dispose of what he has acquired by the sweat of his brow and the toil of his hands" (1:104). Williams's criticism of economic controls is fundamentally a criticism of arbitrary power, which John Phillip Reid identifies as one of the primary fears of British reformists. "To be subject to arbitrary governmental power," he explains, "was to live without liberty."[74] Divested of political influence, the peasant farmer has no say in how power is exercised and therefore lacks control over his own property. The strict censorship laws under which the press operates curtails whatever indirect political influence the unrepresented majority might exert, allowing power to govern unchecked. While in St. Maurice, Williams and her companions notice "a placard stuck on the wall, which stated the various degrees of corporal punishment to be inflicted on those who should indulge themselves in discussions on the principles of Government, or be guilty of the overt act of receiving or reading the [French] papers" (2:182). That those who do challenge the political status quo are subject to the "iron hand of oppression" (2:188) is clearly illustrated through her detailed account of La Harpe's trial as well as her descriptions of the violent suppression of insurgents within the cantons of Uri, Grison, and Berne.[75] Swiss "democracy" is ultimately exposed as an empty signifier where "under the name of liberty, the greatest outrages are committed against the principle" (2:37). Her frequent comparisons between the politically disenfranchised and enslaved peoples (1:126, 202–203, 214–215; 2:48–49) provide a dramatically different image than that of the independent Swiss subject. By detailing the tyrannical ways by which authority is secured and exercised, Williams conveys that the Swiss people deserve liberation with the same urgency as those enslaved within Europe's various empires.[76]

Having established the most flagrant sociopolitical faults of the Swiss Confederacy, Williams proceeds to challenge the purported happiness of its subjects by examining the effects of oppression upon the people. She intentionally explores the expressions of discontent found among the Swiss populace; her tour takes her through spaces of political discontent, allowing her both to see and to sculpt a different reality than previous travel writers. What she finds is a nation fragmented by ongoing hostilities rather than a "happy republic."[77] Williams invalidates the common perception of Swiss happiness by reinterpreting the nation's historical and contemporary internecine conflicts as a symptom of perpetual sociopolitical discontent. Whereas other British travel writers celebrate Switzerland's historical revolts as evidence of the Swiss spirit of independence, she draws her audience's attention to the conditions that enable the recurrence of oppressive power structures. "Were the boasted happiness of the subject classes of Switzerland founded in truth," she argues, "it is not probable that revolts against the sovereign would be so frequent. No people revolt against happiness" (2:88). She suggests that the appearance of national contentment perceived by former travel writers is not an indication of widespread happiness but a measure of the extent to which the Swiss population has normalized their political subjection. "The implicit obedience of the subject," she observes, "never fails of being rewarded by the paternal protection of the state, the members of which, since the event of the French Revolution, have earnestly inculcated the doctrine, that happiness is to be found rather in tranquillity, than in the turbulent freedom of equal rights" (2:224). Her argument specifies that there is a distinction between the happiness borne out of true freedom and the compliance borne out of fear.

By reimagining the history of Swiss uprisings as an indication of ongoing tyranny, she re-presents Switzerland as nation that requires further reform. Williams portrays the incipient revolutionary fervor pervading the nation as a *natural* and *necessary* response to political oppression, and one that carries on Switzerland's celebrated tradition of resistance against despotism. That Britons admired Switzerland's history of democratic reform is manifest in the voices of Coxe, Moore, and Goldsmith, and Williams notes that William Tell's fabled exploits in the service of political liberty are held equally sacred in Britain as in Switzerland. "Tell is in England," she remarks, "as well as Switzerland, the hero of our infancy; the marvellous tale of the apple is one of our earliest lessons" (1:147). British writers hailed the legendary tales of Swiss uprisings against tyranny as examples of the nation's commitment to liberty. Coxe—whose vigorous objections to the French Revolution demonstrate his conservative politics[78]—repeatedly expresses his approbation of Switzerland's tradition of political resistance. "I have frequently remarked with pleasure," he comments, "the national enthusiasm which generally prevails in this country, and greatly admired the fire and animation with which the people discourse of those famous men among their ancestors, to whom they are indebted for that happy state of independence they now enjoy."[79] However, whereas Coxe laments the revolutionary movements spreading across 1790s Switzerland as an abrogation of Swiss liberty,[80] Williams characterizes those to whom she refers as Swiss "patriots" as the natural successors of William Tell. "The Swiss," she states, "have only to consult their own annals . . . and they will probably reflect that the age of heroism is not past with that of chivalry; but that those who march in the steps of an Albert, may find in their path a Verner de Stauffaken, or a William Tell" (1:216–217). Her alignment of contemporary Swiss governments with ancient forms of despotism indicates that Switzerland has departed from its original democratic principles, but it can be revitalized through the revolutionary principles emanating from France. Williams develops a reading of Swiss radicalism that challenges British hostility toward the French invasion of Switzerland. By emphasizing the tyranny exercised by Switzerland's current governing bodies and suggesting the political heritage between past and present rebels, she argues that the revolutionary spirit suffusing the nation should be read as part of Switzerland's legacy of reform and revolution rather than as a foreign assault.

Williams's redefinition of heroes and victims in the unfolding Swiss narrative comes together in her contemplation of the prisoners held in Chillon Castle. The site had become an immensely popular tourist attraction after it was immortalized in Rousseau's *Julie, or the New Heloise* (1761) as the location where the titular character's son nearly drowns; tourists would traipse over the rocks with copies Rousseau's novel and attempt to imaginatively recapture Julie's horror. Williams substitutes fictional anguish with real suffering, contending that the insurgents currently imprisoned within the castle's walls deserve more sympathy than Rousseau's fictional characters:

> All in nature is still romantic, wild, and graceful, as Rousseau has painted it; but the soothing charm associated with the moral feeling, is in some sort dissolved. The soft image of the impassioned Julia no longer hovers around the castle of Chillon; which is now converted into a Swiss Bastile, and guarded by a stern soldiery. The tear of sensibility which has so often been shed over this spot for the woes of fiction, may now fall for sorrows that have the dull reality of existence. It is not the imaginary maternal shriek that pierces the ear, it is the groan of the patriot rising from the floor of his damp dungeon that rends the heart. (2:179–180)

Katherine Turner interprets this passage as a renunciation of sensibility, observing that it is "edged out by political reality."[81] However, I would suggest that sensibility is *shifted* rather than *supplanted* by political reality in this passage. Williams urges her audience to transfer their tears from Julie's imaginary calamity to the real suffering of the Swiss revolutionaries languishing within the castle's walls. She does not appear to be arguing that political reality undermines sentimental experience, but that feeling must be redirected toward the proper objects—to the "patriots" suffering under the heavy hand of an oppressive government. Representing the incarcerated revolutionaries and the people they represent as victims of a despotic system, Williams simultaneously depicts the French Revolutionary Army as the potential heroes of this political drama. They offer the promise of emancipation and restoration, liberating the Swiss people from their master rulers and restoring the nation to "the character it has long usurped, of being the most free in Europe" (2:119).

Through the dual offensive of identifying the egregious shortcomings of Swiss governance and distinguishing Switzerland's present revolutionaries as both the victims of an oppressive system and the direct political successors of the nation's past heroes, Williams invites her audience to extend their sympathy to the nation's current discontents and to revolutionary France, which she depicts as Switzerland's political savior through the figure of Bonaparte. The severe backlash within Britain against France's invasion of Switzerland exemplifies Britons' predisposition to sympathize with the fate of the "mild and paternal governments of Switzerland."[82] "What must we *feel*," laments a critic for *The Analytical Review*, "at the dissolution of a friendly nation[?]"[83] Grief is the feeling to which commentator gestures; they indicate that this can be the only appropriate response to Switzerland's spectacle of ruin. That feeling *for* Switzerland translates into feeling *against* France is made obvious through this reviewer's comparison of the French invasion to a violent tempest: "The flashes and thunder clouds of a storm ris[e] to involve hill, dale, and cottage in undistinguished ruin."[84] Williams disrupts the sociopolitical idealization of Switzerland in order to complicate the demonization of France; by exposing the messy reality behind Switzerland's imagined perfection, she suggests that sympathizing with Switzerland *and* France need not be mutually exclusive.

ELECTRIC FEELINGS: THE MOBILITY OF EMOTION

Williams's portrayal of the circulation of revolutionary affect manifests her belief that feeling *for* and *with* people contained the possibility of total political transformation. Throughout her travelogue she uses the imagery of electricity, lightning, fire, and contagion to convey the way in which revolutionary principles are communicated—metaphors also used by moral philosophers to articulate the operation of sympathy. "The governments of Switzerland," she states in the preface to volume 1, "placed within reach of the electrical fire of that Revolution, flashing around all their borders, behold the subtle spark, which finds a conductor in the human heart, escaping beyond its prescribed limits, and feel its strong concussion in every agitated nerve."[85] The image invoked in this metaphor is the Leyden jar experiment, which was a popular spectacle in the eighteenth century. The performative experiment involved a group of people holding hands in a circle; as the first and last person in the chain touched the inside and outside of an electrified jar, each individual in the group would feel the charge instantaneously.[86] Williams's description of the mobility of revolutionary feeling parallels Hume's discussion of the instantaneous transfer of emotions within a collective. Her comparison of emotional exchange to the inexorable movement of electrical currents mirrors his illustration of affective communication as the unstoppable transfer of sound waves. Explaining the "nature and force of *sympathy*," he asserts, "The minds of all men are similar in their feelings and operations; nor can any one be actuated by any affection, of which all others are not, in some degree, susceptible. As in strings equally wound up, the motion of one communicates itself to the rest; so all the affections readily pass from one person to another, and beget correspondent movements in every human creature."[87] Both metaphors—electrical currents and sound waves—suggest the powerful, transformative potential of feeling. Affective exchange adjusts the internal emotional character of those affected by its relentless pull to mirror the original source of the mobile feelings—impacting the heart, reverberating within the nerves, and resonating throughout the body. Similar to Hume, Williams indicates that political transformation is not accomplished through physical force or even through intellectual debate, but through the spontaneous movement of feeling. It is the heart that responds with "enthusiastic glow" to the history of those "who have struggled for the liberties of mankind" (1:146), and it is "the burst of the heart that swells against oppression" (1:216) that poses the greatest threat to political tyranny. That Williams locates the site of political transformation within the heart indicates the political implications of her sentimental orientation: by addressing her readers' hearts through the language of sensibility, she is attempting to transfer the electric spark of revolution that she and other revolutionaries feel.

The political transformation that Williams hopes to accomplish by this transfer of emotions is not simply Britain's support of France's political program in Switzerland, but the sweeping political transformation of Britain. The established parallels between Switzerland and Britain allow Williams's text to act as a cautionary tale to her British audience, warning the British government that their oppressive practices justify their removal. An apparent misapplication of a couplet in Goldsmith's *The Traveller* provides a moment of productive confusion between Switzerland and Britain that suggests the similarities of their political shortcomings:

> What is remarkable enough in this celebrated land of freedom, where the poet tells us, that

> Even the peasant boasts his rights to scan,
> And learns to venerate himself as man:
>
> All the peasantry in the canton of Basil . . . are literally serfs."
> (1:98–99)

Jones observes that Williams's comment—which is part of her attack on Basel's government—is "rather blunted by the fact that Goldsmith applied the lines to England."[88] Yet could her apparent misapplication be read as a strategic intertextual reference to Britain? By applying lines describing Britain to Switzerland, Williams's condemnation of the superficial nature of Swiss liberty can simultaneously function as a criticism of Britain's analogous faults. Her subsequent parallel between ancient Switzerland's practice of serfdom and Britain's contemporary involvement in the slave trade ties her criticism of the two nations closer together. Turning from a discussion of past Swiss servitude to a contemplation of contemporary British slavery, she asserts that "the execrable traffic belongs almost exclusively to . . . that island which was the birth-place, and the refuge of liberty" (2:73). The idea of liberty corrupted through the abuse of human rights (as understood within an eighteenth-century context) synchronizes with Williams's representation of Switzerland as a nation where "under the name of liberty, the greatest outrages are committed against the principle" (2:37). Although both nations profess to revere liberty, Williams contends that their participation in systems of exploitation reveals the superficial nature of their claims. "Liberty," she observes with reference to Switzerland, "of which so vain a boast has been made, is so little understood" (2:272).

The immediate political subtext for Williams's combined critique of Switzerland's and Britain's oppressive political practices may be the United Irishmen's bid for Irish independence in the late eighteenth century. Williams's acquaintance with Theobald Wolfe Tone during his residence in France would have provided her with intimate knowledge of the revolutionary ideology and aim of the Irish rebels which, according to Tone, was "to break that execrable slavery, by which, under the more plausible name of connexion, we have been chained for six hundred years at the feet of England."[89] In his autobiography, Tone mentions having dined with Williams and John Hurford Stone while in Paris in 1796, and specifically references the political nature of their discussions: "All our politics English" (2:87). Given that Tone was in France to solicit military support for an Irish insurrection, and given Stone's involvement with the United Irishmen, these discussions likely addressed the United Irishmen's project of political independence from Britain.[90] The struggle between the Pays de Vaud region and the Bernese government forms a compelling parallel to similar hostilities between Ireland

and the British government. Like the Vaudois, the members of the United Irishmen were reacting against what they perceived as political oppression from an external governing body; their goals evolved from political reform to Irish separatist republicanism according to the vitalizing example of the French Revolution and to the violence of the British government's attempts at suppression. They subsequently invited the newly instituted French Directory to support their efforts.[91] To a nation facing an internal conflict that could result in an external intervention, Williams demonstrates that oppressive practices invite rather than mitigate conflict. "It requires no great penetration," she observes, "to discover that the abuses which exist in these Swiss governments will be corrected, not so much perhaps from the struggles of the oppressed, as from the conviction in those who govern, how much it behoves their interest to loosen the reins of arbitrary power. The history of every country is full of examples how fatal to tyranny is the burst of the heart that swells against oppression" (1:216). Switzerland illustrates the necessity of political reform for Britain, demonstrating the wisdom of "loosen[ing] the reins of arbitrary power" rather than maintaining authority through violence.

The list of justifications (2:251–271) that Williams provides for France's direct intervention in Swiss affairs clearly demonstrates her support of the impending invasion and gestures toward the subversive subtext running through her travelogue. Given the fears of invasion circulating within Britain at the time of her travelogue's publication, Williams's defense of France's imminent conquest of Switzerland seems intentionally provocative. Her justification of France's aggressive international expansion perhaps should be read as a veiled message to her British audience communicating an alternate course of action for the British government that precludes both domestic and international violence. That she represents France's invasion of Switzerland as a moral obligation rather than as unwarranted aggression indicates that Switzerland is ultimately responsible for its own subjugation; it is the systemic misconduct of Swiss governments that provokes a republican intervention. Her sketch of the conflict between the residents of the Pays de Vaud and the Bernese government is particularly instructive. The experience of political dispossession at the hands of the Bernese government initially motivates the Vaudois to seek restitution, and the severity with which the Bernese government responds to their political appeals incites them to seek political independence with the aid of a foreign power (2:252). By characterizing France's invasion of Switzerland as a response to an "invitation" (2:269), Williams insinuates that it is the will of the Swiss people—*not* the Directory's imperial desire—that motivates France's involvement. The implication is that Switzerland has the power to avert a foreign invasion through reform rather than through the force of arms; France's intervention would be unnecessary if Switzerland's governing institutions would evolve according to the general will. Williams may, indeed, share the opinion of Lord Carlisle that "the Swiss, in some degree, were in a similar situation with ourselves [the British],"[92] but suggests that the right response is to adopt rather than to resist France's influence in accordance with the emerging sentiments of the nation.

"THE NOBLEST EXAMPLES OF FORTITUDE": WOMEN AND THE NATION

Included in Williams's attention to the stories of the dispossessed are the stories of women. Her travelogues build a significant archive of narratives that relate the universal strength and struggles of women, collectively asserting their significance within the sociopolitical life of nations. The political empowerment of women is central to the revolutionary project that she supports. In line with Janet Schaw's *Journal of a Lady of Quality*, the anonymous Lady's *A Journey to the Highlands of Scotland*, and Mary Morgan's *A Tour to Milford Haven*, Williams revises the cultural definition of femininity in order to transform the role women play within society. Her recuperation of sensibility as a site of political transformation is key to this redefinition. Implicit in Williams's analyses of Robespierre's administration and of the Swiss and British governments is the argument that it is the absence of feeling—and particularly the absence of sympathy—that creates the conditions for political domination. The preponderance of reason enables the violence of the Reign of Terror (1:83); avarice interferes with the principles of liberty in Switzerland (1:215; 2:36, 39); and an obsession with personal gain results in the perpetuation of slavery within Britain's Empire (2:73). Whereas personal interest engenders suffering, sympathy mitigates suffering. Madame C—supports the aims of the French Revolution due to her sympathy with the oppressed (1:288); the abbot in Engelberg moderates the violence of French émigrés through "gentle counsels and acts of beneficence" (2:106); and Johann Casper Lavater's "effusion[s] of the heart" (1:68) succeed in "soothing" Williams's feelings, which have been "so long stunned with the cavils of French philosophers" (1:72). The ability to sympathize instills a community-mindedness that obviates the selfish imperatives of exploitation. It is upon this understanding of sensibility that she constructs female sensibility as a source of strength rather than weakness and suggests the constitutive role of women within the project of nation building.

Williams's chronicling of her emotional response to the sublime in Swiss nature thus functions as a sign of her unique fitness for participation within the new political order: "Never, never can I forget the sensations of that moment! when with a sort of annihilation of self, with every past impression erased from my memory, I felt as if my heart were bursting with emotions too strong to be sustained.—Oh, majestic torrent! which hast conveyed a new image of nature to my soul . . . thy course is coeval with time, and thou wilt rush down thy rocky walls when this bosom, which throbs with admiration of thy greatness, shall beat no longer!" (1:60–61). Her ability to perceive and respond to sublime nature contrasts with the indifference of the local residents, who are "inattentive to those thundering sounds which seem calculated to suspend all human activity in solemn and awful astonishment" (1:63). The cold skepticism of French philosophers (1:72) and the apathy of Swiss peasantry (2:224–225) disqualify both from political leadership, as each lead to the institution or to the toleration of tyranny. "Williams," Kelly observes, "has a manifest capacity for the sublime, showing that she and readers who feel with her are qualified subjectively to constitute the cultural and political nation."[93] Her emotional receptivity to the sublime aligns her with the emerging political leadership of the sentimentalized Bonaparte, whose responsiveness to the sublime in the Ossian cycle of poems marks him as the leader who can lead an effective revolution.

Her representation of women's emotional and intellectual strength throughout *A Tour in Switzerland* reinforces her defense of women as capable political subjects. Recounting a narrative told to her by a local Swiss woman of a legendary battle in which Switzerland won independence from Austria, Williams is careful to incorporate the unrecorded contributions of women to the success of the campaign: "'There,' said she, 'on the brow of that hill we stood, dressed in carter's frocks, and the Austrians thought we were a fresh army of soldiers.' By *we* were meant the women of that day, who, according to local tradition, for it does not appear to be recorded in any history, made use of this stratagem to multiply the appearance of the confederated forces" (1:125). She includes the heroics of these female warriors to demonstrate women's active participation in the development of the Swiss nation. The image of women standing in the gap or compensating for male weakness is repeated throughout Williams's works, indicating women's particular firmness of character. In the narrative of Madame and Monsieur C—, Madame C—evinces strength of character in the face of personal disaster that emphasizes her husband's weakness. He emotionally and physically collapses under the strain of loss, rendering him susceptible to Madame de—'s manipulations and forcing his wife to assume the role of protector and provider. Indeed, Williams's personal narrative of political commitment provides a compelling subtext of female resilience. Her fierce attachment to the original principles of the revolution despite the threat of imprisonment and death demonstrates the admirable "constancy" and "fidelity" (1:40) that she attributes to women in all her works.

Her brief mention of the official exclusion of women from French politics suggests a context for her persistent advocacy of women. "Upon the whole," she bitterly observes, "the women of France, to whom, by the Constitutional Act, all rights have been denied, find that they still hold a tolerably despotic empire over their lords and masters, the sovereign people" (1:26). Refused political rights within the new French Republic, women are forced to exercise their influence on behalf of their "friends, lovers, or husbands" in informal and underhanded ways, using the "formidable artillery of bright eyes, gay smiles, lively sallies, and animated graces" (1:25) to gain political advantages for their associates. Williams's caustic tone suggests her criticism of a system that uses women for political purposes yet refuses to formally acknowledge their political participation. That she characterizes French women's influence as "despotic" suggests the corrosive effects of inequality and reiterates the political message found throughout her reflections on Switzerland: that structures of domination invite and perpetuate violence. Women respond to their oppression by attempting to dominate men; their exercise of power ultimately mirrors the authority to which they are subjected—not entirely dissimilar from the continuity Williams sees between the ancien régime and the Jacobins. The absence of authentic feeling within relationships enables the flourishing of self-interest that manifests itself in the abuse of power.

THE SPARK OF REVOLUTION

In *Letters Containing a Sketch of the Politics of France*, Williams characterized her stay in Switzerland as a period of renewal, stating: "My mind is full of those scenes of beauty and grandeur which have calmed my troubled spirit, and in which I have found a renovation of existence" (1:39). *A Tour in Switzerland* records both the regeneration of her faith in the revolution and a renewal of her commitment to the potentialities of feeling—with particular emphasis on the transformative and restorative possibilities of fellow feeling. Although Switzerland's political landscape does not offer an encouraging alternative to France's messy implementation of liberty, it restores her faith in the French Revolution through negative rather than positive example. The abuse of power that she discovers in Switzerland provides Williams with a stark reminder of the necessity of political revolution; it brings her back to her ideological roots and provides a new zeal for the French cause—loosely understood as exporting liberty through the establishment of republican governments. The fresh revolutionary spirit pervading both the citizenry of Switzerland (represented by La Harpe) and the French Revolutionary Army (represented by Bonaparte) offer her hope that the French Revolution might accomplish what it had originally set out to achieve: "equality, fraternity, and the rights of man" (1:99). Her political tourism once again provides her with a cause. She returns to Paris with a renewed political vision for France, Britain, and Europe of an international revolution grounded in sympathy—offering freedom from exploitation to the dispossessed within nations and peace rooted in a shared political purpose between nations.

Williams's implicit desire throughout her narrative is that her reignited passion for political revolution will prove to be the spark that would "kindle into flame" the "combustible materials" (2:275) in both Switzerland and Britain. Her travelogue becomes the means of conducting the revolutionary spark to the hearts of her British readers, which she attempts to accomplish through the cultivation of sympathy. Williams's emphasis on the significance of contiguity or familiarity in the transfer of emotions echoes Hume's conviction that these qualities assist the operation of sympathy and suggests the strategy undergirding her self-appointed role as a mediator between her British audience and the French nation. That she speaks of the Swiss hearing the "shouts of equality, fraternity, and the rights of man" (1:99) and the "shouts of liberty that filled the plains of Lombardy" (1:48) indicates the threat France's proximity poses to Swiss despotism, as does her image of the "principles of independence" simply vaulting over "the dyke which separates Switzerland from France" (2:230). "It is natural to conclude," she states, "that the principles of that mighty revolution . . . cannot fail to expand in those countries which are placed immediately within their influence" (2:270). Williams affirms the contagious nature of emotions, suggesting that they ultimately act as an organic purveyor of revolutionary sentiment. Although the transmission of emotion is here accomplished through proximity, Williams also makes it clear that written communication can achieve similar ends. Given the "imitative nature" of the human mind, Hume contends that "where any set of men, scattered over distant nations, maintain a close society or communication together, they acquire a similitude of manners."[94] Williams's attribution of the improbable "tie of sympathy" (2:77) between the democratic canton of Glaris and ancien régime France to the "habitual intercourse [that] sometimes changes repugnance into friendship" (2:78) suggests her intellectual debt to Hume. She opens the possibility of turning British "repugnance" toward the French into "friendship" by projecting her travelogue as an indirect means of communication between the hostile nations—a "line of connection across the divided world" (*Letters Written in France*, 149). Williams renders sympathetic relations with France imaginable by humanizing the new French Republic, providing Britons with the conditions necessary to form mutually transformative sentimental identifications. Similar to Janet Schaw, the anonymous Lady of *A Journey*, and Mary Morgan, Williams understands that travelers and their texts can act as conduits for national feeling, negotiating intranational or international sympathies by bringing the familiar and the foreign into contact through their itinerant bodies.

EPILOGUE

"An Affair of the Heart"

DILYS POWELL'S *AN AFFAIR OF THE HEART* (1957) is a twentieth-century travelogue by a British author that recounts her lifelong love affair and political entanglement with Greece. I serendipitously chanced upon a worn copy of the travelogue some years ago while in a crammed bookshop in Europe; the title stuck out to me from the shelf as it reminded me of a line from Helen Maria Williams's first travelogue, *Letters Written in France*, where she excuses her "political creed" as "entirely an affair of the heart."[1] After delving into Powell's text, I realized that the parallels with Williams did not stop at the title; she also justifies her controversial political choices by pleading the exigencies of friendship: "Often enough in England, struggling to do work for which a deep disinterest in politics fitted me poorly, I had been accused of partisanship; but then the accusation had been that I was a Royalist, a Tory, one of the Red-bogey brigade. Years later I met an English diplomat whose toga I must once or twice have twitched in the war. 'I could never make out,' he said, 'which side you were on.' 'I was,' I answered, borrowing I fancy someone else's phrase, 'on the side of the Greeks.' And so I was."[2] Her bundling of political decisions within personal feeling echoes Helen Maria Williams's insistence that the best "system of politics" is that "by which those I love are made happy."[3] As Powell goes on to show throughout her travelogue, she supports the political parties and ideologies that benefit those in whom she is emotionally invested—who are, as she states above, Greeks. As her response to the English diplomat indicates, sympathy becomes Powell's means of navigating the complex political relations both between Greece and Britain and between Greece's various political factions following World War II. Her "especial affection" for Greece and its people not only repeatedly draws her back to the nation, it also draws her into political debates and activism despite her purported "deep disinterest in politics."[4] Powell's text illustrates two significant points about the life of the sentimental travelogue after its genesis in the eighteenth century: that the sentimental travelogue survived the demise of the culture of sensibility and continues to flourish as a literary mode, and that the intersections of fact with feeling and distance with intimacy offered by the sentimental travelogue continue to help women negotiate political issues and values within their texts.

Although the language of Powell's text is distinctly twentieth-century, the literary continuity between Powell and eighteenth-century female sentimental travel writers is undeniable; the same anecdotal form, emphasis on emotional responsiveness, and tendency toward sympathy is found in Powell's travelogue as it is in the travel narratives of the four women covered in this book. This continuity indicates that the history of the sentimental travelogue diverges from that of the eighteenth-century sentimental novel. While the sentimental novel more or less fell out of fashion in the nineteenth century, the practice of sentimental travel and travel writing persists into the twenty-first. This persistence speaks to the flexibility of the form; the sentimental mode in travel writing is characterized by a set of stylistic and ideological approaches that can be readily adapted to a range of discourses and experiences, as can be seen in contemporary travel literature. The current division of travel literature into guidebooks and literary memoirs has perhaps even intensified the anecdotal style and the subjective and relational approach inaugurated by eighteenth-century sentimental travelers. Contemporary literary travelogues largely dispense with the technical particulars of travel—the "dull details of post-stages, and churches, and picture-catalogues"[5]—and focus on the journey's emotional, spiritual, and interpersonal dimensions.

A cursory glance through best-selling women's travelogues from the past few decades reveals their sentimental provenance. For instance, Elizabeth Gilbert's journey to enlightenment through both spiritual and cultural experiences in *Eat, Pray, Love: One Woman's Search for Everything across Italy, India and Indonesia* (2006), Tanya Shaffer's pursuit of meaning through humanitarian work in *Somebody's Heart Is Burning: A Woman Wanderer in Africa* (2003), and Rita Golden Gelman's quest for sympathetic identifications that transcend national boundaries in *Tales of a Female Nomad: Living at Large in the World* (2002) all give precedence to the emotional dimensions of travel and to a relational approach to cultural encounters. In their introduction to *Amazonian: The Penguin Book of Women's New Travel Writing* (1998), Dea Birkett and Sara Wheeler state that "the writer's inner journey is the most important part—and certainly the most interesting part—of any travel book. It doesn't make any difference where you go; it's your interpretation of it that matters."[6] Although eighteenth-century sentimental female travel writers would vigorously object to the idea that place is immaterial, the claim that the subjective experience is a vital component of travel would not have struck them as odd. Janet Schaw's proclamation in *Journal of a Lady of Quality* that "every subject will be guided by my own immediate feelings" and that her "opinions and descriptions will depend on the health and the humor of the moment in which I write"[7] aligns with Birkett and Wheeler's assertion of the importance of the traveler's emotional experience and subjective interpretation in current women's travel writing.

This focus on the "inner journey" in contemporary women's travel writing has prompted Bernard Schweizer to identify what he calls a "political gender gap" in twenty-first-century travel writing, with male travel writers being three times more likely than women to write politically engaged travel narratives.[8] Female travel writers, he asserts, have a greater tendency to write in a personal register that seems to abjure politics. However, in her study of cultural governance in twentieth-century women's travel writing, Hager Weslati reminds us that in contemporary women's travelogues as in those of their eighteenth-century counterparts, the personal more often than not encodes the political. She argues that readers must be alert to the "cartographies of *affects* and maps of 'selves in transit'" in women's travel writing in order to uncover the political dimensions encrypted within their apparently apolitical texts.[9] Sentiment is still used to mystify political engagement in contemporary women's travel writing; this is made abundantly clear in Schweizer's struggle to find political content amidst the personal detail in contemporary women's travel writing and in Weslati's insistence upon developing alternate reading strategies to identify the political dimensions of feeling and mobility in these texts. This indicates that the interpretive strategies we develop for reading eighteenth-century women's sentimental travelogues are relevant for women's travel writing today.

Maureen Moynagh, on the other hand, examines the ways in which twentieth-century travel writers use feeling to intensify the political content of their texts. In *Political Tourism and Its Texts* (2008), she describes the "affectively resonant processes of identification and affiliation" in which contemporary political tourists engage to "combat indifference in the public sphere" and rouse support for their political (and specifically revolutionary) agendas.[10] Her specific investigation of the travel narratives of women involved in Nicaragua's Sandinista Revolution reveals that sympathy functions within these texts as both personal incentive and political tool—motivating their political tourism and vivifying their political argument. The political possibilities of sympathy—so well understood by eighteenth-century sentimental travel writers—continue to inform the ways in which travel writers (and specifically female travel writers) represent their political engagement.

Understood as a particular way of approaching and recording foreign or unfamiliar spaces and experiences, the sentimental traveler has become enshrined as a normative mode of travel within contemporary Western culture. The desire to experience travel as self-realization, or as an authentic experience, or as a form of cultural bridging roughly corresponds with eighteenth-century sentimental travelers' determination to be guided by their "immediate feelings," to see with the "eyes of their own understanding," and to provide "just representations" of the countries they visit.[11] Even Western culture's current interest in slum, humanitarian, or responsible tourism can be seen to have its roots in the emphasis on the social and moral dimensions of travel in eighteenth-century sentimental travel writing. Examining, clarifying, and problematizing the mechanism of sympathy in eighteenth-century sentimental travel writing may help us identify and understand the use of sympathy in current travel practices, forcing us to confront the complex and often uncomfortable relationships between exploration and exploitation, privilege and power, self and other, home and abroad. It may also facilitate the examination of our own emotional responses to the sentimentalized or "affectively resonant" literary representations of the foreign and unfamiliar in current travel writing[12]—enabling us some measure of awareness over our own sympathies and the political ideologies they engender and support.

ACKNOWLEDGMENTS

I begin—like many of the female travel writers whose works I study—by acknowledging the many and varied contributions of my community to this project. Gary Kelly's work on Helen Maria Williams inspired this project while I was still doing my master's, and I was fortunate to benefit from his intellectual curiosity and excellent advice while under his supervision at the University of Alberta. Corrinne Harol and Sylvia Brown read the dissertation manuscript in its various stages and provided unfailing support and incisive commentaries. I extend thanks of a more personal nature to the warm scholarly community I found at the University of Alberta, with particular thanks to Dorothy Woodman and David Buchanan, who can always be relied upon for rich conversation and much laughter.

My wonderful colleagues at Concordia University of Edmonton have sustained me through the final stages of this project. I am deeply grateful for the advice and encouragement provided by Conrad van Dyk, Reginald Wiebe, Trevor Cook, Laura Sydora, and Tim McNamara (among many others). This book has also benefited from a number of Concordia University of Edmonton Teaching Reduction Awards and Internal Research Grants.

The guidance offered by numerous editors and readers at various stages of this project has helped to sculpt this book into its final form. Chapter 2 is derived, in part, from an article published in *Studies in Travel Writing* 20, no. 4 (2016), and a version of Chapter 4 was first published in *ABO: Interactive Journal for Women in the Arts, 1640–1830* 9, no. 2 (2019). The advice and knowledge generously shared by Tim Youngs, editor of *Studies in Travel Writing*, Mona Narain, editor of *ABO*, and the anonymous readers at both journals honed my argument. The editors at Bucknell University Press and Rutgers University Press have shepherded this manuscript through the publication process with generosity and enthusiasm. My thanks go out to Suzanne Guiod, Miriam L. Wallace, and Pamelia Dailey at Bucknell University Press and Michelle Scott at Westchester Publishing Services, all of whom have provided wonderful support. The thoughtful and perceptive feedback of the anonymous readers provided through the press modeled effective scholarly criticism; the opportunity to see the manuscript through their eyes has been incredibly helpful.

I reserve special thanks for my closest social circles. My parents, Tjitte Van Netten and Tiedsje Pruiksma Van Netten, taught me to value literature and education, and their love and hard work has provided me with a profound sense of home. I am inspired by the examples of my sisters, Jannie Van Netten, Lucy Pease, and Evelien Lupo, and continue to want to be like them when I grow up. Leslie and Paul Blimke have contributed to the completion of this book through their valuable support in the form of childcare; their cheerful donation of time has been a boon. Brianna Wells, Leigh Dyrda, Allison Peters, Laura Kerslake, and Laura Sydora—known in local curling rinks as the "Blazing Kiltz"—have provided me with uproarious laughter, moral support, and thoughtful advice. Theresa Meinders and I have been talking about literature and life since our undergraduate years, and I forever look forward to our animated discussions and desultory travels.

My deepest thanks go out to my most immediate social circle. Matthew Blimke is the great gift of my life, and his fierce support has always given me the confidence to do what I think is impossible. Clementine and Magnolia Van Netten Blimke have enriched my life in immeasurable ways, and continuously energize me to help create a world in which they can flourish. Home is where you are.

NOTES

INTRODUCTION

1. Mary Douglas, *Notes of a Journey from Berne to England, through France. Made in the Year 1796* (London, 1797), 1, *Eighteenth Century Collections Online* (ECCO).
2. Andrew Douglas, *Notes of a Journey from Berne to England, through France. Made in the Year 1796* (London, 1797), 26, ECCO.
3. For a helpful overview of the multiple discourses available in the eighteenth-century travelogue genre, see Katherine Turner, *British Travel Writers in Europe, 1750–1800: Authorship, Gender, and National Identity* (Burlington, VT: Ashgate, 2001), 49–54.
4. Although *A Journey to the Highlands of Scotland* was for some time attributed to Mary Ann(e) Hanway—who wrote several novels in the late eighteenth and early nineteenth centuries—recent scholarship has cast doubt on the travelogue's authorship. Betty Hagglund concludes that the absence of references to *A Journey to the Highlands of Scotland* in Hanway's subsequent work and the fact that she is described as "an unpracticed" author (*Tourists and Travellers: Women's Non-Fictional Writing about Scotland, 1770–1830* [Bristol: Channel View Publications, 2010], 156) in reviews of her first novel suggest that Hanway is not the author of the travelogue. Barbara Britton Wenner sides with Hagglund's conclusion, basing her suspicions on the twenty-two-year gap between the travelogue's publication and the publication of Hanway's first novel, the difference in style between the travelogue and Hanway's novels, and the fact that the British Museum Library appears to have attributed the travelogue to Hanway sometime between 1872 and 1890 (introduction to *A Journey to the Highlands of Scotland, by a Lady*, ed. Barbara Britton Wenner [Kansas City, MO: Valancourt Books, 2010], xvii–xvii). Both scholars refer to the author as "the Lady" as a result of their well-founded suspicions; I have chosen to do the same.
5. For celebratory and/or biographical approaches to early female travelers, see Barbara Hodgson, *No Place for a Lady: Tales of Adventurous Women Travellers* (Vancouver: Greystone Books, 2002); Jane Robinson, *Wayward Women: A Guide to Women Travellers* (Oxford: Oxford University Press, 1990); and Marion Tinling, *Women into the Unknown: A Sourcebook on Women Explorers and Travelers* (New York: Greenwood Press, 1989). More recently, Mick Conefrey's *How to Climb Mont Blanc in a Skirt: A Handbook for the Lady Adventurer* (Oxford: Oneworld Publications, 2011) has followed in this celebratory strain, providing rollicking accounts of early female travelers' derring-do.
6. Sara Mills, *Discourses of Difference: An Analysis of Women's Travel Writing and Colonialism* (London: Routledge, 1993), 197.
7. Jane West, *A Tale of the Times* (London, 1799), 3:387, ECCO.
8. Turner, *British Travel Writers in Europe*, 128.
9. For example, Mary Wollstonecraft describes the typical eighteenth-century female tourist as more concerned with "the impression that she may make on her fellow travellers; and . . . on the care of the finery that she carries with her" (*A Vindication of the Rights of Women*, ed. Miriam Brody [London: Penguin Books, 2004], 130), and Mick Conefrey is quick to use the words "brave," "reckless," "fascinating," and "eccentric" (*How to Climb*

Mont Blanc in a Skirt, ix) to describe female travelers, reinforcing common contemporary interpretations of early female travelers as "eccentric creatures" and "exceptional spinsters" (Mills, *Discourses of Difference*, 6).

10. See, for instance, Lynn Festa, *Sentimental Figures of Empire in Eighteenth-Century Britain and France* (Baltimore: Johns Hopkins University Press, 2006), ch. 4; Deborah Weiss, "Suffering, Sentiment, and Civilization: Pain and Politics in Mary Wollstonecraft's *Short Residence*," *Studies in Romanticism* 45, no. 2 (Summer 2006): 199–221, https://doi.org/10.2307/25602044; and Gary Kelly, *Women, Writing, and Revolution, 1790–1827* (Oxford: Clarendon Press, 1993), ch. 2. Two studies that do examine the language of sensibility within the context of travel or mobility are Ingrid Horrocks, *Women Wanderers and the Writing of Mobility, 1784–1814* (Cambridge: Cambridge University Press, 2017), esp. ch. 4, and Chris Jones, "Travelling Hopefully: Helen Maria Williams and the Feminine Discourse of Sensibility," in *Romantic Geographies: Discourses of Travel, 1775–1844*, ed. Amanda Gilroy (Manchester: Manchester University Press, 2000), 93–107.
11. Katrina O'Loughlin, *Women, Writing, and Travel in the Eighteenth Century* (Cambridge: Cambridge University Press, 2018), 116.
12. Festa, *Sentimental Figures of Empire*, 6.
13. West, *A Tale of the Times*, 3:387. It is important to note that West's criticism was directed at Helen Maria Williams—a female sentimental traveler whose Swiss travelogue is the subject of Chapter 5. Williams's careful integration of sentimental rhetoric and the conventions of the travelogue produced disarming contemplations on the progress of the French Revolution.
14. Thomas Gisborne, *An Inquiry into the Duties of the Female Sex* (London, 1797), 293, 291, ECCO.
15. Gisborne, *Duties of the Female Sex*, 293.
16. Gisborne, *Duties of the Female Sex*, 293–294.
17. Gisborne, *Duties of the Female Sex*, 294.
18. John Donne, "A Valediction: Forbidding Mourning," in *The Complete Poetry and Selected Prose of John Donne and the Complete Poetry of William Blake*, ed. John Hayward and Geoffrey Keynes (New York: Modern Library, 1941), 34. For more on the emerging ideal of female stasis in the eighteenth century, see Turner's excellent summary in *British Travel Writers in Europe*, ch. 4.
19. Karen Lawrence, *Penelope Voyages: Women and Travel in the British Literary Tradition* (Ithaca, NY: Cornell University Press, 1994), 1.
20. Gisborne, *Duties of the Female Sex*, 21.
21. Amanda Gilroy, introduction to Gilroy, *Romantic Geographies*, 5–6.
22. *A Journey*, 22.
23. Elizabeth Justice, *A Voyage to Russia* (York, 1739), ECCO; and Mary Wortley Montagu, *The Turkish Embassy Letters*, ed. Teresa Heffernan and Daniel O'Quinn (1763; repr. Peterborough, ON: Broadview Press, 2013). For more on the comparative scarcity of women's travel writing in the long eighteenth century, see Benjamin Colbert's pragmatic breakdown of the number of travelogues published by women in "British Women's Travel Writing, 1780–1840: Bibliographical Reflections," *Women's Writing* 24, no. 2 (2017): 151–169, https://doi.org/10.1080/09699082.2016.1207913.
24. Turner, *British Travel Writers in Europe*, 144.
25. The estimates regarding the number of travelogues written by women in the long eighteenth century vary, contingent upon what scholars count as travel literature and whether or not they include unpublished material. Turner estimates that twenty travelogues were published by women between 1770 and 1800; however, she also acknowledges the publication of Lady Mary Wortley Montagu's and Elizabeth Justice's travelogues prior to

1770, bringing Turner's total estimate to twenty-two (*British Travel Writers in Europe*, 127). Benjamin Colbert's estimate is slightly more generous; between 1780 and 1800, he counts twenty-six narrative travelogues and guidebooks published by women ("British Women's Travel Writing," 160).

26. "*Prospects and Observations; on a Tour in England and Scotland, Natural, Economical, and Literary*," *The Analytical Review* 11 (September 1791), 301, *HathiTrust*, https://hdl.handle.net/2027/njp.32101065085373. The critic for *The Analytical Review* lists these topics as the primary modes of inquiry for the travelogue genre.
27. Chloe Chard, *Pleasure and Guilt on the Grand Tour: Travel Writing and Imaginative Geography, 1600–1830* (Manchester: Manchester University Press, 1999), 36.
28. Laurence Sterne, *A Sentimental Journey through France and Italy*, ed. Katherine Turner (Peterborough, ON: Broadview Press, 2010), 137.
29. Gisborne, *Duties of the Female Sex*, 291.
30. Ulrike Brisson, "Introduction: Naked Politics in Travel Writing," in *Not So Innocent Abroad: The Politics of Travel and Travel Writing*, ed. Ulrike Brisson and Bernard Schwiezer (Newcastle upon Tyne: Cambridge Scholars Publishing, 2009), 5.
31. William Reddy, *The Navigation of Feeling: A Framework for the History of Emotions* (Cambridge: Cambridge University Press, 2004), 323–324; Barbara Rosenwein, *Emotional Communities in the Early Middle Ages* (Ithaca, NY: Cornell University Press, 2006), 2.
32. William Reddy, "Against Constructionism: The Historical Ethnography of Emotions," *Current Anthropology* 38, no. 3 (1997): 335, https://doi:10.1086/204622.
33. Jonathan Flatley, "How a Revolutionary Counter-Mood Is Made," *New Literary History* 43, no. 3 (Summer 2012), 504, JSTOR.
34. Flatley, "Revolutionary Counter-Mood," 507.
35. See *Doing Emotions History*, ed. Susan J. Matt and Peter N. Stearns (Chicago: University of Illinois Press, 2014).
36. For a discussion of contemporary critics' confused or embarrassed responses to the eighteenth-century culture of sensibility, see Claudia Johnson, *Equivocal Beings: Politics, Gender, and Sentimentality in the 1790s: Wollstonecraft, Radcliffe, Burney, Austen* (Chicago: University of Chicago Press, 1995), 1.
37. Brycchan Carey, *British Abolitionism and the Rhetoric of Sensibility: Writing, Sentiment, and Slavery, 1760–1807* (New York: Palgrave Macmillan, 2005), 2.
38. Reddy, *The Navigation of Feeling*, 322.
39. Nicole Eustace, *Passion Is the Gale: Emotion, Power, and the Coming of the American Revolution* (Williamsburg, VA: Omohundro Institute of Early American History and Culture, 2008), 12.
40. See Barbara Rosenwein, *Generations of Feeling: A History of Emotions, 600–1700* (Cambridge: Cambridge University Press, 2016); Eustace, *Passion Is the Gale*; Rosenwein, *Emotional Communities*; Reddy, *The Navigation of Feeling*; and Peter N. Stearns and Carol Z. Stearns, "Emotionology: Clarifying the History of Emotions and Emotional Standards," *The American Historical Review* 90 (October 1985): 813–836, https://doi.org/10.2307/1858841. Julie Ellison also points to the historical specificity of the very terms we use to discuss emotion, which "vary according to their usage in distinct historical contexts" (*Cato's Tears and the Making of Anglo-American Emotion* [Chicago: University of Chicago Press, 1999], 5).
41. Markman Ellis, *The Politics of Sensibility: Race, Gender and Commerce in the Sentimental Novel* (Cambridge: Cambridge University Press, 1996), 7.
42. Chris Jones, *Radical Sensibility: Literature and Ideas in the 1790s* (New York: Routledge, 1993), 7, 5.

43. Samuel Johnson, *A Dictionary of the English Language*, vol. 2 (London, 1755–1756), s.v. "Sensibility," ECCO; Festa, *Sentimental Figures of Empire*, 7; Stephen Ahern, *Affected Sensibilities: Romantic Excess and the Genealogy of the Novel, 1680–1810* (New York: AMS Press, 2007), 12.
44. Johnson, *Dictionary*, s.v. "Sympathy."
45. Juliet Shields, *Sentimental Literature and Anglo-Scottish Identity, 1745–1820* (Cambridge: Cambridge University Press, 2010), 3.
46. Ahern, *Affected Sensibilities*, 25.
47. For two influential formulations of the causal relationship between physical environment and national character, see Abbé Dubos's *Critical Reflections on Poetry, Painting, and Music*, trans. Thomas Nugent, vol. 2 (London, 1748), ECCO; and Charles Montesquieu, *The Spirit of the Laws*, trans. Thomas Nugent (1750; repr. Kitchener, ON: Batoche Books, 2001).
48. David Hume, *A Treatise of Human Nature*, ed. Ernest C. Mossner (London: Penguin Books, 1985), 367. Subsequent references will be cited parenthetically in the text.
49. Janet Todd, *Sensibility: An Introduction* (London: Methuen, 1986), 27.
50. David Hume, "Of National Characters," in *Selected Essays*, ed. Stephen Copley and Andrew Edgar (Oxford: Oxford University Press, 2008), 115. Subsequent references will be cited parenthetically in the text.
51. Adam Smith, *The Theory of Moral Sentiments*, ed. Ryan Patrick Hanley (New York: Penguin Books, 2009), 13. Subsequent references will be cited parenthetically in the text.
52. Evan Gottlieb, *Feeling British: Sympathy and National Identity in Scottish and English Writing, 1701–1832* (Lewisburg, PA: Bucknell University Press, 2007), 22.
53. John Mullan, *Sentiment and Sociability: The Language of Feeling in the Eighteenth Century* (Oxford: Clarendon Press, 1988), 25.
54. Carey, *British Abolitionism*, 18.
55. Ahern, *Affected Sensibilities*, 12, 25.
56. Pamela Cheek, *Sexual Antipodes: Enlightenment, Globalization, and the Placing of Sex* (Stanford, CA: Stanford University Press, 2003), 12.
57. Nathaniel Wraxall, *Cursory Remarks Made in a Tour through Some of the Northern Parts of Europe, Particularly Copenhagen, Stockholm, and Petersburgh, in a Series of Letters* (Vienna, 1797), 3, ECCO.
58. George Dekker, *The Fictions of Romantic Tourism: Radcliffe, Scott, and Mary Shelley* (Stanford, CA: Stanford University Press, 2005), 6.
59. Dugald Stewart, "Account of the Life and Writings of Adam Smith LL.D.," in *Essays in Philosophical Subjects* (London, 1795), 33, *Google Books*, https://www.google.ca/books/edition/Essays_on_Philosophical_Subjects_To_whic/x6lcAAAAcAAJ?hl=en&gbpv=0.
60. Stewart, "Life and Writings of Adam Smith," 34.
61. Hugh F. Rankin, *The North Carolina Continentals* (Chapel Hill: University of North Carolina Press, 2005), 29.
62. "*Letters from the Island of Teneriffe, Brazil, the Cape of Good Hope, and the East Indies* by Mrs. Kindersley," *The Monthly Review* 57 (September 1777), 243, *HathiTrust*, https://hdl.handle.net/2027/hvd.hxjfhc.
63. For more on the eighteenth-century perception of novels as potentially corrupting, see M. O. Grenby, *The Anti-Jacobin Novel: British Conservatism and the French Revolution* (Cambridge: Cambridge University Press, 2001), 17–18.
64. Hester Chapone, *Letters on the Improvement of the Mind, Addressed to a Young Lady* (London, 1790), 188, *Google Books*, https://www.google.ca/books/edition/Letters_on_the_improvement_of_the_mind/h5QDAAAAQAAJ?hl=en&gbpv=0.

65. James Fordyce, *Sermons to Young Women*, 14th ed. (London, 1814), 1:214, *Google Books*, https://www.google.ca/books/edition/Sermons_to_young_women/EPvotQIhvH8C?hl=en&gbpv=0.
66. Chapone, *Letters*, 188.
67. Fordyce, *Sermons*, 1:214.
68. "*The Beauties of Nature and Art Displayed: In a Tour through the World*," *The Critical Review* 18 (1764), 375–376, *Google Books*, https://www.google.ca/books/edition/The_Critical_Review_Or_Annals_of_Literat/X8APAAAAQAAJ?hl=en&gbpv=0.
69. Nigel Leask, *Curiosity and the Aesthetics of Travel Writing, 1770–1840* (Oxford: Oxford University Press, 2002), 14.
70. Susan Lamb, *Bringing Travel Home to England: Tourism, Gender, and Imaginative Literature in the Eighteenth Century* (Newark: University of Delaware Press, 2008), 17.
71. Lamb, *Bringing Travel Home*, 24.
72. Janet Schaw, *Journal of a Lady of Quality*, ed. Evangeline Walker Andrews and Charles MacLean Andrews (Lincoln: University of Nebraska Press, 2005), 189.
73. Samuel Johnson, "Letter XXII—To the Same. Skie, Sept. 21st, 1773," in *The Works of Samuel Johnson, LL. D.: With an Essay on His Life and Genius by Arthur Murray, Esq.* (New York: George Dearborn, 1837), 1:509.
74. "*Travels from Hamburg, Through Westphalia, Holland, and the Netherlands, to Paris*," *The Critical Review* 3, no. 1 (April 1804), 361, *HathiTrust*, https://hdl.handle.net/2027/nyp.33433066596903.
75. Linda Colley, *Britons: Forging the Nation 1707–1837*, rev. ed. (New Haven, CT: Yale University Press, 2008), 7.
76. Colley characterizes the political atmosphere of the late eighteenth and early nineteenth centuries as having a "distinctively *sturm-und-drang* quality . . . a special kind of emotionalism and violence" (*Britons*, 151).
77. Holcroft, *Travels from Hamburg through Westphalia, Holland, and the Netherlands to Paris* (London, 1804), vii–viii, *Google Books*, https://books.google.ca/books?id=G3-7jgEACAAJ&printsec=frontcover&source=gbs_ge_summary_r&cad=0#v=onepage&q&f=false. Holcroft, it should be noted, used his own sentimental works to influence British political opinion and was eventually tried for treason in 1794.
78. Mary Fairclough, *The Romantic Crowd: Sympathy, Controversy and Print Culture* (Cambridge: Cambridge University Press, 2013), 4.
79. Flatley, "Revolutionary Counter-Mood," 504.
80. Rosmarie Zagarri, *Revolutionary Backlash: Women and Politics in the Early American Republic* (Philadelphia: University of Pennsylvania Press, 2007), 44. See also Mary Beth Norton, *Liberty's Daughters: The Revolutionary Experience of American Women, 1750–1800* (Boston: Little, Brown, 1980); Holly A. Mayer, "Bearing Arms, Bearing Burdens: Women Warriors, Camp Followers and Home-Front Heroines of the American Revolution," in *Gender, War and Politics: Transatlantic Perspectives, 1775–1830*, ed. Karen Hagemann, Gisela Mettele, and Jane Rendall (New York: Palgrave Macmillan, 2010), 169–187; and Edith Patterson Meyer, *Petticoat Patriots of the American Revolution* (New York: Vanguard Press, 1976).
81. Adriana Craciun and Kari Lokke, "British Women Writers and the French Revolution, 1789–1815," in *Rebellious Hearts: British Women Writers and the French Revolution*, ed. Adriana Craciun and Kari Lokke (Albany: State University of New York Press, 2001), 16. See also Stephanie Russo, *Women in Revolutionary Debate: Female Novelists from Burney to Austen* (Houten, The Netherlands: Hes and De Graaf Publishers, 2012); Kelly, *Women, Writing, and Revolution*; Eleanor Ty, *Unsex'd Revolutionaries: Five Women Novelists of the 1790s*

(Toronto: University of Toronto Press, 1993); and *Rebel Daughters: Women and the French Revolution*, ed. Sara E. Melzer and Leslie W. Rabine (Oxford: Oxford University Press, 1992).

82. Orianne Smith, *Romantic Women Writers, Revolution, and Prophecy: Rebellious Daughters, 1786–1826* (Cambridge: Cambridge University Press, 2013), 6; and Emma Major, *Madam Britannia: Women, Church, and Nation, 1712–1812* (Oxford: Oxford University Press, 2012), chs. 7–8.
83. Brisson, "Naked Politics in Travel Writing," 5.
84. Paul Theroux, *The Tao of Travel: Enlightenments for Lives on the Road* (Toronto: McClelland and Stewart, 2011), 16.
85. O. Smith, *Romantic Women Writers*, 5.
86. *A Journey*, 22.

CHAPTER 1 — "ALTOGETHER OF A DIFFERENT CAST"

1. Laurence Sterne, "Sermon V: The Prodigal Son," in *The Sermons of Mr. Yorick*, vol. 3 (London: J. Dodsley, 1775), 121, *Internet Archive*, https://archive.org/details/sermonsofmryoric03ster. Subsequent references will be cited parenthetically in the text.
2. "*Another Traveller! Or, Cursory Remarks and Tritical* [*sic*] *Observations Made upon a Journey through Part of the Netherlands, in the Latter End of the Year 1766*," *The Monthly Review* 39 (December 1768): 434, *HathiTrust*, https://babel.hathitrust.org/cgi/pt?id=njp.32101064253915&view=1up&seq=7.
3. Sterne, *A Sentimental Journey*, 65. Subsequent references will be cited parenthetically in the text.
4. Lamb, *Bringing Travel Home*, 154.
5. Turner, *British Travel Writers in Europe*, 97.
6. "*A Common Place Book for Travellers in Foreign Countries*," *The Critical Review* 43 (May 1777), 399, *HathiTrust*, https://babel.hathitrust.org/cgi/pt?id=chi.79243088&view=1up&seq=7.
7. Philip Fischer, *Hard Facts: Setting and Form in the American Novel* (Oxford: Oxford University Press, 1985), 93.
8. Fischer, *Hard Facts*, 93.
9. Turner, *British Travel Writers in Europe*, 124.
10. Frank Felsenstein, "After the Peace of Paris: Yorick, Smelfungus and the Seven Years' War," in *Guerres et paix: La Grande-Bretagne au XVIIIe siécle*, ed. Paul Gabriel Boucé (Paris: Presses Sorbonne Nouvelle, 1998), 322. To be clear: this is not to say that Yorick's exercise of sympathy is unproblematic, or even that he is represented as the model of tolerance. For a more critical reading of Yorick's deployment of sensibility, see Robert Markley, "Sentimentality as Performance: Shaftesbury, Sterne, and the Theatrics of Virtue," in *The New Eighteenth Century: Theory, Politics, English Literature*, ed. Laura Brown and Felicity Nussbaum (New York: Methuen, 1987), 210–230.
11. Felsenstein, "After the Peace of Paris," 319.
12. J.C.T. Oates, *Shandyism and Sentiment, 1760–1800* (Cambridge: Cambridge Bibliographic Society, 1968), 14; Percy G. Adams, *Travel Literature and the Evolution of the Novel* (Lexington: University Press of Kentucky), 198.
13. See Oates, *Shandyism and Sentiment*, 14; and Adams, *Travel Literature and the Evolution of the Novel*, 198.
14. Kathleen Turner, introduction to Sterne, *A Sentimental Journey*, 19.
15. See Turner, *British Travel Writers in Europe*, 101–103.
16. *The Monthly Review*, 39, 434.

17. "*A Trip to Kilkenny, from Durham, by Way of Whitehaven and Dublin, in the Year 1776*," *The Monthly Review* 60 (1779), 191, *HathiTrust*, https://hdl.handle.net/2027/hvd.hxjfhf.
18. "*A Sentimental Journey to Bath, Bristol, and Its Environs*," *The Critical Review* 45 (April 1778), 311. *Google Books*, https://www.google.ca/books/edition/The_Critical_Review_Or_Annals_of_Literat/7cIPAAAAQAAJ?hl=en&gbpv=0.
19. Scholars often provide a few general characteristics of the sentimental traveler/travelogue but stop short of a working definition. For example, Turner highlights sentimental travelers' relational approach to foreigners and their enactment and appreciation of individuality (*British Travel Writers in Europe*, ch. 3). Carl Thompson identifies resistance to convention and an emphasis on subjectivity as components of the sentimental traveler, who he says "made a point of being playful and whimsical rather than practical and empirical, and explored—often in highly digressive prose—not so much the scenes around them as their reactions to those scenes" (*The Suffering Traveller and the Romantic Imagination* [Oxford: Oxford University Press, 2007], 35–36).
20. The following three characteristics are based on readings of late eighteenth-century travel texts that are overtly labeled "sentimental" by the author or are categorized as such by contemporary and/or current critics, or whose use of sentimental idioms suggests the influence of Sterne's form. In addition to the four travelogues featured within this book, these texts include, but are not limited to, Samuel Paterson, *Another Traveller!*, 2 vols. (London, 1767–1769), *Eighteenth Century Collections Online* (ECCO); John Armstrong, *A Short Ramble through Some Parts of France and Italy* (London, 1771), ECCO; John Barnard's series "A Sentimental Journey" in *The Lady's Magazine* (1770–1777), *Google Books*; Cornelius Cayley, *A Tour through Holland, Flanders, and Part of France* (Leeds, 1773), ECCO; Nathaniel Wraxall, *Cursory Remarks Made in a Tour through Some of the Northern Parts of Europe, Particularly Copenhagen, Stockholm, and Petersburgh* (London, 1775), ECCO; Samuel Jackson Pratt, *Travels for the Heart*, 2 vols. (London, 1777), ECCO; Peregrine Phillips, *A Sentimental Diary, Kept in an Excursion to Little Hampton, near Arundel, and to Brighthelmstone in Sussex* (London, 1778), *Google Books*; James Douglas, *Travelling Anecdotes through Various Parts of Europe*, 2 vols. (London, 1782), ECCO; John-Baptiste Mercier Dupaty, *Sentimental Letters on Italy*, 2 vols. (London, 1789), ECCO; Helen Maria Williams, *Letters Written in France*, ed. Neil Fraistat and Susan S. Lanser (1790; Peterborough, ON: Broadview Press, 2001); Jane Harvey, *A Sentimental Tour through Newcastle* (Newcastle, 1794), ECCO; John Gabriel Stedman, *The Narrative of a Five Years Expedition against the Revolted Negroes of Surinam*, 2 vols. (London, 1796), ECCO; Mary Wollstonecraft, *Letters Written during a Short Residence in Sweden, Norway, and Denmark*, ed. Ingrid Horrocks (1796; Peterborough, ON: Broadview Press, 2013); Charlotte Biggs, *A Residence in France, during the Years 1792, 1793, 1794, and 1795*, 2 vols. (London, 1797), ECCO; Mary Douglas, *Notes of a Journey from Berne to England through France: Made in the Year 1796* (London, 1797), ECCO; and Thomas Holcroft, *Travels from Hamburg, through Westphalia, Holland, and the Netherlands, to Paris*, 2 vols. (London, 1804), *Google Books*. The inclusion of Barnard in this list is admittedly eccentric. However, Barnard's series—while fictional—provides useful insights into how the sentimental mode was understood and adapted within eighteenth-century society.
21. See S. J. Pratt, *Travels for the Heart*; and Barnard, "A Sentimental Journey."
22. It is important to clarify here that although emotional response may be privileged, it does not necessarily take the place of scientific, sociopolitical, or aesthetic assessment. See Nigel Leask's discussion of the emergence of "affective" realism and the fine balance between subjectivity and objectivity in late eighteenth- and nineteenth-century travel writing in *Curiosity and the Aesthetics of Travel Writing, 1770–1840* (Oxford: Oxford University Press, 2002), ch. 1.

23. S. J. Pratt, *Travels for the Heart*, 1:xxxiii; Williams, *Letters Written in France*, 91; Schaw, *Journal*, 20.
24. Thompson, *The Suffering Traveller*, 36.
25. Paterson, *Another Traveller!*, 1:34.
26. Cayley, *A Tour*, 24.
27. Dupaty, *Sentimental Letters*, 1:10.
28. *The Monthly Review* 39, 434.
29. John Barnard, "A Sentimental Journey," *The Lady's Magazine* 4 (January 1773), 3. *Google Books*, https://www.google.ca/books/edition/The_Lady_s_Magazine_Or_Entertaining_Comp/bZ1PAQAAMAAJ?hl=en&gbpv=0.
30. S. J. Pratt, *Travels for the Heart*, 1:53.
31. Wollstonecraft, *Short Residence*, 51.
32. *A Journey*, 4; S. J. Pratt, *Travels for the Heart*, 1:x.
33. Paterson, *Another Traveller!*, 2:174.
34. *The Monthly Review* 60, 191.
35. Take, for example, Bernard Mandeville's *Treatise of Hypochondriack and Hysterick Passions* (London, 1730), ECCO, which argues that women's nerves were structurally different than men's, and George Cheyne's *The English Malady* (Dublin, 1733), ECCO, which characterizes physical firmness as masculine and physical weakness as feminine.
36. S. J. Pratt, *Travels for the Heart*, 1:61.
37. Francis Hutcheson, *A Short Introduction to Moral Philosophy* (Glasgow, 1747), 260, ECCO.
38. Lord Henry Home Kames, *Sketches of the History of Man*, 2nd ed. (Edinburgh, 1778), 2:3. ECCO.
39. John Barnard, "A Sentimental Journey," *The Lady's Magazine* 1 (October 1770), 100, *Google Books*, https://www.google.ca/books/edition/The_Lady_s_Magazine_Or_Entertaining_Comp/1iJNAAAAcAAJ?hl=en&gbpv=0.
40. James Fordyce, *Sermons to Young Women*, 14th ed. (London, 1814), 1:211–212, *Google Books*, https://www.google.ca/books/edition/Sermons_to_young_women/EPvotQIhvH8C?hl=en&gbpv=0.
41. For scholarly investigations of the evolving definition and roles of women within the culture of sensibility, see G. J. Barker-Benfield, *The Culture of Sensibility: Sex and Society in Eighteenth-Century Britain* (Chicago: University of Chicago Press, 1992); Ellis, *The Politics of Sensibility*; and Karen O'Brien, *Women and Enlightenment in Eighteenth-Century Britain* (Cambridge: Cambridge University Press, 2009).
42. Wollstonecraft, *A Vindication of the Rights of Women*, 130.
43. Tobias Smollett, *The Expedition of Humphrey Clinker*, ed. Lewis M. Knapp (Oxford: Oxford University Press, 1998), 128.
44. Turner, *British Travel Writers in Europe*, 128.
45. Maria first appears in Laurence Sterne's *Tristram Shandy*, vol. 9.
46. Chard, *Pleasure and Guilt*, 153.
47. Paterson, *Another Traveller!*, 1:61–62, 73–79, 91–96.
48. *The Gentleman's Magazine* 46 (January 1775), 24n, *Google Books*, https://books.google.ca/books?id=SB49AAAAYAAJ&printsec=frontcover&dq=gentlemans+magazine+46+1776&hl=en&sa=X&redir_esc=y#v=onepage&q&f=true.
49. Wraxall, *Cursory Remarks*, 401–404.
50. Dupaty, *Sentimental Letters*, 1:21, 202, 203.
51. Dupaty, *Sentimental Letters*, 1:117.
52. Stedman, *Five Years Expedition*, 1:iv.
53. Stedman, *Five Years Expedition*, 1:iv. It is also significant that Stedman compares Joanna to the tragic figure of Maria. Upon his departure for Holland, Stedman describes Joan-

na's emotional state in terms similar to those used by Sterne to describe Maria: "The unfortunate Joanna (now but nineteen) gazing on me, and holding me by the hand, with a look ten thousand times more dejected than *Sterne's Maria*,—was unable to utter one word!!!—I perceived she was distracted" (2:379). Just as Maria's madness is instigated by the abandonment of her lover, Stedman describes Joanna as going mad with grief upon his departure.

54. It may be more accurate to say that male sentimental tourists' interest in foreign females is more explicitly presented as erotic, whereas earlier Grand Tourists and explorers present their interest in females as ethnographic, although scholars have argued that their "ethnographic" approach to women obscures an erotic interest. See Chard's discussion of women as signifiers of the foreign in *Pleasure and Guilt*, ch. 3.
55. Markley, "Sentimentality as Performance," 211.
56. C. Johnson, *Equivocal Beings*, 1–19; Ingrid Horrocks, *Women Wanderers*, 1–38.
57. Markley, "Sentimentality as Performance," 211.
58. A. Smith, *Moral Sentiments*, 288, 175, 245.
59. Wollstonecraft, *A Vindication of the Rights of Women*, 110, 131.
60. Wollstonecraft, *A Vindication of the Rights of Women*, 131.
61. Wollstonecraft, *A Vindication of the Rights of Women*, 6.
62. Markley, "Sentimentality as Performance," 211.
63. *A Journey*, 16.
64. Mary Morgan, *A Tour to Milford Haven, in the Year 1791* (1795; ECCO Print Editions, 2010), ix.
65. Schaw, *Journal*, 113; *A Journey*, 16; M. Morgan, *Milford Haven*, 32–50; 15, 38, 321; Helen Maria Williams, *A Tour in Switzerland* (London, 1798), 2:125, ECCO.
66. Schaw, *Journal*, 82; *A Journey*, 8.
67. Festa, *Sentimental Figures of Empire*, 52.

CHAPTER 2 — "I AM SURE YOU WILL SHARE MY FEELINGS"

1. The "contact zone" is a term coined by Mary Louise Pratt (*Imperial Eyes: Travel Writing and Transculturation* [London: Routledge, 1992], 6) to describe the spaces in which colonizers and colonized interact.
2. Schaw, *Journal*, 21. Subsequent references will be cited parenthetically in the text.
3. Edmund Burke, "Letters on a Regicide Peace: Letter III," in *The Works of the Right Honourable Edmund Burke*, vol. 5 (London: George Bell and Sons, 1877), 272.
4. Allan Ramsay, *Letters on the Present Disturbances in Great Britain and Her American Provinces* (London, 1777), 20, *Eighteenth Century Collections Online* (ECCO).
5. E. Burke, "Letters on a Regicide Peace," 210.
6. Evangeline Walker Andrews, introduction to Schaw, *Journal*, 9–10, 106–107.
7. E. W. Andrews, introduction to Schaw, *Journal*, 3.
8. In the 1939 edition of *Journal of a Lady of Quality*, E. W. Andrews includes a letter from Mrs. W. H. Nelson that provides this additional biographical material (Janet Schaw, *Journal of a Lady of Quality*, ed. Evangeline Walker Andrews and Charles MacLean Andrews, 3rd ed. [New Haven, CT: Yale University Press, 1939]), 343 (all other citations of *Journal* in this book are to the 2005 edition).
9. E. W. Andrews was the first to suggest the potentially broad scope of Schaw's audience, asserting that the letters were "probably copied many times for circulation among relatives and friends" (introduction to Schaw, *Journal*, 3). Katrina O'Loughlin agrees with E. W. Andrews, citing the wide circulation of manuscripts in the period as her basis for believing that Schaw's texts were written with an "extended social audience in mind"

("'In Brazen Bonds': The Warring Landscapes of North Carolina, 1775," in *Emotions and War: Medieval to Romantic Literature*, ed. Stephanie Downes, Andrew Lynch, and Katrina O'Loughlin [Basingstoke, UK: Palgrave Macmillan, 2015], 223).

10. Margaret Ezell, *Social Authorship and the Advent of Print* (Baltimore: John Hopkins University Press, 2003), 38.
11. Ezell, *Social Authorship*, 39.
12. Ezell, *Social Authorship*, 39.
13. Turner, *British Travel Writers in Europe*, 135.
14. Schaw mentions her close friendship with Lord Mansfield (89), and her impressive social networks in the West Indies, North Carolina, and Lisbon further reveal her prominent political connections.
15. Hugh F. Rankin, *The North Carolina Continentals* (1971; repr. Chapel Hill: University of North Carolina Press, 2005), 29.
16. O'Loughlin, *Women, Writing, and Travel*, 167.
17. Sterne, *A Sentimental Journey*, 70.
18. David Hume, "Of National Characters," in *Selected Essays*, ed. Stephen Copley and Andrew Edgar (Oxford: Oxford University Press, 2008), 115.
19. Hume, *A Treatise*, 389.
20. Hume, *A Treatise*, 645; A. Smith, *Moral Sentiments*, 13.
21. Troy Bickham, *Making Headlines: The American Revolution as Seen through the British Press* (DeKalb: Illinois University Press, 2009), 67.
22. E. W. Andrews, introduction to *Journal*, 65.
23. Edmund Burke, "Speech on Conciliation with America," in *On Empire, Liberty, and Reform: Speeches and Letters* (New Haven, CT: Yale University Press, 2000), 37.
24. Edmund Burke, "Speech on American Taxation," in *The Portable Edmund Burke*, ed. Isaac Kramnick (New York: Penguin Books, 1999), 254–255.
25. James E. Bradley, *Popular Politics and the American Revolution in England: Petitions, the Crown, and Public Opinion* (Macon, GA: Mercer University Press, 1986), 93.
26. Stephen Conway, *The British Isles and the American War of Independence* (Oxford: Oxford University Press, 2002), 131–132. Compelling examinations of Britons' conflicted response to the American Revolution and of colonial Americans' contested identity can also be found in Julie Flavell, *When London Was Capital of America* (New Haven, CT: Yale University Press, 2011); Colley, *Britons*; Linda Colley, *Captives: Britain, Empire, and the World, 1600–1850* (New York: Anchor Books, 2004); Stephen Conway, "From Fellow-Nationals to Foreigners: British Perceptions of the Americans, circa 1739–1783," *The William and Mary Quarterly* 59, no. 1: 65–100, https://doi.org/10.2307/3491638; Kathleen Wilson, *The Sense of the People: Politics, Culture and Imperialism in England, 1715–1785* (Cambridge: Cambridge University Press, 1998); Kathleen Wilson, *The Island Race: Englishness, Empire, and Gender in the Eighteenth-Century* (New York: Routledge, 2003); Dror Wahrman, "The English Problem of Identity in the American Revolution," *The American Historical Review* 106, no. 4 (October 2001): 1236–1262, https://doi.org/10.2307/2692947; Eliga H. Gould, *The Persistence of Empire* (Chapel Hill: University of North Carolina Press, 2000); and Bradley, *Popular Politics*.
27. Wahrman, "The English Problem of Identity," 1256.
28. Ramsay, *Letters*, 17.
29. Ramsay, *Letters*, 19–20.
30. Ramsay, *Letters*, 19.
31. John Erskine, *Shall I Go to War with My American Brethren?* (London, 1769), 10, ECCO; Richard Price, *Observations on the Nature of Civil Liberty* (Dublin, 1776), 5, ECCO; E. Burke, "Conciliation," 128.

32. Erskine, *Shall I Go to War?*, 10.
33. John Knox, *The American Crisis, by a Citizen of the World* (London, 1777), 3:28–29, ECCO.
34. J. Knox, *The American Crisis*, 29.
35. J. Knox, *The American Crisis*, 31.
36. Ramsay, *Letters*, 23–24.
37. Ramsay, *Letters*, 24.
38. Adam Ferguson, *An Essay on the History of Civil Society*, 2nd ed. (London, 1768), 36, ECCO.
39. Josiah Tucker, *A Series of Answers to Certain Popular Objections against Separating from the Rebellious Colonies and Discarding Them Entirely* (Gloucester, 1776), 16, ECCO.
40. Bickham, *Making Headlines*, 67.
41. Adam Smith, *An Inquiry into the Nature and Causes of the Wealth of Nations*, ed. Jonathan B. Wight (Petersfield, UK: Harriman House, 2007), 619.
42. Colley, *Britons*, 121.
43. Colley, *Britons*, 123.
44. David Dobson, *Scottish Emigration to Colonial America, 1607–1785* (Athens: University of Georgia Press, 1994), 4; Douglas J. Hamilton, *Scotland, the Caribbean and the Atlantic World, 1750–1820* (Manchester: Manchester University Press, 2005), 23.
45. Leith Davis, *Acts of Union: Scotland and the Literary Negotiation of the British Nation, 1707–1830* (Stanford, CA: Stanford University Press, 1999), 74.
46. Ian Graham, *Colonists from Scotland: Emigration to North America, 1707–1783* (Ithaca, NY: Cornell University Press, 1956), 154.
47. Hamilton, *Scotland*, 161.
48. Excellent discussions of the complex nature of Anglo-Scottish relations in the eighteenth century can be found in Rivka Swenson, *Essential Scots and the Idea of Unionism in Anglo-Scottish Literature, 1603–1832* (Lewisburg, PA: Bucknell University Press, 2015); Shields, *Sentimental Literature and Anglo-Scottish Identity*; Gottlieb, *Feeling British*; Colley, *Britons*; Leith Davis, Ian Duncan, and Janet Sorensen, eds., *Scotland and the Borders of Romanticism* (Cambridge: Cambridge University Press, 2004); Davis, *Acts of Union*; and Katie Trumpener, *Bardic Nationalism: The Romantic Novel and the British Empire* (Princeton, NJ: Princeton University Press, 1997).
49. Ramsay, *Letters*, 20.
50. Steven Thomas, "Doctoring Ideology: James Grainger's *The Sugar Cane* and the Bodies of Empire," *Early American Studies: An Interdisciplinary Journal* 4, no. 1 (2006): 85, JSTOR.
51. When Schaw visited Antigua and St. Christopher in 1774, the islands' plantations were more often than not in the hands of overseers. Absentees represented 80 percent of Antigua's planter population and 50 percent of St. Christopher's (Andrew O'Shaughnessy, *An Empire Divided: The American Revolution and the British Caribbean* [Philadelphia: University of Pennsylvania Press, 2000], 5).
52. Richard Cumberland, *The West Indian, a Comedy. As It Is Performed at the Theatre Royal in Drury-Lane* (London, 1771), 50, ECCO.
53. Cumberland, *The West Indian*, 60.
54. See Kames, *Sketches*, 1:210–215.
55. Edward Long, *The History of Jamaica. Or, General Survey of the Antient and Modern State of That Island* (London, 1774), 1:261–262, ECCO.
56. Hans Sloane, *A Voyage to the Islands Madera, Barbados, Nieves, S. Christophers and Jamaica* (London, 1707), 1:xi, ECCO.
57. O'Shaughnessy, *An Empire Divided*, 14.

58. "Creole" is here being used to designate Britons who were born and raised within the West Indies.
59. Sarah Scott, *The History of Sir George Ellison*, ed. Betty Rizzo (Lexington: University Press of Kentucky, 1996), 10–20.
60. Wilson, *The Island Race*, 130.
61. A. Smith, *Moral Sentiments*, 264.
62. Wilson, "The Island Race," 130.
63. Thomas Bicknell and Thomas Day, *The Dying Negro, a Poem*, 3rd ed. (London, 1775), 15, http://www.brycchancarey.com/slavery/dying.htm (accessed July 3, 2015).
64. John Singleton, *A Description of the West-Indies. A Poem, in Four Books. By Mr. Singleton. During His Excursions among Those Islands* (London, 1776), 18, ECCO.
65. Ferguson, *History of Civil Society*, 171.
66. Corey E. Andrews, "'Ev'ry Heart Can Feel': Scottish Poetic Responses to Slavery in the West Indies, from Blair to Burns," *International Journal of Scottish Literature* 4 (Spring–Summer 2008): 2, http://www.ijsl.stir.ac.uk/issue4/andrews.htm (accessed August 15, 2015).
67. Bicknell and Day, advertisement to *The Dying Negro*, n.p.
68. Carey, *British Abolitionism*, 38.
69. Bicknell and Day, advertisement to *The Dying Negro*, n.p.
70. *A Sentimental Journey* features a scene in which Yorick imagines the acute suffering of an enslaved man until he [Yorick] dissolves into sympathetic tears, unable to "sustain the picture of confinement which my fancy had drawn" (127). Yorick's tears produced by simply imagining the suffering of enslaved peoples emphasizes the cruelty of Schaw's figurative shrug after witnessing the actual suffering of the West Indies' enslaved population.
71. See Hume, "Of National Characters," n120; Kames, *Sketches*, 1:1–10; and Long, *The History of Jamaica*, 356–380.
72. I am indebted to Festa's illuminating analysis of Schaw's representation of the West Indies' enslaved population, in which she details the ways that Schaw effectively dehumanizes those enslaved by portraying them as incapable of feeling, thereby justifying her own failure of sympathy while simultaneously obviating the circulation of sympathy between her metropolitan audience and the West Indies' enslaved population (*Sentimental Figures of Empire*, 171–187).
73. Festa, *Sentimental Figures of Empire*, 2.
74. Duane Meyer, *The Highland Scots of North Carolina 1732–1776* (Chapel Hill: University of North Carolina Press, 1961), 138.
75. Graham, *Colonists from Scotland*, 158.
76. Festa, *Sentimental Figures of Empire*, 176; Carey, *British Abolitionism*, 41. Festa defines the "labor of unfeeling" as "the work necessary to justify the failure of sympathy" (*Sentimental Figures of Empire*, 176). Carey explains that what he refers to as "sentimental diversion" occurs when "the sufferings of one person or group of people are invoked in order to divert attention away from the sufferings of another" (*British Abolitionism*, 41).
77. Ramsay, *Letters*, 17.
78. Bradford J. Wood, *This Remote Part of the World: Regional Formation in Lower Cape Fear, North Carolina, 1725–1775* (Columbia: University of South Carolina Press, 2004), 18.
79. Scotus Americanus, *Informations concerning the Province of North Carolina* (Glasgow, 1773), 16, *Google Books*, https://www.google.ca/books/edition/Informations_Concerning_the_Province_of/QpVpuAAACAAJ?hl=en.
80. Alexander Hewatt, *An Historical Account of the Rise and Progress of the Colonies in South Carolina and Georgia* (London, 1779), iii, *Google Books*, https://www.google.ca/books/edition/An_Historical_Account_of_the_Rise_and_Pr/2q5bAAAAQAAJ?hl=en&gbpv=0.

81. For additional eighteenth-century accounts of and commentaries on North Carolina, see John Lawson, *A New Voyage to Carolina* (London, [1709] 1714), ECCO; John Brickell, *The Natural History of North Carolina* (Dublin, 1737), ECCO; Arthur Young, *Political Essays concerning the Present State of the British Empire* (London, 1772), ECCO; and John Mitchell, *The Present State of Britain and North America: With regard to Agriculture, Population, Trade, and Manufactures, Impartially Considered* (London, 1767), ECCO. Mitchell's negative depiction of North Carolina is an exception to the largely positive accounts of the colony.
82. Americanus, *Informations*, 9, 32.
83. Americanus, *Informations*, 30, 26.
84. For early nonfictional accounts that represent America in Edenic terms, see Christopher Columbus, "The Letter of Columbus to Luis de Santángel, Announcing his Discovery," in *Travel Narratives from the Age of Discovery*, trans. Albert Bushnell Hart and Edward Channing, ed. Peter Mancall (Oxford: Oxford University Press, 2006); and Thomas Harriot's "A Briefe and True Report of the New Found Land of Virginia" in *Travel Narratives from the Age of Discovery*, trans. Albert Bushnell Hart and Edward Channing, ed. Peter Mancall (Oxford: Oxford University Press, 2006). For nonfictional eighteenth-century accounts that perpetuate this tradition, see Thomas Nairn, *A Letter from South Carolina* (London, 1710), ECCO; John Lawson, *A New Voyage to Carolina*; John Brickell, *The Natural History of North Carolina*; William Burke, *An Account of the European Settlements in America*, 4th ed. (Dublin, 1762), ECCO; and William Smith, *Information to Emigrants* (Glasgow, 1773), ECCO. For additional examples of this trope in eighteenth-century fiction, see Unca Eliza Winkfield's (pseud.), *The Female American*, ed. Michelle Burnham and James Freitas, 2nd ed. (Peterborough, ON: Broadview Press, 2014). For scholarly examinations of this trope, see Wil Verhoeven, *Americomania and the French Revolution Debate in Britain, 1789–1802* (Cambridge: Cambridge University Press, 2014); Zachary McLeod Hutchins, *Inventing Eden: Primitivism, Millennialism, and the Making of New England* (Oxford: Oxford University Press, 2014); and Pam Perkins "Paradises Lost: Ann Grant and Late Eighteenth-Century Idealizations of America," *Early American Literature* 40, no. 2 (2005): 315–340, JSTOR.
85. Americanus, *Informations*, 31, 32.
86. Mitchell, *Great Britain and North America*, 178.
87. Mitchell, *Great Britain and North America*, 184.
88. Ramsay, *Letters*, 17.
89. Brett Mizelle specifically notes that eighteenth-century representations of monkeys emphasized their long limbs and flexibility. For more on the eighteenth-century representation of monkeys and the use of anthropoid apes in period debates regarding racial distinction, see Mizelle's article, "'Man Cannot Behold It without Contemplating Himself': Monkeys, Apes and Human Identity in the Early American Republic," *Pennsylvania History: A Journal of Mid-Atlantic Studies*, 66 (1999): 144–173, JSTOR.
90. Hume, *A Treatise*, 75.
91. A. Smith, *Moral Sentiments*, 19, 35.
92. Sara Knott, *Sensibility and the American Revolution* (Chapel Hill: University of North Carolina Press, 2009), 157.
93. Graham, *Colonists from Scotland*, 155.
94. E. Burke, "Conciliation," 104, 45.
95. Ramsay, *Letters*, 19–20.
96. Elizabeth Kim, "Complicating Complicity/Resistance in Janet Schaw's *Journal of a Lady of Quality*," *Auto/Biography Studies* 12, no. 2 (Fall 1997): 181, https://doi.org/10.1080/08989575.1997.10815105.

97. Laura Brown, "The Romance of Empire: Oroonoko and the Trade in Slaves," in *The New Eighteenth-Century: Theory, Politics, and English Literature*, ed. Felicity Nussbaum and Laura Brown (London: Methuen, 1987), 54.
98. Deirdre Coleman, "Janet Schaw and the Complexions of Empire," *Eighteenth-Century Studies* 36, no. 2 (Winter 2003): 180, JSTOR.
99. Elizabeth Bohls, "The Aesthetics of Colonialism: Janet Schaw in the West Indies, 1774–1775," *Eighteenth-Century Studies* 27, no. 3 (Spring 1994): 390, https://doi.org/10.2307/2739361.
100. Kames, *Sketches*, 168.
101. Kames, *Sketches*, 168.
102. Hume, "Of National Characters," 248.
103. Eve Tavor Bannet, "Trading Routes and Eighteenth-Century Migrations: Reframing Janet Schaw," in *Recording and Reordering*, ed. Dan Doll and Jessica Munns (Lewisburg, PA: Bucknell University Press, 2006), 150.
104. Edmund Burke, "A Letter to the Sheriffs of Bristol on the Affairs of America," in *On Empire*, 150.
105. Ramsay, *Letters*, 20.

CHAPTER 3 — THE TIES THAT BIND

1. To avoid confusion with Samuel Johnson's *A Journey to the Western Islands of Scotland*, I will abbreviate *A Journey to the Highlands of Scotland* as *A Journey* and will reference the full title of Johnson's travelogue throughout.
2. Wilson, *The Island Race*, 96.
3. For more on the origins and itinerary of the "Short Tour" of Scotland, see Peter Womack, *Improvement and Romance: Constructing the Myth of the Highlands* (London: Macmillan Press, 1989), 62–63; and Malcolm Andrews, *The Search for the Picturesque: Landscape Aesthetics and Tourism in Britain, 1760–1800* (Aldershot, UK: Scolar Press, 1989), 206.
4. "*A Journey to the Highlands of Scotland*," *The Monthly Review* 57 (September 1777), 242, *HathiTrust*, https://hdl.handle.net/2027/inu.30000093224917.
5. On the development of tourism in Scotland in general and/or in the Scottish Highlands specifically, see Hagglund, *Tourists and Travellers*; Kenneth McNeil, *Scotland, Britain, Empire: Writing the Highlands, 1760–1860* (Columbus: Ohio State University Press, 2007); Martin Rackwitz, *Travels to Terra Incognita: The Scottish Highlands and Hebrides in Early Modern Travellers' Accounts c. 1600–1800* (New York: Waxmann Munster, 2007); E. Mairi MacArthur, "Fresh Fields for Inquiry: Travellers to the Highlands," in *Crossing the Highland Line: Cross-Currents in Eighteenth-Century Scottish Writing, Selected Papers from the 2005 ASLS Annual Conference*, ed. Christopher McLachlan (Glasgow: Assocation for Scottish Literary Studies, 2009), 153–160; and John Glendening, *The High Road: Romantic Tourism, Scotland and Literature, 1720–1820* (New York: Palgrave Macmillan, 1996).
6. Rackwitz, *Terra Incognita*, 131.
7. "*A Journey to the Highlands of Scotland*," *The Critical Review* 43 (March 1777), 238, *HathiTrust*, https://hdl.handle.net/2027/chi.79243088; *The Monthly Review* 57, 242; "*A Journey to the Highlands of Scotland*," *The Scots Magazine* 39 (March 1777), 153, *HathiTrust*, https://hdl.handle.net/2027/nyp.33433081660478.
8. *The Monthly Review* 57, 242.
9. Hagglund, *Tourists and Travellers*, 49. See also Marie E. McAllister, "Women on the Journey: Eighteenth-Century British Women's Travel in Fact and Fiction" (PhD diss., Princeton University, 1988).

10. *A Journey*, 3. All subsequent references will be cited parenthetically in the text.
11. Sterne, *A Sentimental Journey*, 96.
12. Sterne, *A Sentimental Journey*, 70.
13. Daniel Defoe, *A Tour thro' the Whole Island of Great Britain*, 4 vols. (London, 1748), *Eighteenth Century Collections Online* (ECCO); Samuel Johnson, *A Journey to the Western Islands of Scotland* (1775, repr. New York: Dover Publications, 2008); Thomas Pennant, *A Tour in Scotland 1769* (Chester, 1771), ECCO; and Thomas Pennant, *A Tour in Scotland, and Voyage to the Hebrides, 1772*, 2 vols. (London, 1776), ECCO.
14. Sterne, *A Sentimental Journey*, 81.
15. Richard Brinsley Sheridan and Israel Pottinger, *The General Fast; a Lyric Ode: With a Form of Prayer Proper to the Occasion, and a Dedication to the King* (London, 1776), ECCO; John Witherspoon, *An Address to the Natives of Scotland Residing in America: Being an Appendix to a Sermon Preached at Princeton on a General Fast* (London, 1778), ECCO; and the anonymous *The Delusive and Dangerous Principles of the Minority, Exposed and Refuted. In a Letter to Lord North* (London, 1778), ECCO.
16. Additional examples of political works on the American Revolution published by Fielding and Walker include A. Charles Dodd, *The Contrast: Or, Strictures on Select Parts of Doctor Price's Additional Observations on Civil Liberty, &c.* (London, 1777), ECCO; Israel Mauduit, *Remarks upon General Howe's Account of His Proceedings on Long Island in the Extraordinary Gazette of October 10th, 1776* (London, 1778), *Google Books*, https://www.google.ca/books/edition/Remarks_Upon_Gen_Howe_s_Account_of_His_P/RLE6AAAAcAAJ?hl=en&gbpv=0; and the anonymous *An Epistle from Edward, and American Prisoner in England, to Harriet, in America* (London, 1779), *Google Books*, https://www.google.ca/books/edition/An_Epistle_from_Edward_an_American_Priso/BllpAAAAcAAJ?hl=en&gbpv=0.
17. Gottlieb, *Feeling British*, 101.
18. Adam Ferguson, *Remarks on Dr. Price's "Observations on the Nature of Civil Liberty"* (London, 1776), 39, ECCO.
19. Holly Brewer, *By Birth or Consent: Children, Law, and the Anglo-American Revolution in Authority* (Williamsburg, VA: Omohundro Institute of Early American History and Culture, 2005), 320.
20. Contemporary responses that oppose Lord Hardwicke's Marriage Act of 1753, some of which are anonymous, include Rev. Alexander Keith, *Observations on the Act for Preventing Clandestine Marriages* (London, 1753), ECCO; Dr. Henry Stebbing, *An Inquiry into the Force and Operation of the Annulling Clauses in the Late Act for the Better Preventing of Clandestine Marriages, with Respect to Conscience* (London, 1754), ECCO; *Reflections on the Marriage Act; With Some Hints for a New Law: Humbly Offered to the Consideration of Parliament* (London, 1764), ECCO; and *Reflections on the Repeal of the Marriage-Act Now under Consideration of Parliament* (London, 1765), ECCO. For contemporary responses that support the act, see *A Letter to the Public: Containing the Substance of What Hath Been Offered in the Late Debates upon the Subject of the Act of Parliament, for the Better Preventing of Clandestine Marriages* (London, 1753), ECCO; and Edmund Burke, "On the Second Reading of a Bill for the Repeal of the Marriage Act," in *The Works of the Right Honourable Edmund Burke*, vol. 6 (1781; London, 1869), 168–172.
21. For scholarly considerations of the Marriage Act, see Brewer, *By Birth or Consent*, ch. 8; Rebecca Probert, "The Impact of the Marriage Act of 1753: Was It Really 'A Most Cruel Law for the Fair Sex?," *Eighteenth-Century Studies* 38, no. 2 (Winter 2005): 247–262, https://doi.org/10.1353/ecs.2005.0015; David Lemmings, "Marriage and the Law in the Eighteenth Century: Hardwicke's Marriage Act of 1753," *The Historical Journal* 39, no. 2 (1996): 339–360, JSTOR; R. B. Outhwaite, *Clandestine Marriage in England, 1500–1850*

(London: Hambledon Press, 1995); and Lawrence Stone, *Road to Divorce: England, 1530–1987* (Oxford: Oxford University Press, 1990), chs. 2–5.

22. Henry Gally, *Some Considerations upon Clandestine Marriages* (London, 1750), 12, 13, ECCO.
23. Gally, *Clandestine Marriages*, 11.
24. Richard Brinsley Sheridan, "On the Bill to Explain and Amend the Marriage Act," in *The Speeches of the Right Honourable Richard Brinsley Sheridan: With a Sketch of His Life* (London: Henry G. Bohn, 1842), 1:16, *Google Books*, https://books.google.ca/books?id=Ck4JAAAAQAAJ&pg+PP1#v+onepage&q&f=false.
25. Fox's rebuttal is included at the end of Sheridan's "On the Bill," 1:17.
26. *Reflections on the Marriage Act*, 38–39.
27. Thomas Paine, "Common Sense," in *Rights of Man, Common Sense and Other Political Writings*, ed. Mark Philp (Oxford: Oxford University Press, 2008), 22.
28. *Reflections on the Repeal of the Marriage-Act*, 1–2.
29. Jay Fliegelman's comparison of eighteenth-century family dynamics and the familial rhetoric deployed during the American Revolution yields the conclusion that "the relationship of the American colonies to England had long been accepted by both the British government and its subjects in America as analogous to that of a child's relationship to its parent" (*Prodigals and Pilgrims: The American Revolution against Patriarchal Authority* [Cambridge: Cambridge University Press, 1982], 93). For more on the familial metaphor in the discourse of the American Revolution, see also Gordon S. Wood, *The Radicalism of the American Revolution* (New York: Vintage Books, 1991), 145–168.
30. R. Price, *Observations*, 16.
31. *Reflections on the Marriage Act*, 38.
32. R. Price, *Observations*, 16.
33. Fox in Sheridan, "On the Bill," 1:17.
34. R. Price, *Observations*, 51–52.
35. Ferguson, *Remarks on Dr. Price's "Observations,"* 3.
36. Ferguson, *Remarks on Dr. Price's "Observations,"* 6.
37. Sheridan, "On the Bill," 17.
38. Ferguson, *Remarks on Dr. Price's "Observations,"* 15.
39. Ferguson, *Remarks on Dr. Price's "Observations,"* 18.
40. Ferguson, *Remarks on Dr. Price's "Observations,"* 68, 18.
41. Schaw, *Journal*, 157.
42. The Irishman and Englishwoman appear violently in love when Matthew Bramble and his companions initially encounter them; their passion has led them to escape her parents in the pursuit of everlasting love. However, upon finding out that her intended is but a humble tailor, the young lady immediately resolves to elope with Jery Melford's silver-tongued servant—whom she has known for the whole of a day (Smollett, *The Expedition of Humphrey Clinker*, 210–213). The entire exchange exposes the young lovers' passion as fickle and based entirely on appearances and economics rather than on authentic feeling, while also suggesting the wisdom of a law that attempts to prevent such thoughtless unions.
43. R. Price, *Observations*, 16.
44. "Leading strings" were a common eighteenth-century contraption for young children, not dissimilar from a leash. They were composed of ribbons of fabric attached to a child's clothing and would be held by the caretaker in order to help toddlers walk and to prevent young children from straying too far.
45. Francis Hopkinson, "Dissertation IV," in *Four Dissertations, on the Reciprocal Advantages of a Perpetual Union between Great-Britain and Her American Colonies: Written for Mr. Sargent's Prize Medal* (London, 1766), 108, ECCO.

46. Ferguson, *Remarks on Dr. Price's* Observations, 6.
47. Benjamin Franklin, "Examination of Dr. Franklin," in *The Life and Essays of Dr. Benjamin Franklin: Carefully Collected from His Own Papers, Containing All His Miscellaneous Pieces*, ed. Henry Stueber (London, 1838), 375, emphasis added, *Google Books*, https://books.google.ca/books?id=BylCAAAAIAAJ&printsec=frontcover#v=onepage&q&f=false.
48. Franklin, "Examination," 375.
49. Ferguson, *Remarks on Dr. Price's "Observations,"* 49, emphasis added.
50. John Phillip Reid argues that "licentiousness" was a word bandied about during the American Revolution, and commonly denoted unrestrained liberty, or liberty running into excess (*The Concept of Liberty in the Age of the American Revolution* [Chicago: University of Chicago Press, 1988], 32).
51. R. Price, *Observations*, 129.
52. The quote is from John Dryden's *The Spanish Fryer, or The Double Discovery* (1681), which was written and performed during the Exclusion Crisis.
53. McAllister, "Women on the Journey," 109.
54. R. Price, *Observations*, 125–126.
55. Fliegelman, *Prodigals and Pilgrims*, 14.
56. A. Smith, *Moral Sentiments*, 25–30.
57. Schaw, *Journal*, 210.
58. Bradley, *Popular Politics*, 93.
59. Samuel Johnson, *Taxation No Tyranny; an Answer to the Resolutions and Address of the American Congress*, 4th ed. (London, 1775), 87, ECCO.
60. Samuel Estwick, *A Letter to the Reverend Josiah Tucker: D. D., Dean of Glocester* (London, 1776), 10, ECCO.
61. Erskine, *Shall I Go to War?*, 21.
62. Edmund Burke, "A Letter to the Sheriffs of Bristol on the Affairs of America," in *On Empire*, 149.
63. E. Burke, "A Letter to the Sheriffs of Bristol," 149.
64. Zoë Kinsley, *Women Writing the Home Tour, 1682–1812* (Aldershot, UK: Ashgate, 2008), 54.
65. McAllister, "Women on the Journey," 115.
66. Recent criticism on Johnson's travelogue has revealed the complex nature of Johnson's representation of Scotland. While on one hand the text can be read as a colonial encounter that seeks to repress difference and impose a new, homogenous English identity, scholars have increasingly focused on the complex representative strategies within Johnson's work as sign of his attempt to engage with Scotland sympathetically. For scholarship that falls within the former category, see Trumpener, *Bardic Nationalism*. For work that falls into the latter category, see Gottlieb, *Feeling British*; Davis, *Acts of Union*; John Glendening, *The High Road*; and Martin Wechelblatt, "Finding Mr. Boswell: Rhetorical Authority and National Identity in Johnson's *A Journey to the Western Islands of Scotland*," *ELH* 60, no. 1 (Spring 1993): 117–148, JSTOR.
67. Johnson, *A Journey to the Western Islands of Scotland*, 27. Subsequent references will be cited parenthetically in the text.
68. Trumpener, *Bardic Nationalism*, 68.
69. Gottlieb, *Feeling British*, 122.
70. Gottlieb, *Feeling British*, 122.
71. "Remarks on a Voyage to the Hebrides, in a Letter to Samuel Johnson, LL.D," in *Samuel Johnson: The Critical Heritage*, ed. James T. Boulton (London: Routledge, 1971), 240.
72. Note that both "approbation" and "edifying" are meant here in a purely mocking manner.

73. A. Smith, *Moral Sentiments*, 82.
74. The Lady here paraphrases the Duke of Gloucester, the future Richard III, in William Shakespeare's *King Henry VI, Pt. 3*: "Why, I can smile, and murder whiles I smile" (*The Oxford Shakespeare: The Complete Works*, ed. Stanley Wells et al., 2nd ed. [Oxford: Clarendon Press, 2005], 3.3.182).
75. Rackwitz, *Terra Incognita*, 522.
76. A. Smith, *Moral Sentiments*, 11.
77. For more on the productive trading network between Scotland (and specifically Glasgow) and the American colonies, see Arthur Herman, *How the Scots Invented the Modern World: The True Story of How Western Europe's Poorest Nation Created Our World and Everything in It* (New York: Three Rivers Press, 2001); Alexander Murdoch, *Scotland and America, c. 1600–c. 1800* (New York: Palgrave Macmillan, 2010); Colley, *Britons*; and Dalphy I. Fagerstrom, "Scottish Opinion and the American Revolution," *The William and Mary Quarterly* 11, no. 2 (April 1954): 252–275, https://doi.org/10.2307/1922041.
78. Murdoch, *Scotland and America*, 76.
79. Herman, *How the Scots Invented the Modern World*, 169.
80. Gisborne, *An Inquiry into the Duties of the Female Sex*, 291.
81. Penny Fielding, *Scotland and the Fictions of Geography: North Britain, 1760–1830* (Cambridge: Cambridge University Press, 2008), 81.
82. Fielding, *Fictions of Geography*, 81.
83. Defoe, *A Tour*, 4:46–47.
84. Pennant, *A Tour in Scotland 1769*, 40.
85. Pennant, *A Tour in Scotland 1769*, 41.
86. Fielding, *Fictions of Geography*, 79.
87. E. Burke, "A Letter to the Sheriffs of Bristol," 155.
88. A. Smith, *Moral Sentiments*, 26.
89. E. Burke, "A Letter to the Sheriffs of Bristol," 155.
90. E. Burke, "Conciliation," 128.
91. Turner, *British Travel Writers in Europe*, 201.

CHAPTER 4 — REVITALIZING SENSIBILITY

1. Benedict Anderson, *Imagined Communities* (London: Verso, 1983), 7.
2. Vicesimus Knox, *The Spirit of Despotism* (London, 1795), 68, *Eighteenth Century Collections Online* (ECCO).
3. V. Knox, *The Spirit of Despotism*, 68.
4. Joanna Innes, *Inferior Politics: Social Problems and Social Politics in Eighteenth-Century Britain* (Oxford: Oxford University Press, 2009), 179.
5. In regard to the push for the reformation of the elite, Hannah More's pamphlet *Thoughts on the Importance of the Manners of the Great to General Society* argues that "reformation must begin with the GREAT, or it will never be effectual. *Their* example is the fountain from whence the vulgar draw their habits, actions, and characters. To expect to reform the poor while the opulent are corrupt, is to throw odours into the stream while the springs are poisoned" (4th ed. [London, 1788], 116, ECCO).
6. Grenby, *The Anti-Jacobin Novel*, 159. For another discussion regarding the reformation of the elite in the 1790s, see Colley, *Britons*, ch. 4. For more general discussions of the reformation of manners campaign in late eighteenth century, see Innes, *Inferior Politics*, ch. 5; and M.J.D. Roberts, *Making English Morals: Voluntary Association and the Moral Reform Movement in England, 1688–1886* (Cambridge: Cambridge University Press, 2004), chs. 1–2.

7. That Morgan was familiar with Burke's *Reflections* is also evident from her direct (mis)quotation of his line "The age of chivalry is gone" (*A Tour to Milford Haven, in the Year 1791* [1795; ECCO Print Editions, 2010], 387). Subsequent references to *Milford Haven* will be cited parenthetically in the text.
8. See, for example, William Gilpin, *Observations on the River Wye, and Several Parts of South Wales, &c. Relative Chiefly to Picturesque Beauty: Made in the Summer of the Year 1770*, 5th ed. (London, 1800), ECCO; Henry Penruddocke Wyndham, *A Gentleman's Tour through Monmouthshire and Wales, in the Months June and July, 1774* (London, 1775), ECCO; Thomas Pennant, *A Tour in Wales*, 2 vols. (London, 1778–1781), ECCO; Arthur Aikin, *Journal of a Tour through North Wales and Part of Shropshire; with Observations in Mineralogy, and Other Branches of Natural History* (London, 1797), ECCO; and John Evans, *A Tour through Part of North Wales: In the Year 1798, Principally Undertaken with a View to Botanical Researches. Interspersed with Observations on Its Scenery, Agriculture, Manufactures, Customs, History, and Antiquities* (London, 1800), ECCO.
9. "*A Tour to Milford Haven, in the Year 1791*," *The Monthly Review* 18 (November 1795), 274, *HathiTrust*, https://hdl.handle.net/2027/inu.30000093233157.
10. Rev. Morgan's most overtly political sermons include *The Duty of Patriotism Vindicated and Enforced: A Sermon Preached in the Cathedral Church of Ely* (London, 1780), ECCO; *A Sermon Preached in the Cathedral Church of Ely, on Wednesday, February the 21st, 1781: Being the Day Appointed for a General Fast* (London, 1781), ECCO; *A Sermon Preached in the Cathedral Church of Ely, on Thursday, April 23, 1789: Being the Day Appointed for a General Thanksgiving to Almighty God for His Majesty's Happy Recovery* (Cambridge, 1789), ECCO; and *A Sermon on Public Spirit: Preached at Wisbech, the Isle of Ely, on Sunday, April 29, 1798* (Cambridge, 1798), ECCO.
11. For more on Matthew Montagu's Tory politics, see R. G. Thorne, *The House of Commons 1790–1802* (Woodbridge, UK: Boydell and Brewer, 1986), 617.
12. "Obituary, with Anecdotes, of Remarkable Persons," *The Gentleman's Magazine* 75 (August 1808), 751, *Google Books*, https://www.google.ca/books/edition/The_Gentleman_s_Magazine/8LlCAQAAMAAJ?hl=en&gbpv=0. My knowledge of Morgan's little-known chapbook comes from Emily Spunaugle's excellent article, "A Travel Writer Reconsidered: Recovering Mary Morgan's *Mary, The Osier-Peeler*," *ABO: Interactive Journal for Women in the Arts, 1640–1830* 10, no. 2, art. 2 (2020), n.p., https://scholarcommons.usf.edu/abo/vol10/iss2/2.
13. There is a wealth of excellent scholarship on eighteenth-century bluestockings. The resources to which I am indebted include Emma Major, *Madam Britannia: Women, Church, and Nation, 1712–1812* (Oxford: Oxford University Press, 2012); Elizabeth Eger and Lucy Peltz, *Brilliant Women: 18th-Century Bluestockings* (New Haven, CT: Yale University Press, 2008); *Reconsidering the Bluestockings*, ed. Nicole Pohl and Betty A. Schellenberg (San Marino, CA: Huntington Library, 2003); and Gary Kelly, "General Introduction: Bluestocking Feminism and Writing in Context," in *Bluestocking Feminism: Writings of the Bluestocking Circle, 1738–1785* (London: Pickering and Chatto, 1999), 1:ix–lix.
14. Eger and Peltz, *Brilliant Women*, 47.
15. Eger and Peltz, *Brilliant Women*, 16.
16. *The Knyghte of the Golden Locks: An Ancyent Poem, Applicable to the Present Times*, ed. Mary Morgan (Wisbech, 1799), 3, ECCO.
17. For scholarship on women and the Anglican Church see Major, *Madam Britannia*; Karen O'Brien, *Women and Enlightenment in Eighteenth-Century Britain* (Cambridge: Cambridge University Press, 2009), ch. 1; Norma Clark, "Bluestocking Fictions: Devotional Writings, Didactic Literature and the Imperative of Female Improvement," in *Women, Gender and*

Enlightenment, ed. Barbara Taylor and Sarah Knott (New York: Palgrave Macmillan, 2005), 460–473; Susan Staves, "Church of England Clergy and Women Writers," *Huntington Library Quarterly*, 65, nos 1–2 (2000): 81–103, JSTOR; and Harriet Guest, *Small Change: Women, Learning, Patriotism, 1750–1810* (Chicago: University of Chicago Press, 2000), ch. 6.

18. *The Gentleman's Magazine* 75, 751.
19. *The Gentleman's Magazine*75, 751.
20. *The Gentleman's Magazine* 75, 751. For more on Morgan's active philanthropy, see Spunaugle, "A Travel Writer Reconsidered," 4–5.
21. O'Brien, *Women and Enlightenment*, 39.
22. "*A Tour to Milford Haven, in the Year 1791*," *The Gentleman's Magazine* 65, no. 5, pt. 2 (November 1795), 943, *HathiTrust*, https://hdl.handle.net/2027/mdp.39015018405426.
23. Sterne, *A Sentimental Journey*, 81.
24. Sterne, *A Sentimental Journey*, 84.
25. *The Gentleman's Magazine* 65, 943.
26. "*A Tour to Milford Haven, in the Year 1791*," *The British Critic* 6 (August 1795), 160, *Hathitrust*, https://hdl.handle.net/2027/mdp.39015056066775.
27. *The Monthly Review* 18, 269.
28. *The Monthly Review* 18, 269.
29. Turner, *British Travel Writers in Europe*, 201.
30. Jones, *Radical Sensibility*, 3.
31. Markman Ellis incisively contests the dominant narrative of sensibility's downward trajectory during the 1790s, arguing that the discourse of sensibility survives into the nineteenth century (*The Politics of Sensibility*, 220–221), and Janet Todd sees the "sentimental strain" continue to manifest itself in the genres of drama and fiction well after its supposed decease (*Sensibility*, 147).
32. Edmund Burke, *Reflections on the Revolution in France*, ed. L. J. Mitchell (Oxford: Oxford University Press, 1993), 86–87. Subsequent references are cited parenthetically in the text.
33. For more on Burke's contribution to the Revolution Debate, see David Bromwich, "Burke, Reflections on the Revolution in France," in *Cambridge Companion to British Literature of the French Revolution in the 1790s*, ed. Pamela Clemit (Cambridge: Cambridge University Press, 2011); Gregory Claeys, *The French Revolution Debate in Britain: The Origins of Modern Politics* (New York: Palgrave Macmillan, 2007); and Marilyn Butler, *Burke, Paine, Godwin, and the Revolution Controversy* (Cambridge: Cambridge University Press, 1984).
34. Williams, *Letters Written in France*, 148.
35. Williams, *Letters Written in France*, 90, 147.
36. Williams, *Letters Written in France*, 91.
37. John Thelwall, *The Peripatetic; or, Sketches of the Heart, of Nature and Society; in a Series of Politico-Sentimental Journals* (Southwark, 1793), 2:178–179, ECCO.
38. Thelwall, *The Peripatetic*, 1:143.
39. Thelwall, *The Peripatetic*, 1:viii.
40. Helen Maria Williams's sentimental advocacy and defense of the French Revolution has been extensively studied; see, for instance, Adriana Craciun, *British Women Writers and the French Revolution: Citizens of the World* (New York: Palgrave Macmillan, 2005); Stephen Blakemore, *Crisis in Representation: Thomas Paine, Mary Wollstonecraft, Helen Maria Williams, and the Rewriting of the French Revolution* (London: Associated University Presses, 1997); Jones, *Radical Sensibility*; Mary Favret, *Romantic Correspondence: Women, Politics, and the Fiction of Letters* (Cambridge: Cambridge University Press, 1993);

and Kelly, *Women, Writing, and Revolution*. There are also a handful of fine studies on John Thelwall's interpolation of sensibility and radical politics; these include Claeys, *The Revolution Debate in Britain*; Michael Henry Scrivener, *Seditious Allegories: John Thelwall and Jacobin Writing* (University Park: Pennsylvania State University Press, 2001), ch. 6; and Fairclough, *The Romantic Crowd*, ch. 2.

41. There is a wealth of scholarship on the radical polemic launched against Burke and the cult(ure) of sensibility by Wollstonecraft and Godwin. See, for instance, Morgan Rooney, *The French Revolution Debate and the British Novel, 1790–1814: The Struggle for History's Authority* (Lewisburg, PA: Bucknell University Press, 2013), ch. 2; Blakemore, *Crisis in Representation*; Evan Radcliffe, "Arguing Benevolence: Wordsworth, Godwin, and the 1790s," in *The French Revolution Debate in English Literature and Culture*, ed. Lisa Plummer Crafton, (London: Greenwood Press, 1997), 59–82; Jones, *Radical Sensibility*; and Butler, *Revolution Controversy*.
42. Mary Wollstonecraft, *A Vindication of the Rights of Men*, ed. Sylvana Tomaselli (Cambridge: Cambridge University Press, 1995), 5.
43. William Godwin, *Enquiry concerning Political Justice and Its Influence on General Virtue and Happiness* (London, 1793), 1:82, ECCO.
44. Nicola J. Watson, *Revolution and the Form of the British Novel* (Oxford: Clarendon Press, 1994), 28.
45. George Canning, "New Morality," in *Poetry of the Anti-Jacobin*, 2nd ed. (London, 1800), 225, 220–240, ECCO.
46. Maria Edgeworth and R. L. Edgeworth, *Practical Education*, 2nd ed. (London, 1801), 2:4, *Google Books*, https://www.google.ca/books/edition/Practical_Education/3kj4Xqw6cxEC?hl=en&gbpv=0.
47. Ellis, *The Politics of Sensibility*, 190.
48. Jones, *Radical Sensibility*, 13.
49. Butler, *Revolution Controversy*, 1.
50. Thomas Rennell, *The Connexion of the Duties of Loving the Brotherhood, Fearing God, and Honoring the King. In a Sermon Preached at Saint Magnus the Martyr, London Bridge* (Winton, 1791), 2, ECCO.
51. Rennell, *Connexion*, 3.
52. Rennell, *Connexion*, 2.
53. O'Brien, *Women and Enlightenment*, 38.
54. Emma Major has fruitfully explored bluestocking women's use of Anglicanism as an anti-revolutionary practice in Chapter 7 of *Madam Britannia*.
55. Richard Price, *A Discourse on the Love of Our Country*, 3rd ed. (London, 1790), 24, *Google Books*, https://www.google.ca/books/edition/A_Discourse_on_the_Love_of_Our_Country/92QNAAAAIAAJ?hl=en&gbpv=0.
56. R. Price, *Discourse*, 22.
57. R. Price, *Discourse*, 23.
58. R. Price, *Discourse*, 50.
59. For studies that deal specifically with Burke's *and* Price's early contributions to the French Revolution debate, see Rooney, *The French Revolution Debate and the British Novel*, ch. 1; Verhoeven, *Americomania*, ch. 1; Claeys, *The French Revolution Debate in Britain*, ch. 1; John Faulkner, "Burke's Perception of Richard Price," in *The French Revolution Debate in English Literature and Culture*, ed. Lisa Plummer Crafton (London: Greenwood Press, 1997), 1–26; and Butler, *Revolution Controversy*, chs. 2–3.
60. John Barrell, *The Spirit of Despotism: Invasions of Privacy in the 1790s* (Oxford: Oxford University Press, 2006), 4. For more on the nature and effect of Pitt's policies over the course of the 1790s, see Clive Emsley, "An Aspect of Pitt's Terror: Prosecutions for Sedition

in the 1790s," *Social History* 6, no. 2 (May 1981): 155–184; and Steve Poole, "Pitt's Terror Reconsidered: Jacobinism and the Law in Two South-Western Counties, 1791–1803," *Southern History* 17 (1995): 65–87.

61. Thelwall, *The Peripatetic*, 1:vii.
62. V. Knox, *The Spirit of Despotism*, 68.
63. Turner, *British Travel Writers in Europe*, 206.
64. Carl Thompson, *The Suffering Traveller*, 34.
65. Kelly, *Women, Writing, and Revolution*, 28.
66. Virginia C. Kenny, *The Country-House Ethos in English Literature, 1699–1750: Themes of Personal Retreat and National Expansion* (Brighton, UK: Harvester Press, 1984), 210.
67. Elizabeth Montagu to Gilbert West, 1 November 1755, qtd. in Eve Tavor Bannet, "The Bluestocking Sisters: Women's Patronage, *Millenium Hall*, and 'The Visible Providence of a Country,'" *Eighteenth-Century Life* 30, no. 1 (2005): 35–36, Project MUSE.
68. For more descriptions of Montagu's philanthropic initiatives, see Steve Hindle, "Representing Rural Society: Labor, Leisure, and the Landscape in an Eighteenth-Century Conversation Piece," *Critical Inquiry* 41 (Spring 2015): 615–654, http://doi.org/10.1086/680205; Bannet, "The Bluestocking Sisters"; Peter Denney, "'Unpleasant, tho' Arcadian Spots': Plebeian Poetry, Polite Culture, and the Sentimental Economy of the Landscape Park," *Criticism* 47, no. 4 (Fall 2005): 493–514,JSTOR; Zoë Kinsley, "*A Tour to Milford Haven* and *Millenium Hall*: Female Charity and the Example of Elizabeth Montagu," in *Eighteenth-Century Women: Studies in Their Lives, Work, and Culture*, ed. Linda Troost (New York: AMS Press, 2003), 3:199–224; and Elizabeth Child, "Elizabeth Montagu, Bluestocking Businesswoman," *Huntington Library Quarterly* 65, nos. 1–2 (2002): 153–173, JSTOR.
69. Elizabeth Montagu, December 4, 1781, in *A Lady of the Last Century (Mrs. Elizabeth Montagu): Illustrated in Her Unpublished Letters; Collected and Arranged, with a Biographical Sketch, and a Chapter on Blue Stockings*, ed. John Doran (R. Bentley and Son, 1873), 306, *Google Books*, https://books.google.ca/books/about/A_Lady_of_the_Last_Century_Mrs_Elizabeth.html?id=fBSiAQAACAAJ&redir_esc=y.
70. See Denney, "'Unpleasant, tho' Arcadian Spots,'" 508, and Hindle, "Representing Rural Society," 648.
71. Elizabeth Montagu to Gilbert West, qtd. in Bannet, 36.
72. Major, *Madam Britannia*, 248.
73. Major, *Madam Britannia*, 233.
74. Denney, "Unpleasant, tho' Arcadian Spots," 509.
75. Denney, "Unpleasant, tho' Arcadian Spots," 508.
76. James Woodhouse, "The Life and Lucubrations of Crispinus Scriblerus," in *The Life and Poetical Works of James Woodhouse*, ed. Rev. R. L. Woodhouse (London: Leadenhall Press, 1896), 1:68, 165–168, 170–178, *Google Books*, https://www.google.ca/books/edition/The_Life_and_Poetical_Works_of_James_Woo/ino4AAAAYAAJ?hl=en&gbpv=0.
77. Woodhouse, *Life and Lucubrations*, 166.
78. Denney, "Unpleasant, tho' Arcadian Spots," 509.
79. Kinsley, "Female Charity and the Example of Elizabeth Montagu."
80. Major, *Madam Britannia*, 233.
81. Cynthia Wall, *Grammars of Approach: Landscape, Narrative, and the Linguistic Picturesque* (Chicago: University of Chicago Press, 2019), 11.
82. Mrs. Montagu to Miss H. More, Sandleford 1784, in *Memoirs of the Life and Correspondence of Hannah More*, ed. William Roberts, Esq., 2nd ed. (London, 1834), 1:372, *Google Books*, https://www.google.com/books/edition/_/oB46AAAAcAAJ?gbpv=1.
83. Denney, "Unpleasant, tho' Arcadian Spots," 493.

84. Uvedale Price, *Essays on the Picturesque, as Compared with the Sublime and the Beautiful; and, on the Use of Studying Pictures, for the Purpose of Improving the Landscape* (London, 1810), 1:340, *Google Books*, https://books.google.ca/books?id=Al0AAAAAYAAJ&dq.
85. Nathaniel Kent, *General View of the Agriculture of the County of Norfolk* (London, 1796), 132, ECCO.
86. Uvedale Price, *Thoughts on the Defence of Property. Addressed to the County of Hereford* (Hereford, 1797), 19–20, ECCO.
87. Kent, *General View*, 172.
88. Denney details the shuffling of "objects of utility" under Brown's leadership, noting that the "offices and barns were moved where they obstructed the prospect" and that the "outbuildings and kitchen garden were also relocated" ("'Unpleasant, tho' Arcadian Spots,'" 506). It is important to clarify that although these buildings and spaces were moved, they were not removed—a fact that Morgan appears to deliberately emphasize in her description of Montagu's estate.
89. Morgan's description of Montagu's unique hiring practices bears a striking resemblance to the employment of the disabled in Scott's *Millenium Hall*: "The cook cannot walk without crutches, the kitchen maid has but one eye, the dairy maid is almost stone-deaf, and the house maid has but one hand" (*A Description of Millenium Hall*, ed. Gary Kelly [Peterborough, ON: Broadview Press, 1995], 169). Kinsley also notes the parallels between the fictional Millenium Hall and the real-life Sandleford, and observes that this similarity demonstrates the principle of inclusion operating both in Scott's fictional estate and in Montagu's real-life estate: "Millenium Hall, like the Sandleford of Morgan's description, constitutes a society where disability or infirmity actually provides access into the community: the atmosphere is one of positive cooperation rather than exclusion or isolation" ("Female Charity and the Example of Elizabeth Montagu," 209).
90. A. Smith, *Moral Sentiments*, 265.
91. U. Price, *Defence of Property*, 1:340.
92. See *Milford Haven*, 38 and 112, for Morgan's references to *Millenium Hall*.
93. Scott, *A Description of Millenium Hall*, 222.
94. David Green, *Blenheim Palace* (London: Country Life, 1951), 43.
95. James Legard, "Queen Anne, Court Culture and the Construction of Blenheim Palace," *Journal for Eighteenth-Century Studies* 37, no. 2 (2014): 185, https://doi.org/10.1111/1754-0208.12158.
96. Green, *Blenheim Palace*, 183.
97. Kenny, *Country-House Ethos*, 210.
98. Alexander Pope, "Upon the Duke of Marlborough's House at Woodstock," in *Complete Poetical Works of Alexander Pope*, ed. Henry Walcott Boynton (New York: Houghton, Mifflin, 1903), 101–102, *Internet Archive*, https://archive.org/details/completepoetica04unkngoog.
99. John Loveday, "The Diary of a Tour in 1732," in *John Loveday of Caversham 1711–1789: The Life Tours of an Eighteenth-Century Onlooker*, ed. Sarah Markham (Salisbury, UK: Michael Russell Publishing, 1984), 80.
100. Montagu, December 4, 1781, 306. Montagu's reference to "temples" and "bridges" suggests two of Blenheim's prominent embellishments. The estate features the Temple of Diana, which was built in 1773 by William Chambers. It also boasts a famously extravagant bridge that, prior to Brown's lake, vaulted over a series of modest canals. Jane Brown also notes the striking similarities between Montagu's descriptive statement and Blenheim's famous features and concludes that Montagu and Brown must have discussed his design of the Duke of Marlborough's estate. "Surely," she argues, "'the proud bridges over humble rivulets' meant they had talked of Blenheim and other of Lancelot's

achievements; did he confess to her that some of his clients spent too much money and that places were spoilt by this[?]" (*The Omnipotent Magician: Lancelot 'Capability' Brown, 1716–1783* [London: Chatto and Windus, 2011], 297).

101. Montagu, December 4, 1781, 306.
102. Carole Fabricant, "The Literature of Domestic Tourism and the Public Consumption of Private Property," in *The New Eighteenth-Century: Theory, Politics, English Culture*, ed. Felicity Nussbaum and Laura Brown (London: Methuen, 1987), 266.
103. V. Knox, *The Spirit of Despotism*, 357.
104. Grenby, *The Anti-Jacobin Novel*, 168.
105. William F. Mavor, *Blenheim, a Poem. To Which Is Added, a Blenheim Guide* (London, 1787), 34, ECCO.
106. Mrs. Montagu to Miss H. More, 372.
107. Edmund Burke, *A Philosophical Enquiry into the Origin of Our Ideas of the Sublime and Beautiful*, 5th ed. (London, 1767), 206, *Google Books*, https://www.google.ca/books/edition/A_Philosophical_Enquiry_into_the_Origin/LJ1gAAAAcAAJ?hl=en&gbpv=0.
108. E. Burke, *Sublime and Beautiful*, 66–67.
109. E. Burke, *Sublime and Beautiful*, 206–207.
110. E. Burke, *Sublime and Beautiful*, 99.
111. E. Burke, *Sublime and Beautiful*, 206, 205, 206.
112. Morgan's sense of being overwhelmed by Blenheim mirrors Burke's description of the astonishment evoked by the sublime: "The passion caused by the great and sublime in *nature*, when those causes operate most powerfully, is astonishment; and astonishment is that state of the soul, in which all its motions are suspended, with some degree of horror" (*Sublime and Beautiful*, 95).
113. E. Burke, *Sublime and Beautiful*, 206.
114. Lodestones were used in compasses for navigational purposes due to their magnetic quality.
115. M. Andrews, *The Search for the Picturesque*, 46.
116. Whereas Jean-Jacques Rousseau idealizes the isolated condition of primitive man and envisages societal progress as moral degeneration (see *Discourse on the Origin of Inequality* [1755; London, 1761], ECCO), Morgan's emphasis on the corrupting effects of isolation and on the violence of primitive societies underscores the benefits of modern culture and equates societal progress with moral improvement.
117. Jacqueline Pearson, "Crushing the Convent and the Dread Bastille: The Anglo-Saxons, Revolution, and Gender in Women's Plays of the 1790s," in *Literary Appropriations of the Anglo-Saxons from the Thirteenth to the Twentieth Century*, ed. Donald Scragg and Caroline Weinburg (Cambridge: Cambridge University Press, 2000), 123.
118. Morgan's idealization of Wales as a stable society grounded in mutual obligations and loyalties was not unique in her time. Malcolm Andrews observes that this comforting perception of Wales was increasingly linked to the presence of political unrest throughout England in the late eighteenth century. "The idealisation of a remote, peaceful rural existence," he asserts, "intensified at a time when there was conspicuous social unrest in the English counties. The Welsh peasantry were seen as . . . uncontaminated by such mob grievances" (*The Search for the Picturesque*, 111).
119. C. Morgan, *A Sermon on Public Spirit*, 11.
120. Knox's vigorous condemnation of war can be found in *The Spirit of Despotism* and his *Sermon XXV: The Prospect of Universal and Perpetual Peace to Be Established on the Principles of Christian Philanthropy*, in *The Works of Vicesimus Knox* (London, 1824), 6:351–371, *Google Books*, https://www.google.ca/books/edition/The_Works_of_Vicesimus_Knox_D_D/3kkVAAAAYAAJ?hl=en&gbpv=0.

121. V. Knox, *The Spirit of Despotism*, 213. Knox argues that war is pursued for "sordid or vain-glorious purposes of the governors, with little regard to the real, substantial happiness of the governed" (213).
122. To be clear: although Montagu is portrayed within the domestic space in Morgan's travelogue, she was an avid traveler and not defined by domestic stasis.
123. E. Radcliffe, "Arguing Benevolence," 221.

CHAPTER 5 — "A RENOVATION OF EXISTENCE"

1. Williams, *A Tour in Switzerland*. Subsequent references to both volumes of this work will be cited parenthetically in the text.
2. Kelly, *Women, Writing, and Revolution*, 79.
3. Williams, *Letters Written in France*, 149. Subsequent references to this work will be cited parenthetically in the text.
4. Helen Maria Williams, *Letters Containing a Sketch of the Politics of France, from the Thirty-first of May 1793, till the Twenty-eighth of July 1794, and of the Scenes which have Passed in the Prisons of Paris* (London, 1795), 1:174, *Eighteenth Century Collections Online* (ECCO). There are four volumes of *Letters Containing a Sketch of the Politics of France*; the first two volumes were published in 1795 and the second two volumes were published in 1796. Subsequent references to all volumes of this work will be cited parenthetically in the text.
5. "*A Tour in Switzerland*," *The British Critic* 12 (July 1798), 24, *HathiTrust*, https://hdl.handle.net/2027/chi.63735473.
6. Although the details of Stone's political purpose on the Continent are somewhat murky, Adriana Craciun and Chris Jones both affirm that Stone was traveling in some capacity for the new French Republic, with Craciun asserting that Stone was "charged by the Committee of Public Safety with the task of gathering intelligence on English politics and obtaining English newspapers in Hamburg" (*British Women Writers and the French Revolution: Citizens of the World* [New York: Palgrave Macmillan, 2005], 207), and Jones more generally remarking that Stone was "travelling as a commissary of the French government" (*Radical Sensibility*, 152). Also see Deborah Kennedy, *Helen Maria Williams and the Age of Revolution* (Lewisburg, PA: Bucknell University Press, 2002), 126.
7. "*A Tour in Switzerland*," *Analytical Review* 27 (June 1798), 562, *HathiTrust*, https://hdl.handle.net/2027/nyp.33433087364802.
8. A reviewer for *The Monthly Review* notes that he can attest to the "fidelity of Mr. Coxe's topographical descriptions" as he has "travelled through Switzerland with his former work in [his] hands" ("*Travels in Switzerland*," [January 1790], 26, *HathiTrust*, https://hdl.handle.net/2027/hvd.hxjg9i).
9. *The London Review and Literary Journal* 33 (June 1798), 390.
10. *The Monthly Review* 27 (October 1798), 140, *HathiTrust*, https://hdl.handle.net/2027/nyp.33433082491006.
11. *The London Review and Literary Journal* 33, 390.
12. *The Analytical Review* 27, 561.
13. *The British Critic* 12, 24.
14. *The Monthly Review* 27, 144.
15. *The Monthly Review*, 27, 140.
16. "*Letters Written in France, in the Summer 1790, to a Friend in England*," *The Monthly Review* 3 (December 1790), 429, *HathiTrust*, https://hdl.handle.net/2027/nyp.33433082490826.
17. "*Letters Written in France, in the Summer 1790, to a Friend in England*," *The Gentleman's Magazine* 61 (January 1791), 63, *HathiTrust*, https://hdl.handle.net/2027/mdp.39015018060841; "*Letters Written in France, in the Summer 1790, to a Friend in England*," *The*

General Magazine, and Impartial Review 4 (December 1790), 541, *HathiTrust*, https://hdl.handle.net/2027/nyp.33433104886621.

18. "*Letters Written in France, in the Summer 1790, to a Friend in England*," *The English Review* 17 (January 1791), 23, *HathiTrust*, https://hdl.handle.net/2027/nyp.33433081645321.
19. William Wordsworth, "Sonnet on Seeing Miss Helen Maria Williams Weep at a Tale of Distress," *The European Magazine* 11 (1787), 202, *HathiTrust*, https://hdl.handle.net/2027/njp.32101065086231; Edward Jerningham, "On Reading 'Letters Written in France in the Summer 1790, to a Friend in England, by Helen Maria Williams,'" in Williams, *Letters Written in France*, 221.
20. Jerningham, "On Reading 'Letters Written in France in the Summer 1790,'" 221.
21. Laetitia Matilda Hawkins, *Letters on the Female Mind, Its Powers and Pursuits: Addressed to Miss H. M. Williams, with Particular Reference to Her Letters from France* (London, 1793), 1:35, *Google Books*, https://www.google.ca/books/edition/Letters_on_the_Female_Mind/SeIFVXD7Y_MC?hl=en&gbpv=0.
22. Hawkins, *Letters on the Female Mind*, 1:45.
23. Jones, "Travelling Hopefully," 101.
24. Jones, "Travelling Hopefully," 101.
25. Jones, *Radical Sensibility*, 159.
26. *The Gentlemen's Magazine* 61, 218.
27. *The Monthly Review* 27, 144.
28. Hawkins, *Letters on the Female Mind*, 1:35.
29. Burke, *Reflections on the Revolution in France*, 76–77.
30. Jones, *Radical Sensibility*, 159.
31. Williams is familiar with *A Sentimental Journey* and Sterne's classification of travellers, at one point referring to "that class of travellers whom Sterne describes as sailing and posting through the politer kingdoms of the globe, in order to see sights and look into discoveries" (*A Tour in Switzerland*, 2:130).
32. Jones, *Radical Sensibility*, 152.
33. Thelwall, *The Peripatetic*, 1:viii.
34. Maureen Moynagh, *Political Tourism and Its Texts* (Toronto: University of Toronto Press, 2008), 26.
35. Festa, *Sentimental Figures of Empire*, 17.
36. Anna Seward, "Anna Seward to Helen Maria Williams, 17 January 1793," in *Letters*, ed. Walter Scott (1811), 3:208, http://spenserians.cath.vt.edu (accessed September 29, 2015).
37. Seward, "Anna Seward to Helen Maria Williams," 208.
38. Edmund Burke, "Letters on a Regicide Peace: Letter I," in *Edmund Burke on Revolution*, ed. Robert A. Smith (New York: Harper and Row, 1968), 252.
39. "The beast that ascendeth out of the bottomless pit shall make war against them, and shall overcome them, and kill them" (Revelation 11:7 [King James Version]).
40. Williams's eight volumes of letters about the French Revolution are collectively known as *Letters from France*.
41. Biggs, *A Residence in France*, 1:xxv.
42. Biggs, *A Residence in France*, 1:xxvii.
43. Samuel Jackson Pratt, *Gleanings through Wales, Holland, and Westphalia; with Views of Peace and War at Home and Abroad*, 2nd ed. (London, 1796), 3:270, ECCO.
44. S. J. Pratt, *Gleanings*, 3:286.
45. *London Review* 33, 390.
46. Philip Harling, "A Tale of Two Conflicts: Critiques of the British War Effort, 1793–1815," in *Resisting Napoleon: The British Response to the Threat of Invasion, 1797–1815*, ed. Mark Philp (Aldershot, UK: Ashgate, 2006), 25.

47. Biggs, *A Residence in France*, 1:xxvi.
48. Helen Maria Williams, *Memoirs of Mons. and Madame du F. in a Series of Letters, Extracted from Her Letters on the French Revolution* (Boston, 1794).
49. Helen Maria Williams, *Letters Containing a Sketch of the Scenes which Passed in Various Departments of France, during the Tyranny of Robespierre, and of the Events which Took Place in Paris on the Tenth of Thermidor* (London, 1795), 3:194. ECCO.
50. For more on the parallel between the ancien régime and Robespierre in Williams's writing, see Jones, "Travelling Hopefully," 97.
51. Williams, *Letters Containing a Sketch of the Scenes which Passed in Various Departments of France, during the Tyranny of Robespierre*, 3:194.
52. Ann Radcliffe, *A Journey Made in the Summer of 1794, through Holland and the Western Frontier of Germany, with a Return Down the Rhine: to Which Are Added Observations during a Tour to the Lakes of Lancashire, Westmoreland, and Cumberland* (Zurich: Georg Olms Verlag, 1975), 114.
53. S. J. Pratt, *Gleanings*, 3:270.
54. Dafydd Moore, *Enlightenment and Romance in James Macpherson's 'The Poems of Ossian': Myth, Genre and Cultural Change* (Aldershot, UK: Ashgate, 2003), 144.
55. Kelly, *Women, Writing, and Revolution*, 70.
56. Jones, *Radical Sensibility*, 152–153.
57. *The Critical Review* 23 (May 1798), 9, *HathiTrust*, https://hdl.handle.net/2027/nyp.33433066596325.
58. *The Analytical Review* 27, 561.
59. Oliver Goldsmith, *The Traveller: A Poem*, illustrated by Burket Foster (London: George Routledge and Sons, 1868), 179–182.
60. William Coxe, *Travels in Switzerland. In a Series of Letters to William Melmouth, Esq.* (London, 1789), 1:4–5, ECCO.
61. Coxe, *Travels in Switzerland*, 1:232; 2:79, 113, 390.
62. See John Moore's *A Journal during a Residence in France, from the Beginning of August, to the Middle of December, 1792*, 2 vols. (London, 1793); and William Coxe's *A Letter to the Rev. Richard Price* (London, 1790), ECCO.
63. John Moore, *A View of Society and Manners in France, Switzerland, and Germany*, 7th ed. (London, 1789), 1:150, ECCO.
64. Helen Maria Williams, "An Epistle to Dr. Moore," in *Poems*, 2nd ed. (London, 1791), 1:19, 45, *Google Books*, https://www.google.ca/books/edition/Poems_by_Helen_Maria_Williams/MPy0tgAACAAJ?hl=en.
65. "Proceedings in the Last Session of Parliament, 1797–8, March 28," in *The Gentleman's Magazine* (November 1798), 955, *HathiTrust*, https://hdl.handle.net/2027/mdp.39015018405202.
66. Colley, *Britons*, 283, 284. For more on the British response to the threat of a French invasion, see Philp, *Resisting Napoleon*.
67. U. Price, *Defence of Property*, 19–20.
68. Johann Casper Lavater, *Remonstrance Addressed to the Executive Directory of the French Republic* (Belfast, 1798), 4, ECCO.
69. Fitzgerald frequented Williams's salons in 1791, where he was introduced to his future wife through Williams. Tone fraternized with Stone and Williams while in Paris in 1796, recording at least one of their meetings in his autobiography (*The Autobiography of Theobald Wolfe Tone, 1763–1798*, ed. R. Barry O'Brien, 2 vols. [London: T. Fisher Unwin, 1893], 2:87).
70. E. Burke, *Reflections*, 227.
71. Williams quotes from Coxe (1:63, 114, 222; 2:119, 201, 221) and Goldsmith (98) throughout her travelogue, and both her friendship with Moore and her poetic tribute to his

travels and travel reflections provides evidence of her familiarity with his writings on Switzerland.

72. Jones, *Radical Sensibility*, 153.
73. E. Burke, *Reflections*, 227.
74. Reid, *The Concept of Liberty*, 109.
75. La Harpe was sentenced to death *in absentia* and was divested of his property for organizing a celebration of the two-year anniversary of the fall of the Bastille.
76. Williams's anti-slavery platform was well known by the time she wrote *A Tour*; her abolitionist sentiments can be found throughout her work, most notably in "A Poem on the Bill Lately Passed for Regulating the Slave Trade" (London, 1788), ECCO.
77. J. Moore, *A View of Society and Manners*, 150.
78. For his objections to the French Revolution, see Coxe, *A Letter to the Rev. Richard Price*, and William Coxe, "Additions to 'Travels in Switzerland': Containing an Historical Sketch and Notes on the Late Revolution" in *Travels in Switzerland*, 4th ed. (London, 1801), 1:v–lxx, *Google Books*, https://www.google.com/books/edition/_/EqZDAAAAYAAJ?sa=X&ved=2ahUKEwimvuvC2KnxAhWSs54KHc77DvQQre8FMBR6BAgfEB0.
79. Coxe, *Travels in Switzerland*, 1:292.
80. For Coxe's conservative response to France's invasion of Switzerland, see "Additions to 'Travels in Switzerland.'"
81. Turner, *British Travel Writers in Europe*, 222.
82. *The British Critic* 17 (June 1801), 583, *HathiTrust*, https://hdl.handle.net/2027/hvd.hxjg4i.
83. *The Analytical Review* 27, 561, emphasis added.
84. *The Analytical Review* 27, 561.
85. Williams was not the only one to imagine the movement of revolutionary fervor in terms of electricity. "Claims for electricity's vital function," Mary Fairclough explains, "were incorporated into literary and political discourse in the 1790s, as electricity was increasingly often evoked as a symbol of political vitality" (*Electricity, Literature and Politics, 1740–1840: "Electrick Communication Every Where"* [New York: Palgrave Macmillan, 2017], 121). For more on this topic, see Fairclough's chapter "Animal Electricity, Vitality, and Revolution" in the above (121–169).
86. Paola Bertucci offers a good overview of the spectacle of electricity in "Sparks in the Dark: The Attraction of Electricity in the Eighteenth Century," *Endeavor* 31, no. 3 (August 2007): 88–93, https://doi.org/10.1016/j.endeavour.2007.06.002.
87. Hume, *A Treatise*, 626–627.
88. Jones, *Radical Sensibility*, 157.
89. Theobald Wolfe Tone, *An Address to the People of Ireland on the Present Important Crisis* (Belfast, 1796), 16, *Google Books*, https://www.google.ca/books/edition/An_Address_to_the_People_of_Ireland_on_t/V6dbAAAAQAAJ?hl=en&gbpv=0.
90. For more on Tone's residence and political activity in France, see Sylvie Kleinman, "A Rough Guide to Revolutionary Paris: Wolfe Tone as an Accidental Tourist," in *The United Irishmen, Rebellion and the Act of Union: 1791–1803*, ed. John Gibney (Yorkshire: Pen and Sword Books, 2018), 56–64; and Marianne Elliott, *Wolfe Tone*, 2nd ed. (Liverpool: Liverpool University Press, 2012).
91. More details on the transition from Irish reform to radicalism during the 1790s can be found in a number of excellent studies including James G. Patterson, *In the Wake of the Great Rebellion: Republicanism, Agrarianism, and Banditry in Ireland after 1798* (Manchester: Manchester University Press, 2008); and Stephen J. Small, *Political Thought in Ireland, 1776–1798: Republicanism, Patriotism, and Radicalism* (Oxford: Clarendon Press, 2002).

92. "Proceedings in the Last Session of Parliament," 955.
93. Kelly, *Women, Writing, and Revolution*, 73.
94. Hume, "Of National Characters," 248, 250.

EPILOGUE

1. Williams, *Letters Written in France*, 91.
2. Dilys Powell, *An Affair of the Heart* (London: Hodder and Stoughton, 1957), 38.
3. Williams, *Letters Written in France*, 140.
4. Powell, *An Affair of the Heart*, 21, 38.
5. "*Another Traveller!*," *The Monthly Review* 39, 434.
6. Dea Birkett and Sara Wheeler, introduction to *Amazonian: Penguin Book of Women's New Travel Writing*, ed. Dea Birkett and Sara Wheeler (New York: Penguin Books, 1998), viii.
7. Schaw, *Journal of a Lady of Quality*, 20.
8. Bernard Schweizer, "The Politics of Travel Writing in 2006," in Brisson and Schweizer, *Not So Innocent Abroad*, 28.
9. Hager Weslati, "Travel in Disguise: On Travel Writing and Cultural Governance," in Brisson and Schweizer, *Not So Innocent Abroad*, 105.
10. Moynagh, *Political Tourism*, 3, 252.
11. Respectively: Schaw, *Journal*, 20; M. Morgan, *Milford Haven*, 268; *A Journey*, 2.
12. Moynagh, *Political Tourism*, 3.

BIBLIOGRAPHY

Adams, Percy G. *Travel Literature and the Evolution of the Novel.* Lexington: University Press of Kentucky, 1983.

Ahern, Stephen. *Affected Sensibilities: Romantic Excess and the Genealogy of the Novel, 1680–1810.* New York: AMS Press, 2007.

Aikin, Arthur. *Journal of a Tour through North Wales and Part of Shropshire; with Observations in Mineralogy, and Other Branches of Natural History.* London, 1797. ECCO.

Americanus, Scotus. *Informations concerning the Province of North Carolina: Addressed to Emigrants from the Highlands and Western Isles of Scotland.* Glasgow, 1773. *Google Books.* https://www.google.ca/books/edition/Informations_Concerning_the_Province_of/QpVpuAAACAAJ?hl=en.

Anderson, Benedict. *Imagined Communities.* London: Verso, 1983.

Andrews, Corey E. "'Ev'ry Heart Can Feel': Scottish Poetic Responses to Slavery in the West Indies, from Blair to Burns." *International Journal of Scottish Literature* 4 (Spring–Summer 2008): 1–22. https://www.ijsl.stir.ac.uk/issue4/andrews.htm (accessed August 15, 2015).

Andrews, Evangeline Walker. Introduction to Janet Schaw, *Journal of a Lady of Quality,* edited by Evangeline Walker Andrews and Charles McLean Andrews, 1–18. Lincoln: University of Nebraska Press, 2005.

Andrews, Malcolm. *The Search for the Picturesque: Landscape Aesthetics and Tourism in Britain, 1760–1800.* Aldershot, UK: Scolar Press, 1989.

"*Another Traveller! Or, Cursory Remarks and Tritical* [*sic*] *Observations Made upon a Journey through Part of the Netherlands, in the Latter End of the Year 1766.*" *The Monthly Review* 39 (December 1768): 434–448. *HathiTrust.* https://babel.hathitrust.org/cgi/pt?id=njp.32101064253915&view=1up&seq=7.

Armstrong, John. *A Short Ramble through Some Parts of France and Italy. By Lancelot Temple, Esq.* London, 1771. ECCO.

Bannet, Eve Tavor. "The Bluestocking Sisters: Women's Patronage, Millenium Hall, and 'The Visible Providence of a Country.'" *Eighteenth-Century Life* 30, no. 1 (2005): 25–55. Project MUSE.

———. "Trading Routes and Eighteenth-Century Migrations: Reframing Janet Schaw." In *Recording and Reordering,* edited by Dan Doll and Jessica Munns, 137–157. Lewisburg, PA: Bucknell University Press, 2006.

Barker-Benfield, G. J. *The Culture of Sensibility: Sex and Society in Eighteenth-Century Britain.* Chicago: University of Chicago Press, 1992.

Barnard, John. "A Sentimental Journey." *The Lady's Magazine or Entertaining Companion for the Fair Sex* 1 (October 1770): 97–104. *Google Books.* https://www.google.ca/books/edition/The_Lady_s_Magazine_Or_Entertaining_Comp/1iJNAAAAcAAJ?hl=en&gbpv=0.

———. "A Sentimental Journey." *The Lady's Magazine or Entertaining Companion for the Fair Sex* 4 (January 1773): 3–8. *Google Books.* https://www.google.ca/books/edition/The_Lady_s_Magazine_Or_Entertaining_Comp/bZ1PAQAAMAAJ?hl=en&gbpv=0.

Barrell, John. *The Spirit of Despotism: Invasions of Privacy in the 1790s.* Oxford: Oxford University Press, 2006.

"*The Beauties of Nature and Art Displayed: In a Tour through the World.*" *The Critical Review* 18 (1764): 375–376. *Google Books*. https://www.google.ca/books/edition/The_Critical_Review_Or_Annals_of_Literat/X8APAAAAQAAJ?hl=en&gbpv=0.

Bertucci, Paola. "Sparks in the Dark: The Attraction of Electricity in the Eighteenth Century." *Endeavor* 31, no. 3 (August 2007): 88–93. https://doi.org/10.1016/j.endeavour.2007.06.002.

Bickham, Troy. *Making Headlines: The American Revolution as Seen through the British Press*. DeKalb: Illinois University Press, 2009.

Bicknell, Thomas, and Thomas Day. *The Dying Negro, a Poem*. 3rd ed. London, 1775. http://www.brycchancarey.com/slavery/dying.htm (accessed July 3, 2015).

Biggs, Charlotte. *A Residence in France, during the Years 1792, 1793, 1794, and 1795*. 2nd ed., vol. 1. London, 1797. ECCO.

Birkett, Dea and Sara Wheeler. Introduction to *Amazonian: Penguin Book of Women's New Travel Writing*, edited by Dea Birkett and Sara Wheeler, vii–xii. New York: Penguin Books, 1998.

Blakemore, Stephen. *Crisis in Representation: Thomas Paine, Mary Wollstonecraft, Helen Maria Williams, and the Rewriting of the French Revolution*. London: Associated University Presses, 1997.

Bohls, Elizabeth A. "The Aesthetics of Colonialism: Janet Schaw in the West Indies, 1774–1775." *Eighteenth-Century Studies* 27, no. 3 (Spring 1994): 363–390. https://doi.org/10.2307/2739361.

———. *Women Travel Writers and the Language of Aesthetics 1716–1818*. Cambridge: Cambridge University Press, 1995.

Bradley, James E. *Popular Politics and the American Revolution in England: Petitions, the Crown, and Public Opinion*. Macon, GA: Mercer University Press, 1986.

Brewer, Holly. *By Birth or Consent: Children, Law, and the Anglo-American Revolution on Authority*. Williamsburg, VA: Omohundro Institute of Early American History and Culture, 2005.

Brickell, John. *The Natural History of North Carolina*. Dublin, 1737. ECCO.

Brisson, Ulrike. "Naked Politics in Travel Writing." In *Not So Innocent Abroad: The Politics of Travel and Travel Writing*, edited by Ulrike Brisson and Bernard Schwiezer, 1–16. Newcastle upon Tyne: Cambridge Scholars Publishing, 2009.

Bromwich, David. "Burke, Reflections on the Revolution in France." In *Cambridge Companion to British Literature of the French Revolution in the 1790s*, edited by Pamela Clemit, 16–30. Cambridge: Cambridge University Press, 2011.

Brown, Jane. *The Omnipotent Magician: Lancelot 'Capability' Brown, 1716–1783*. London: Chatto and Windus, 2011.

Brown, Laura. "The Romance of Empire: Oroonoko and the Trade in Slaves." In *The New Eighteenth-Century: Theory, Politics, and English Literature*, edited by Felicity Nussbaum and Laura Brown, 41–61. London: Methuen, 1987.

Burke, Edmund. "A Letter to the Sheriffs of Bristol on the Affairs of America." In *On Empire, Liberty, and Reform: Speeches and Letters*, 135–184. New Haven, CT: Yale University Press, 2000.

———. "Letters on a Regicide Peace: Letter I." In *Edmund Burke on Revolution*, edited by Robert A. Smith, 248–282. New York: Harper and Row, 1968.

———. "Letters on a Regicide Peace: Letter III." In *The Works of the Right Honourable Edmund Burke*, vol. 5, 261–354. London: George Bell and Sons, 1877.

———. "On the Second Reading of a Bill for the Repeal of the Marriage Act." In *The Works of the Right Honorable Edmund Burke*, vol. 6, 168–172. London, 1869.

———. *A Philosophical Inquiry into the Origin of Our Ideas of the Sublime and Beautiful*. 5th ed. London, 1767. *Google Books*. https://www.google.ca/books/edition/A_Philosophical_Enquiry_into_the_Origin/LJ1gAAAAcAAJ?hl=en&gbpv=0.

———. *Reflections on the Revolution in France.* Edited by L. J. Mitchell. Oxford: Oxford University Press, 1993.

———. "Speech on American Taxation." In *The Portable Edmund Burke,* edited by Isaac Kramnick, 254–255. New York: Penguin Books, 1999.

———. "Speech on Conciliation with America." In *On Empire, Liberty, and Reform: Speeches and Letters,* 62–135. New Haven, CT: Yale University Press, 2000.

Burke, William. *An Account of the European Settlements in America. In Six Parts.* 4th ed. Dublin, 1762. ECCO.

Butler, Marilyn. *Burke, Paine, Godwin, and the Revolution Controversy.* Cambridge: Cambridge University Press, 1984.

Canning, George. "New Morality." In *Poetry of the Anti-Jacobin,* 2nd ed., 220–240. London, 1800. ECCO.

Carey, Brycchan. *British Abolitionism and the Rhetoric of Sensibility: Writing, Sentiment, and Slavery, 1760–1807.* New York: Palgrave Macmillan, 2005.

Cayley, Cornelius. *A Tour through Holland, Flanders, and Part of France.* Leeds, 1773. ECCO.

Chapone, Hester. *Letters on the Improvement of the Mind, Addressed to a Young Lady.* London, 1790. *Google Books.* https://www.google.ca/books/edition/Letters_on_the_improvement_of_the_mind/h5QDAAAQAAJ?hl=en&gbpv=0.

Chard, Chloe. *Pleasure and Guilt on the Grand Tour: Travel Writing and Imaginative Geography, 1600–1830.* New Haven, CT: Yale University Press, 1999.

Cheek, Pamela. *Sexual Antipodes: Enlightenment, Globalization, and the Placing of Sex.* Stanford, CA: Stanford University Press, 2003.

Cheyne, George. *The English Malady: or, a Treatise of Nervous Diseases of All Kinds, as Spleen, Vapours, Lowness of Spirits, Hypochondriacal, and Hysterical Distempers, &c.* Dublin, 1733. ECCO.

Child, Elizabeth. "Elizabeth Montagu, Bluestocking Businesswoman." *Huntington Library Quarterly,* 65, nos. 1–2 (2002): 153–173. JSTOR.

Claeys, Gregory. *The French Revolution Debate in Britain: The Origins of Modern Politics.* New York: Palgrave Macmillan, 2007.

Clark, Norma. "Bluestocking Fictions: Devotional Writings, Didactic Literature and the Imperative of Female Improvement." In *Women, Gender and Enlightenment,* edited by Barbara Taylor and Sarah Knott, 460–473. New York: Palgrave Macmillan, 2005.

Coleman, Deirdre. "Janet Schaw and the Complexions of Empire." *Eighteenth-Century Studies* 36, no. 2 (Winter 2003): 176–193. JSTOR.

Colley, Linda. *Britons: Forging the Nation, 1707–1837.* Rev. ed. New Haven, CT: Yale University Press, 2005.

———. *Captives: Britain, Empire, and the World, 1600–1850.* New York: Anchor Books, 2004.

Conefrey, Mick. *How to Climb Mont Blanc in a Skirt: A Handbook for the Lady Adventurer.* Oxford: Oneworld Publications, 2011.

Conway, Stephen. *The British Isles and the American War of Independence.* Oxford: Oxford University Press, 2002.

———. "From Fellow-Nationals to Foreigners: British Perceptions of the Americans, circa 1739–1783." *The William and Mary Quarterly* 59, no. 1: 65–100. http://doi.org/10.2307/3491638.

Colbert, Benjamin. "British Women's Travel Writing, 1780–1840: Bibliographical Reflections." *Women's Writing* 24, no. 2 (2017): 151–169. https://doi.org/10.1080/09699082.2016.1207913.

Columbus, Christopher. "The Letter of Columbus to Luis de Santángel, Announcing His Discovery." In *Travel Narratives from the Age of Discovery,* translated by Albert Bushnell Hart and Edward Channing, edited by Peter Mancall, 207–213. Oxford: Oxford University Press, 2006.

"*A Common Place Book for Travellers in Foreign Countries*." *The Critical Review* 43 (May 1777): 399. *HathiTrust*. https://babel.hathitrust.org/cgi/pt?id=chi.79243088&view=1up&seq=7.

Coxe, William. "Additions to 'Travels in Switzerland': Containing an Historical Sketch and Notes on the Late Revolution." In *Travels in Switzerland*, 4th ed., vol. 1, v–lxx. London, 1801. *Google Books*. https://www.google.com/books/edition/_/EqZDAAAAYAAJ?sa=X&ved=2ahUKEwimvuvC2KnxAhWSs54KHc77DvQQre8FMBR6BAgfEB0.

———. *A Letter to the Rev. Richard Price*. London, 1790. ECCO.

———. *Travels in Switzerland. In a Series of Letters to William Melmouth, Esq*. Vol. 1. London, 1789. ECCO.

———. *Travels in Switzerland. In a Series of Letters to William Melmouth, Esq*. Vol. 2. London, 1789. ECCO.

Craciun, Adriana. *British Women Writers and the French Revolution: Citizens of the World*. New York: Palgrave Macmillan, 2005.

Craciun, Adriana, and Kari Lokke. "British Women Writers and the French Revolution, 1789–1815." In *Rebellious Hearts: British Women Writers and the French Revolution*, edited by Adriana Craciun and Kari Lokke, 3–30. Albany: State University of New York Press, 2001.

Cumberland, Richard. *The West Indian, a Comedy. As It Is Performed at the Theatre Royal in Drury-Lane*. London, 1771. ECCO.

Davis, Leith. *Acts of Union: Scotland and the Literary Negotiation of the British Nation, 1707–1830*. Stanford, CA: Stanford University Press, 1999.

Davis, Leith, Ian Duncan, and Janet Sorensen, eds. *Scotland and the Borders of Romanticism*. Cambridge: Cambridge University Press, 2004.

Defoe, Daniel. *A Tour thro' the Whole Island of Great Britain*. 4th ed., vol. 4. London, 1748. ECCO.

Dekker, George. *The Fictions of Romantic Tourism: Radcliffe, Scott, and Mary Shelley*. Stanford, CA: Stanford University Press, 2005.

The Delusive and Dangerous Principles of the Minority, Exposed and Refuted. In a Letter to Lord North. London, 1778. ECCO.

Denney, Peter. "'Unpleasant, tho' Arcadian Spots': Plebeian Poetry, Polite Culture, and the Sentimental Economy of the Landscape Park." *Criticism* 47, no. 4 (Fall 2005): 493–514. JSTOR.

Dobson, David. *Scottish Emigration to Colonial America, 1607–1785*. Athens: University of Georgia Press, 1994.

Dodd, A. Charles. *The Contrast: Or, Strictures on Select Parts of Doctor Price's Additional Observations on Civil Liberty, &c*. London, 1777. ECCO.

Donne, John. "A Valediction: Forbidding Mourning." In *The Complete Poetry and Selected Prose of John Donne and the Complete Poetry of William Blake*, edited by John Hayward and Geoffrey Keynes, 34. New York: Modern Library, 1941.

Douglas, Andrew. *Notes of a Journey from Berne to England, through France. Made in the Year 1796*. London, 1797. ECCO.

Douglas, James. *Travelling Anecdotes through Various Parts of Europe*. 2nd ed. 2 vols. London, 1785. ECCO.

Douglas, Mary. *Notes of a Journey from Berne to England, through France. Made in the Year 1796*. London, 1797. ECCO.

Dubos, Jean-Baptiste. *Critical Reflections on Poetry, Painting, and Music*. Translated by Thomas Nugent. Vol. 2. London, 1748. ECCO.

Dupaty, Jean-Baptiste Mercier. *Sentimental Letters on Italy*. Translated by J. Povoleri. 2 vols. London, 1789. ECCO.

Dwyer, John. "Enlightened Spectators and Classical Moralists: Sympathetic Relations in Eighteenth-Century Scotland." In *Sociability and Society in Eighteenth Century Scotland*, edited by John Dwyer and Richard B. Sher, 96–118. Edinburgh: Mercat Press, 1993.

Edgeworth, Maria, and R. L. Edgeworth. *Practical Education*. 2nd ed. Vol. 2. London, 1801. *Google Books*. https://www.google.ca/books/edition/Practical_Education/3kj4Xqw6cxEC?hl=en&gbpv=0.

Eger, Elizabeth, and Lucy Peltz. "The Nine Living Muses of Great Britain." In *Brilliant Women: 18th-Century Bluestockings*, edited by Elizabeth Eger and Lucy Peltz, 94–126. New Haven, CT: Yale University Press, 2008.

Elliott, Marianne. *Wolfe Tone*. 2nd ed. Liverpool: Liverpool University Press, 2012.

Ellis, Markman. *The Politics of Sensibility: Race, Gender and Commerce in the Sentimental Novel*. Cambridge: Cambridge University Press, 1996.

Ellison, Julie. *Cato's Tears and the Making of Anglo-American Emotion*. Chicago: Chicago University Press, 1999.

Emsley, Clive. "An Aspect of Pitt's Terror: Prosecutions for Sedition in the 1790s." *Social History* 6, no. 2 (May 1981): 155–184.

An Epistle from Edward, and American Prisoner in England, to Harriet, in America. London, 1779. *Google Books*. https://www.google.ca/books/edition/An_Epistle_from_Edward_an_American_Priso/BllpAAAAcAAJ?hl=en&gbpv=0.

Erskine, John. *Shall I Go to War with My American Brethren?* London, 1769. ECCO.

Estwick, Samuel. *A Letter to the Reverend Josiah Tucker: D. D., Dean of Glocester*. London, 1776. ECCO.

Eustace, Nicole. *Passion Is the Gale: Emotion, Power, and the Coming of the American Revolution*. Williamsburg, VA: Omohundro Institute of Early American History and Culture, 2008.

Evans, John. *A Tour through Part of North Wales: In the Year 1798, Principally Undertaken with a View to Botanical Researches. Interspersed with Observations on Its Scenery, Agriculture, Manufactures, Customs, History, and Antiquities*. London, 1800. ECCO.

Ezell, Margaret. *Social Authorship and the Advent of Print*. Baltimore: John Hopkins University Press, 2003.

Fabricant, Carole. "The Literature of Domestic Tourism and the Public Consumption of Private Property." In *The New Eighteenth-Century: Theory, Politics, English Culture*, edited by Felicity Nussbaum and Laura Brown, 254–275. London: Methuen, 1987.

Fagerstrom, Dalphy I. "Scottish Opinion and the American Revolution." *The William and Mary Quarterly* 11, no. 2 (April 1954): 252–275. https://doi.org/10.2307/1922041.

Fairclough. Mary. *Electricity, Literature and Politics, 1740–1840: "Electrick Communication Every Where."* New York: Palgrave Macmillan, 2017.

———. *The Romantic Crowd: Sympathy, Controversy and Print Culture*. Cambridge: Cambridge University Press, 2013.

Favret, Mary. *Romantic Correspondence: Women, Politics, and the Fiction of Letters*. Cambridge: Cambridge University Press, 1993.

Faulkner, John. "Burke's Perception of Richard Price." In *The French Revolution Debate in English Literature and Culture*, edited by Lisa Plummer Crafton, 1–26. London: Greenwood Press, 1997.

Felsenstein, Frank. "After the Peace of Paris: Yorick, Smelfungus and the Seven Years' War." In *Guerres et paix: La Grande-Bretagne au XVIIIe Siécle*, edited by Paul Gabriel Boucé, 310–323. Paris: Presses Sorbonne Nouvelle, 1998.

Ferguson, Adam. *An Essay on the History of Civil Society*. 2nd ed. London, 1768. ECCO.

———. *Remarks on Dr. Price's Observations on the Nature of Civil Liberty*. London, 1776. ECCO.

Festa, Lynn. *Sentimental Figures of Empire in Eighteenth-Century Britain and France*. Baltimore: Johns Hopkins University Press, 2006.

Fielding, Penny. *Scotland and the Fictions of Geography: North Britain, 1760–1830*. Cambridge: Cambridge University Press, 2008.

Fischer, Philip. *Hard Facts: Setting and Form in the American Novel.* Oxford: Oxford University Press, 1985.

Flatley, Jonathan. "How a Revolutionary Counter-Mood Is Made." *New Literary History* 43, no. 3 (Summer 2012): 503–525. JSTOR.

Flavell, Julie. *When London Was Capital of America.* New Haven, CT: Yale University Press, 2011.

Fliegelman, Jay. *Prodigals and Pilgrims: The American Revolution against Patriarchal Authority.* Cambridge: Cambridge University Press, 1982.

Fordyce, James. *Sermons to Young Women.* 14th ed. Vol. 1. London, 1814. *Google Books.* https://www.google.ca/books/edition/Sermons_to_young_women/EPvotQIhvH8C?hl=en&gbpv=0.

Franklin, Benjamin. "Examination of Dr. Franklin." In *The Life and Essays of Benjamin Franklin: Carefully Collected from His Own Papers, Containing All His Miscellaneous Pieces*, edited by Henry Stueber, 370–402. London, 1838. *Google Books.* https://books.google.ca/books?id=BylCAAAAIAAJ&printsec=frontcover#v=onepage&q&f=false.

Gally, Henry. *Some Considerations upon Clandestine Marriages.* London, 1750. ECCO.

The Gentleman's Magazine 46 (January 1775): 24n. *Google Books.* https://www.google.ca/books/edition/The_Gentleman_s_Magazine/55E3AAAAYAAJ?hl=en&gbpv=0.

Gilpin, William. *Observations on the River Wye, and Several Part of South Wales, &c. Relative Chiefly to Picturesque Beauty: Made in the Summer of the Year 1770.* 5th ed. London, 1800. ECCO.

Gilroy, Amanda. Introduction to *Romantic Geographies: Discourses of Travel 1775–1844*, edited by Amanda Gilroy, 1–18. Manchester: Manchester University Press, 2000.

Gisborne, Thomas. *An Inquiry into the Duties of the Female Sex.* London, 1797. ECCO.

Glendening, John. *The High Road: Romantic Tourism, Scotland and Literature, 1720–1820.* New York: Palgrave Macmillan, 1996.

Godwin, William. *Political Justice: And Its Influence on General Virtue and Happiness.* Vol. 1. London, 1793. ECCO.

Goldsmith, Oliver. *The Traveller: A Poem.* Illustrated by Burket Foster, 179–182. London: George Routledge and Sons, 1868.

Gottlieb, Evan. *Feeling British: Sympathy and National Identity in Scottish and English Writing, 1707–1832.* Lewisburg, PA: Bucknell University Press, 2007.

Gould, Eliga H. *The Persistence of Empire: British Political Culture in the Age of the American Revolution.* Chapel Hill: University of North Carolina Press, 2000.

Graham, Ian Charles Cargill. *Colonists from Scotland: Emigration to North America, 1707–1783.* Ithaca, NY: Cornell University Press, 1956.

Green, David. *Blenheim Palace.* London: Country Life, 1951.

Grenby, M. O. *The Anti-Jacobin Novel: British Conservatism and the French Revolution.* Cambridge: Cambridge University Press, 2001.

Guest, Harriet. *Small Change: Women, Learning, Patriotism, 1750–1810.* Chicago: University of Chicago Press, 2000.

Hagglund, Betty. *Tourists and Travellers: Women's Non-Fictional Writing about Scotland, 1770–1830.* Bristol: Channel View Publications, 2010.

Hamilton, Douglas J. *Scotland, the Caribbean and the Atlantic World, 1750–1820.* Manchester: Manchester University Press, 2005.

Harling, Philip. "A Tale of Two Conflicts: Critiques of the British War Effort, 1793–1815." In *Resisting Napoleon: The British Response to the Threat of Invasion, 1797–1815*, edited by Mark Philp, 19–40. Aldershot, UK: Ashgate, 2006.

Harriot, Thomas. "A Briefe and True Report of the New Found Land of Virginia." In *Travel Narratives from the Age of Discovery*, translated by Albert Bushnell Hart and Edward Channing, edited by Peter Mancall, 312–321. Oxford: Oxford University Press, 2006.

Harvey, Jane. *A Sentimental Tour through Newcastle*. Newcastle, 1794. ECCO.

Hawkins, Laetitia Matilda. *Letters on the Female Mind, Its Powers and Pursuits: Addressed to Miss H. M. Williams, with Particular Reference to Her Letters from France*. Vol. 1. London, 1793. *Google Books*. https://www.google.ca/books/edition/Letters_on_the_Female_Mind/SeIFVXD7Y_MC?hl=en&gbpv=0.

Herman, Arthur. *How the Scots Invented the Modern World: The True Story of How Western Europe's Poorest Nation Created Our World and Everything in It*. New York: Three Rivers Press, 2001.

Hewatt, Alexander. *An Historical Account of the Rise and Progress of the Colonies in South Carolina and Georgia*. London, 1779. *Google Books*. https://www.google.ca/books/edition/An_Historical_Account_of_the_Rise_and_Pr/2q5bAAAAQAAJ?hl=en&gbpv=0.

Hindle, Steve. "Representing Rural Society: Labor, Leisure, and the Landscape in an Eighteenth-Century Conversation Piece." *Critical Inquiry* 41 (Spring 2015): 615–654. https://doi.org/10.1086/680205.

Hodgson, Barbara. *No Place for a Lady: Tales of Adventurous Women Travellers*. Vancouver: Greystone Books, 2002.

Holcroft, Thomas. *Travels from Hamburg through Westphalia, Holland, and the Netherlands to Paris*. London, 1804. *Google Books*. https://books.google.ca/books?id=G3-7jgEACAAJ&printsec=frontcover&source=gbs_ge_summary_r&cad=0#v=onepage&q&f=false.

The Holy Bible: Authorized King James Version. Charlotte: Bible House, 1976.

Hopkinson, Francis. "Dissertation IV." In *Four Dissertations, on the Reciprocal Advantages of a Perpetual Union between Great-Britain and Her American Colonies. Written for Mr. Sargent's Prize Medal*. London, 1766. ECCO.

Horrocks, Ingrid. *Women Wanderers and the Writing of Mobility, 1784–1814*. Cambridge: Cambridge University Press, 2017.

Hume, David. "Of National Characters." In *Selected Essays*, edited by Stephen Copley and Andrew Edgar, 113–125. Oxford: Oxford University Press, 2008.

———. *A Treatise of Human Nature*. Edited by Ernest C. Mossner. London: Penguin Books, 1985.

Hutcheson, Francis. *A Short Introduction to Moral Philosophy, in Three Books; Containing the Elements of Ethicks and the Law of Nature*. Glasgow, 1747. ECCO.

Hutchins, Zachary McLeod. *Inventing Eden: Primitivism, Millennialism, and the Making of New England*. Oxford: Oxford University Press, 2014.

Innes, Joanna. *Inferior Politics: Social Problems and Social Policies in Eighteenth-Century Britain*. Oxford: Oxford University Press, 2009.

Jerningham, Edward. "On Reading 'Letters Written in France in the Summer 1790, to a Friend in England, by Helen Maria Williams.'" In *Letters Written in France*, by Helen Maria Williams, edited by Neil Fraistat and Susan S. Lanser, 221. Peterborough, ON: Broadview Press, 2001.

Johnson, Claudia. *Equivocal Beings: Politics, Gender, and Sentimentality in the 1790s: Wollstonecraft, Radcliffe, Burney, Austen*. Chicago: University of Chicago Press, 1995.

Johnson, Samuel. *A Dictionary of the English Language*. 2nd ed. Vol. 2. London, 1755–1756. ECCO.

———. *A Journey to the Western Islands of Scotland*. New York: Dover Publications, 2008.

———. "Letter XXII—To the Same. Skie, Sept. 21st, 1773." In *The Works of Samuel Johnson, LL.D. With an Essay on His Life and Genius by Arthur Murray, Esq.*, vol. 1, 509. New York: George Dearborn, 1837.

———. *Taxation No Tyranny; an Answer to the Resolutions and Address of the American Congress*. 4th ed. London, 1775. ECCO.

Jones, Chris. *Radical Sensibility: Literature and Ideas in the 1790s*. New York: Routledge, 1993.

———. "Travelling Hopefully: Helen Maria Williams and the Feminine Discourse of Sensibility." In *Romantic Geographies: Discourses of Travel, 1775–1844*, edited by Amanda Gilroy, 93–107. Manchester: Manchester University Press, 2000.

A Journey to the Highlands of Scotland, by a Lady. Edited by Barbara Britton Wenner. Kansas City, MO: Valancourt Books, 2010.

"*A Journey to the Highlands of Scotland, by a Lady*." *The Critical Review* 43 (March 1777): 238. *HathiTrust*. https://hdl.handle.net/2027/chi.79243088.

"*A Journey to the Highlands of Scotland, by a Lady*." *The Monthly Review* 57 (September 1777): 241–242. *HathiTrust*. https://hdl.handle.net/2027/inu.30000093224917.

"*A Journey to the Highlands of Scotland*." *The Scots Magazine* 39 (March 1777): 153. *HathiTrust*. https://hdl.handle.net/2027/nyp.33433081660478.

Justice, Elizabeth. *A Voyage to Russia*. York, 1739. ECCO.

Kames, Lord Henry Home. *Sketches of the History of Man*. 2nd ed. Vol. 1. Edinburgh, 1778. ECCO.

———. *Sketches of the History of Man*. 2nd ed. Vol. 2. Edinburgh, 1778. ECCO.

Keith, Alexander. *Observations on the Act for Preventing Clandestine Marriages*. London, 1753. ECCO.

Kelly, Gary. "Bluestocking Feminism and Writing in Context." In *Bluestocking Feminism: Writings of the Bluestocking Circle, 1738–1785*, vol. 1, ix–liv. London: Pickering and Chatto, 1999.

———. Introduction to Sarah Scott, *A Description of Millenium Hall*, edited by Gary Kelly, 11–43. Peterborough, ON: Broadview Press, 1995.

———. *Women, Writing, and Revolution, 1790–1827*. Oxford: Clarendon Press, 1993.

Kennedy, Deborah. *Helen Maria Williams and the Age of Revolution*. Lewisburg, PA: Bucknell University Press, 2002.

Kenny, Virginia. *The Country-House Ethos in English Literature 1688–1750: Themes of Personal Retreat and National Expansion*. Sussex: Harvester Press, 1984.

Kent, Nathaniel. *General View of the Agriculture of the County of Norfolk*. London, 1796. ECCO.

Kim, Elizabeth. "Complicating Complicity/Resistance in Janet Schaw's *Journal of a Lady of Quality*." *Auto/Biography Studies* 12, no. 2 (Fall 1997): 166–188. https://doi.org/10.1080/08989575.1997.10815105.

Kinsley, Zoë. "*A Tour to Milford Haven* and *Millenium Hall*: Female Charity and the Example of Elizabeth Montagu." In *Eighteenth-Century Women: Studies in Their Lives, Work, and Culture*, edited by Linda Troost, vol. 3, 199–224. New York: AMS Press, 2003.

———. *Women Writing the Home Tour, 1682–1812*. Aldershot, UK: Ashgate, 2008.

Kleinman, Sylvie. "A Rough Guide to Revolutionary Paris: Wolfe Tone as an Accidental Tourist." In *The United Irishmen, Rebellion and the Act of Union: 1791–1803*, edited by John Gibney, 56–64. Yorkshire: Pen and Sword Books, 2018.

Knott, Sarah. *Sensibility and the American Revolution*. Chapel Hill: University of North Carolina Press, 2009.

Knox, John. *The American Crisis, by a Citizen of the World*. Vol. 3. London, 1777. ECCO.

Knox, Vicesimus. *Sermon XXV. The Prospect of Perpetual and Universal Peace to Be Established on the Principles of Christian Philanthropy*. In *The Works of Vicesimus Knox*, vol. 6, 351–371. London, 1824. *Google Books*. https://www.google.ca/books/edition/The_Works_of_Vicesimus_Knox_D_D/3kkVAAAAYAAJ?hl=en&gbpv=0.

———. *The Spirit of Despotism*. London, 1795. ECCO.

Lamb, Susan. *Bringing Travel Home to England: Tourism, Gender, and Imaginative Literature in the Eighteenth Century*. Newark: University of Delaware Press, 2008.

Lavater, Johann Casper. *Remonstrance Addressed to the Executive Directory of the French Republic*. Belfast, 1798. ECCO.

Lawrence, Karen. *Penelope Voyages: Women and Travel in the British Literary Tradition*. Ithaca, NY: Cornell University Press, 1994.

Lawson, John. *A New Voyage to Carolina*. London, 1709. ECCO.

Leask, Nigel. *Curiosity and the Aesthetics of Travel Writing, 1770–1840*. Oxford: Oxford University Press, 2002.

Legard, James. "Queen Anne, Court Culture and the Construction of Blenheim Palace." *Journal for Eighteenth-Century Studies* 37, no. 2 (2014): 185–197. https://doi.org/10.1111/1754-0208.12158.

Lemmings, David. "Marriage and the Law in the Eighteenth Century: Hardwicke's Marriage Act of 1753." *The Historical Journal* 39, no. 2 (1996): 339–360. JSTOR.

A Letter to the Public: Containing the Substance of what hath been offered in the late Debates upon the Subject of the Act of Parliament, For the Better Preventing of Clandestine Marriages. London, 1753. ECCO.

"*Letters from the Islands of Teneriffe, Brazil, the Cape of Good Hope, and the East Indies* by Mrs. Kindersley." *The Monthly Review* 57 (September 1777): 243. *HathiTrust*. https://hdl.handle.net/2027/hvd.hxjfhc.

"*Letters Written in France, in the Summer 1790, to a Friend in England*." *The English Review; or, an Abstract of English and Foreign Literature* 17 (January 1791): 21–23. *HathiTrust*. https://hdl.handle.net/2027/nyp.33433081645321.

"*Letters Written in France, in the Summer 1790, to a Friend in England*." *The General Magazine, and Impartial Review* 4 (December 1790): 541–543. *HathiTrust*. https://hdl.handle.net/2027/nyp.33433104886621.

"*Letters Written in France, in the Summer 1790, to a Friend in England*." *The Gentleman's Magazine* 61 (January 1791): 62–63. *HathiTrust*. https://hdl.handle.net/2027/mdp.39015018060841

"*Letters Written in France, in the Summer 1790, to a Friend in England*." *The Monthly Review* 3 (December 1790): 429–430. *HathiTrust*. https://hdl.handle.net/2027/nyp.33433082490826.

Long, Edward. *The History of Jamaica. Or, General Survey of the Antient and Modern State of That Island*. Vol. 1. London, 1774. ECCO.

Loveday, John. *The Diary of a Tour in 1732*. In *John Loveday of Caversham 1711–1789: The Life Tours of an Eighteenth-Century Onlooker*, edited by Sarah Markham. Salisbury, UK: Michael Russell Publishing, 1984.

MacArthur, E. Mairi. "Fresh Fields for Inquiry: Travellers to the Highlands." In *Crossing the Highland Line: Cross-Currents in Eighteenth-Century Scottish Writing, Selected Papers from the 2005 ASLS Annual Conference*, edited by Christopher McLachlan, 153–160. Glasgow: Association for Scottish Literary Studies, 2009.

Major, Emma. *Madam Britannia: Women, Church, and Nation, 1712–1812*. Oxford: Oxford University Press, 2012.

Mandeville, Bernard. *A Treatise of the Hypochondriack and Hysterick Diseases*. London, 1730. ECCO.

Markley, Robert. "Sentimentality as Performance: Shaftesbury, Sterne, and the Theatrics of Virtue." In *The New Eighteenth-Century: Theory, Politics, English Literature*, edited by Felicity Nussbaum and Laura Brown, 210–230. New York: Methuen, 1987.

Matt, Susan J., and Peter N. Stearns, eds. *Doing Emotions History*. Chicago: University of Illinois Press, 2014.

Mauduit, Israel. *Remarks upon General Howe's Account of His Proceedings on Long Island in the Extraordinary Gazette of October 10th, 1776*. London, 1778. *Google Books*. https://www.google.ca/books/edition/Remarks_Upon_Gen_Howe_s_Account_of_His_P/RLE6AAAAcAAJ?hl=en&gbpv=0.

Mavor, Rev. William F. *Blenheim, a Poem. To Which Is Added, a Blenheim Guide*. London, 1787. ECCO.

Mayer, Holly A. "Bearing Arms, Bearing Burdens: Women Warriors, Camp Followers and Home-Front Heroines of the American Revolution." In *Gender, War, and Politics: Transatlantic Perspectives, 1775–1830*, edited by Karen Hagemann, Gisela Mettele, and Jane Rendall, 169–187. New York: Palgrave Macmillan, 2010.

McAllister, Marie E. "Women on the Journey: Eighteenth-Century British Women's Travel in Fact and Fiction." PhD Diss., Princeton University, 1998.

McNeil, Kenneth. *Scotland, Britain, Empire: Writing the Highlands, 1760–1860*. Columbus: Ohio State University Press, 2007.

Melzer, Sara E., and Leslie W. Rabine, eds. *Rebel Daughters: Women and the French Revolution*. Oxford: Oxford University Press, 2012.

Meyer, Duane. *The Highland Scots of North Carolina 1732–1776*. Chapel Hill: University of North Carolina Press, 1961.

Meyer, Edith Patterson. *Petticoat Patriots of the American Revolution*. New York: Vanguard Press, 1976.

Mills, Sara. *Discourses of Difference: An Analysis of Women's Travel Writing and Colonialism*. London: Routledge, 1993.

Mitchell, John. *The Present State of Great Britain and North America*. London, 1767. ECCO.

Mizelle, Brett. "'Man Cannot Behold It without Contemplating Himself:' Monkeys, Apes and Human Identity in the Early American Republic." *Explorations in Early American Culture: A Supplemental Issue of Pennsylvania History* 66: 144–173. JSTOR.

Montagu, Elizabeth. "December 4, 1781." In *A Lady of the Last Century (Mrs. Elizabeth Montagu): Illustrated in Her Unpublished Letters; Collected and Arranged, with a Biographical Sketch, and a Chapter on Blue Stockings*, edited by John Doran, 306. Bentley and Son, 1873. *Google Books*. https://books.google.ca/books/about/A_Lady_of_the_Last_Century_Mrs_Elizabeth.html?id=fBSiAQAACAAJ&redir_esc=y.

———. Elizabeth Montagu to Gilbert West, 1 November 1755, quoted in Eve Tavor Bannet, "The Bluestocking Sisters: Women's Patronage, *Millenium Hall*, and 'The Visible Providence of a Country.'" *Eighteenth-Century Life* 30, no. 1 (2005): 25–55. Project MUSE.

———. Mrs. Montagu to Miss H. More. Sandleford, 1784. In *Memoirs of the Life and Correspondence of Hannah More*, edited by William Roberts, Esq. 2nd ed. Vol. 1, 372. London, 1834. *Google Books*. https://www.google.com/books/edition/_/oB46AAAAcAAJ?gbpv=1.

Montagu, Lady Mary Wortley. *The Turkish Embassy Letters*. Edited by Teresa Heffernan and Daniel O'Quinn. Peterborough, ON: Broadview Press, 2012.

Montesquieu, Charles. *The Spirit of the Laws*. Translated by Thomas Nugent. Kitchener: Batoche Books, 2001.

Moore, Dafydd. *Enlightenment and Romance in James Macpherson's 'The Poems of Ossian': Myth, Genre and Cultural Change*. Aldershot, UK: Ashgate, 2003.

Moore, John. *A Journal during a Residence in France, from the Beginning of August, to the Middle of December, 1792*. 2 vols. London, 1793. ECCO.

———. *A View of Society and Manners in France, Switzerland, and Germany*. 7th ed. Vol. 1. London, 1789. ECCO.

More, Hannah. *Thoughts on the Importance of the Manners of the Great to General Society*. 4th ed. London, 1788. ECCO.

Morgan, Caesar. *The Duty of Patriotism Vindicated and Enforced: A Sermon Preached in the Cathedral Church of Ely*. London, 1780. ECCO.

———. *A Sermon on Public Spirit: Preached at Wisbech, the Isle of Ely, on Sunday, April 29, 1798*. Cambridge, 1798. ECCO.

———. *A Sermon Preached in the Cathedral Church of Ely, on Thursday, April 23, 1789: Being the Day Appointed for a General Thanksgiving to Almighty God for His Majesty's Happy Recovery*. Cambridge, 1789. ECCO.

———. *A Sermon Preached in the Cathedral Church of Ely, on Wednesday, February the 21st, 1781: Being the Day Appointed for a General Fast*. London, 1781. ECCO.

Morgan, Mary. "The Editor to the Reader." In *The Knyghte of the Golden Locks: An Ancyent Poem, Applicable to the Present Times, Selected from Many Others in the Possession of Mrs. Morgan*, edited by Mary Morgan. Wisbech, 1799. ECCO.

———. *Mary, the Osier-Peeler: A Simple but True Story: A Poem*. John White, 1798. *Google Books*. https://www.google.ca/books/edition/Mary_the_Osier_peeler/_AuJtgAACAAJ?hl=en.

———. *A Tour to Milford Haven, in the Year 1791*. 1795. Reprint, ECCO Print Editions, 2010.

Moynagh, Maureen. *Political Tourism and Its Texts*. Toronto: University of Toronto Press, 2008.

Mullan, John. *Sentiment and Sociability: The Language of Feeling in the Eighteenth Century*. Oxford: Clarendon Press, 1988.

Murdoch, Alexander. *Scotland and America, c. 1600–c. 1800*. New York: Palgrave Macmillan, 2010.

Nairn, Thomas. *A Letter from South Carolina*. London, 1710. ECCO.

Norton, Mary Beth. *Liberty's Daughters: The Revolutionary Experience of American Women, 1750–1800*. Boston: Little, Brown, 1980.

Oates, J.C.T. *Shandyism and Sentiment, 1760–1800*. Cambridge: Cambridge Bibliographic Society, 1968.

"Obituary, with Anecdotes, of Remarkable Persons." *The Gentleman's Magazine* 75 (August 1808): 751. *Google Books*. https://www.google.ca/books/edition/The_Gentleman_s_Magazine/8LICAQAAMAAJ?hl=en&gbpv=0.

O'Brien, Karen. *Women and Enlightenment in Eighteenth-Century Britain*. Cambridge: Cambridge University Press, 2009.

O'Loughlin, Katrina. "'In Brazen Bonds': The Warring Landscapes of North Carolina, 1775." In *Emotions and War: Medieval to Romantic Literature*, edited by Stephanie Downes, Andrew Lynch, and Katrina O'Loughlin, 218–234. New York: Palgrave Macmillan, 2015.

———. *Women, Writing, and Travel in the Eighteenth Century*. Cambridge: Cambridge University Press, 2018.

O'Shaughnessy, Andrew Jackson. *An Empire Divided: The American Revolution and the British Caribbean*. Philadelphia: University of Pennsylvania Press, 2000.

Outhwaite, R. B. *Clandestine Marriage in England, 1500–1850*. London: Hambledon Press, 1995.

Paine, Thomas. "Common Sense." In *Rights of Man, Common Sense and Other Political Writings*, edited by Mark Philp, 1–60. Oxford: Oxford University Press, 2008.

———. "Rights of Man." In *Rights of Man, Common Sense and Other Political Writings*, edited by Mark Philp, 83–198. Oxford: Oxford University Press, 2008.

Paterson, Samuel. *Another Traveller! Or Cursory Remarks and Tritical* [*sic*] *Observations Made upon a Journey through Part of the Netherlands in the Latter End of the Year 1766*. Vol. 1. London, 1767–1769. ECCO.

———. *Another Traveller! Or Cursory Remarks and Tritical* [*sic*] *Observations Made upon a Journey through Part of the Netherlands in the Latter End of the Year 1766*. Vol. 2. London, 1767–69. ECCO.

Patterson, James G. *In the Wake of the Great Rebellion: Republicanism, Agrarianism, and Banditry in Ireland after 1798*. Manchester: Manchester University Press, 2008.

Pearson, Jacqueline. "Crushing the Convent and the Dread Bastille: The Anglo-Saxons, Revolution, and Gender in Women's Plays of the 1790s." In *Literary Appropriations of the Anglo-Saxons from the Thirteenth to the Twentieth Century*, edited by Donald Scragg and Caroline Weinburg, 122–137. Cambridge: Cambridge University Press, 2000.

Pennant, Thomas. *A Tour in Scotland 1769*. Chester, 1771. ECCO.

———. *A Tour in Scotland, and Voyage to the Hebrides, 1772*. 2 vols. London, 1776. ECCO.

———. *A Tour in Wales*. 2 vols. London, 1778. ECCO.

Perkins, Pam. "Paradises Lost: Ann Grant and Late Eighteenth-Century Idealizations of America." *Early American Literature* 40, no. 2 (2005): 315–340. JSTOR.

Phillips, Peregrine. *A Sentimental Diary, Kept in an Excursion to Little Hampton, near Arundel, and to Brighthelmstone, in Sussex*. London, 1778. *Google Books*. https://www.google.ca/books/edition/A_Sentimental_Diary_kept_in_an_excursion/vhtbAAAAcAAJ?hl=en&gbpv=0.

Philp, Mark, ed. *Resisting Napoleon: The British Response to the Threat of Invasion, 1797–181*. Aldershot, UK: Ashgate, 2006.

Pohl, Nicole, and Betty A. Schellenberg, eds. *Reconsidering the Bluestockings*. San Marino, CA: Huntington Library, 2003.

Poole, Steve. "Pitt's Terror Reconsidered: Jacobinism and the Law in Two South-Western Counties, 1791–1803." *Southern History* 17: 65–87.

Pope, Alexander. "Upon the Duke of Marlborough's House at Woodstock." In *Complete Poetical Works*, edited by Henry Walcott Boynton, 101–102. New York: Houghton Mifflin, 1903. *Internet Archive*. https://archive.org/details/completepoetica04unkngoog.

Powell, Dilys. *An Affair of the Heart*. London: Hodder and Stoughton, 1957.

Pratt, Mary Louise. *Imperial Eyes: Travel Writing and Transculturation*. London: Routledge, 1992.

Pratt, Samuel Jackson. *Gleanings through Wales, Holland, and Westphalia; With Views of Peace and War at Home and Abroad*. 2nd ed., vol. 3. London, 1796. ECCO.

———. *Travels for the Heart. Written in France*. Vol. 1. London, 1777. ECCO.

Price, Richard. *A Discourse on the Love of Our Country*. 3rd ed. London, 1790. *Google Books*. https://www.google.ca/books/edition/A_Discourse_on_the_Love_of_Our_Country/92QNAAAAIAAJ?hl=en&gbpv=0.

———. *Observations on the Nature of Civil Liberty*. Dublin, 1776. ECCO.

Price, Uvedale. *Essays on the Picturesque, as Compared with the Sublime and the Beautiful; and, on the Use of Studying Pictures, for the Purpose of Improving Real Landscape*. Vol. 1. London, 1810. *Google Books*. https://books.google.ca/books?id=Al0AAAAAYAAJ&dq.

———. *Thoughts on the Defence of Property. Addressed to the County of Hereford*. Hereford, 1797. ECCO.

Probert, Rebecca. "The Impact of the Marriage Act of 1753: Was It Really 'A Most Cruel Law for the Fair Sex?" *Eighteenth-Century Studies* 38, no. 2 (Winter 2005): 247–262. https://doi.org/10.1353/ecs.2005.0015.

"Proceedings in the Last Session of Parliament, 1797–8, March 28." *The Gentleman's Magazine* (November 1798): 955. *HathiTrust*. https://hdl.handle.net/2027/mdp.39015018405202.

"*Prospects and Observations; on a Tour in England and Scotland, Natural, Economical, and Literary*." *The Analytical Review* 11 (September 1791): 293–301. *HathiTrust*. https://hdl.handle.net/2027/njp.32101065085373.

Radcliffe, Ann. *A Journey Made in the Summer of 1794, through Holland and the Western Frontier of Germany, with a Return down the Rhine: To Which Are Added Observations during a Tour to the Lakes of Lancashire, Westmoreland, and Cumberland*. Zurich: Georg Olms Verlag, 1975.

Radcliffe, Evan. "Arguing Benevolence: Wordsworth, Godwin, and the 1790s." In *The French Revolution Debate in English Literature and Culture*, edited by Lisa Plummer Crafton, 59–82. London: Greenwood Press, 1997.

Rackwitz, Martin. *Travels to Terra Incognita: The Scottish Highlands and Hebrides in Early Modern Travellers' Accounts c. 1600–1800*. New York: Waxmann Munster, 2007.

Ramsay, Allan. *Letters on the Present Disturbances in Great Britain and Her American Provinces*. London, 1777. ECCO.

Rankin, Hugh. *The North Carolina Continentals*. Chapel Hill: University of North Carolina Press, 2005.

Reddy, William. "Against Constructionism: The Historical Ethnography of Emotions." *Current Anthropology* 38, no. 3 (1997): 327–351. https://doi.org/10.1086/204622.

———. *The Navigation of Feeling: A Framework for the History of Emotions.* Cambridge: Cambridge University Press, 2004.

Reflections on the Marriage Act: with Some Hints for a New Law: Humbly Offered to the Consideration of Parliament. London, 1764. ECCO.

Reflections on the Repeal of the Marriage-Act Now under Consideration of Parliament. London, 1765. ECCO.

Reid, John Phillip. *The Concept of Liberty in the Age of the American Revolution.* Chicago: Chicago University Press, 1988.

"Remarks on a Voyage to the Hebrides, in a Letter to Samuel Johnson, LL.D." In *Samuel Johnson: The Critical Heritage,* edited by James T. Boulton, 237–240. London: Routledge, 1971.

Rennell, Thomas. *The Connexion of the Duties of Loving the Brotherhood, Fearing God, and Honoring the King. In a Sermon Preached at Saint Magnus the Martyr, London Bridge.* Winton, 1791. ECCO.

Roberts, M.J.D. *Making English Morals: Voluntary Association and the Moral Reform Movement in England, 1688–1886.* Cambridge: Cambridge University Press, 2004.

Robinson, Jane. *Wayward Women: A Guide to Women Travellers.* Oxford: Oxford University Press, 1990.

Rooney, Morgan. *The French Revolution Debate and the British Novel, 1790–1814: The Struggle for History's Authority.* Lewisburg, PA: Bucknell University Press, 2014.

Rosenwein, Barbara. *Emotional Communities in the Early Middle Ages.* Ithaca, NY: Cornell University Press, 2006.

———. *Generations of Feeling: A History of Emotions, 600–1700.* Cambridge: Cambridge University Press, 1999.

Rousseau, Jean Jacques. *Discourse on the Origin of Inequality.* London, 1761. ECCO.

Russo, Stephanie. *Women in Revolutionary Debate: Female Novelists from Burney to Austen.* Houten, The Netherlands: Hes and De Graaf Publishers, 2012.

Schaw, Janet. *Journal of a Lady of Quality.* Edited by Evangeline Walker Andrews and Charles MacLean Andrews. Lincoln: University of Nebraska Press, 2005.

———. *Journal of a Lady of Quality.* Edited by Evangeline Walker Andrews and Charles MacLean Andrews. 3rd ed. New Haven, CT: Yale University Press, 1939.

Schlick, Yaël. *Feminism and the Politics of Travel after the Enlightenment.* Lewisburg, PA: Bucknell University Press, 2012.

Schweizer, Bernard. "The Politics of Travel Writing in 2006." In *Not So Innocent Abroad: The Politics of Travel and Travel Writing,* edited by Ulrike Brisson and Bernard Schweizer, 17–37. Newcastle upon Tyne: Cambridge Scholars Publishing, 2009.

Scott, Sarah. *The History of Sir George Ellison.* Edited by Betty Rizzo. Lexington: University Press of Kentucky, 1996.

———. *Millennium Hall.* Edited by Gary Kelly. New York: Broadview Press, 1995.

Scrivener, Michael Henry. *Seditious Allegories: John Thelwall and Jacobin Writing.* University Park: Pennsylvania State University Press, 2001.

"*A Sentimental Journey to Bath, Bristol, and its Environs.*" *The Critical Review* 45 (April 1778): 311. *Google Books.* https://www.google.ca/books/edition/The_Critical_Review_Or_Annals_of_Literat/7cIPAAAAQAAJ?hl=en&gbpv=0.

Seward, Anna. "Anna Seward to Helen Maria Williams, 17 January 1793." In *Letters,* edited by Walter Scott, vol. 3, 202–209. 1811. http://spenserians.cath.vt.edu.

Shakespeare, William. *King Henry VI, Pt. 3.* In *The Oxford Shakespeare: The Complete Works,* edited by Stanley Wells et al., 2nd ed., 91–124. Oxford: Clarendon Press, 2005.

Sheridan, Richard Brinsley. "On the Bill to Explain and Amend the Marriage Act." In *Speeches of the Right Honourable Richard Brinsley Sheridan: With a Sketch of His Life*. Vol. 1, 16–17. London: Henry G. Bohn, 1842. *Google Books*. https://books.google.ca/books?id=Ck4JAAAAQAAJ&pg+PP1#v+onepage&q&f=false.

Sheridan, Richard Brinsley, and Israel Pottinger. *The General Fast; a Lyric Ode: with a Form of Prayer Proper to the Occasion, and a Dedication to the King*. London, 1776. ECCO.

Shields, Juliet. *Sentimental Literature and Anglo-Scottish Identity, 1745–1820*. Cambridge: Cambridge University Press, 2010.

Singleton, John. *A Description of the West-Indies. A Poem, in Four Books. By Mr. Singleton. During His Excursions among Those Islands*. London, 1776. ECCO.

Sloane, Hans. *A Voyage to the Islands Madera, Barbados, Nieves, S. Christophers and Jamaica*. Vol. 1. London, 1707. ECCO.

Small, Stephen J. *Political Thought in Ireland, 1776–1798: Republicanism, Patriotism, and Radicalism*. Oxford: Clarendon Press, 2002.

Smith, Adam. *An Inquiry into the Nature and Causes of the Wealth of Nations*. Edited by Jonathan B. Wight. Petersfield, UK: Harriman House, 2007.

———. *The Theory of Moral Sentiments*. Edited by Ryan Patrick Hanley. New York: Penguin Books, 2009.

Smith, Orianne. *Romantic Women Writers, Revolution, and Prophecy: Rebellious Daughters, 1786–1826*. Cambridge: Cambridge University Press, 2013.

Smith, William. *Information to Emigrants, Being the Copy of a Letter from a Gentleman in North America*. Glasgow, 1773. ECCO.

Smollett, Tobias. *The Expedition of Humphrey Clinker*. Edited by Lewis M. Knapp. Oxford: Oxford University Press, 1998.

Spunaugle, Emily D. "A Travel Writer Reconsidered: Recovering Mary Morgan's *Mary, the Osier-Peeler*." *ABO: Interactive Journal for Women in the Arts, 1640–1830* 10, no. 2, art. 2 (2020). https://scholarcommons.usf.edu/abo/vol10/iss2/2.

Staves, Susan. "Church of England Clergy and Women Writers." *Huntington Library Quarterly*, 65, nos. 1–2 (2000): 81–103. JSTOR.

Stearns, Peter N., and Carol Z. "Emotionology: Clarifying the History of Emotions and Emotional Standards." *American Historical Review* 90 (October 1985): 813–836. https://doi.org/10.2307/1858841.

Stebbing, Henry. *An Inquiry into the Force and Operation of the Annulling Clauses in the Late Act for the Better Preventing of Clandestine Marriages, with Respect to Conscience*. London, 1754. ECCO.

Stedman, John Gabriel. *Narrative of a Five Years' Expedition against the Revolted Negroes of Surinam, in Guiana, on the Wild Coast of South Africa, from the Year 1772 to 1777*. Vol. 1. London, 1796. ECCO.

———. *Narrative of a Five Years' Expedition against the Revolted Negroes of Surinam, in Guiana, on the Wild Coast of South Africa, from the Year 1772 to 1777*. Vol. 2. London, 1796. ECCO.

Sterne, Laurence. *A Sentimental Journey through France and Italy*. Edited by Katherine Turner. London: Broadview Press, 2010.

———. "Sermon V: The Prodigal Son." In *The Sermons of Mr. Yorick*, 103–128. London: J. Dodsley, 1775. *Internet Archive*. https://archive.org/details/sermonsofmryoric03ster.

Stewart, Dugald. "Account of the Life and Writings of Adam Smith LL.D." In *Essays in Philosophical Subjects*, 9–95. London, 1795. *Google Books*. https://www.google.ca/books/edition/Essays_on_Philosophical_Subjects_To_whic/x6lcAAAAcAAJ?hl=en&gbpv=0.

Stone, Lawrence. *Road to Divorce: England, 1530–1987*. Oxford: Oxford University Press, 1990.

Swenson, Rivka. *Essential Scots and the Idea of Unionism in Anglo-Scottish Literature, 1603–1832*. Lewisburg, PA: Bucknell University Press, 2015.

Thelwall, John. *The Peripatetic; or, Sketches of the Heart, of Nature and Society; in a Series of Politico-Sentimental Journals*. Vol. 1. Southwark, 1793. ECCO.

———. *The Peripatetic; or, Sketches of the Heart, of Nature and Society; in a Series of Politico-Sentimental Journals*. Vol. 2. Southwark, 1793. ECCO.

Theroux, Paul. *The Tao of Travel: Enlightenments for Lives on the Road*. Toronto: McClelland and Stewart, 2011.

Thomas, Steven. "Doctoring Ideology: James Grainger's *The Sugar Cane* and the Bodies of Empire." *Early American Studies: An Interdisciplinary Journal* 4, no. 1 (2006): 78–111. JSTOR.

Thompson, Carl. *The Suffering Traveller and the Romantic Imagination*. Oxford: Oxford University Press, 2007.

Thorne, R. G. *The House of Commons 1790–1802*. Boydell and Brewer, 1986.

Tinling, Marion. *Women into the Unknown: A Sourcebook on Women Explorers and Travelers*. New York: Greenwood Press, 1989.

Todd, Janet. *Sensibility: An Introduction*. London: Methuen, 1986.

Tone, Theobald Wolfe. *An Address to the People of Ireland on the Present Important Crisis*. Vol. 5. Belfast, 1796. ECCO.

———. *The Autobiography of Theobald Wolfe Tone, 1763–1798*. Edited by R. Barry O'Brien. 2 vols. London: T. Fisher Unwin, 1893.

"*A Tour to Milford Haven, in the Year 1791*." *The British Critic and Quarterly Theological Review* 6 (August 1795): 160–164. *Hathitrust*. https://hdl.handle.net/2027/mdp.39015056066775.

"*A Tour to Milford Haven, in the Year 1791*." *The Gentleman's Magazine* 65, no. 5, pt. 2 (November 1795): 943. *HathiTrust*. https://hdl.handle.net/2027/mdp.39015018405426.

"*A Tour to Milford Haven, in the Year 1791*." *The Monthly Review* 18 (November 1795): 269–274. *HathiTrust*. https://hdl.handle.net/2027/inu.30000093233157.

"*A Tour in Switzerland*." *The Analytical Review* 27 (June 1798): 561–571. *HathiTrust*. https://hdl.handle.net/2027/nyp.33433087364802.

"*A Tour in Switzerland*." *The British Critic* 12 (July 1798): 24–29. *HathiTrust*. https://hdl.handle.net/2027/chi.63735473.

"*A Tour in Switzerland*." *The London Review and Literary Journal* 33 (June 1798): 390–392.

"*A Tour in Switzerland*." *The Monthly Review* 27 (October 1798): 131–144. *HathiTrust*. https://hdl.handle.net/2027/nyp.33433082491006.

"*Travels from Hamburg, through Westphalia, Holland, and the Netherlands, to Paris*." *The Critical Review* 3, no. 1 (April 1804): 361. *HathiTrust*. https://hdl.handle.net/2027/nyp.33433066596903.

"*Travels in Switzerland*." *The Monthly Review* (January 1790): 24–32. *HathiTrust*. https://hdl.handle.net/2027/hvd.hxjg9i.

"*A Trip to Kilkenny, from Durham, by way of Whitehaven and Dublin, in the Year 1776*." *The Monthly Review* 60 (1779): 191–196. *HathiTrust*. https://hdl.handle.net/2027/hvd.hxjfhf.

Trumpener, Katie. *Bardic Nationalism: The Romantic Novel and the British Empire*. Princeton, NJ: Princeton University Press, 1997.

Tucker, Josiah. *A Series of Answers to Certain Popular Objections against Separating from the Rebellious Colonies and Discarding Them Entirely*. Gloucester, 1776. ECCO.

Turner, Katherine. *British Travel Writers in Europe, 1750–1800: Authorship, Gender, and National Identity*. Burlington, VT: Ashgate, 2001.

———. Introduction to Lawrence Sterne, *A Sentimental Journey through France and Italy*, 11–46. Edited by Katherine Turner. Peterborough, ON: Broadview Press, 2010.

Ty, Eleanor. *Unsex'd Revolutionaries: Five Women Novelists of the 1790s*. Toronto: University of Toronto Press, 1993.

Verhoeven, Wil. *Americomania and the French Revolution in Britain, 1789–1802*. Cambridge: Cambridge University Press, 2014.

Watson, Nicola J. *Revolution and the Form of the British Novel.* Oxford: Clarendon Press, 1994.

Wechelblatt, Martin. "Finding Mr. Boswell: Rhetorical Authority and National Identity in Johnson's *A Journey to the Western Islands of Scotland.*" *ELH* 60, no. 1 (Spring 1993): 117–148. JSTOR.

Weiss, Deborah. "Suffering, Sentiment, and Civilization: Pain and Politics in Mary Wollstonecraft's *Short Residence.*" *Studies in Romanticism* 45, no. 2 (Summer 2006): 199–221. https://doi.org/10.2307/25602044.

Wenner, Barbara Britton. Introduction to *A Journey to the Highlands of Scotland, by a Lady*, edited by Barbara Britton Wenner, vii–xvii. Kansas City, MO: Valancourt Books, 2010.

Weslati, Hager. "Travel in Disguise: On Travel Writing and Cultural Governance." In *Not So Innocent Abroad: The Politics of Travel and Travel Writing*, edited by Ulrike Brisson and Bernard Schweizer, 85–109. Newcastle upon Tyne: Cambridge Scholars Publishing, 2009.

West, Jane. *A Tale of the Times.* Vol. 3. London, 1799. ECCO.

Wharman, Dror. "The English Problem of Identity in the American Revolution." *The American Historical Review* 106, no. 4 (October 2001): 1236–1262. https://doi.org/10.2307/2692947.

Williams, Helen Maria. "An Epistle to Dr. Moore." In *Poems*, 2nd ed., vol. 1, 35–52. London, 1791. *Google Books.* https://www.google.ca/books/edition/Poems_by_Helen_Maria_Williams/MPy0tgAACAAJ?hl=en.

———. *Letters Containing a Sketch of the Politics of France, from the Thirty-first of May 1793, till the Twenty-eighth of July 1794, and of the Scenes which Have Passed in the Prisons of Paris.* Vols. 1–2. London, 1795. ECCO.

———. *Letters Containing a Sketch of the Politics of France, from the Thirty-first of May 1793, till the Twenty-eighth of July 1794, and of the Scenes which have Passed in the Prisons of Paris.* Vols. 3–4. London, 1796. ECCO.

———. *Letters Containing a Sketch of the Scenes which passed in Various Departments of France During the Tyranny of Robespierre.* Vol. 3. London, 1795. ECCO.

———. *Letters Written in France, in the Summer 1790, to a Friend in England; Containing Various Anecdotes Relative to the French Revolution.* Edited by Neil Fraistat and Susan S. Lanser. Peterborough, ON: Broadview Press, 2001.

———. *Memoirs of Mons. and Madame du F. in a Series of Letters, Extracted from Her Letters on the French Revolution.* Boston, 1794.

———. *A Poem on the Bill Lately Passed for Regulating the Slave Trade.* London, 1788. ECCO.

———. *A Tour in Switzerland.* Vol. 1. London, 1798. ECCO.

———. *A Tour in Switzerland.* Vol. 2. London, 1798. ECCO.

Wilson, Kathleen. *The Island Race: Englishness, Empire, and Gender in the Eighteenth–Century.* New York: Routledge, 2003.

———. *A Sense of the People: Politics, Culture and Imperialism in England, 1715–1785.* Cambridge: Cambridge University Press, 1998.

Winkfield, Unca Eliza. *The Female American.* Edited by Michelle Burnham and James Freitas. 2nd ed. Peterborough, ON: Broadview Press, 2014.

Witherspoon, John. *An Address to the Natives of Scotland Residing in America: Being an Appendix to a Sermon Preached at Princeton on a General Fast.* London, 1778. ECCO.

Wollstonecraft, Mary. *Letters Written during a Short Residence in Sweden, Norway, and Denmark.* Edited by Ingrid Horrocks. Peterborough, ON: Broadview Press, 2013.

———. *A Vindication of the Rights of Men.* Edited by Sylvana Tomaselli. Cambridge: Cambridge University Press, 1995.

———. *A Vindication of the Rights of Women.* Edited by Miriam Brody. London: Penguin Books, 2004.

Womack, Peter. *Improvement and Romance: Constructing the Myth of the Highlands.* London: Macmillan Press, 1989.

Wood, Bradford J. *This Remote Part of the World: Regional Formation in Lower Cape Fear, North Carolina, 1725–1775*. Columbia: University of South Carolina Press, 2004.

Wood, Gordon S. *The Radicalism of the American Revolution*. New York: Vintage Books, 1991.

Woodhouse, James. "The Life and Lucubrations of Crispinus Scriblerus." In *The Life and Poetical Works of James Woodhouse*, edited by Rev. R. I. Woodhouse, vol. 1, 9–223. London: Leadenhall Press, 1896. *Google Books*. https://www.google.ca/books/edition/The_Life_and_Poetical_Works_of_James_Woo/ino4AAAAYAAJ?hl=en&gbpv=0.

Wordsworth, William. "Sonnet on Seeing Miss Helen Maria Williams Weep at a Tale of Distress." *European Magazine* 11 (1787): 202. *HathiTrust*. https://hdl.handle.net/2027/njp.32101065086231.

Wraxall, Nathaniel. *Cursory Remarks Made in a Tour through Some of the Northern Parts of Europe, Particularly Copenhagen, Stockholm, and Petersburgh*. London, 1775. ECCO.

Wyndham, Henry Penruddocke. *A Gentleman's Tour through Monmouthshire and Wales, in the Months June and July, 1774*. London, 1775. ECCO.

Young, Arthur. *Political Essays concerning the Present State of the British Empire*. London, 1772. ECCO.

Zagarri, Rosemarie. *Revolutionary Backlash: Women and Politics in the Early American Republic*. Philadelphia: University of Pennsylvania Press, 2007.

INDEX

ABOUT THE AUTHOR

LINDA VAN NETTEN BLIMKE is an associate professor of English at Concordia University of Edmonton, where she teaches in the areas of eighteenth- and nineteenth-century literature. She has published articles on the travelogues of Janet Schaw and Mary Morgan and has coedited an early twentieth-century travel journal entitled *Crossing Canada, 1909: Hope Hook's Diary.*